Louis Tikas.
Courtesy of the Library, State Historical Society of Colorado.

BURIED UNSUNG

Louis Tikas and the Ludlow Massacre

Zeese Papanikolas

Foreword by Wallace Stegner

University of Utah Press
Salt Lake City, Utah
1982

Volume fourteen of the University of Utah Publications
in the American West, under the editorial direction of
the American West Center.
S. Lyman Tyler, Director

Library of Congress Cataloging in Publication Data

Papanikolas, Zeese.
    Buried unsung.

    (The University of Utah publications in the American
West; v. 14)
      Bibliography: p.
      Includes index.
      1. Tikas, Louis, d. 1914.   2. Coal Strike, Colorado,
1913–1914.   3. Trade-unions—Colorado—Officials
and employees—Biography.   4. Greek Americans—Biography.
I. Title.   II. Title: Ludlow Massacre.   III. Series.
HD6509.T54P36   1982   331.89'3822334'0924 [B] 82–13475
ISBN 0–87480–211–3

For permission to reprint the following copyrighted and unpublished material the
author gratefully acknowledges these sources:

The Denver Public Library, Department of Western History for unpublished por-
tions of the Edward L. Doyle and John R. Lawson Collections.

Eric Margolis for interview material from the *Life of the Western Coal Miner
Project* video tapes, Institute of Behavioral Science, Boulder, Colorado.

The American Folklore Society for "When will the Skies Clear?" from Ellen Frye,
The Marble Threshing Floor (University of Texas Press, Austin and London, 1973).

Edward B. Marks Music Corporation for "The Argentines, the Portuguese and the
Greeks," by Carey Morgan and Arthur M. Swanstrom, c.

Harcourt Brace Jovanovich, Inc. for a portion of Walter Benjamin's *Illuminations*,
translated by Harry Zohn (Harcourt, Brace & World, Inc., 1968).

Alan Lomax for lines from "Damn the Filipinos," from *American Ballads and Folk
Songs* by John A. Lomax and Alan Lomax (The MacMillan Company, 1934).

Endsheets: Louis Tikas' funeral in Trinidad, Colorado. Courtesy of the Library,
State Historical Society of Colorado, Dold Collection.

For you, Louis

CONTENTS

ILLUSTRATIONS

MAPS

ACKNOWLEDGMENTS

Many people have contributed to the making of this book. Barron B. Beshoar and Leonard F. Guttridge, historians of the 1913–14 Colorado coal strike, were prompt in answering my questions and in making available their research. Readers of this book will readily see how much indebted I am to their works both for their insights and information. And I am indebted to Mary Thomas O'Neal, whose lively book remains the only one written by a participant in the great Colorado strike. Alan Kent Powell, Philip Notarianni, and Joseph Stipanovich passed on documents which came to be cornerstones of this work and without which, it is fair to say, I could not have proceeded. Mark Griffiths, Joanna Karvonides, Vangelis Frangiadikis, and Terry Mousalimas performed services that were real kindnesses, and my cousin Amy Theodore was the essence of hospitality on my trips to Denver. My wife, Ginna Allison, as always, deserves my thanks for her encouragement and interest during all phases of this undertaking.

The staffs of the Western History Department of the Denver Public Library, the State Historical Society of Colorado, and the National Archives have been generous with their time and resources, as have Eric Margolis and Ron McMahan of the Life of the Western Coal Miner Project at the University of Colorado, and George Warren, Archivist of the Colorado Division of State Archives and Public Records.

I have been fortunate in my readers. I thank all those who read my manuscripts in whole or in excerpt and whose thoughts and comments have become part of the texture of this book, but especially I thank Frank Bergon, John Vernon, and Joseph Butwin who went through my early drafts with patience and insight when what I had was closer to an idea of a book than a book itself. Michael Nagler took time to read and comment on my appendix on Greek Oral Poetry and History, and Wallace Stegner encouraged me at an early stage in this project and read the completed manuscript with the kind of sensitivity that not only illuminates a book, but enriches it, as is shown by the foreword.

A manuscript is one thing, a book another, and so I am indebted to the staff of the University of Utah Press for making this into a book and especially to Paula Roberts, who first read it for the Press and saw promise in it. And I would like to thank those two anonymous scholar-readers who were willing to report favorably on a work that sometimes deserts the conventional ways of writing history to tell its story.

Throughout the researching and writing of this book my mother has been my chief translator, my closest reader, and a source for much of the lore and history of the Greek laborers in the Rocky Mountains, while my father has looked on with encouragement and perceptive comment. I can only thank them with these pages. Finally, I must express my deep gratitude to Emmanuel Marangoudakis and the people of Loutra and to all those survivors of the tumultuous events of the 1913–14 strike who were willing to speak for this record. The simple listing of their names in this book and its notes must stand as a poor token of how much I owe them. I would, however, like to single out for special thanks Louis R. Dold (1888–1980) and Gus Papadakis, who became not only major sources for this history, but my friends.

FOREWORD

by Wallace Stegner

Every American traveling in Greece has met them: the gnarled, dura-
ble old men in dark suits who rise from their coffeehouse chairs or
from their benches in the public square and come forward and make
themselves known when a visibly-American stranger appears. I have
been greeted by them under the orange trees in the sun-whitened square
of Sparta, on the dock at Khalkis on Euboea, in the nightingale-haunted
grove among the ruins of Olympia. They are grave and friendly, their
characteristic Greek xenophilia enhanced by a certain controlled eagerness. In English, they tell you that they have spent many years in
America. They wonder if you know their cousin Joe Kosmos in Joliet,
Illinois, or if by chance you come from Paterson, New Jersey, or
Denver, Colorado, places where they have lived and have friends.

They are never pests, they don't hold you with their skinny hands.
But they have an air of remote and diffident hunger; they are like the
shades that Odysseus summoned with the black blood of sacrificed
sheep; they ask word of the world they went out to as young men,
lost themselves in, and now have returned from, doubly lost. They take
pride in greeting you in your own language—you sense that this pro-
ficiency gives them status and authenticity. They tell you scraps of
their experience in America, places they have seen. They are assiduous
to give you the directions they hope you need. When you must go, they
part from you with visible reluctance and go back among the coffeehouse sitters or the sitters in the shade of the square, no more fully

at home there than they were quite at home with you. They are the lost ones, the ones who were tempted by the new world but were never willing to give up the old, and so lost both.

Changed by strangeness and wandering, supported now by social security checks from another country, they bear the taints of difference and privilege, they are half-strangers, "Americans," like the old returned emigrant in Silone's novel, the one the village knew as Sciatap because *sciatap* was the only American word he had brought home, the only one he had apparently clearly understood. *Sciatap*. Shut up.

Those old men with blurred identities are products of the human currents of force that fed cheap labor, usually through the means of crooked padrones, into the land of opportunity. Though divided in mind and heart, they survive. Many of their companions did not, but are now unknown names on unvisited graves in America's industrial cities and mining camps—as Louis Tikas, who was born to another name in the village outside of Rethymnon, in Crete, is an unknown name on an unvisited grave in the Knights of Pythias cemetery in Trinidad, Colorado.

There is a third kind, those who both stayed and survived, who married American women or sent home for picture brides, who found steady jobs or created little businesses—coffeehouses, restaurants, shoe-shine parlors—and fathered children who grew up American and fathered another generation of children. By the normal routines of acculturation and assimilation, that third generation could be expected to have forgotten their grandfathers' hardships along with their grand-fathers' language, and to have replaced nostalgia with the preoccupa-tions and busy-nesses of the new country.

Zeese Papanikolas is of that generation, but has never been easy in it. He was a sensitive and listening child. In Congoleum kitchens where his grandfather and his grandfather's friends sat around bare tables over wine glasses or coffee cups, talking, talking, he learned the strangeness of being stretched out between a half-unwilling past and a half-reluctant present, between the Greek that was and the American that is. The way to revive the glory of ancient Greece, says one Greek–American, is to destroy every chair in modern Greece. But that would destroy much else, for that endless sitting, that interminable remembering, that talking, weaves the net that holds the past and so gives meaning to the present.

A Greek is nothing without a past, a cultural continuity, a flow of relationships and customs. Without the talk of the old men around their kitchen tables in Bingham Canyon or Magna, Zeese Papanikolas might never have developed the hunger for a clear and acceptable identity. His hunger started him on a search that lasted many years, a search that fairly early focused on the figure of Louis Tikas, one of those anonymous ones who "pressed very lightly on the earth," one who might serve as a representative and symbol of all his kind and thus, as Papanikolas says, for a part of himself.

Once, speaking before the Association of Greek Writers in Athens, I tried to tell them how it felt to grow up without history; what it was like to be a boy on a frontier where there was no past, but only a present and (we hoped) a future, where Americans and Scandinavians and Russians, Cockney Englishmen and Ontario Orangemen and French–Indian halfbreeds, Syrian peddlers and Chinese restaurant-keepers and Texas cowboys, were thrown into a place with no remembered past, and asked to make a town out of the disparate and often irreconcilable scraps of the cultures they had brought with them. The Greek writers were fascinated. It had never occurred to them that there might be a problem in having too little past. Their problem had always been having too much.

Zeese Papanikolas, born in America, understands the problem of too little past. Being of Greek parentage, he perhaps feels it more than some of us do. His thirst is not different in kind from the thirst that sent me back to Norway, or Alex Haley back to Africa, but it is intensified by the sense of all the past glory to which he is heir. Modern Greece is a Balkan nonentity altered by centuries of domination by Romans, Franks, and Venetians, and debased by four hundred years of Ottoman oppression. A great civilization has declined to the status of a folk culture. But it is no less compelling—perhaps it is more so—for its decline. It is a country that its children love, even when they have to leave it in order to live; a country that the ages have been at work on. And the country that invented, among many other things, history.

In his life of Louis Tikas, Zeese Papanikolas has had to re-invent history, or re-create it. History does not exist until it is formulated and given permanence either in oral tradition (as in the Icelandic sagas) or in writing. Left to human memory, it fades in a generation or two, and in three or four has either been transmuted into legend or has been lost entirely. Migrant laborers, especially those used as strikebreakers, especially those who at first could not break into the society that fed and oppressed them, left few tracks. The history of labor itself in America has been relatively neglected; that of migrant, immigrant, gang-labor imported for the breaking of strikes has been essentially ignored.

Writing the history of the I.W.W. organizer and martyr Joe Hill (like Louis Tikas he used a different name in America than the one he was christened with), I found only six or seven people who had incontrovertibly known him, and a pitiful little pile of authenticated facts supplemented by an enormous pile of misinformation, rumor, labor and capitalist propaganda, and plain mis-remembering. Writing the history of the man who called himself Louis Tikas, Papanikolas is even more deprived, for his subject was a martyr more minor (though more authentic) than Joe Hill, and he left no songs to be remembered by.

What he left was a fading memory among men growing old and unreliable, a few notices in newspapers and union records, a few photographs. One shows Louis Tikas, "already half a ghost," standing among other labor leaders during the Ludlow strike. One is a photograph of his corpse, propped up on a slab in the Trinidad morgue. A third is a photograph of a mile-long, sullen procession—his funeral procession— moving down Commercial Street. As Papanikolas discovers him, he was not an important leader in that or any other strike; he rose above namelessness primarily because he learned English faster than most of his companions, and could represent them in meetings. He was not a hero, he led no gallant charges, last stands, or stirring confrontations. He tried to make peace, he tried to mediate, he tried to keep talking. Nevertheless, Thucydides' epitaph for the Spartans at Thermopylæ would apply to him, and perhaps Papanikolas was thinking of them as he wrote. "Having done what men could, they suffered what men must."

The search for Louis Tikas is a search for a shadow, an almost-vanished memory. Like a hound on a cold scent, Papanikolas circles, stops, changes directions, starts again, is led aside, returns to the track: from the kitchens of Utah copper camps to Colorado boarding houses, from town to cemetery, from newspaper files to photographic archives, from court testimony to the fallible memories of old men, from the grandfathers to John D. Rockefeller II, from Colorado back to Crete. Never quite sure what it is he seeks, he sniffs out labor contractors, militiamen, company detectives, union leaders, politicians, Old World relatives and childhood companions. Little by little, piece by piece, he fills in the jigsaw mosaic that is the history of Greek immigrants in the American West.

At every stage of the search, the passionate involvement of Papanikolas himself is apparent. This is a poet at work; the book he has produced is at once a cultural history, an elegy, and a lyrical autobiography. He hunts inward as well as outward; even as the search takes him in widening circles, the personal core is steadily consolidating, firming, becoming sure of itself. In finding Louis Tikas and men like him and tracing their harsh Argosy, this third-generation Greek–American defines himself.

Central to his story of Louis Tikas and his friends is the 1913 strike in the Colorado coal mines whose bloody climax has come to be known as the Ludlow Massacre. It was the event in which Louis Tikas died, and it was a watershed event. One of the bleakest and blackest episodes of American labor history, it killed many people, including many women and children burned to death in the firing of the strikers' camp; and in annihilating the strikers it also all but killed the union in Colorado and set back the cause of unionism there for a generation. It may or may not have touched the conscience of John D. Rockefeller II, dominant director of Colorado Fuel and Iron—he seems to have been more misled and confused than personally guilty. But it did touch the conscience of the nation, and if it did not make raw corporate gun-law impossible, it gave it a bad name. At the very least, it made corporations more careful.

That was Louis Tikas' contribution: his life, lost in the effort to find a degree of justice, a portion of security, a moiety of self-respect, for himself and the Greeks, Italians, Austrians, and South Slavs who were his companions in America. The story is a little Iliad from the losers' side—a confrontation, a catalog of leaders and champions, shifting tactics, reinforcements, hopes lifted and hopes dashed, preparations, desperations, a siege, a battle, catastrophe, choral comment. It is a credit to Papanikolas' artistic conscience that his reconstruction of these people and events is not a whitewash. Sympathetic as he is, he does not try to make Louis Tikas and his companions more than they were. They were working men, fallible, ignorant, many of them illiterate, all of them disadvantaged by their inability in English and their initial role as scabs, all of them heir to the peculiarly Greek weakness of argumentativeness and disunion, none of them a hero. But all of them oppressed, cheated, used, and driven by the arrogance of bosses, foremen, and labor padrones to the final desperation of the strike, out of which was to develop the martyrdom of some and the possibility of permanent relocation in America for others.

People of small importance, their Iliad an event worth only a few paragraphs in the history books. But what Papanikolas makes of these materials is a fascinating search for his ethnic and historical roots and his personal identity. The book is electric with its author's personal involvement and luminous with the felicity of his language. It is a book about the real, not the mythic West. Eastern critics would do well to read it (though I am afraid few will) instead of bemusing themselves further with the romantic figure of the cowboy. Cowboys didn't make the West; they only created the image by which it is mis-known. People like Louis Tikas made the West, and in the process made modern Westerners such as Zeese Papanikolas.

All the time I was reading this sensitive, poetic, and profound examination of one Westerner's roots, I kept thinking of a poem by George Seferis. It is called "The King of Asine," and its subject is a king mentioned once in the *Iliad* and mentioned nowhere else, a name sounded and then forever silent: a burial mask, and beneath the mask a void. It is in history itself, among the ruins of an ancient acropolis, that Seferis hunts for the King of Asine, and not among the blank spaces of uncreated history where Papanikolas has had to seek Louis Tikas. But their search is mystically the same.

> And the poet lingers, looking at the stones, and asks himself
> does there really exist
> among these ruined lines, edges, points, hollows, and curves
> does there really exist
> here where one meets the path of rain, wind, and ruin

does there exist the movement of the face, shape of the tenderness
of those who've shrunk so strangely in our lives . . .

His answer comes like a clang of bronze from the age of heroes:

> Shieldbearer, the sun climbed warring,
> and from the depths of the cave a startled bat
> hit the light as an arrow hits a shield:
> "'Ασίνην τε 'Ασίνην τε." Would that it were the king of Asine
> we've been searching for so carefully on this acropolis
> sometimes touching with our fingers his touch upon the stones.*

Fugitive as that bat, Louis Tikas reveals himself in this book. He
is the arrow, Zeese Papanikolas the shield. In the end, the search is
nearly fruitless, there seems so little to be found. And yet our fingers
have touched his very touch on the stones. Greek-immigrant casualty
and third-generation Greek–American, between them, somehow make
a whole and a brotherhood. They can teach us that there are better
places to hunt the self than in the self's own crevices. Greek, American,
or some hyphenated hybrid, we are most surely discoverable in what
we share with others, in the story of our own kind.

---

*George Seferis, *Collected Poems*, translated, edited, and introduced by
Edmund Keeley and Philip Sherrard, expanded ed. (Princeton University Press,
Princeton, N.J., 1981).

Notes begin on p. 273 and are located by page number and an identifying word or phrase from the text.

Judge Advocate: Where did he come from?
Lawson: Greece, as far as I know.

1. BEGINNINGS

They lived above the town's one drugstore in rented rooms. The rooms were almost empty. A few pots and pans, thin beds, a few Greek newspapers. It was not poverty. It was simply a kind of austerity born out of a lifetime of habit. And what would they spend money for anyway, these two old men, in Oak Creek, Colorado? For these were men who pressed very lightly on the world. Their rooms had a look of being somehow improvised, temporary, as if at any minute one of these old bachelors could stuff a few shirts into a suitcase and disappear down the canyon with no mark of his passing left behind. Barba John Tsanakatsis, with his round peasant face, his sporty cap and marvelous laugh, went to Las Vegas toward the end of October to get warm. Old Mr. Papadakis stuck it out through the winter, a few miles up the road from the ski resort with its bars and restaurants and new plywood chalets for those comfortable enough to play with the season. In Mr. Papadakis' room there was one obvious center. It was not the bed or the table or the gas stove, but a steamer trunk. He opened it for me, showed me its elaborate compartments, its pressers for trousers and suits. He had bought it in the '30s for his first trip back to Crete.

"He used to have some new suitcases," Barba John said, winking slyly, "for the airplane. The best."

"I give them up," Mr. Papadakis said. "They were light, you know. Special made for the airplane. There was something about them. I just didn't like them." The few possessions in Barba John's room had been tumbled about in a genial disorder. Mr. Papadakis kept his room immaculate. He was a few years older than Barba John, a slender

1

man with a white mustache. He held himself straight. When he spoke English, the words had a tart Cretan twang to them. That afternoon Barba John and I had driven down the canyon looking for him. We found him a few miles out of town where the remains of the mines stuck out of the brush and scrub oak, a rusted coal car, the stump of the tipple, here and there the black smudge of a dump. He was gathering chokecherries to make into wine. He was eighty-five years old.

We sat in his room drinking the sweet homemade wine and he was telling me what he knew of the man I was searching for.

". . . There was not too many of us speaking very much then. Louis, he didn't speak very much neither, but good enough to get by. But there was not too many to take the speakers' stand and speak and all that. Louis, he done pretty well. He got the appointment around Denver. I don't know who appointed him."

"Did you know him before?"

"I seen him, but I didn't know too much about him. A young, nice, pretty good man, that's all I can say."

"So anyway, he was sort of your spokesman?"

"Yes. More like he give us the dope and mix with the higher-ups, you know, and talk things over."

Barba John laughed and pushed back his cap and adjusted his thick glasses to look at the photograph I handed him. "Yes, yes, yes," Barba John said with his devilish chuckle, "here he is. Sure I knew Louis. Had a little coffeehouse in Denver."

"That was on Market Street?"

"Yeah, Market Street."

"What kind of place was it?"

"A coffeehouse. Like them coffeehouses. Maybe you seen them coffeehouses. Have you? Chairs, you know, couple of tables. Serve coffee, little *ouzo*, stuff like that . . ."

"No *ouzo*," Mr. Papadakis interrupted. It was important to him for things to be accurate.

"Sometimes," Barba John went on, "sometimes they have a dance, you know. Let them play the *laouto* . . . Have that two, three times . . ."

He stands beside the other men almost shyly, posing a little diffi- dently for the photographer, a big, slightly incongruous checkered motoring cap in his hand, a tin star pinned for some reason to his coat. His name is Louis Tikas. In 1906 he had left a village near Rethymnon, Crete, for the United States. He had passed his twentieth birthday at sea on his way to New York. Now, seven years later, he stands in front of the tent city the strikers have built on the Ludlow plain smiling, already, it seems, half a ghost, lingering only momentarily on the curve of the camera lens. Beside him John Lawson, the United Mine Workers organizer, is calm, solid, squinting a little into the sun. He stands a head taller than Louis Tikas and the other two men. One of these men is an officer in the National Guard, the other wears the derby hat and protruding vest of some city man—mine official or editor or politician. The wind blows a little, kicking up a spume of dust that brings with it the acrid tang of sage, the smell of the horses. Louis Tikas smiles. Caught in that incredible, fragile innocence of all such photographs, which know only the present, none of these men realizes that in a few months Tikas will be dead, shot down by the soldiers and the company gunmen while the tent city burns around him.

I have seen two other photographs. A blurred indoor shot of Tikas lying dead in a Trinidad, Colorado, mortuary, his face already sliding into the terrible formlessness of death; the other the long procession of silently marching men that winds for a mile down Commercial Street behind his funeral coach. Sixty years later this is almost all he has left on the surface of history.

How do you write about a ghost? No doubt the thing I was searching for was really a fragment of myself.

Sifting through the thin walls of Gus Papadakis' room from some radio down the hall came the sound of the Grateful Dead. There was the dim, sweet odor of marijuana in the air. Long-hairs had drifted into Oak Creek, spill off from Aspen or Boulder or wherever the scene was in Colorado that summer. On the street as we were going up to the hotel, a big-breasted girl with dirty hair had waved to Barba John from the midst of a bunch of scruffy hitchhikers on a flat-bed truck and called him by his first name. So they lived now, the rootless young who had no history, these uprooted old men who had nothing else, in a sudden convergence in this seedy hotel in a dying town in the year 1973.

"Louis, you know, Tikas," Barba John was saying, his cap pushed back on his head, "he joined the union, see, behind with the miners.

He was one of the most quiet men I had ever known and a man you could have absolute confidence in. . . . —John Lawson on Tikas. Lawson, left, Tikas with star. Courtesy of the Library, State Historical Society of Colorado, Dold Collection.

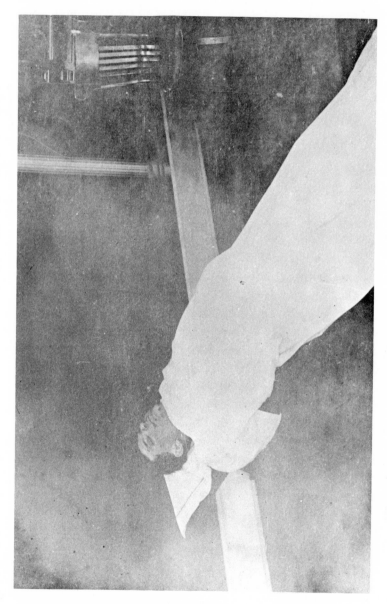

They stepped on his face. We have a photograph . . . it shows plain the prints of the heel in his face. —Pearl Jolly. Louis Tikas in the mortuary. Courtesy of the Library, State Historical Society of Colorado, Dold Collection.

And he come over to Lafayette, you know. And I tell him, 'Now, you better move from here.' Because he come over to the boardinghouse. And the guy that opened up said, 'Louis, you better run because the guards are after you . . .' He run from the back door. And I was right there that time. And after that, he went south. And he was happy to get there . . ."

A year later I would listen to this passage again on my tape recorder. If Tikas was in Lafayette, in the northern coalfields, it would have been before the big strike in the south, before the fall of 1913. And I would remember how Barba John had said of Tikas in the Northern Field, "They shoot him." But who had shot him and why? For a moment, in the heat of an August afternoon, I caught a glimpse of Louis Tikas, a young man in 1911 or '12, running for his life out the back door of a boardinghouse in Lafayette, Colorado. It was one of those glimpses I would try to confirm. And as with so many other glimpses, it would perhaps elude me and leave me in that uneasy twilight place betwen history and some old man's memory, between what I knew and what I had to guess.

And yet I smiled when Louis escaped the nets of history as he escaped the gunmen that day in Lafayette. He ran through the twilight and into a kind of legend. He became a hero. Not the sort of hero it was usual to speak of, maybe, but a hero cut to my own size—smiling, congenial, clever. And, it could be, baffled too—for what else could I read in that diffident look of his, that retreating smile? In the summer heat there was a geometry, three sides to a puzzle which I was trying to solve: those old men with their memories and that music coming through the wall, which was all at once so foreign to me, and the small pressure of Louis' absence, were part of some unresolved figure, in which I thought I could locate what I was. If Louis Tikas had been alive he would have been Gus Papadakis' age, my grandfather's age. I could have been speaking with him there and drinking that wine. There was nothing left now but that drop of wine and the harsh smell of summer's burnt grass up there in Oak Creek Canyon. In such emptiness, who was to say what was important and not important? The name of a coffeehouse, a remembered anecdote, a laugh, Louis' checkered cap might be of profound significance.

What I am about to write is hardly fiction, nor is it quite history. It is the story of a search, personal, at times tentative, into the fragments of the life of one man, a union organizer called Louis Tikas, who was killed in the fighting at Ludlow, Colorado, on April 20, 1914. He was not the most important of the miners' leaders in the big strike, nor was he the only one to die at Ludlow. Let him stand for a whole generation of immigrant workers who found themselves, in the years before the First World War, caught between the realities of industrial America and their aspirations for a better life. They are an anonymous generation, factory hands, pick-and-shovel men, some union organizers like Tikas. And they are men without biographies. Their stories are not found in the volumes of labor and immigration statistics. They are barely sketched in by those grimmer relics, the tallies of the dead and maimed in mine disasters and mill accidents or in the bleak rows of headstones in industrial town cemeteries. Few had come with the idea of settling permanently in America. Many—perhaps almost half of them—returned to their native lands. The rest were able to make their peace with the new land, to settle into some more or less steady work, to buy a shop, open a restaurant, make a foremanship, or possibly arrive at real prosperity, and perch there somewhat warily at the edge of American life, waiting to see what their sons and daughters would do with their opportunities. That was all. The immigrants of Louis Tikas' generation were not literate men. They had not brought with them that special consciousness of their place in history that forms the habit of keeping one's documents about one, of setting down one's justifications. They were farmers and shepherds who were struggling with an industrial world few of them had even imagined before their arrival. Their business was one of survival, not history. And yet, paradoxically —and I speak of the Greeks now, though others would fit this mold— they were extravagantly historical in their outlook. It was a history not of books and documents but of things they carried inside them, and it informed every gesture, every inflection of their voices and summed up their whole notion of what it was to be a man in the world. They brought it with them in the packets of Greek earth they had sewn to their clothing like amulets, in the Old Country costumes they would bring from their trunks on feast days, and in the songs of the *Turkomachia*—the Turk wars—carried down from generation to generation, which they would sing in America not with some vague nostalgia, but with the sense of an epic and living presence more real, even, than the machines and pits they worked among and the men who drove them. It was against this history that they played out their sense of the present—a present that enlarged itself and became, in their eyes, a theater for heroic action. It was a view of life that did not fit the terms of the industrial war that had to be fought, a view misunderstood and defied by an America caught up in an unreal martial vision of its own; at Ludlow it would have its part in the making of a massacre.

This book, then, is an attempt to rescue Tikas for history, and maybe more important it is an attempt to rescue him from it—to bring to life, if only provisionally, the sense of a man, with his flesh and his individuality, allowed to escape for a moment his part in the scheme of his times. This book is speculative and it is full of doubts, a work of reconstruction, of guesses as well as facts. And so it is a work of the imagination. And—for it would not be possible to write it any other way—a book about a part of myself. If it leaves as many questions as it answers, then so does the brief life of Louis Tikas the man. I did not know when I first set out on this search what I would find. But in the end I would catch more than one glimpse of this man—this shadow— caught against the flow of history. I would come to recognize something familiar in his ways. And for one brief moment I would hear his voice.

The coffee houses are as exact a reproduction of those in Greece . . . as one could hope to find. . . . There is the same vile atmosphere and the same crowd of big, able-bodied loafers with apparently nothing to do all day but smoke, drink, play cards and talk. . . .

Professor Henry Pratt Fairchild
1911

2. 1746 MARKET STREET

In the winter of the depression year of 1907 a bunch of Greeks were living in a shack on the outskirts of Pueblo, Colorado. Among them was a tall young man from the mountains of Roumeli. He had worked for the Colorado Fuel and Iron Company for a while shoveling coke at the Minnequa mill. The pay was $1.75 for a twelve-hour day. On his first day of work he had beaten a Bulgarian almost senseless. The Bulgarian had hidden the shovel in a pile of coke when the shift changed, as the custom was, and the young Greek thought he was trying to get him fired. In the shack the Greeks ate beans and lentils and waited for the coal trains to come by so they could jump on the moving cars and throw out coal for their stove. It was bitterly cold. Of the seven in the shack only one was working. Already the tall Greek had taken to carrying the pistol he had bought a few months before in his first days in America.

The tall Greek was my grandfather, George Zeese—Yorgis Zisimopoulos, of Klepa in Nafpaktias. Louis Tikas had arrived in America the year before. He had landed in New York in March of 1906 and six months later had arrived in Colorado. The two men never met, but they had been born in the same year, 1886. They had come to the United States within eighteen months of each other, and they would find themselves, for a time, foreigners in the same western city. Perhaps my grandfather's story can stand for a part of Louis Tikas'.

In the spring George Zeese and another Greek paid a labor agent a dollar each for a job on a section gang repairing track in the desert 175 miles out of Pueblo. It was nearly midnight when they arrived

9

at the camp and the section boss told them he didn't need any labor, hadn't ordered any. The agent in Pueblo had lied. The Greeks had no coats or blankets and the dollar they'd given the labor agent had been the last of their money. The section boss let them spend the night shivering in the station house. They caught the first freight heading out.

But the train didn't stop at Pueblo as they thought it would. It veered off at a branch in the track and ran them straight through to Denver, and so they found themselves in a strange city, hungry and friendless and a hundred miles from help.

They tried to hook another freight south, but a policeman spotted them and chased them out of the yard. They tried again, and again they were chased. Finally they gave up. George Zeese went over to the policeman and asked him in halting English to tell them where Greek town was.

So they came to it, that little Greek world, that sanctuary, as other lost and hungry men had. Here in a coffeehouse George Zeese met Angelo Raïkos, a small-time straw boss and interpreter who was to stand godfather to the tall Greek's youngest child. Raïkos' father had come from the same mountain district as George Zeese and such ties were important. Raïkos went off with the two hungry young Greeks and introduced them to another man, a white-haired baker, who fed them bread and beans in his shop. Every day the baker cooked a meal for those of his countrymen who were without work. The baker's name has been lost, and it is unfortunate; it is well to remember such men. Raïkos and the baker were able to scrape together enough money to send one of the homeless men back to Pueblo. George Zeese stayed awhile with Raïkos in a dirty boardinghouse, waiting for his chance to get back.

On Holy Friday George Zeese went with the others to the small Greek Orthodox Church on Lafayette Street. He stood before the flower-covered bier shoulder to shoulder with other young men and listened to the chanting of the dirges for the Saviour's death.

How shall I bury thee, O my God? Or with what winding sheet shall I enshroud thee? With what hands shall I touch thy body incorruptible? Or what songs shall I sing at thy forthgoing . . . ? Now and then the dense Byzantine language parted to reveal a word, a moment familiar to them, and they tasted the pain of their exile.

Perhaps as they waited there they thought of their own deaths, which must have seemed so near in this alien land. The young men had come to the New World without women. Before there would be the need to celebrate a wedding or a baptism there would be that more urgent need, should death take them in this foreign place, not to be buried unsung, mourned without blessing or chant in some mining town coffeehouse or saloon. Death had founded their churches.

An Angel stood before the Myrrh-bearing Women at the tomb, the chanter sang, *crying Spices are meet for the dead, but Christ hath revealed himself as a stranger to corruption. . . .* The attendants raised the bier to their shoulders and carried it outside, and the young men followed with their candles, singing. In the darkness they walked three times around the church shielding the frail lights. The procession stopped. The bier was raised high above the door of the church and one by one the men bowed and passed under it—Raïkos, the baker, my grandfather, Louis Tikas. George Zeese would survive the road gang and the mining town, live to found a family and enter the long struggle with old age. Louis Tikas would die a martyr, cut off from both his past and his posterity.

They went once more into the church where the service ended and they were blessed. They thought of their sins, forgave each other, and embraced. As my grandfather left the church the baker slipped something into his pocket. It was a five-dollar gold piece.

In April 1908 an extra gang went out to Cripple Creek to work on the Denver and Rio Grande Western line. George Zeese went with them. He would not spend much more time in Denver after that starving spring. From now on he would be a railroad builder, foreman of work crews, a labor contractor, eventually an owner of businesses. He would never take a dollar from a man to buy a job, and he would never (except for one brief moment) turn back to the Old Country. Once, twice, three times at least, he would pull his gun—the gun he referred to as his six brothers—in anger. And in the end, it was only when he was an old man that he could finally be persuaded to put it away. He had made his success. But that is his story.

As for Louis Tikas, he had been in Colorado since the middle of September 1906. What had brought him there, how he had lived in the intervening six months, I do not know. He had not come alone, however, for with him were others from his village. Perhaps there were Greeks from their district already in Colorado. Perhaps the rumor of work had lured them west, as it had my grandfather. I think of them on the train that was taking them west looking at the groups of men standing sweltering beside the track, backs burnt, sledgehammers and tie tampers for a moment stilled, trying to catch a bit of breeze from the cars speeding by. The young men on the train would have known they were their countrymen. A few years later an educated Greek named Canoutas would travel these same western tracks and remember the little groups of his own people who seemed to stand at every mile. The sight filled him with grief. "All these have left their beloved fatherland," he wrote, "their families, their fellow countrymen and their lands, and have come here to build and repair railroads in the hope of acquiring a few thousand francs—instead of which they acquire rheumatism, tuberculosis, venereal diseases, and those other ills, while others are deprived of feet, hands, eyes, and some their lives. . . ." Who knows what Louis Tikas thought? He had turned twenty on the boat bringing him to America and had not had time to shed his old Greek name. I like to think that since he was young he was hopeful.

In those first years in Colorado Tikas may have rustled a job in the steel mill in Pueblo, as George Zeese had done, or in the mines or on a road crew. Or gone out with other Greeks to thin the endless acres of sugar beets in the shimmering heat of the Arkansas River Valley. There are rumors, too, from Americans who knew him only during the great strike that he had worked for an insurance agency or kept a saloon or was head of a syndicate of bootblacks. This last rumor may be tantalizingly significant. It was at just about this time that a gang of Greek bootblacks who had been working for five cents an hour and sleeping in straw above a Denver shine parlor walked out for a ten-cent an hour raise. Was this Louis Tikas' first strike?

So Tikas may have done these things. Or he may have done none of them. But four years after his arrival in America we find him taking the first step toward a permanent accommodation with the new land. On April 1, 1910, he went into District Court in Denver and made out his Declaration of Intention.

> I, Louis Tikas, aged twenty-four years, occupation merchant, do declare on oath that my personal description is: Color, white; com-

plexion, medium; height, five feet eight inches; wei₎
fifty-one pounds; color of hair, dark brown; color
other visible distinctive marks, none;
    I was born eight miles west of Retimo, Crete, on ₎
day of March, anno Domini 1886; I now reside at ₎
Street, Denver, Colorado. It is my bona fide intention ₎
forever all allegiance and fidelity to any foreign prince,
state or sovereignty, and particularly to George I, Kin₎
Greeks, of which I am now a subject; I arrived at the port
York on or about the twenty-fifth day of March, anno Domin.
I am not an anarchist; I am not a polygamist nor believer ₎
practice of polygamy; and it is my intention in good faith to be₎
a citizen of the United States of America and to permanently re₎
therein:

SO HELP ME GOD

He signed his name with the careful hand of a man not much us₎
writing. America had swallowed the old Greek name. He was L₎
Tikas now, merchant. He was part owner of a coffeehouse at 17₎
Market Street.

It is difficult to tell how 1746 Market Street once looked. By the
1970s its face had been plastered over and it had become some nameless parts distributor or auto repair shop. But I remember such places
from childhood: a flyspecked pot of basil in the window, a few cheap
prints on the walls of the mustachioed heroes of '21 and of the King of
Greece—or Venizelos if they were Cretans—a half-dozen tables and
rickety chairs where old men huddled over their cups of sweet coffee
and the Greek papers. In old photographs you see the same pictures on
the walls of the coffeehouses, the same improvised, rickety ambience.
Only the men posing for the camera are young and careless, full of the
vanity of their years and displaying their new-found American wealth.
Here one wears a rakish cap, another is dressed in a Norfolk jacket
buttoned to the chin, someone else, some twenty-four-year-old card-
shark is wearing, miraculously, spats. I remember them at Stellios'—
that good Cretan—on Salt Lake City's Second West Street, the *sportis*
of days gone by, shuffling rheumatically back into the kitchen to peer
under the lids of the pans.
    Such places did not rise out of the ground whole. How they came
to be built, and the Greek Towns around them, could tell us a good

Maybe you seen them coffeehouses. Have you? Chairs, you know,
couple of tables. Serve coffee, little ouzo, stuff like that. . . . —John

Tsanakatsis. Greek coffeehouse in Ogden, Utah, early 1900s. Courtesy of Mrs. George Soteras, Ogden, Utah.

deal about the early years of Greek immigration in this country.

George Allison (some stories would have his name originally Krouskos) is the name one reads again and again in the early history of Greek Denver—the *tselingas*, the head shepherd of the flock. He arrived in Colorado from his native Sparta at the age of twelve in the year 1883. The date alone would make him a pioneer, one of those first adventurous Peloponnesians to set out for America. By 1897, when there were probably fewer than fifteen thousand Greeks in all of the United States, we read of George Allison valiantly trying to scrape together enough money from Denver's tiny Greek colony to send fifteen of her men to the Greco–Turkish war.

But the great rush of Greek immigration was about to begin. The crash in the market for Greek currants in 1898 only drove it on all the more rapidly. Between 1901 and 1910 perhaps 170,000 Greeks entered the United States, and this from a country whose official population was not much more than two and a half million people. Reports from Greek officials in those years would find entire provinces almost totally deserted by their men and boys. They had left a country whose rocky, exhausted fields could no longer support them. There were simply too many of them and they were too hungry and there was not enough land.

America was their goal. Since the Civil War this country had become a formidable power and she was being built on two things, both, it seemed, inexhaustible: immense natural resources and the cheap labor necessary to turn these resources into commodities. The immigrants were that cheap labor. By 1901 Denver papers were already beginning to print news of the Greeks who were filtering into the West.

> *The Rocky Mountain News*   January 26, 1901
>
> One hundred and fifty Greeks arrived in Pueblo this morning and were at once employed as laborers by the Colorado Fuel and Iron company at the Bessemer steel works. This action on the part of the company is rather an unusual one for heretofore when it has been necessary to import labor the men have been colored steel workers from Alabama and Tennessee. Just at the present time the company could have found plenty of laborers in Pueblo, for there are a number of idle men here who have come in from railroad grading camps in various parts of the state.

They came in gangs such as this at first, as other immigrants had before them, brought in by the carload by some labor agent to work on a road gang or in a smelter or a mine. Yet in Pueblo there were men waiting for work, there were blacks experienced in steel making ready to be imported from the South. Why, the article asked, bring in the Greeks? The answer was unspoken: the Greeks were newcomers, unorganized, tractable, willing to work for the lowest wages. It was a pattern cut deep in American industry of new immigrants displacing the old, breaking their strikes, driving them, as the nativists would have it, from their jobs. (Indeed, a year later you would see the smelter operators of Salida firing "white men" to fill their places with Greeks, now called "the best in the business.")

A month after the Greeks were sent to the steel mill in Pueblo we find sixty-six Greeks who had been grading the Colorado and Wyoming road leaving Trinidad by coach for work on the Rio Grande and Sangre de Cristo line at Crestone. We next hear of the Greeks in a grim little story that tells us something of such gangs and their life. In July of 1901 two Greeks, Gus Geanakos and George Karakatseanes, and Joseph Zurtos, an "Austrian," were recovering from dangerous knife wounds in St. Joseph's Hospital in Denver. It had happened on the Nebraska plains near Sidney. A gang of a hundred Greeks working on the Union Pacific track had fought with a gang of Austrians and Italians over possession of a handcar. The Greeks had been running the handcar down the tracks when Zurtos, the Austrian, waved a pistol at them and ordered them to stop. Karakatseanes jumped at him with a knife and in a few minutes two hundred men were battling with knives and clubs along the tracks.

But the battles were not only fought among club-and-knife-wielding Greeks and Slavs and Italians along the barren reaches of a railroad section. Already Denver's Greek colony held enough members for serious feuding within its own ranks.

On February 4, 1901, there was a row in the colony. George Allison's authority as "mayor" of the Greeks was being challenged by a rival faction led by one Stratis Cokanes. A week later Cokanes and his gang were again in the news accused of the theft of two shirts, an overcoat, a pair of shoes, and a bed. The newspaper accounts of the feud are interesting for what they tell us in passing of the Denver Greeks; it seems they had become pullers of candy and poppers of corn.

Denver Times   February 11, 1901

> Some of the Greeks preside over popcorn stands at night and the others run candy stores during the daytime. The popcorn men are home during the days and the candy men at night, and while the poppers are away working the candy pullers steal the clothing and beds, and while the candy pullers are doing business the popcorn men steal them back again. In the mix-up it is evident that there has not been a fair deal somewhere along the line. The division of property has not been even, and one side having given up hope of getting a square deal, has taken the matter into the courts.

No doubt the courts were as unsuccessful as the Greeks had been in meting out justice in the case. Yet the hint the newspaper gives of the Greeks' lives, of their work, is important. They were leaving the railroad gangs and road crews with those small sums of money that would allow them to settle in a city such as Denver and buy a popcorn cart or open a hole-in-the-wall candy stand. They were former villagers, farmers, shepherds, goatherds. It was an impressive thing to own your own business, to work with clean hands.

And they worked. A sad little item tells this story.

Denver Times August 11, 1902

GREEK ROBBED FOR SIXTH TIME

As Fast as He Saves Up a Small
Sum of Money Thieves Take it From
Him. Complains to the Police—
Works Early and Late.

The Greek's name was Leo Condon. A neighbor named Louis Lake told the *Times* reporter of the five previous robberies and of this latest theft.

> "Last night they broke in at the same window," resumed Lake, "and they searched his trunk and took those Greekish papers that he thinks a whole lot of."
> Besides the papers, the thieves got away with a number of plaster of paris images and some candy and peanuts. Condon is much disturbed over his failure to get a good start in business in this country. He came to Denver from his native home only a few years ago, and

accumulated $500 by selling popcorn on the streets. This money he loaned to one of his countrymen. Now, having lost the notes, he cannot collect the cash, and is trying again to save up his money. A few weeks ago he started out to sell popcorn at nights. He runs his shop from 6 a.m. until 8 p.m., and then sells popcorn from 8 p.m. until 10 o'clock and sometimes later. He believes that a gang of street arabs who are acquainted with his habits are responsible for the burglaries in his shop, all of which have been committed while he was out in the evenings selling popcorn on the streets.

Works early and late. That is what they had come to this country for, to work early and late, to run that popcorn stand, to save money. They were saving the money for their sisters' dowries and for paying off the mortgages on the family farms and for their own return to Greece. (For they would return, of that even those taking out citizenship papers were sure.) And so they clustered in the cities and towns. They built their own colonies, their way stations and fortresses in the New World. They came off the railroad gangs or out of the mines and smelters with their small stakes or they borrowed money from a friend or relative a little better established in this country than they were or a padrone sent them out on the streets selling candy or flowers or put them to work shining shoes. By 1910, when Louis Tikas took out his first papers, there were 240 Greeks noted in the Denver census. But in reality there were hundreds more, itinerants moving from job to job, newcomers shining shoes or washing dishes in their countrymen's restaurants, men trying to catch on in some small business they could collapse to the size of a suitcase overnight if disaster overtook them or a new opportunity called in another town. In the winter, with the end of railroad work, still more Greeks flocked to the city. They filled the transient hotels and boardinghouses and haunted the labor agencies looking for a job. Turning Sybarite, they went in gangs to the public baths, scraping the dirt of the roads away in the hot water, steaming out stiffened muscles—you see them caricatured in the papers as "Modern Apollos," dripping and oily. They gambled and visited the women on Market Street. And they went to the coffeehouse. In the midst of them was Louis Tikas.

Think now of a night in the winter of 1911 and Louis Tikas' coffeehouse in Denver. The men who fill the room are young and most are Cretans—of all the Greeks the most clannish, the closest to their medieval roots. They sit in a cloud of cigarette smoke, cursing and arguing above the roll of the dice of the backgammon players. They are miners, gamblers, *sportis* with their hats pushed back on their heads like the Americans. In the village most of them would have been too young to sit carousing in a coffeehouse, but they are ripped from the villages now and from the omnipresent eyes of their elders, who demanded modesty of young men and respect. So they frisk with their newfound freedom, they strut. Danger has added its particular spices to their leisure. They like to tell a newcomer how the Greeks had been saved from the Victor–American mine explosion in Delagua, Colorado, the November before. Had they not taken the day off in honor of St. Demetrios, whose celebration it was, they would have gone up with the Mexicans and the Italians and the rest of them when the mine caught fire. Such narrow escapes had not kept them from going into the mines again. They were, after all, fatalists, and they would put their trust in St. Demetrios or the Holy Virgin or in some personal and mysterious form of luck. They feared rockfall and explosion and firedamp; they feared desperately the mutilation of the body. But what they feared more than any of this was failure. For they had come to America not for safety but for dollars.

At a table someone pounds his fist, blasphemes passionately. "Andreas, I screw your Holy Virgin!" Another picks up the dice "*Ela, you little cuckolds . . .*"

Words: *He who hurries shits himself. Stars fell and the pigs ate them. They send us to let a fart and we shit all over the cosmos. Him? He'd argue with his own pants* . . . They'd stepped from a wooden-plow economy into the most industrialized nation in the world and this is what they'd sent them to fight with: a handful of proverbs, two dozen songs of vendetta and the Turk wars, the *Erotokritos*, a few *amanes*. This was their education.

So they contend with one another, bargain, shout. And among them goes Louis, smiling, affable, a man to trust. He does errands for the Cretans, goes to the post office to fill out a money order for them or to the bank. For he has always been deft at such things, quick to catch on to new ways. His English is a little better than that of most of them—not much. And yet that is power. One tips his cap to the man who knows a few words of English and who can speak confidentially

to the policeman or the boss. Such a man is—a Turkish word—
an *afentis*, a boss himself. But Louis Tikas is no boss. He is a patriot.

"Two of them? Really?"

"I swear it *vre*. Two of them. American girls . . ."

The sports and cardsharks cast their eyes about, sipping sweet
coffee, smoking cigarettes, while Louis goes here and there, wiping a
table, bringing another cream soda, offering advice. He is twenty-four
years old, and, as I imagine him, even then smartly dressed, as the
women in the tent colonies were to remember him. A *kafedzhis* must
be a man of parts, must know how to get along. For before there
were Greek churches in this country, before there were clubs and
patriotic societies, there were these smoky little shrines to Hellenism.
A long-handled pot of coffee brewing on a stove, a table or two—
it was enough. Here a Greek left word of his whereabouts for a friend
or a fellow villager; here is where the letters from home come, the
pleas for money, the warnings against the beguilements of the foreigners, the black-bordered messages telling of a death. Tikas reads
these letters to the illiterates—and not a few are illiterate. He takes
down their replies. Perhaps, if the story is to be believed, this is why
that nameless Cretan who preceded him left the coffeehouse to Louis,
although they were neither relatives nor fellow villagers. Perhaps he
had recognized in Louis Tikas this ability to deal with men.

But sing me another song now, in the year 1911, in Louis' coffeehouse. With them in that year is a young Cretan dishwasher from the
town of Spili named Louloudakis. He had come over just a year before.
He'd washed dishes for John Kavas and had been one of the Greeks
who was celebrating St. Demetrios' day in Delagua when the mine
blew up.

Mr. Loulos likes to be called by his uncut name, Louloudakis,
which in Greek means "Little Flower." And there is in fact something
flower-like about him, this small and smiling old man with the thick
glasses who sits in front of his air conditioner on a hot day in Chicago
telling me about Denver in the old days.

"Louis Tikas, he had a coffeehouse at that time. Seventeen Market
Street. In Denver we was maybe two hundred Cretans, work in coal
mines around there—Lafayette, Frederick, Louisville, Delagua, Ludlow.

And every night or so those Cretans come flocking to the coffeehouse. He done pretty good. Sit down, play cards, drink coffee, you know. Denver was dry 1911. He was serving a little ice cream. He was doing pretty good . . ."

The letter said he had known Tikas, that Tikas was a good man. As a newcomer he had slept in the same bed as Louis in a hotel on Larimer Street. "He was a good patriot," he had written to the editor of the Cretan paper. "Now I beg you to forgive me because I am not so good with letters. I am sixty-three years in this American world. My name is Pericles Louloudakis, from Spili, Rethymnon, but now I have cut my name . . ."

Sitting before me he is almost apologetic that he had so little for me.

"He helped me out sometime I was short of money, you know, hungry. So he helped me out. Give me a chance. He was a very good man. He was hundred percent Cretan."

A hundred percent Cretan. It is the kind of praise only one who knows the Cretans can appreciate. It speaks of generosity and a kind of dash, of a zest for life and for heroics. There is nothing to forgive Mr. Louloudakis as he sits telling me of those days.

By the winter of 1911 young Louloudakis had gone on to another dishwashing job—this time in a downtown cafeteria owned by an American. Working with the Cretan was a girl from St. Louis named Ora Williams. She was older than Louloudakis—twenty-seven to his seventeen. But he was lively, handsome (to judge from old photographs), and charming. And, I suspect, ingenious. Now Tikas had a new role, that of go-between. He translated the love notes exchanged betwen Ora, who of course knew no Greek, and the romantic English-less Little Flower. I imagine Little Flower writing out his ardent letters in his careful clerk's hand (he'd been trained to be secretary to the court in Spili when he was fifteen) and Tikas rendering them into somewhat inaccurate English. But accurate enough. On Christmas Eve 1911 the Cretan dishwasher and Ora Williams went before a Baptist minister in Golden, Colorado, and were married. Ora, it turned out, was the daughter of a Missouri department store owner and a woman of some means. She brought to the marriage five choice acres of land between Golden and West Colfax, cash, and the cafeteria itself. For when the old woman who owned the place let it be known she disapproved of dishwashers marrying white help, Ora simply bought her out.

In the meantime the dishwasher had become something of a celebrity among his own people, even landing in the New York Greek–American press for his foray into the heart of a millionaire's daughter. The Greeks sat around Tikas' coffeehouse enjoying their friend's notoriety. What would you expect, the sports said. She was, after all, an *Americanidha* . . . They pushed their hats back on their heads and winked.

But as in all fairy tales such fortune does not come without a price. Thirty days after the wedding Ora Loulos lay dead with a ruptured appendix. And the dishwasher was left not with an inheritance but a lawsuit.

They went to court twice, the rich father suing the upstart Greek to break the legacy. At last there came a treacherous Greek bearing the Anglo–Saxon name of Frye—Nick Frye. It was Frye who convinced Louloudakis to sign a certain paper, and so one morning the dishwasher woke up to realize he'd been betrayed. The paper he'd signed was a quitclaim to the cafeteria. But Louloudakis was determined to rescue something, and the cafeteria basement was filled with food. "Boys," he said, standing up in the coffeehouse, "you come tomorrow morning about four o'clock. Louis, make a good breakfast for about fifty or sixty Cretans." And that is what happened. Louloudakis hired three wagons and in fifteen minutes the Cretans had cleared out the cafeteria basement, unloaded the food at Louis', and were sitting down to breakfast and laughing about the whole thing. And so the Little Flower managed to salvage something from his brief career as an American husband.

Louis Tikas looks out on Market Street and being Greek he sees it with Greek eyes. He sees how ambitious these Americans are, how much they have done. There is a will behind the soft manners of the men in the offices, a relentlessness behind those smooth, pale faces. The women too are wonders. They go about alone, ride on streetcars, stop on the open street to speak with men they happen to know. In the village they would be called shameless; the young Cretans call them worse that that. All this Louis Tikas takes in. But above all what he takes in is the almost dizzy sense of opportunity for a Greek with brains. His partner is now a Corinthian named Gus Kutsofes. The Kotopoulos brothers own a restaurant nearby, as does John Kavas. A few doors down Pete Colaris and Nick Trahanas run a saloon. Chris Kayas owns a grocery store at 1501 19th and George Pappas has a lunchroom on Curtis. And on Curtis and 15th is George Allison's candy store. It is an impressive place with two entrances and a counter that reflects the rows of glass jars, the light from the mirrors, the polished spigots. In the candy store, Allison is surrounded by important Americans, politicians, and campaign workers. He speaks to them all and everyone in Denver knows him. Louis Tikas would have listened to Allison's advice to the Greeks and he would have pondered his success. It was probably the example of progressive men such as Allison that had prompted him to take out his first papers in April 1910. The papers could be a token of embracing American progress, of throwing in your lot with it. But they were more importantly a kind of camouflage, like Anglicizing or cutting your name, a hedge against the nativists and bigots. The memory was still fresh in 1910 of the South Omaha riots of the year before when a mob of striking slaughterhouse workers and hangers-on, bitter over Greek strikebreakers, had seized the pretext of a Greek killing a policeman to burn Greek Town to the ground and drive twelve-hundred Greeks out of the city.

But there was another man, a Spartan like Allison, who could be seen going in and out of his office across the street from Tikas' coffeehouse when he was in town.

I believe Louis Tikas would have watched this man, Leonidas Skliris, through the windows of the coffeehouse, and I believe he would have thought of him often in those days. For Skliris was a padrone and like Louis Tikas an organizer of men. But he organized them in order to bleed them.

A Corinthian tells of his first meeting with Skliris in a Trinidad, Colorado, restaurant on the Fourth of July 1907. There was a band of them, all fresh to the country, up from an extra gang at Raton to take in the horse race and parade. I think of the young Greeks talking a little too loudly, looking green and out of place in their cheap new American clothes. At another table a man was watching them. He was young himself, just under thirty, and like them a Greek. But his clothes were not the cheap suits of the railroad workers. The man questioned the sixteen-year-old Corinithian.

"Do you know who I am?"

The Corinthian said he didn't know.

"I'm Louis Skliris. You ever hear of him?"

The boy shook his head. No, he had never heard of him. And the man smiled.

Am I inventing that smile? Maybe so. But it is for me a sign of the man, of his ability to master these Greeks. His name is still remembered in Greek households in the Rockies. He is still hated, and, in a strange way, still admired. For almost two decades he touched the lives of the Greeks in the West.

It was not long after the young Corinthian, John Rougas, had met this man Skliris that he learned who he was. Working at the Colorado Fuel and Iron Company plant in Pueblo he would hear Greeks say, "We're going over to Skliris to work on the railroad." Others would set out for Utah or Nevada where a job they had bought from him awaited them in the mines. There is a photograph of Skliris published a year after his meeting with young Rougas in Trinidad on that Fourth of July. He looks out at the camera with calm, wide-set eyes. His face is the broad, square face of the Peloponnesos, a cleft chin, wide mouth. It is the sort of face that will grow jowly in time, but he is only thirty now and already a master of his world. By the time the photograph was taken he controlled much of the Greek labor in at least three western states. In the Utah coal towns and the copper camps of eastern Nevada, he was their final authority. More important was his hold over the Greek laborers at the cluster of Utah Copper Company mines at Bingham Canyon, where steam shovels and dynamite were gouging out an immense amphitheater in a mountain of copper ore. The railroad workers, too, were under his thumb, for he held labor contracts for the Union Pacific, the Western Pacific, and the Denver and Rio Grande. When my grandfather found himself blackballed and his railroad gang out of work in Montpelier, Idaho, it was Skliris he wired. A short time later he was working his crew among the switchbacks and tunnels of the Western Pacific line at Portola, California. *O Ergatis*, the newspaper which published Skliris' photograph, called him *sidherous anthropos*—a man of iron.

I'm Louis Skliris. You ever hear of him? —Leonidas G. Skliris. Photograph of Skliris at about 30. Courtesy of Helen Zeese Papanikolas, Salt Lake City, Utah.

When he looked at the sixteen-year-old greenhorn who didn't recognize his name, he smiled.

He had been born in Bresthenon, Sparta, in 1878. He claimed to be the son of a former governor of the province; the claim was an exaggeration, but in fact the Greek he spoke was that of the educated classes and not that of the poor villagers. When he was sixteen or seventeen he stowed away on a liner and came to America. By his own account he sold violets in the lobby of an office building in New York then moved west to work on the labor gangs of the Illinois Central Railroad. In May 1900 a small notice appeared in the *Denver Times* of a gang of Greeks sent to work on the Cripple Creek line. It may be these were Skliris' men, for at about this time he had undertaken, "on nerve alone," a contract on the Cripple Creek road. But the notice points to Skliris with more than just a coincidence of dates; for the 130 Greeks had been lied to, the money they paid to the Chicago employment agency for their transportation was gone, and the labor contractor was demanding four months' work from them before he'd give them half the fare back. It was the pattern of gouging Skliris would exhibit in all his dealings with laboring men. But whatever Skliris' part in the troubles of the Greeks on the Cripple Creek gang— if he had a part at all—by the time the ambitious young Spartan was finished with his labor contract he was principal labor agent for the Denver and Rio Grande Western railroad. Now he would set up his headquarters in Salt Lake City and enter the market for labor in the coal and copper mines of Utah and eastern Nevada. He would open branch offices of his agency in New York, St. Paul, Chicago, Kansas City, San Francisco, Sacramento, and on Denver's Market Street. He would move into a suite in the newly-built Hotel Utah, taking an entire floor on one wing, and there would be shares of stock, a commission store in San Francisco, a California ranch, a steamship line agency, a store concession in the camps of Utah Copper. And always the stories of his heartlessness and greed.

For the poor man there is always this mystery about power: power cleanses. It puts one out of the reach of the everyday world. Out of the reach of hunger and uncertainty and the need to bow. Power imparts its aura to the meanest of gestures. It places the man who possesses it beyond the touch of law and common things. More than a few Greek laborers had murder stored up in their bellies for Skliris, who had cheated them out of their wages or sold their jobs to another man. In 1915 a Cretan he had swindled would come at him with a gun as he was leaving the Hotel Utah, seriously wounding him. But for a time it looked as if he were invulnerable.

At 1746 Market Street the coffee house knows the buzz of speculation when Skliris is in town. It hums with the reason for his meeting with his nephew, the tall and imposing Gus Economou, conjectures on his doings with the Americans, weighs up grain by grain the sum of his influence. For the Cretans in the coffeehouse, Skliris is a man with *mesa*—with "means"—the almost supernatural power to accomplish things. And so they must go to wait upon him, hat in hand. Ten dollars, twenty dollars to buy a job, a dollar a month to keep it—if another man did not outbid you for it. All this Skliris himself exacts. Then there are the fees and the bribes to his lieutenants in each mining town, on each road gang. You tip your hat and call the powerful man *afentis*.

Skliris listens to the Cretans with ill-disguised contempt for their country dialect. For he is both above them and necessary to them. It was he who made sense of the anarchy of life in the mines and on the railroads. He filled a void in the crude workings of the industrial system and brought his men jobs as scabs and menials. He sent them out to work for $1.75 a day when a good German or Welshman could get $2.50, but this was the work the Greeks needed, the work America held out to them. And they needed Skliris because they knew him. He was the bey, the landowner, the Ottoman with his hand out to take a bribe or dispense a favor. They had always known these things.

In the coffeehouse someone begins to sing. The voice clears a way for itself in the smoky air, insistent and droning.

> Theos mou, *give me light! A heart like a cauldron*
> *To sit here and think of Master John . . .*

The men at the tables pause. They listen to the singer.

> *I will not give the tribute, I will not pay the taxes*
> *Let the Sultan bring against us battle flags in the thousands,*
> *Let the Sultan bring against us his pashas and his armies,*
> *Sphakia has men, men and castle-wreckers,*
> *Sphakia has worthy and gallant warriors . . .*

It is eerie to think of it. They sit in the coffeehouse singing the song their great-great-grandfathers knew as if that boiling industrial world of twentieth-century America had been all at once stopped, frozen in time like a castle in a fairy tale. All history compresses to the same moment for them: Skliris and the Sultan are one, noble Daskaloyiannis of Sphakia stands poised on the edge of action, as he had stood in 1770. His spirit fills the coffeehouse, expands in the heavy air. They had heard the pop of muskets in the hills themselves, these Cretans, they remembered the flash of sabers in the village square. They were no good at looking at the mines and mills and railroads and seeing their brutal lives as part of some system, of some deep disorder in the world. Suffering and heroism, pain and joy were personal things. Eleven hundred years of Arab pirates and Venetian overlords and Turkish conquerors had taught them this. If they fought, it would not be for some abstraction. It would be for personal vengeance. And it would have the swift, sharp taste of gunpowder and blood.

When Louis Tikas watched Skliris the padrone from the windows of his coffee house, a man of the sixteenth century was looking out at a man of the twentieth. Yet already Tikas was preparing to step beyond. He had, after all, his start. He had signed his first papers.

In the mind of the average American, the modern immigrants are generally regarded as inferior peoples —races which he looks down on, and with which he does not wish to associate on terms of social equality. Like the negroes, they are brought in for economic reasons to do the hard and menial work to which an American does not care to stoop. The business of the alien is to go into the mines, the foundries, the sewers, the stifling air of factories and work shops, out on the roads and railroads in the burning sun of summer, or the driving sleet and snow. If he proves himself a man, and rises above his situation, and acquires wealth, and cleans himself up—very well, we receive him after a generation or two. But at present he is far beneath us, and the burden of proof rests with him.

Professor Henry Pratt Fairchild
1911

You have no right to be poor. It is your duty to be rich.

Reverend Russell H. Conwell
1901

3. A LESSON IN ECONOMICS

The towns lay up the stark canyons huddled around the workings of the mines: the spindly-legged tipple, the fan house, the corrugated iron sheds of the stables and powerhouses and shops. The entrances of the mines were carved out of the sides of the bluffs, the numbers painted on the concrete shoring around their mouths. Culm bearded the denuded slopes and lay heaped up everywhere in slatey mounds. Everywhere were smoking piles of slack. At night the rows of coke ovens flared luridly along the tracks. And among the piles of rock and slack, following the narrow lines of the railroad with its endless strings of coal cars, or climbing the steep hills, were the buildings of the town: the company store, the mine offices, the bleak, identical rows of company

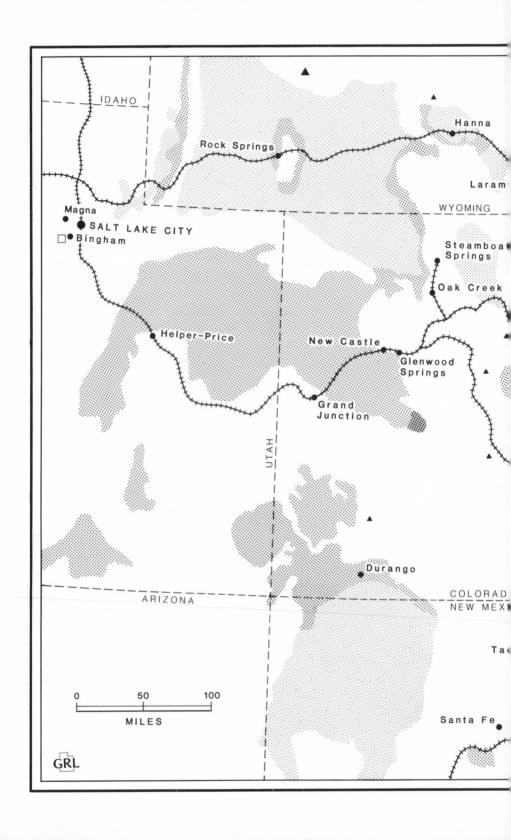

IDAHO

Rock Springs

Hanna

Laram

WYOMING

Magna

SALT LAKE CITY

Bingham

Steamboat
Springs

Oak Creek

Helper–Price

New Castle

Glenwood
Springs

Grand
Junction

UTAH

Durango

COLORAD

ARIZONA

NEW MEX

Tae

0   50   100

MILES

Santa Fe

GRL

COLORADO COALFIELDS

Sunrise

Cheyenne

NEBRASKA

Greeley

oulder
Lafayette

NORTHERN COALFIELD (INSET)

DENVER

K
A
N
S
A
S

Colorado Springs

Cripple Creek

anyon City

Pueblo

SOUTHERN COALFIELD

Walsenburg

Aguilar

Trinidad

Raton

COAL DEPOSITS

- ANTHRACITE
- BITUMINOUS
- SUBBITUMINOUS

IRON ORE DEPOSITS

- ▲ PRIMARY
- ▲ SECONDARY

COPPER DEPOSITS

- ☐ PRIMARY

NORTHERN COALFIELD

0 2 4
MILES

■ MINES

Longmont

St. Vrain

Frederick Mine

Dacono

Ft. Lupton

BOULDER CO.

Boulder Creek

Erie

Dry Creek

Boulder

Lafayette

WELD CO.
ADAMS CO.

Brighton

Louisville

Vulcan Mine

Marshall

Coal Creek

Monarch Mine

Platte River

houses, little cubes of clapboard or brick and inside cardboard partitions nailed over the studs. Up the sides of the bluffs the powder-box shanties and adobe huts perched so steeply, sometimes, that where a man's front porch fell off, his neighbor's chimney cap began. Now and then there was the sagging porch of an unpainted boardinghouse or cheerless hotel. There was never a sidewalk, a decent street, hardly a tree. The camps were closed, many of them. That is, they were surrounded by barbed-wire fences and a guard who would stop a stranger and ask him hard questions about his business and his friends. Perhaps the town had a church or a meeting hall on company land. There was a school. In Sopris there was a saloon for every seventeen men.

In 1911 a young Greek from the desolate coast of Sphakia, in southern Crete, came up to the Hastings mine. His name was Kostas Papadakis and he was twenty-three years old. His father had died when he was nine and had left him with a mother, sister, and younger brother to provide for. He had struggled in his family's olive grove, herded other people's sheep. Those who imagine such rocky villages through the haze of a visit or two to a Greek nightclub should talk to men like him: he never learned to dance. He never had time. Once he cut down a bunch of the scrubby oaks that grew among the rocks of his family's land. He learned how to stack the limbs into ricks and keep them burning slowly under a mound of earth. He kept the fire alive through three or four days of continuous watching while his mother and sister brought him food. In the end he made a ton and a half of charcoal and sold it for half a cent a pound. People thought he had done well. He had earned fifteen dollars for more than a week of constant work, but it was enough to make up what he needed to get to America. In 1911 he left for the United States. He had to wait ten days for a ship at the port of Patras and starved himself the whole time, trying to save the ten or fifteen dollars of show money he needed to get into the United States. He landed in New York, then got a letter from someone he knew that sent him down to Anderson, South Carolina, to work in a factory making nets. He stayed there a while, making $1.20 for working a twelve-hour day. He was set to go home in disgust with a few of the other Greeks when they ran into a labor agent in Norfolk who said they were crazy—he could send them to a place where they could make some money. The labor agent fed them a couple of days, talked to them, then gave them a few dollars and put them on a train for Colorado.

Papadakis ended up at the Victor–American camp of Hastings. They sent him over to the company store to get outfitted: pick and shovel, hank of fuse, electric lamp, roll of waxed paper to wrap the charge in. He signed up for a can of double F black powder. He was already well in debt to the store. The next day he went up to the mine and got the numbered brass checks he would attach to the coal cars for weighing. If there was an accident, it would be the check that would identify his burned or mangled body.

He went to work with an old timer, a black man named Dave. Dave kept a wad of tobacco in his cheek, spat, showed the Greek the ropes. He showed him how to test the roof of the room with the blade of a pick, listening for the clean ring of metal against stone that meant it was solid. He showed him how to set a prop. It didn't take many words between them, the old timer and the green foreigner. Dave pointed his finger above his head at the treacherous roof and the Greek kid didn't need a translation. They set to work loading the first of the day's cars, shoveling the loose coal until it rose over the car's sides, sometimes using their picks to break the pieces that were too big to handle. They trimmed the cars with the heavy chunks of coal, wrestling the slabs into the car against their knees. Together they could load seven or eight cars on a good day. They were paid fifty cents a ton.

When the loose coal was loaded, they dressed the face of the room, undercut the bottom of the coal seam with their picks, then set to work drilling the holes for the next round of charges. Four along the roof, two on each side, four on the bottom with a thread bar and box, twelve turns to the inch, six feet for each charge. It could take both of them, using all their strength, to turn the bar. Then they placed the charges and stuck in the clay-filled dummies for the shot firers to tamp. They drove each room two hundred fifty feet then had to quit, for the air was bad at Hastings. Every time they moved they had to scavenge the mine for old rails, rip them up and set them again, since the Victor-American Company did not allow them to use new rails. They were not paid for this. They were moving sixteen-pound rails, five or six hundred feet of them. Every time they'd move a rail they'd sit down and curse.

There is an essential silence in a mine, and the echoless, thick air smothers the sound of machinery or the tamp of picks or boots on a floor. The dark too is without resonance, so that the beam of a pit lamp ends abruptly in the blackness as in a dead-end tunnel. Now and then the light picks up the dark, sweating sheen of a wall, glimmering like the flow of a river. This is the coal. Or it catches the surprised flash of a mule's eyes, or the sudden appearance of a group of men, their blackened faces ghastly in the chalky light. They squatted there, not trying to talk much, Old Dave and the Greek, resting after moving a rail or waiting for the mule to come by to take a loaded car. In the quiet the sounds of their breath and their pounding hearts gave way to listening. Beneath the weight of silence they heard the creaking of the pillars around them, the "working" of the mine. Sometimes, deep in the strata of rock above them, something would give way with a sharp crack that could make them suddenly stiffen with fear. And almost imperceptible, so that they had to listen hard for it, with a faint, far-away noise like the murmur of water trickling over the pebbles in a brook, was the sound of the gas seeping through the crevices of the coal. It was what they couldn't hear that was more threatening; those tiny particles of coal dust filling their lungs and the tinder-dry air, infinitely fine and infinitely combustible.

At the weigh boss' shack Dave and the young Greek watched the cars move over the scales. They checked their numbers against the weights marked next to them on the coal-smudged bulletin. The cars they had figured at two tons lined up on the sheet at 3,800 pounds, 3,7000 pounds. Dave spat tobacco juice on the side of one of the cars. "See, I tol' you," he said, "I tol' you they was cheatin' us."

In the years before the great strike of 1913–14 a fiction was created by the coal operators of Colorado that the men who dug in their mines were not simply employees, as much a part of the machinery for mining coal as the mules and the washers and the trains, but independent contractors, free to come and go as they pleased. It was a fiction that allowed them to exact much from their men and that absolved them of much. The men worked the mine in rooms, two of them together usually, cutting into the face of the seam between pillars of standing coal. The room was doled out by the pit boss, and it was crucial. How thick your coal seam was, how full of rock, how much water you had to stand in or how low you had to bend to get at the coal —for a man working with his back, working to feed himself and often a family, all this was vital. There was more to it than that. The independent contractors—men like Gus Papadakis and Dave—were paid by the ton. They were paid for the coal they mined, not for the coal they couldn't get to or for the rails they lifted or the rooms they timbered or the walls they "brushed" back from the tracks, the "dead work" in a mine. And they were ultimately responsible for their own safety. The room-and-pillar system of digging coal and the piecework wage might not have been the most efficient ways of working the mines, but they were the most effective means of exploiting men.

A bit of folklore has come down to us that tells how these men saw the companies that worked them. The story might attach itself to any of the mine disasters of those years. A pit boss is sitting in the company office when someone brings him news that the mine has gone up and every man and beast with it, and his first words are "How many mules?" A mule had to be bought and fed. The men replaced themselves. They flooded in, foreigners ignorant of mining, willing to break each other's strikes or undercut a wage, eager to make their seven cars, to take a chance on a poorly-timbered room or a dummy filled with coal dust instead of the clay they would not be paid for unloading. Between 1910 and 1913—in those three years—618 Colorado coal diggers lost their lives in mine accidents. In the disaster year of 1910, the cost of mining coal in terms of men came out to a life given for every 38,000 tons. It didn't take the greenhorn Gus Papadakis long to see what a death trap like the Hastings mine could do. On June 19, 1912, a windy shot set off a pocket of gas and the explosion caught thirteen men on the night shift before they knew what had happened. Twelve of them, including one of the two Greeks on the shift, died of suffocation. The other Greek, George Pappas, was luckier. The rescue team pulled him stunned and broken from behind a wall. He was horribly burned.

The immigrants were cheap and they were expendable. In all the years of coal mine deaths and mutilations, seldom in the memories of the people of the Southern Field had the company-controlled coroners' juries found the corporations to blame. The average death benefit was around $700; many families settled for less. Colorado Fuel and Iron Company attorney Fred Herrington told one widow she ought to be satisfied with a twenty-dollar coffin. Mother Jones said that before she ever came to Colorado she read that a reporter from a Pittsburgh paper asked a C. F. and I. manager why his mine wasn't correctly timbered. The manager answered "Oh, damn it, Dagoes are cheaper than props."

But there was another fiction growing up in Colorado in those years, the dream of the company town itself. You can see the dream in halftone photographs in the C. F. and I. magazine, *Camp and Plant*— the neat ranks of houses, each with its own privy, like a sentry post in back, the interiors of the miners' recreation rooms with their billiard tables and gramophones; you can read the chatty notes from the women's clubs (there are also articles in Spanish and Slavic and Italian); review Professor Keating's lantern slide lecture on "Art in the Decoration of Homes and School Rooms" . . . Where once there had been only scrub cedar and sagebrush, now there were mines, railroads, schools, houses. A city of paper rose in the offices of the coal companies in Denver and Pueblo, blueprints for mine rescue cars, bulletins on safety, and sociological surveys. And always the circulars reminding the superintendents and store managers of the company's policies of noninterference in politics, of freedom of trade, of adherence to laws that had been on the state's books before the turn of the century upholding the rights of men to organize in unions and to have their own checkweighmen and to work an eight-hour day . . . But the circulars stopped short at the barbed-wire fences around the camps. Between the dream and the reality there was a radical disjunction. "We don't care whether you are a member or not," the pit boss might tell a man with a union card. But the next morning the man would find water at his place or be moved to one that did have water, or he wouldn't get his timber or his rails wouldn't be delivered or something else, and he would finally pick up his bucket and go home. Just before the strikers went out in 1913 C. F. and I. Superintendent Charlie O'Neill went up to union coal digger Jim Fyler with a petition and said if he could get anyone to sign it the company would put on a checkweighman and furnish him with bulletins and lead pencils. "It is too late in the day for me," Fyler said. Above C. F. and I. manager Weitzel's desk in Pueblo hung a picture of William A. Pinkerton. The company town was a dream that needed to be policed.

It was policed—sometimes by the very ministers and social workers and saloon keepers and company doctors the men who owned the mines had turned out to lubricate the towns' parts when they grated and repair them when they broke down. More directly it was policed by men like C. F. and I. Chief of Detectives Billy Reno and red-haired Sheriff Jeff Farr, who ran Huerfano County's politics from his string of whorehouses and saloons; by men like Segundo Marshal Bob Lee, laid out cold behind a Dago saloon by someone who'd had enough of his bullying; and by Charlie O'Neill, a former striker turned company man, who answered Weitzel's circular on saloons by saying it might be a good thing for a miner to go on a drunk once in a while since he worked all the harder to make up for lost time when he got to the face of his room. If the company town was a vision to capitalists like John Osgood, who had founded the C. F. and I., and to engineers like Weitzel, who laid it out with their economic rulers, to the men who worked there it was a machine to cheat them of their dignity and their wages. They saw the money they hacked out of the coal with shovels and picks siphoned back to the company itself in the charges they paid for powder and tools and blacksmithing and lamps, in the dollar a month they paid to the company doctor and the rent they paid for a company house. The pair of overalls you could buy at an Aguilar dry goods store for fifty cents cost a dollar and a quarter in the company store—and let a man try to take his trade elsewhere. At Lester they sold water for thirty-five cents a barrel. "It is not what a man earns in Colorado that counts," the union's John Lawson said. "It is what he gets when they get through with him." In 1913, in spite of the years of state law forbidding it, some of the miners were still being paid in scrip.

But to the miners the truth of the company town was more than what could be measured in money. An Italian miner remembered it. "We were called Dago, garlic snapper, all kinds of words. But never the name. Never Bazanelle, Victor Bazanelle." He remembered having to toss scrip into a pit boss' cap as tribute and how, if a man borrowed money against his wages the pit boss would throw it on the ground so that he would have to stoop to pick it up. "A poor man has got no law," one of the immigrants said. Still the dream did not die in the minds of the rich men who made it. In 1903 some poet in *Camp and Plant* described Sopris as a Rocky Mountain gem with lace curtains fluttering in the windows and pianos and sewing machines in the parlors and even, here and there, a patch of lawn. Eleven years later the Sopris doctor went up to Wop Town where the Italian coke pullers were patching together their own community out of dry goods boxes and barrel staves and old pieces of corrugated iron and anything that would stop a hole. The privies were a few boards laid across a pit with a gunnysack for a door and the children didn't even bother with them. Typhus was endemic. Once the doctor had to move a woman in childbirth to get her out of the water falling through the roof of her shack. It had not been that long since the C. F. and I. had looked at its camps, its kindergartens and libraries and schools, the new hospital at Pueblo, and the $10,000 mission it was building as a refuge for the unemployed, where "floaters" could make a temporary living chopping wood, and had proclaimed "It is the announced purpose of this corporation to solve the social problem."

In 1903 the coal miners of Colorado joined the striking hard-rock men of the Western Federation of Miners to rise up in their first important strike, a strike broken by beatings and deportations and the National Guard, and by the Japanese and Mexican and Italian scabs brought in by the carload to work in mines other immigrants were trying to shut down. But although the union was crushed in that strike, it would go out again. Because this is something that had never been explained to those city men who clung to the towns and the mines with the tenacity and selfishness of all dreamers: that a generation had grown up on those denuded slopes, in those bleak and crowded schools, in those unheated boardinghouses, in those shacks. And that they thought of them as their homes. By the end of 1903 *Camp and Plant* had ceased publication and the Colorado Fuel and Iron Company had passed into the hands of a new entrepreneur. Sure the immigrants had heard of John D. Rockefeller. Rockefeller was President of the United States.

The world never ceases its obligation to pay back the poor boy. Yet what it pays is not enough, be it ten thousand-fold the wage it has taken. One serves the world back by shaming it with charity, with dignity, with austerity. These things the world cannot abide.

There was always something dry and hard about John D. Rockefeller. His jokes, when they are recounted by his biographers, have a certain poverty about them, the strained merriment of a child who has never learned to play. Ida Tarbell said he had the soul of a bookkeeper, but it wasn't that. Under the skin was something larger, more ferocious than bookkeeping. It was a terrible sense of order, of efficiency and strength raised to world mastery. He was the first corporate man.

There was something almost aesthetic about it, this sense of order. It was self-willed and severe and, in its complexity, in the intricate maneuvers that had shaped it, in its relentless concern with detail, it had a kind of beauty. It had cost much. "Don't let good fellowship get the least hold on you," he wrote. And again: "I never had a craving for tobacco, or tea or coffee. I never had a craving for anything." In the care he took not to know too much about the means by which certain parts of his great scheme had been accomplished there may have been a splitting of himself that was a species of madness. Long after he was many times a millionaire, he would waken out of a nightmare of his days as a clerk exclaiming "I can't collect so-and-so's account!" On his estates he would raise a flag each year to mark the anniversary of his first coming into business.

But he had been charitable. There is a rather touching artifact of his days as a poor clerk, Ledger A, in which the evidence of his early giving is kept. Five cents to the Sunday School, seventy-five cents to the Mite Society, six cents to the Missionary Cause, ten cents to the poor in church. Cent by cent laying up treasures in heaven. He was not acquisitive of money in itself, nor was he ostentatious in its spending. His whole effort may have been to strip his soul as dry and clean as possible. By 1915 he had given about a quarter of a billion dollars to public benefactions.

He firmly believed God gave him his money. It was not a defiant statement, but a pious one. Through him was the stewardship of great projects, projects to the benefit of all society, not least the working man. He had proved with his great trust, the Standard Oil Company, what few industrialists had even guessed before him, that combination was a fundamental economic law. Yet he would deny the right to combine to the workers themselves. He quoted scripture: A laborer is worthy of his hire." But added, lest he be misunderstood, "*No less, but no more . . .*" Once he commended Henry Frick for the courage and firmness he had displayed at bloody Homestead.

In 1911 the best of the Colorado coal miners would make around $696. Three years later the Colorado Fuel and Iron Company's supporters would point out—it was cause for some congratulations on his altruism—that in the eleven years John D. Rockefeller had controlled the company he had received only $960,000 in dividends: a rate of only a dollar in dividends for every hundred dollars in wages.

In the summer of 1906, about the time twenty-year-old Louis Tikas was making his way to Colorado, John D. Rockefeller, Sr., was vacationing in France, in the town of Compiègne. He bicycled about the countryside or walked through the town asking questions of the natives concerning their habits, their work, their savings. He had received a cable that an indictment had been handed down against him in Ohio concerning violation of that state's antitrust laws. It was expected, for the Interstate Commerce Commission was not alone in its crusade against his combination. Still he continued his amiable chats with his doctor and strolled about the streets, evincing a strong interest in the local heroine (herself a visionary much hounded by courts and commissions), Joan of Arc.

One day a reporter for the *New York American*, who had followed Rockefeller to France, watched an interesting exchange. A barefoot and ragged urchin stepped before Rockefeller and held out his hand. There was a moment of tension. The American looked at the boy steadily, but made no move. The boy himself stood his ground, hand out. It was as if, for that moment, neither the beggar nor the millionaire could move from his attitude, the one staring, the other frozen to his extended hand. At last a bystander came up and spoke sharply to the boy and the boy slunk off.

"What did you say to him?" Rockefeller asked.

"I asked him if he had no self-respect," the Frenchman answered.

"That was fine!" said Rockefeller. "Self-respect—that's it! That's the way we make citizens of the immigrants who come to our country."

During this period my work in the interest of per-fecting your organization among my people took me over the entire Northern Coal Field of the State of Colorado.

Louis Tikas

4. THE NORTHERN FIELD:
THE MAKING OF AN ORGANIZER

On the twenty-fifth of October 1912 the Greeks gathered on Champa Street in East Denver. More than 400 of them fell into a marching column on the street. At the column's head was George Allison, the patriarch, in his forty-first year. Behind him came a brass band, then Father Isaias Paschopoulos, full bearded, with the tall black hat and flowing vestments of the Greek Orthodox clergy. Behind Paschopoulos came two color-bearers, one with the blue and white St. George's Cross of the Kingdom of Greece, the other with the Stars and Stripes. Then came the War Committee and the reserves, 232 men from the Greek army classes of 1900 through 1910. After these came 200 of the unfortunate Greeks who would have to stay behind. I think of the air that day being filled with the giddiness and high solemnity of young men going to a war they believed in.

On October eighth Montenegro had declared war on Turkey. Ten days later Greece, Serbia, and Bulgaria joined her. On the twentieth, in an emotional meeting, the Greeks of Denver subscribed $2,500 to the cause and declared three thousand Colorado Hellenes were ready to fight. So they marched down Champa Street, waving at each side of the column Greek flags, American flags. In their lapels, too, were small American flags, for they were eager to show the dual patriotism they claimed and, perhaps now, in the ardor of the first days of the war, truly felt.

Outside Union Depot they passed under the Welcome Arch and knelt on the pavement of 17th Street. The band played the anthem of Greece, then the "Star Spangled Banner." The men cheered. Father

Isaias presented a Greek flag to Andrew Rally, the leader of the reserves. Then the reserves formed up and marched into the station to board their special train while those who remained behind cheered them wildly. Later that night another special with five hundred war-bound Greeks from California passed through.

It is hard to think of that ardent young man, Louis Tikas, not being in the crowd that cheered the special going east. In the coaches there would have been men he knew well, maybe good friends. He had taken out his first papers for American citizenship, but now that the war had come, little thought was given to such technicalities—or to the old rivalries between Mainlander and Cretan. They were Greeks—all of them. They were striving now for the Great Idea, that dream of remaking the Byzantine Empire which was to cost them so much blood and treasure. I think of Louis Tikas grinding his teeth with the others who had been left behind.

In the weeks leading up to that war which would bring on the final dismantling of the Ottoman Empire, in the copper camps of northern Utah another empire had been crumbling. And if it was a lesser empire it was crumbling just as swiftly and just as dramatically and not without its own whiff of gunpowder. On September 17, the Western Federation of Miners had gone out on strike at the Utah Copper Company mines around Bingham, Utah. At the heart of the strike were the most militant of the miners and the largest single ethnic group, the Cretans. They had not gone out for more pay or for better conditions or for an ideology, but in a bitter vendetta against that haughty, self-possessed man Louis Tikas had watched going back and forth to his office across the street from the coffeehouse, Skliris, the padrone. For almost two years the Utah Greeks had attempted to expose Skliris' extortion. When the Western Federation of Miners began its organizing drive in Bingham Canyon, seven hundred of them had joined in one night. Now, with the Slavs and Italians and Japanese who had gone out with them, they dug in on the hillside above the mines, raking the mine workings with rifle any time the deputy sheriffs or railroad men made a move to enter the grounds. Skliris combed Idaho and Colorado for out-of-work men to break the strike, and then he made a terrible miscalculation. The workers he brought into Utah by the boxcar were men from the Peloponnesos. He had sunk to his lowest, pitting Greek against Greek. And he had touched that one nerve deepest in the Cretans, their honor. The men on the hills held firm. Once while the strike leaders were carousing and the picket line was left to a couple of raw boys, Skliris was able to sneak into Bingham Canyon dressed as a woman to assess the situation, but courage alone couldn't save him, and a week after the strike began he was forced to resign, as the strikers demanded. The Greeks still patrolled the hills above the mines, wary of Skliris' return and heeding the Federation's plea to stay out. The strike spread to the Guggenheim properties in eastern Nevada. Then, in mid-October, the shooting started again. By the time the strike began to die out in early November, two Greeks had been killed in gun battles between strikers, scabs, and deputy sheriffs at Bingham and two unarmed Greek picketers had been shot down by mine guards in McGill, Nevada.

In Denver the Greeks fed on the news of the strike at Utah Copper telephoned from coffeehouse to coffeehouse around the West from the headquarters of the Cretan insurgents, the Leventis brothers' own coffeehouse in Bingham Canyon. And they avidly watched the progress of the war in the Old Country. By October twenty-seventh Old Serbia had been cleared of the Turks and the Bulgarians were at the gates of Adrianople. On November eighth, the day of its patron, Saint Demetrios, Salonika fell to the Greeks. Ten days earlier the *Denver Times* had published a cartoon showing a terrified Turkish soldier being chased by a bayonet-wielding Balkan on whose shirt was pinned a badge reading "Greek from Denver, Colorado."

But Louis Tikas had stayed behind. Family duty, the need to get dowries or pay a debt or his own ambition had restrained him. Yet soon, without willing it, he would become involved in his own war. Sometime that fall he took the train north to the coalfields of Weld County and the beginning of a new career. He had been listed in the *Denver City Directory* of the summer of 1912 as proprietor of the coffeehouse at 1746 Market Street. With winter coming on and the railroad crews moving in from the prairies, the coffeehouse would be full of men, business would prosper. Did the coffeehouse somehow go sour? Or did he sell out and go off to the easy money promised by the employment agents who swelled Market Street? Perhaps he simply left for a month or two to scrape together the extra dollars needed to meet some family crisis in the Old Country or some new venture. For Tikas it would be a turning point. I remember the old man I first asked about how it came to be that Louis Tikas, up there in the Northern Field, had first joined the union. He looked at me for a moment, then pointed to the spinning reels of my recording machine. "Turn that thing off," he said. Then he smiled a little. "He was a scab."

They were small towns, the coal towns of the Northern Field. They lay out in the flat fields of alfalfa and sugar beets with a look of permanence and rural quiet. West of the fields the Rockies rose out of the prairies sudden and snowy as if they had been chipped out of the horizon with a hammer. The towns here were not owned by the coal companies as they were in the south. Many of the men—Cornishmen, Welshmen, experienced miners—had lived here since the opening of the fields. Some operated a store or other small business. Many owned their own homes. They had dug them out of the mine, one super-intendent said. Around the ten mines of the Rocky Mountain Fuel Company and the six other nonunion mines of the district there were stockades of wood and barbed wire. The strike had been going on for two years.

In December of 1910 an out-of-work miner named Charles Snyder ran into Walter Hall, the chief guard for the National Fuel Company, in an employment agency between 17th and 18th Streets in Denver. A few days later Snyder found himself a Baldwin–Felts guard at the Monarch Number One mine in Downer, Colorado. Later he wrote about it. "I found that the majority of the inmates of the camp were the low type of Bulgarians and Greeks, and a few English speaking people. I think there were about two hundred and fifty people in the camp at that time. About 20 per cent. were English speaking. I found in some of the 4 room houses as many as twenty-five people living and sleeping, among them being 1 to 3 women and some small children." In one twelve-by-fourteen-foot room Snyder saw as many as five beds. Men washed and changed in these warrens. At the company store prices were forty percent higher than in Denver. Storekeepers were cashing scrip at seventy-five cents on the dollar. Five weeks later Snyder moved his family into the stockade at the Industrial mine at Superior, where he worked first as a miner and then as a guard. Inside the

Superior stockade liquor ran loose and one crap game in the washhouse went on for forty-eight hours. Some of the guards were veterans of the tough strike at Lead, South Dakota, and they pistol-whipped miners to keep them in line. In those months Snyder watched a man, his wife and baby with only three dollars to their names thrown out of camp and forced to abandon their furniture. He saw another man borrowing money to bury a dead child when the superintendent tied up his wages.

The fences around the camps were more useful in keeping the scabs inside than strikers out. In May of 1910 Eli Gross of the State Free Employment Agency went to the Superior mine to get out a group of men who claimed they were being held in the stockade. At the approach to the tipple he came across a young mine guard armed with a Winchester and six gun. "I imagined that this lad thought I was an official in the Company," Gross said, "because there had been an automobile with some of the officials drive up there a few minutes before. I just leaned over and said to him, I said 'How are things around here?' And I said 'Do you have much trouble keeping the men in camp?' And he said 'No, we don't have any trouble keeping them here. . . . These foreigners, they goes and walks, we run them back. But these Kentuckians and Virginians they are game . . . you cannot run them back at all by pulling a gun on them. . . .'"

In the camp a group of foreigners approached Gross and asked him if he was a state official and if he could get them out. He said he could and the men went for their clothes and dunnage, refusing to be separated. Later on at a boardinghouse at Gorham, Gross watched the men eating their meal while half a dozen armed guards circulated around a gallery above the dining hall. Guards followed him everywhere and no men came up to talk to him in this camp.

In early January of 1912 Paul Paulson, an International organizer from Rock Springs, Wyoming, and an Italian organizer named Gerald Lippiatt managed to get all fifty of the foreign strikebreakers at the Northern Fuel Company's Alpha pit to walk out and effectively shut down the mine. "It means," District 15 President Frank Smith said, "that these foreigners will reach their own countrymen in the Puritan, Frederick, Wills and Baum mines. . . . It is a new solution to the problems up north."

But it was not a solution. It was almost a year later before there would be another such walkout. And this time the impetus came, it seems, not from the union, but from the scabs themselves.

There were thirty-five of them in the Frederick slope mine— Greeks, Italians, and what the *United Mine Workers Journal* report called "Germans"—meaning probably the ubiquitous "Austrians," Italians and South Slavs from the Austro–Hungarian Empire. Most of them lived in the company shacks inside the stockade. I do not know what had brought them there—promise of good money in a scab mine, a desperate need for work—but what they found in the Northern Field was a kind of slavery. They were making thirty-nine and a half cents a ton on the coal they mined and still were cheated at the scales. They furnished their own powder and were forced to lay track to their rooms. They had to carry the rails, ties, and timbers to their work places, and if they couldn't find the supplies they needed they were told to "look around." The mine managers were more accommodating. For five dollars they would find a way to come up with the rails or the timbers. There was no limit on the number of hours a man worked. When the men complained about the dangerous conditions they were told that if they wanted a better place they would have to come across with some money.

On the seventeenth of November, Andrew Rally, the leader of the Denver volunteers, wired his roommate that he and some of the other Colorado Greeks were about to move up to engage the Turks on the Chatalja line. In the dark clay of Macedonia the demoralized Turkish army was driving its ox carts over its own dead. A day after Rally's telegram the fortress of Monastir fell to the Serbians and 50,000 Turkish soldiers surrendered. On that same day a handful of Greeks and Italians and Slavs in the stockade at Frederick, Colorado, struck a small blow of their own.

When he wrote of it two years later, Tikas said he led the walkout with sixty-three fellow Greeks. It is hard to tell how much a part the union had in it, whether the walkout was called by it or came about spontaneously through the men themselves. But the next day, November nineteenth, the entire work force of the Frederick mine, with the exception of three men, met at a hall somewhere outside company property and joined the union in a block.

So Tikas enters his destiny. It is a moment worth considering. In making the turn from scab to striker he was following the path of thousands of immigrants before him, of whole nationalities. In a profound way, more than at that moment when he set foot on Ellis Island, more than at that other moment when he signed his first papers with a new name, walking out of the Frederick stockade was the most American thing he had done. The revolt of the Greeks in the Utah Copper Company mines had been prophetic. For when the Greeks at Bingham, Utah, rose up against Leonidas Skliris, without knowing it they were rising up against a whole ethos, that ignorance, that poverty in their past which had created such men as Skliris and which, in this New World, so desperately needed them. The Bingham strike had not made union men of the Greeks. It was for Tikas and the immigrant organizers like him to take such unformed revolts one step further; to make of the anarchy of the industrial world a map.

Greenhorn, *kafedzhis*, scab . . . the old roles no longer fit, they split like a pair of pants that a man's outgrown. The Greeks at the Frederick mine would have known Tikas from his Denver days, and already he would have something of a position of leadership among them for his better grasp of the English language and American ways. But allegiance to the union did not grow up in a man like that overnight. An opportunist as a scab, the strike at the slope mine might have been at first no more than another opportunity. Some hot words, a chance for action, a chance to play some role. But he was learning. America was teaching him. The next few months of the strike in the Northern Field would see Louis Tikas developing the patience and dedication of the true organizer. Yet for a time, it may be until his death, the two men he now was would exist simultaneously in the same skin: the medieval man—the Greek—and the union organizer. That rash and ardent patriotism which had sent those 232 Colorado Greeks to fight in the Balkans was his inheritance, too, but it was being transmuted in him from the crude and narrow Old Country thing it was and turned toward another loyalty and another fight.

When the Frederick strikers got back from their meeting they found the three remaining scabs and the guards setting fire to a building next to the mine shaft. They rushed in and put the fire out, for they knew they would be blamed for it. Two days later they were paid off and ordered to leave the shacks inside the stockade.

The union hall at Frederick was a two-story building. Upstairs was a meeting room with a stage; downstairs the union had set up cots and mattresses as a temporary lodging for the striking workers until they could be placed in houses or tents. On the twenty-first of November there was more trouble. Around four in the afternoon a union man and a scab ran into each other outside Frederick and traded a few punches. Shortly after the two men parted, an automobile loaded with Baldwin–Felts detectives roared out of the Frederick stockade and made for the union hall.

The Baldwin–Felts men broke down the door of the hall. Upstairs a Greek named Nick Fallas was standing on the stage. Apparently he was the man they were after. F. R. Slater, a Baldwin–Felts gunman from West Virginia, leveled a rifle at Fallas and ordered him off the stage. The Greek put his hands in his pockets and slowly walked down the narrow stairway and into the street.

What happened then is unclear. Slater and a guard named Pointer said they saw Fallas trying to slip a concealed weapon to another Greek. The story as told by organizer Adolph Germer is that Fallas was searched and the guards found nothing. A third guard later admitted that the first time he saw the gun Slater was taking it away from another Greek. That Greek is identified in the account of the incident written for the *United Mine Workers Journal* as "one Tikas."

Aside from the listings in the *Denver City Directory*, this is probably the first time Louis Tikas' name appears in print.

The detectives turned the cots on the first floor upside down and took Fallas to the mine office. At the office another Greek was brought in by a different gang and they chained the two men together. By morning they had brought in four more Greeks. When they found Mike Croclis in his boardinghouse he started to explain that he didn't know about any trouble and one of the detectives hit him in the face. They took the six Greeks to Greeley and put them in the Weld County jail, charged with carrying concealed weapons, disturbing the peace, and assault. On December third the Greeks and two other strikers involved in the melee were brought to trial.

According to Adolph Germer, the trial was a farce. The Baldwin–Felts men never could get their story straight about who had the gun Nick Fallas was supposed to have been carrying, nor could they produce any kind of warrant. When someone asked Pointer what right he had to burst into the hall armed with a shotgun and revolver he replied, blandly, "I just butted in, I guess." We get the outcome of the trial in Ed Doyle's union account book—one union man fined ten dollars and costs, another simply fined. The others let off.

Compared with the frame-ups and murder charges union men would face in the Southern Field, the outrage of such justice is not great. But wherever Louis Tikas was during the trial, it must have set him thinking. Tikas was not the first Greek union man in the Northern Field, but he was to become the most effective. Now he met the union figures who would be important to him in the future: Adolph Germer, the socialist organizer from the Midwest; Ed Doyle, who had been a checkweighman in the Vulcan mine and was now secretary of District 15, jailed twice for his part in the strike; John Lawson, District 15 International organizer. Doyle recalled, a few years later, his first meeting with Tikas. "My first connection with him was when he joined the organization. While he had been working as a strikebreaker in the Northern Field he came out on strike. Seeing he was an active fellow, we made him one of our interpreters through which to speak to the Greek population and do any translation we needed in Greek." And so Louis became a useful man to the union.

On the evening of January 10, 1913, International President White and his party came to the Northern Field from Denver. The night was dark and cold, and White was met at the Marshall station by men carrying lighted pit lamps, who escorted him to a hall where he spoke to an enthusiastic crowd of miners and their families. The next day he went on to Erie and Frederick. On Sunday morning, the twelfth, he spoke to a capacity crowd in Lafayette. The new union man from the Denver coffeehouse may have been in that crowd. He *was* in Lafayette the next day . . . *But Louis, you know, Tikas, he joined the Union, see, behind with the miners. And he come over to Lafayette, you know. And I tell him, "Now, you better run from here." Because he come over to the boardinghouse. And the guy that opened up said,*

*"Louis, you better run because the guards are after you . . ." He run
from the back door. And I was right there that time. . . .*

This old John Tsanakatsis had told me in Oak Creek. And he
had said something else about Louis' stay in the north: "They shoot
him." Six years later I confirmed the shooting in a letter dictated by
Tikas to a secretary or friend. It was an attempt to justify himself to
the union two months before he was killed. "The Louis Tikas upon
whom a cowardly assault was made and who was shot by a Baldwin–
Felts detective in Lafayette, Colorado, on the thirteenth day of January,
1913, is the same Louis Tikas, the writer of this report to you."

That is the last evidence of Louis Tikas in the Northern Field,
a pale and insubstantial figure of a man running between an old
Greek's memory and a sentence in a letter written sixty years before.
There is nothing else. The *United Mine Workers Journal* follows
President White to the next stop on his tour of the strike field without
a trace of the shooting. Nor do any of the newspapers of Denver or
Weld or Boulder counties give so much as a line to this unimportant
young Greek running out of a boardinghouse with the Baldwin–Felts
gunmen after him. Later on Tikas would learn the value of such a
wound to union publicists. But at the time he simply hid it, like a
guerrilla in the Cretan hills, trusting to his own wit to console him.

Flesh heals; but something in a man keeps a wound like that from
closing. Maybe that torn shred of skin was a part of him that had to
be given in order to seal him to his new career. I imagine him running
for his life out that boardinghouse door and think how often, when
I happen to glimpse him, he will be running. After that, old John said,
Louis went south. And he was happy to get there.

I read over my first notes on Louis Tikas.

> The "facts" of his life could be put on a single card in a researcher's
> file. He was in his early thirties when he was killed. He was waiting
> for a picture bride to come from Greece. Almost certainly he was a
> Cretan, like most of the strikers at Ludlow at the time. I once
> thought he was from Rethymnon, but that is probably not the case.
> He may have been from a village near there. There is a persistent
> story that he was a graduate of Athens University, but that is almost
> certainly untrue—he may have made that up, or some reporter . . . he
> may have been from Rethymnon. He may have been a university

graduate. I don't know. He was killed on the night of April 20, 1914, near the crossroads of Ludlow while the tent city was on fire and was numbered in the dead. He was buried in a grave somewhere in Trinidad, with a wooden cross for a marker, if that. The grave has disappeared. Tikas was undoubtedly not his real name. I do not think much more than this will ever be known.

I had come across his name in a pamphlet in a library basement. The pamphlet was one of those grim, self-serving things, a report of a special board of officers of the Colorado National Guard investigating the massacre of striking miners and their women and children at the Ludlow tent colony on April 20, 1914. Among the dead was the leader of the tent colony, Louis Tikas. Louis the Greek. I had gone into the library looking for materials for a fiction. I came out with a name.

There was word from the Greek coffeehouses of the coal country of eastern Utah, where my mother had grown up, that the few old men left remembered his death. They called him *strategos*—"general"— "our brave general Tikas." Yet no one had known him, or even his true name. Who was he? Some cardplayer raked out of a Denver coffeehouse? A martyr? Every time some new rumor, some new fleck of evidence surfaced above the dark hollow of his absence from history, I would be forced to see some new possibility, some new version of his myth. And all I had, really, was that name. A name that was itself part fiction, something invented for the placation of America. Tikas. Did he wear it proudly, I wondered, or was it stiff and somehow cheap, like a first American suit?

I had a friend in the days when I had first begun to think about the story of Louis Tikas, one of those unlikely friends who crop up in your life now and then, with whom you eat and argue and who step out of your life one day leaving not a ripple behind. We walked through my overgrown garden, my friend and I, among the quacking ducks and the trees that are always green on this seasonless California coast, building the towers of our ideas. It was the worst days of the Vietnam War. The country was collapsing upon itself. My friend was electric with hints of secret meetings, contacts with wanted men. I talked of an obscure Greek labor organizer killed sixty years before and a thousand miles away. My friend accused me of being interested only in dead radicals.

Maybe I was. I worked at my little farm, ditched around the field, built a shed for the goats. Mid-century, mid-Vietnam America was drowning in tear gas and rhetoric and out there on my two acres of mud and pastoral in the middle of the redwoods I was trying to find solid ground pulling at the teats of a milk goat. I stayed close to the radio and the typewriter and my failing fictions, trying to peck my way into history.

There was a word the old-time Greeks used to describe the Americans among whom they suddenly found themselves, those soft-spoken men with pink cheeks and repressed tempers, the men behind the counters and desks, well-dressed, courteous to a fault, soft-spoken even while they skinned you. They called them *analatos*—saltless. At thirty I looked at myself, trying to discover how much of the Greek remained. There were a few appetites, remembered tastes, a few words in a language I had once known, but which day by day was retreating from me —all that was thin, without substance. With my hesitations, my isolation, that need I had to make life into some aesthetic object (let it be a book instead of a corporation) I was closer to the Rockefellers than I ever was to that young Greek organizer, Louis Tikas. I was becoming saltless.

I remember the first lamb that died in my little flock. There had been two of them that February, twins. The lambs had wrinkled, ill-fitting skins and black, sharp faces. They looked worn and slightly disreputable, like old bums. When they sucked, their tails wagged frantically behind them like bell ropes. One day I found one of them in the pasture dead. When I lifted it out of the wet grass it felt suddenly very light and dry in my hands, like an empty glove. I remembered a trick the sheepherders used when a ewe whose lamb had died would not accept a strange lamb to suck. They would wrap the skin of her dead lamb around the strange lamb and pen her in with it. The ewe did not really accept the jacketed lamb as her own, but the smell of the skinned pelt was enough to allow it to feed. In bed at night I lay awake, listening to the bells moving softly through my dark pasture. If they rang in a cluster I would tense, but it was only the sheep moving to a new bedding. The bells soon subsided into a soft, low jingling. One night I woke up and on the ridge above the pasture

I imagined I saw the tents of Ludlow in flame. I lay there in the silence and the dark, looking at the black shape of the ridge and the jagged tops of the firs.

Brought together now in one of those increasingly rare reunions, the family sits down to the dining room table. We come back at Christmas, maybe, or in the summer when the mountains are cool, touch down a few days and then scatter to our separate worlds.

I like these cousins of mine, articulate, clever, long-nosed as Assyrian princes carved on a wall. We are an oddly American lot; businessman, young lawyer, computer linguist, whatever I call myself. One of us is missing, the youngest, gone off to play baseball for a season in the big leagues (how strange *that* seems—one fantasy, at least, of the New Land come true). We talk about cybernetics, anthropology. Black holes in space. Are we rushing toward the light of some previous solar system where all the electrical charges have been reversed? The table is our ship, mastless hull of post-Homeric voyagers adrift on a sea of mediocrity. Our adventures are marriage, children, sports, divorce. Our monsters boredom, complacency, money.

My grandfather tells of a dream he has had. In the dream he has invented a sort of machine in the shape of a cross that he has hung around the neck of our missing cousin, the ballplayer. The machine is a transmitter for his voice so that he can call out through the cross "George! This is *Papou* . . . Get a hit!"

One uncle has fallen asleep before the drone of the T.V.

The family has grown old with one another. Our neuroses have become less interesting, less passionate, as have our strengths. Uncles, who used to sit at this table gorging themselves like heroes, have grown torpid and maybe a little sad, reconciled to the world. My grandfather, that six-foot-four *leventis*, is bent over a cane now, deaf and nearly blind. He has outgrown his violence and his success, and waits for death with a patience he never had, forced on him by old age. Once, in the 1930s, comfortable with what he had achieved and probably bored, he grew a mustache and spent a few weeks in Athens at the King George Hotel. He came back. He discovered that he no longer fit into the Old World, that he had become, in ways he had not realized, an American. There was no return. There was just trauma and the Old World cut away as with a knife—only twitching, now and then, with the illusory spasm of some amputated limb.

Looked at from some star (or some library) who knew if there was some order, some pattern to these lurches and troughs and blood-lettings we called America? For us who lived it there was only the slap of our own experience. Each new batch of immigrants wiped the slate clean. There was no American past; there was only the moment of our own discovery. Perhaps we were a people without a history.

The women clear the places. A few crumbs are left on the table-cloth, a stain of wine. We were the survivors, we Greeks. We had survived both this country's and our own violence. We had sat down to America's banquet with all the self-assurance of people who'd been invited. It was a lie. We never were. This food, which has been prepared for us, is the food we were searching for so many years in this country. Now it is too much. It is almost as if America has become something different than we desired at the very moment we achieved its promise. Under this pale fiction of success we were living out there was a darker issue. It was the lives of all those America had not delivered whole. Of men like Louis Tikas, cut off from me now by a posterity they never had. Their stories were evaporating behind them, leaving only a few odd traces here and there. There was only the hole they had left in time.

Then there were the photographs. That summer I went to Colorado. It was a kind of family outing; my mother and father, my sister and her young son. At Ludlow the United Mine Workers had raised a monument to the dead and we read their names and tried to follow the course of the battle. Across the plain an August thunderstorm was coming up, darkening the gashes in the mesa where the ruins of the mines lay. At the mines there was nothing but broken foundations and shoring and the dark smudges of cinders where the rails had once run. The entries to the shafts had been cemented over. At Hastings a row of broken coking ovens lay agape to the sky. It didn't rain. When we opened the car door at the cluster of boarded-up buildings that were what remained of Ludlow station, a flurry of grasshoppers sprayed up with the dry, popping sound of fire. The signs nailed to the smashed

I got a bunch of soldiers and they came back just now from Old Mexico war, and that people is going to fight you dagoes, to clean you out from here. —Louis Tikas quoting K. E. Linderfelt. Soldiers in front of Ludlow saloon. Courtesy of the Library, State Historical Society of Colorado.

Day after day, week after week, and the money almost gone. During a strike all suffer, but I think it must be harder on the wife. . . . She, at home, is planning what and how to feed her children . . . counting and recounting each penny, so much for fuel, so much for water, so much for a soup bone. —Anne Ellis. Strikers' camp near Walsenburg. Winter, 1913–14. Courtesy of the Library, State Historical Society of Colorado.

windows of the buildings warned of poisoned bait. The coyotes had reclaimed the place.

We went back to Denver. While my mother looked through the Historical Society files I stayed in the next room, poring over the photographs of the strike. For years my mother had been writing histories of the Greeks in her own Utah coal country, piecing together the flow and texture of their lives. But I was looking at those photographs and asking of them something that was both more and less than that flow of history, that wanted, it may be, to deny it. Officers staring into the camera smiling. Deputies. Children standing in the snow. Men grouped in front of their tents with bandanas around their necks and rifles in their hands. Ruined tipples, dead and bloated mules, the burned foundations of the tents. And always Tikas, given form now, a gray smear of emulsion on a piece of paper, smiling in front of the Ludlow camp or dead on the slab of a Trinidad mortuary, or going to his burial in a horse-drawn carriage with a double file of men marching endlessly behind him into the silence of the photograph. Sitting with the photographs in front of me I was looking across sixty years. And the men of those days, there on the Ludlow plain they stood, just as the camera had caught them. But the camera's shutter had fallen between us like a blade. Trapped in the terrible, silent light of that shutter click, all they could offer were their shadows. Now they lay frozen and still in their little prisons of time, like those arrows released by Zeno's archer which could fly from the snap of the bowstring but never reach the target.

In Denver the trail to the old-timers went cold. I went home. One day I found myself in the office of *Nea California* on San Francisco's Market Street trying to send an advertisement for news of a dead man across the endless reaches of Greek America. From behind his desk the editor looked at me archly. He was wearing a necktie sensationally modish for an old Greek. "And just who *are* these people who want to know about this man?" he asked in his excellent, accented voice.

I went back to the Denver photographs again and again in the next years, and they would always move me. I did not know then that all the while I was staring into the faces of those long lost Greeks and Italians and Slavs the man who had taken the photographs was living just a few miles away from me, and thus they floated in a kind of mystery, as if they had not been made, but simply appeared, like those wonder-working icons of the Balkans. But for a time there were only the few bits of hearsay left in the coffeehouses of eastern Utah and a few lines in the histories and the photographs themselves.

This is the day of your emancipation. This is the day when liberty and progress come to abide in your midst.

An Appeal to All Mine Workers in District 15
1913

5. ORGANIZING:
THE SOUTHERN FIELD

If I have learned anything about the Colorado coal strike of 1913–14, I learned it from those photographs. The man who took them was named Louis R. Dold. Sixty years after the strike I came to meet him.

In 1913 Dold was making the rounds of the mining camps of Las Animas County with a camera and tripod and a case full of plates. His father was a liquor distributor and plunger in mining claims, a German with a cruel streak in him toward his boys, but he had gone down to Jalisco to run a silver mine and at twenty-five Lou Dold was well rid of him.

Southern Colorado was a tough country, still permeated with the frontier mentality of the days of the ranches and trail drives along the muddy stream the cattlemen called the Picketwire. It had not been so long since Bat Masterson had come over from Dodge City to serve a stint as Trinidad city marshal, and every so often even in the teens of the new century a gang would get hold of a rope and rush the jail in a parody of frontier justice. But the frontier and its mentality mingled with an overshadowing reality. The reality of the industrial world. Now telephone lines sagged above the office buildings and hotels built up the twisting length of Commercial Street, and the sidewalks of Trinidad were filled not only with the cowboys and ranchers and Mexicans of the frontier, but with the crowds of immigrants who had come to dig the coal—Italians, Slavs, Greeks, Bulgarians, Japanese. It was a world in a volatile and sudden transition. A rich place for a man like Lou Dold.

61

He had tried his hand at railroading, shoveling coal into the fire-boxes of the doubleheader engines pulling the grade of Raton Pass, even tried laying brick. But his real talent was the life of Trinidad's West Main, that wild stretch of saloons and cathouses and gambling dens patrolled by an army of prostitutes waiting for miners to come down to play the tenderloin. He shot pool with the featherweight boxer Benny Chavez and the outlaws and camp followers who hung around him and took a couple of turns tending bar in a dive with a murderous bouncer and a legless owner who pulled himself across the sawdust on the floor to ladle two-bits-a-pint liquor to the bums waiting in the alley. Once he carried a gun for a year against a black man he was on the outs with.

There were other pleasures. Sometimes he and a couple of friends would take an old canvas-sided wagon and a span of mules and go over Raton Pass and into the Taos country where they'd hunt and fish and Lou might take a few pictures. Once he built a blind and hid out in the cedars photographing the ritual crucifixion of the Mexican Penitentes.

Wild and exotic world, the Taos country. But no wilder or more exotic than Aguilar, with its anarchist saloon and rumors of the Black Hand. It was a favorite haunt. There were three of them who would go over to Aguilar to make the rounds of the bars. One of them could chord a piano, another was a comic dancer, Lou was a pretty fair acrobat. They'd do their turn and pass the hat. One night Lou went to Aguilar and checked into the hotel Mike Poma kept above his saloon. He lay in bed at Mike Poma's and got thinking, what the hell am I doing here? He left town on the midnight train. A few days later he got a letter.

> Dear Dold, you stay here and no pay. If that's the kind of man you are, O.K. Goodbye
>
> Mike Poma

He laughed about that one a long time.

He got into the photography business. He apprenticed himself to a man named Morrison and the two traveled around the camps doing what they called "kidnapping." They carried a big five-by-seven view camera and when they saw a kid hanging around a house they'd knock on the door and take a picture on the spot.

He spent a good deal of time taking photographs of Slav funerals and weddings. If you didn't drink with the Slavs they'd think you were a prohibitionist and wouldn't let you take their pictures. He would squint through his ground glass and where there were three Bohunks standing around the coffin, holding bottles in their hands and stuffing cigars into the corpse's pockets, he would see, upside down and weaving, six. Once at some Slavic wedding in a saloon the groom didn't arrive. The bride said if he didn't show up in twenty minutes she'd marry the best man. And that's just what she did. They were all pretty drunk from the waiting.

Good times for a footloose young man with a wild hair. But Lou Dold was seeing other things through his ground glass besides those unfocused, drunken figures. He was looking at the men at work. He would set up his camera at the portal of a mine and wait for them to come out at the end of their shift carrying their picks and lard pail lunch buckets and blinking in the sun, their faces blackened and their pit lamps still fixed to their caps. Now and then he would run across a Greek photographer plying his trade in the camps, carrying with him for the use of his clients a collection of what Lou called Greek uniforms —the white pleated kilts of the Mainland or the black loose breeches of Crete.

I would give a good deal to see the photographs Lou Dold took in those days; but I have seen others like them, and they tell a world. They show men posed in front of their shacks and boardinghouses in their new American clothes, with the bottles in their hands that would have symbolized the good life to their countrymen at home. They show men who are not ashamed of their rough work, proud to have it, proud to be miners, wanting to boast of their good luck in America. No one can ever tell you how many hundreds of thousands of immigrants these photographs brought to the new land. In Aguilar the postmaster kidded the young photographer about the string of immigrants who crowded up to the post office window after one of his tours, each with the identical-sized envelope full of pictures. "God damn you Dold," he said, "I can always tell when you've been around. They put trading stamps on the envelopes to send them to Italy." The men standing in front of the mines and boardinghouses were the same men Lou Dold would photograph a year or two later with cartridge bandoliers draping their shoulders and the red bandana insignia of the strike knotted around their necks.

Lou Dold saw still more in the mines and the company towns. He went down into the coal pits for the C. F. and I. and Victor–American, taking pictures of the new and wonderful safety features destined to appear in the glossy pages of *Coal Age*, of shelving built to hold enough rock dust to dampen any explosion. Before he shot off his open flash in these safe and up-to-date mines they'd send a man in with a safety lamp to check for the gas that might be ready to blow them all sky-high. In the towns he saw miners using scrip discounted fifteen, twenty, twenty-five percent to raise some cash. He heard about men being canned for not buying at the company store. Heard how the pit bosses "pinched" the cars—dealt them out to the waiting miners for a bribe. The photographs of the proud men posing in front of the mine or carousing at a wedding or a wake were not all of the story. Years afterwards Lou Dold summed up what he knew about those men and their lives. He used a worked-out phrase, but he meant it: "They treated them worse than slaves."

About the same time Lou Dold was going from camp to camp with his camera and box of plates there was another man working the Southern Field, a tall and nervy young Croatian named Mike Livoda. Livoda had come over in 1903 and found his way to the steel mills of Steubenville, Ohio. He'd lived with a bunch of Slavs in a boarding-house. The men took turns using the beds according to their shifts at the mill. On weekends when they flopped the shift they'd sleep three to a bed. Once Livoda was fired for not contributing beer money to the straw boss: loading pig iron and scrap at seventeen cents an hour was bad enough, he thought. He picked up another job at a rolling mill and stayed on for three years. In 1907 he got the gold fever and set off for Alaska with another young fellow. He'd made it as far as Butte, Montana, when his money ran out. He drifted over to Red Lodge and picked up a union card among the solid union miners there, Finns and Italians and Americans and Slavs, and in the spring of 1910 headed for Denver, then south to the mines. All this time he was talking up the union. On the first of January 1912 he started working for John

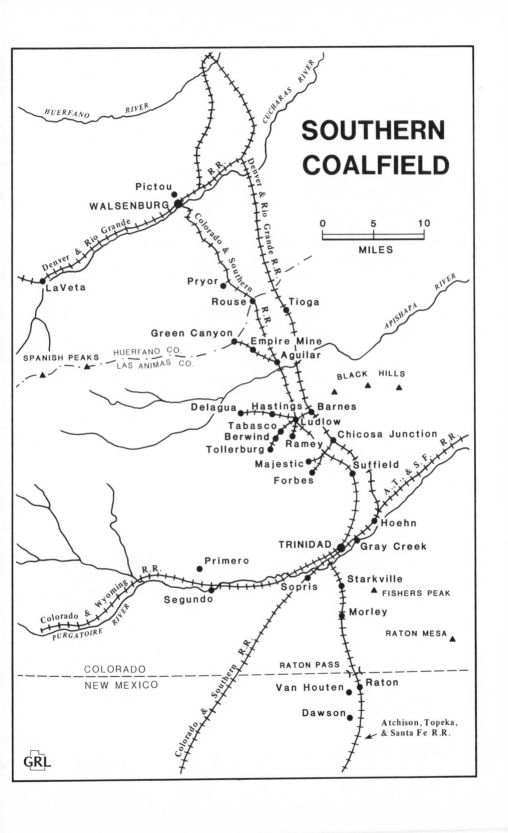

Lawson as an organizer for the United Mines Workers of America. The pay was three and a half dollars a day and expenses.

A month later four men picked him out of a Walsenburg retaurant and took him to Jeff Farr, the beer-bellied Huerfano County sheriff, who was waiting in the back room of a saloon. Farr looked Livoda over then turned to his thugs. "Is that the son of a bitch?" He turned back to Livoda. "You know who I am?" Livoda said he did. "I'm king of this county. And if you want to do any of your dirty work you'll have to do it in Las Animas, not here." The four thugs set Livoda out on the railroad tracks and told him to start walking. He spent the night five miles out of town, sleeping in the shack of a miner he knew while the miner and his son sat up with a shotgun watching the men on horses who'd tailed Livoda in the light of the full moon. The next morning Livoda went into Walsenburg and called the union in Trinidad to tell them that unless he got some help he was quitting.

But he didn't quit. In the middle of June he was back in Huerfano County spending the night with some Slavs who were baching it in the Ravenwood Camp. About midnight someone stuck a flashlight through the door of his room and five men burst in. They threw the light in his face and told him to get up and get dressed. Then they went through his pockets, took out his keys, his money, his books. It was the books they were after. He knew three of them. A couple were deputy sheriffs. One was a superintendent at the Ravenwood mine, another was a boss of the mule drivers. They ordered him to come with them. One of them grabbed him by the belt and they pulled him out of the room. Just as he was stepping out of the house, someone hit him in the face and knocked him down, and when he started to yell for help another man put a hand over his mouth and said, "Shut up, you son of a bitch, or we'll kill you." Then they started hitting and kicking him, smashing in his nose. All he could think of was his eyes. He covered them with his hands while they hammered him. When they were finished they picked him up and walked him out of the camp, kicking him and cursing. At the edge of the camp they fired off their revolvers and told him to get the hell out of Colorado or they would kill him. It took Livoda four hours to walk the five miles into Walsenburg, and when he got there he went to the only safety he knew, the shop of a Jewish tailor. He lay on a mattress in the tailor's coal shed two days before they could get a doctor to him. It was a week before he could get out of bed, and when he did he went back to work organizing.

There is a list District 15 Secretary Ed Doyle kept, and it is only a partial list, of the union organizers beaten or killed in Colorado in the years leading to the strike of 1913. Mike Livoda is on it, and Bob Uhlich and John Lawson and many more. It is a grim list, and it would grow before the strike's end. They had a special kind of toughness, these men, for their task was a more difficult one than mere survival. They not only had to outwit and outrun the Pinkertons and the Baldwin–Felts thugs and company spotters, but they had to do something very nearly impossible: to form a union out of the two dozen jealous nationalities that vied for jobs in the coalfields of the West.

Many of the leaders of the strike in the south were of the same stuff as their organizers. There was John Lawson, forty-two at the time of the strike, a big man, an amateur boxer—he'd learned his unionism from his Scottish father in the coal mines of Pennsylvania where he'd gone to work picking slate at the breaker with the other mining camp urchins at the age of eight. Lawson had been an organizer in the 1903 Colorado strike and had seen his house dynamited, his wife and daughter just escaping death. He'd been shot down by a mine owner named Coryell in that strike and in Walsenburg, he too had had a taste of Jeff Farr's justice. Ed Doyle was younger, twenty-seven when the strike began. In 1894 he'd watched United States troops shoot down miners playing cards under the oaks in Spring Valley, Illinois, and had never forgotten it. He'd gone to work as a trapper boy at the age of twelve. Doyle said his Irish immigrant father had gone mad from the pressures of the mine. He grew up to a bitter, sarcastic wit. In the Northern Field he'd served six months in jail on trumped-up charges. He learned to keep a record of his whereabouts after that. There were others as well: the Scot John McLennan, himself once an immigrant coal digger in the Colorado mines; Bob Uhlich, a German who had wandered from the province of Saxony throughout Europe and at last to Canada and Mexico and the United States, a working man who'd seen enough to turn him radical; Adolph Germer, the Midwestern socialist who'd played a leading role in ousting Big Bill Haywood from the party and sniped at him now from the union journal; affable Billy Diamond who would, perhaps, betray his cause; Frank Hayes, eloquent young International vice-president with a penchant for sentimental verse and a dangerous affinity for the bottle, a former miner, too, who'd once run for governor of Illinois on the Socialist ticket.

But I think most of Lawson and Doyle, for through their testimony I know them best. And I am struck by the power of their formulation. In 1894, not long after John Lawson left for the West, the writer Stephen Crane visited a breaker in Pennsylvania and watched just such boys as John Lawson picking slate from the sluggish stream of coal that poured between their legs. Crane found in the slate pickers not dumb despair, but what he called a kind of "hoodlum valor." They laughed more than the New York gamins he knew, and when they laughed their faces were "a wonder and a terror." While the grimy young slate pickers crowded around Crane trying to find out if he was willing to give away any tobacco, and their boss harangued them, work stopped. Lawson himself recalled, in an unpublished portion of an interview with one of his biographers, that the arrival of a traveling circus found the slate pickers walking out en masse—his first strike. When he was fifteen Ed Doyle saw the inside of a college for the first time. He thought it was a place men went for entertainment. Such men as Doyle and Lawson got their first educations on the hills of culm with their curses and battles with boys from other camps or down in the choked passages of the mines.

The move to organize the Southern Field began in the first months of 1913. While the strike in the north held at a bitter stalemate, Lawson was convincing the International that the key to organizing Colorado was the coal fiefs of the south. Throughout that winter and into the spring Lawson, Doyle, and McLennan organized for a major strike. The union positioned itself for a peaceful solution, but while the union and the operators sparred and the ineffectual, mild-mannered Governor Elias Ammons desperately tried to head them off, the policy committee set up shop in the south. They trained and sent to the field twenty-one pairs of organizers, an active and passive organizer in each pair. The active organizer was open about his work, drawing the fire of mine owners and superintendents. Meanwhile the passive man went down and got work in a mine, receiving his organizer's pay through a dummy real estate firm so that coal company post office men wouldn't know of his union connections. While the active organizer proselytized, the passive man held his job, noted the men ripe for unionizing, and reported the anti-union men to the pit boss as dangerous radicals— "radicals" who were soon fired. Lawson opened a union office in Trinidad, but played down the imminence of a strike. But the mine owners knew what was coming. They were doing some organizing of their own.

On January 16, 1913, Walter Belk of the Baldwin–Felts detective agency was made a deputy sheriff in the south. A month later Albert Felts, a director of the agency, was deputized as well. Seven years later Felts would meet his death on the streets of Matewan, West Virginia, gunned down by men who had had enough of his detective work. Now he was a consultant in the importation of violent men. Perhaps as many as seventy-five Baldwin–Felts men were assigned to southern Colorado in those months, toughs who had made their marks in the Northern Field and in the bloody strike in West Virginia. Nor were the coal companies' own detectives slow to act. By mid-September the lobby of the Dover Hotel in Denver was filled with men from the saloons and barrelhouses of Larimer and 17th Streets waiting for an interview with one of C. F. and I. Chief of Detectives Billy Reno's assistants. They were men whose breaths were strong with whiskey and whose coats bulged over the guns in their hip pockets. The guard duty they were after paid $3.50 a day and only experienced men were wanted. The sheriffs of Las Animas and Huerfano counties, too, were not unprepared for violence; and their law, such as it was, was clearly the law of the coal companies. Between September and October of 1913 Jeff Farr, the king of Huerfano County, recruited 258 deputy sheriffs. He would later admit that, for all he knew, they could have been red-handed murderers. The union took the precaution of having its organizers made game wardens so that they could legally carry guns.

For all their talk of compromise, the union knew the crisis was near. Guns were being imported wholesale on both sides, and the mines and saloons were full of spies. In the months of August and September the Victor–American mine at Bowen was employing at least fourteen men as "spotters." They were paid ten to thirty dollars a month extra and their fees were charged up on their payroll accounts as money for "brushing" and other work. Earlier that summer, if the report of one company spy can be trusted, the editor of the *United*

Mine Workers Journal had come down to the south, taken a look at the situation, and told the organizers to tell their men to arm themselves with the best rifles money could buy, get up on the hills and not be a damned bit particular who they picked off.

By the end of August the union organizers were in place and working. The undercover men were sending in their reports, building a case for the demand for better conditions, adding up the strength of the union in the mines.

Number 52 wrote from Tioga:

> In and around Tioga Camp unionism is quite openly expressed while some are quit and dont say much I should judge about 75 to 85 per cent are only waiting to be called out and are ready to lay down there tools. Most diggers clame they are getting very short weights. The Big Four compel all single men to board at ther boarding house whitch is very bum most of the time. The dinner pail they dont fill is a poor lunch. Friday they only put in the dinner pail two fat meat sandwiches and a piece of poor rhubarb pie and a little green apple. All the Boys Kicked. But its take what they give you or leve the Camp. They worked 8 hours. The wash house is fair but not sanitary.

Delagua paid only fifty-five cents a ton for pick work and the coal would not break at all and it was no place for an American.

> There is about four of five hundred men here. Outside men are mostly American. I think about 50 Japs. The rest are farmers such as Austrians, Slavish, and Mexicans, Greeks and Italians and they all no sava. Of all the places I ever was in my life this is the worst place I ever saw for an American to live unless he is a Boss.
>
> I am sure I cant stand it here eny longer. In the first place I cant make wages. I and the three other Americans are bording at the Jap boarding house. Gee the Japs that swarm around here at night. The bath is a big squair box two ft. deep and 12 feet squair all the Japs, Greeks and Mexicans and all of us have got to wash in the same for they only fill the tub once. Last night one Jap with a lot of open sors on his body jumped in the tub with the rest of us. Now I dont think a senceable white man would stand for this, do you. . . .

Since early August there had been a new organizer in the field. Doyle's minutes of the policy committee for August 7, 1913, contain this note: "L. Tikas, G. Lippiatt, M. V. Hibbs and John Petron sent south as advisors." Two of them, Tikas and Lippiatt, wouldn't come back.

In the north, Tikas had worked diligently for the union collecting what he said were more than twenty-eight affidavits for the Colorado legislature's investigation of the strike in Boulder and Weld counties and producing seventy-two witnesses. Apparently he had done his work well. In April the union again made use of him. On the first day of the month he was sent to the Pike View mine in El Paso County where a 150 men had gone on strike against the Pikes Peak Fuel Company. Before he left Denver Tikas took the time to file his final citizenship papers. On that same day Turkey accepted the peace terms of the Powers and abandoned the last of her claims to Crete.

No doubt Tikas was sent to the Pike View because the men on strike—or a good part of them—were Greek. According to the Colorado Springs papers of the time the strike was a failure and two days after Tikas' arrival at the mines most of the strikers had gone back to work at the old scale. But the union was not ready for a spontaneous walkout in April. A letter from one undercover man, again Number 52, shows him trying to quell a premature strike in Walsenburg at the end of August. So it may be Tikas' claim to have settled the difficulties at the Pike View is true, and his task was not to lead a strike but to get the men back to work, to convince them to wait for the union's word. The union kept him on its payroll until the first of May. He went back to Denver, perhaps still interested in the coffeehouse, perhaps involved in some other business, but still organizing on his own time. Then in the first week of August the union was ready for him again.

There is a curious story you still hear in Colorado about Tikas leaving Denver for the Southern Field. It has the elements of folklore, but the truth is not so easy to come by, nor is it so chaste that you can throw such a legend away. The story has it that the Denver mine owners offered Tikas several thousand dollars not to go south. Had this obscure young Greek organizer made such a name for himself then? Sixty-three years later Nick Matsoukas, a columnist for the Chicago *Greek Press*, remembered talking to Greeks who had been in the Colorado strike of 1913–14. Louis Tikas has been transformed in Matsoukas' account into Leo the Cretan, the bribe has swollen to $10,000, and Leo calls a meeting to stand up on a box and tell his fellow Greeks of the immense sum the Company has offered him to leave the strike-bound camp.

> "What do you want me to do?" asked Leo the Cretan.
> "Do whatever you think is the right thing to do," came back the unanimous reply.
> "I am staying till the end," was Leo's simple answer.

The next day, as Matsoukas tells it, Leo the Cretan was shot in the back.

There exist, in the United Mine Workers of America files, two letters by Tikas. They are practically the only accounts of Tikas in his own words—words strained through the English of whatever American he got to type out his letters and translate them from his immigrant English into standard stuff. One of the letters, written in February 1914, is his justification. The other is dated August 28, 1913. It is to the secretary treasurer of District 15, who would be Ed Doyle. It is from this letter that we get a sense of Tikas' activities for the union in the south.

He says he went to the Southern Field on the first of August. He visited the Pike View again, then went down to the mines of Huerfano and Las Animas counties. (In the spellings of the camps he visited I hear his immigrant accent passing through the American who took down his account: Pike View becomes Pickview, Ravenwood comes out Riverhood, Delagua is written Delacoa.) In all he visited fourteen camps. In Denver and Pueblo he compiled a few statistics on the Greeks in the Southern Field, statistics which are hard to come by from the casual treatment usually given foreigners in company and government reports. He says there were three hundred fifty Greeks in the mines of the Southern Field. Since the first of the year, thirteen had been killed. Many more had been injured.

In Pueblo he went to the Colorado Fuel and Iron Company hospital and walked among the gardens and the mock-Spanish Colonial courtyards collecting what data he could on the injuries. He learned that a Greek was there, Michael Stamatakis. Stamatakis had been hurt badly in a mine accident on the eighteenth day of May. He had lain in the hospital fourteen days before his hands or face were washed. It was the treatment given to miners the Greeks said. Someone sent an attorney to see Stamatakis but the doctor in charge refused to let him in. The doctor warned Stamatakis that if he talked to anyone about his case they'd put him out of the hospital and leave him on the sidewalk to take care of himself.

Tikas talked to other Greeks. In Trinidad Eleftharios Motakis told him that he'd gone to see his brother at the Frederick mine and the superintendent had had him arrested by two detectives and put out of camp. Nick Saris and James Ganos, the official interpreter of the Pueblo Greeks, told him of the exorbitant prices the miners had to pay at the companies' stores. Saris and Ganos had worked for the C. F. and I. for five or six years. They had watched coal weighed in the same cars they had used when they'd first gone to work drop from 5,500 or 6,000 pounds to 3,000 or 3,500 pounds on the company's scales. Tikas concluded his letter to Doyle in a way that was more significant than he knew at the time. He said that the spirit among his 350 countrymen in the south was that of war.

> They are ready at any time unless conditions improve to engage in an industrial war and to fight, just as their fathers and brothers in the fatherland have fought the Turks until their freedom has been obtained, so these men are ready even at the sacrifice of their lives to fight until their industrial freedom has been obtained.

"Industrial war" was not an idle metaphor. For the Greeks would see the confrontation between themselves and a complex industrial system played out in the terms of a revolt—of the wars against the Turks. It was a dangerous and clumsy metaphor with which to fight the grip of something as vast and as powerful as the American corporation, but it was the only one they had, and the Greeks and the other strikers would suffer bitterly for it.

So Tikas did not create the spirit of militancy in the Greeks of the south; he found it. Already in Segundo, the C. F. and I. camp run by such bullying gunmen as George Titsworth, Sr., and Bob Lee, they were boiling. They saw themselves as the lowest on the scale of privilege, friendless, with no one to back them up. Worse off, even, than the Italians. They would put the Greeks to work four or five days a week, then pull them; the superintendents would give the extra days to their friends. "It is not right," said Pete Katsulis, a Greek who would come to rival Tikas for his organizer's job. "All I know is that they try to protect themselves, to show the people whether they got a right to be a man like a man, to stand like a man, that is all. This country they don't care much about the Greeks. . . ." And in Delagua, too, the Greeks were angry. On September first, after two or three of them had been fired for loading dirty coal, all of the Greeks came out. They milled around the mine office with their tools and their pit lamps in their hands, twenty or so of them, and in a body demanded their time. Like any good organizer, Tikas would exploit this discontent, would strive to channel it into unionism. But a year before his trip to the Southern Field there were already Greeks in Las Animas and Huerfano counties who had secretly joined the union. Kostas Papadakis, the young Sphakiote, was one of those who had gone quietly up to a hotel room in Trinidad to hear Bob Uhlich talk. It was the black man, Old Dave, who had first told him about the union. Papadakis heard how the union would fight for better working conditions, better pay. It would cost them a dollar a month. There were fifteen Greeks at Hastings. They all joined.

Before Tikas left the Southern Field to make his report in Denver, the coming strike claimed its first death. Gerald Lippiatt, the Italian organizer who had worked in the strike in the north and who, like Louis Tikas, was sent south in the first week of August, had come into Trinidad on the 8:00 P.M. Colorado Southern train from Rugby the night of August fifteenth. With him were five foreign miners. He had come to attend the State Federation of Labor convention which would begin the next week. It was Saturday and the streets of Trinidad were crowded with shoppers and men down from the mines. At the corner of Elm and Commercial, Lippiatt ran into George Belcher and Walter Belk, two of the West Virginia gunmen who had been in southern Colorado a month on the Baldwin–Felts payroll. Lippiatt accused the pair of being spotters for the C. F. and I. and there were some words exchanged. Lippiatt went into the union headquarters in the Packer Building. In a few minutes he was back. Belcher and Belk were waiting for him. There were more words and Belk made a pass for his gun. Lippiatt drew a .45 automatic and said, "Keep your gun in your pocket." Then the shooting started. Lippiatt fired once at Belcher, then ran into the street and fired again. His bullet hit Belcher above the knee, but the Baldwin–Felts men had gotten off eight shots, and four of them had gone home. Lippiatt died instantly. The five foreign miners scattered. The killing would not be forgotten by the union and the Italians of the Southern Field.

They buried Gerald Lippiatt in Colorado Springs on August twenty-second with his American fiancée standing at the grave. He was thirty-two. By August twenty-seventh Louis Tikas was back in Denver. So much was the killing of Gerald Lippiatt in the air he does not mention it in his report.

Now, at the end of August the push for a strike was drawing to its climax. First blood had been let and Governor Ammons' attempts to get the sides to negotiate had met with failure. The operators were inalterably opposed to negotiating with the union. To do so would have been, in their eyes, as much as recognizing it. By September fourth, L. M. Bowers, experiencing a dyspeptic old age (he would live, nevertheless, to be ninety-six) and a ruined vacation, wrote John D. Rockefeller, Jr., from Binghamton, New York, in glowing terms of the profits of the past year for the Colorado Fuel and Iron Company. Then he mentioned the news that had spoiled his holiday.

> There has been a group of labor-union agitators in southern Colorado for more than a month threatening to call a strike for the purpose of securing a recognition of the Western Federation of Miners, but protests have come from nearly all the State officials from the governor on down, together with the protests from the boards of trade and of commercial bodies, so that the matter has quieted down, though their national officials are still in Colorado.
>
> This has kept us all in a state of unrest, so that my vacation has been a season of worry. A disaster of this sort would put us up against a fight that would be serious indeed.

Bowers was wrong about the name of the union. He was right about the fight.

By September twelfth things were already on virtual strike footing and Tikas received fifty-four dollars relief from the union for eighteen Greeks—no doubt men who had moved from their homes to stand duty in the coming strike. The union's organizing efforts were complete. On Sunday September fourteenth Louis Tikas was back in El Paso County. There, along with organizers Paul Paulson and Dan O'Leary, he addressed a mass meeting of miners he had helped bring into the union. It may have been the young Greek's first public speech.

On September sixteenth the United Mine Workers of America held a special convention in Trinidad. In Doyle's accounts and in the convention roll are the names of nine of the Greeks who attended. Louis Tikas was among them. In the West Theater Tikas listened to the delegates from the camps read their reports. It was a catalog of bad work and poor wages and bribes to the pit bosses and of being robbed at the store and the tipple scales, of bad timbering and accidents and death. He sat with the other foreigners and watched Mother Jones pace up and down the stage, a frail-looking old lady with her hair up in a bun and her cold blue eyes darting out from under her steel-rimmed spectacles. I wonder how much of her wild and rambling speech the immigrants got. But maybe it wasn't necessary to understand the words exactly. She told them there were no Dagos in this country. She told them that whenever the immigrant commission passed on a man and let him into the country he was immediately an American citizen. She said that the Italian was as dear to her as any other nationality, that the Polish fellow was too—he didn't get a chance to be born maybe where he wanted to. He had to take what he could get. Christ was born in a stable. She went on to talk of West Virginia, speaking rapidly as she did when she was excited, an incoherent account of guards and Gatling guns along Cabin Creek, then talked about Montana and New Mexico. She had been everywhere . . . "When I get Colorado, Kansas and Alabama organized, I will say, God almighty take me to my rest if you want to, but not until then. . . . I want you as a body to pledge yourselves in this convention that we will stand as one solid mass with the voice of human liberty . . . this fight is going on, and if there is anybody going to keep it on, I am going to do it." The miners framed their resolutions and issued a list of demands: recognition of the union, ten percent advance in the tonnage rate of wages, an eight-hour day, pay for dead work, checkweighmen, the right to trade at any store they wanted, the right to choose their own boardinghouse and doctor, enforcement of the mining laws, abolition of the guard system. The scabs of 1903 and 1904, those ignorant foreigners brought in ten years before by the carload to break other foreigners' strike, had seized something important in the smoky air of that theater. At the end of the convention they issued the strike call. They would give the operators a week to answer their demands.

But they knew what the answers would be. Already Doyle had leased ground at the mouths of the canyons anticipating the eviction of the miners from their company houses. Tents had been ordered from the Utah and West Virginia coalfields to shelter men and families. The strike had begun.

At Coal Creek, Colorado Fuel and Iron Company manager E. H. Weitzel waited at Odd Fellows Hall to address the miners of the Radiant pit. The entire force of the mine, 135 men, walked upstairs and, in the United Mine Workers office over Weitzel's head, signed up en masse for union cards. Dr. Schwegel, the Austrian consul, came down to the Southern Field and toured the coal camps, passing out cigars from the porches of the company stores and urging the men not to strike. Under the eyes of the company guards the miners kept quiet. But when a gang of these "Austrians"—Slavs and Hungarians and North Italians—who cordially hated Franz Joseph and his Empire, came upon Schwegel on the streets of Trinidad, it took an escort of United Mine Workers organizers to hustle him to the safety of a Denver-bound train.

A delegation of newspaper reporters descended from Denver to capture the events of the mass exodus from the mining camps. Gus Papadakis and his friends moved up to LaVeta and looked for a place to board for the duration of the strike. Lou Dold began making plans to set up his camera in front of the miners' tent colonies.

6. THE STRIKE BEGINS

On the twenty-third of September 1913 the strike officially began. Don MacGregor of the *Denver Express* was one of the reporters who watched the strikers and their families stream out of their company houses in the canyons to the tent colonies the union had set up for them on the plains. Those lucky enough to have been able to hire a wagon hunched over their piled-up household goods trying to avoid the wind-driven rain that had been coming down all day. When they came to the hills, they all got out, the men, women, and sometimes the children, and tried to push the carts along, straining against the wheels. In the hour's drive between Trinidad and the Ludlow colony, MacGregor counted fifty-seven wagons; more were pouring down to the main road from every canyon. While he watched, he was filled with bitterness at all those cheery lies in the coal companies' magazines with their glossy photos, at all the optimistic gas in the speeches coming out of the owners of the mines. "Prosperity!" he wrote,

Little piles of miserable looking straw bedding! Little piles of kitchen utensils! And all so worn and badly used they would have been the scorn of any second-hand dealer on Larimer Street.

Prosperity! With never a single article even approaching luxury, save once in a score of wagons a cheap gaily painted gramophone! With never a bookcase! With never a book! With never a single article that even the owners thought worth while trying to protect from the rain!

79

And as he counted the stream of homeless people, it seemed to him that even the horses dragging the loaded wagons through the mud looked weary and worn and shamefaced.

John Lawson went from colony to colony, mud-spattered, in high-topped boots, rallying the strikers, helping to pull the balked carts from the mud. At Ludlow he set up a canteen at the edge of the colony and had milk and hot coffee doled out to the soaked and exhausted families as they straggled in. Only sixteen tents had been pitched. The rail-roads had deliberately delayed the tents coming in from West Virginia. Little piles of furniture lay scattered over the prairie with the rain falling on them. In spite of the storm, a thousand strikers stood in the open and cheered the speakers at the meeting. The union housed as many as it could in the big central tent, in its halls, and in the homes of sympathizers. That night the rain turned to snow. The Greeks camped out in the storm.

There was trouble in Segundo. The union had established a camp on the outskirts of the town. When the miners sent wagons for the belongings they had left in the company houses, the mine guards turned them back. The next day the wagons were turned back again, and the harassed, bitter miners let anyone who cared know that they would get their pots and pans and bedding, gunmen or no gunmen. That afternoon one of the coalfield marshals found out it was no bluff.

Bob Lee was one of those primitives scratched up by the industrial West to police its machine, a leftover of the frontier. The C. F. and I. liked to think of him as some courtly Southerner "of the Lee family of Virginia." He was a Kentuckian brought up in New Mexico. In 1904 Bob Lee had come up to Colorado to pick up a badge as a company guard with a reputation as a tough customer. The coal companies brought in men like Lee by the carload for the strike of that year, and in the rough camps of the Southern Field these men found their place.

But there were other hard men in these camps as well, primitives themselves, though in a different style from the company marshals and three-dollar-a-day gunmen. The frontier they had come from, like the one in which they now found themselves, was a social one. Those starving south European villages of the immigrants had their own code of behavior, their own name for that value deepest in a man. It was what the Greeks called *philotimo*—the love of honor. There is a report that a few months before the strike Bob Lee had beaten up some of the Segundo Greeks and that they had been seen plotting against him in a saloon. The Greeks did not need the excuse of a beating to turn their sense of grievance into action. They saw themselves as the most abused of the camp workers in Segundo. It had cut them to the quick. In 1903 the Italians of the Southern Field had been brought into the union by the brilliant socialist organizer Carlo Demolli. Newspapers such as *Il Proletario* from New York, or Trinidad's *Il Lavoratore Italiano*, promoted class consciousness among them. At the Aguilar saloon named "The 29th of July" the Italians were rumored to use a knife and a he-goat to demonstrate how on that date the anarchist Bresci had assassinated King Umberto I. The Greeks were no such theorists. They had come to this country untouched by social ideals. They were men with the skin peeled off, quick to detect a slight, to burn under it, and they cherished their revenge with an almost sexual intensity. Vendetta was part of their lives. They did not kill for aesthetics or for an idea, but to even up an imbalanced internal world.

Around noon on the twenty-fourth, after the miners had had their traps turned back from Segundo a second time, Bob Lee got word that a gang of Greeks was tearing up the new footbridge the company had put across Las Animas Creek just below the coke ovens. The Greeks were armed. If the company refused them its road, they would tear down the bridge the company put up for its scabs. When Lee got to the bridge he ordered the Greeks away and started backing them off, muscling his horse against them. They got as far as the coke ovens and the Greeks stopped and began milling around the horse. Lee started to pull his rifle out of its scabbard. All at once one of the Greeks raised his shotgun and fired and Lee dropped from his horse, his jugular vein severed by the blast. When the people of the camp got to him they discovered his rifle on the ground. It was still cocked.

Almost before the report of that old single-barreled shotgun had stopped ringing, Tom Larius and the four other Greeks had slipped into the scrub cedar, heading for the New Mexico line. A mounted posse fanned into the hills, but Larius was never caught. On the streets of Trinidad they nodded and summed up Bob Lee's career in a phrase that was already beginning to sound a little hollow in the fading West:

"He lived by gun law, and now he has died by gun law." An independent mine owner named Abercrombie said with a little more humor that it seemed to him Bob Lee had died of natural causes.

A strike is no abstraction. It is a sum of grievances stored up, made manifest. The Greeks thought of their lot in Hastings and Segundo and Delagua. They added up, each man to himself, the humiliations, the extortions. They passed the stories around. Someone remembered the three bakers, Trakaniaris, Loulos, and Harry Pagonia. Not even strikers. Kicked out of Delagua before they could even collect their bills just because they were Greeks. That $350 the bakers lost burned into the Greeks. They brooded on it as if it were a personal affront. And there was Angelo Zikos. Caught in his testimony to a grand jury months later is a sense of that personal grievance, and it is more pertinent to such strikes and their violence than all the pages of tables and statistics in the world.

Zikos was an oddity among the Greeks, older than most of them at thirty-four, not a coal miner, but a skilled company man, a machinist. He'd been a sailor, knew the world. Shortly after the strike broke out he went up to Old Segundo to get his mail. Just outside the C. F. and I. office company gunman George Titsworth, Sr., stuck a .45 revolver into Zikos' chest and told him to put up his hands. He called the Greek a son of a bitch, some foreigner who had come over to kill American citizens. A guard had been beaten by the strikers. Zikos said he didn't have anything to do with it.

"I been Greek citizen, American citizen, I been square for any country," Zikos said. "I been all over this world for twenty years, I never be troubled. I have been in India, West Indies, South Africa, China, England, Germany, Italy and France . . ."

Titsworth told him to shut up. He shook his revolver at the Greek.

"I don't be afraid of revolver," Zikos said. "Go ahead. Shoot."

Titsworth put him under arrest and they went into the mine office. They stood in a little room with work clothes hanging on the walls. In one corner was the telegraph operator's desk. Mining equipment lay strewn about. They brought in Frank Miller, master mechanic Dan Collins, the machinist, the chief chemist. These were men Zikos knew. He had worked at Segundo five years. Corey, the captain of the guards, came in. He was the one who had been beaten. Corey looked at the Greek and said, "That is the man."

"You big mistake, Corey," Zikos said.

Corey looked at Zikos' high-topped boots. He asked the Greek if he had worn those boots the other day and the Greek said yes. Corey didn't know whether he had the right man or not. He thought it might be.

In the other room the clerks were working at their desks. The mine superintendent was with them and Zikos called to him. The superintendent came to the door.

"What do you take me for?" Zikos said. "You never know me for five years whether I am a square man or trouble man?"

He called the superintendent twice. The superintendent didn't answer. He just looked at the Greek. Then he went back inside. Zikos called to Dan Collins. "Dan, what is the matter? Anything wrong for me over here? What do I trouble to you fellows over here?"

Collins answered him. "I don't know, Angelo," he said. "Somebody pointed to you, said you did the trouble." Collins told the Greek he'd better beat it from the camp.

"I can't leave this camp," Zikos said. "I can't beat this camp, not now, no time. I have to live in this camp."

Collins said he would feel pretty sorry to see the Greek get arrested, to see him get killed over there.

"Well, you no my brother, you no my father or any relation, but you only good friend between five years," Zikos said.

'If you want it," Collins told him, "I'll send you some place to work. New Mexico or any place. Or Utah. I have plenty of friends."

"I refuse all that," Zikos said. "I have to remain here in Segundo. I have to see this business out."

Now, in the first week of October, the camp at Ludlow was put in order. It had been laid out on the prairie that spread beneath the twin canyons that led up the cedar-covered mesas to the mines; Delagua Canyon to the north, Berwind to the south. It was, John Lawson thought, the biggest industrial colony in the world. There were as many as 1,300 people in the colony—500 men, 300–400 women, the rest children who played now among the neat rows of tents with their

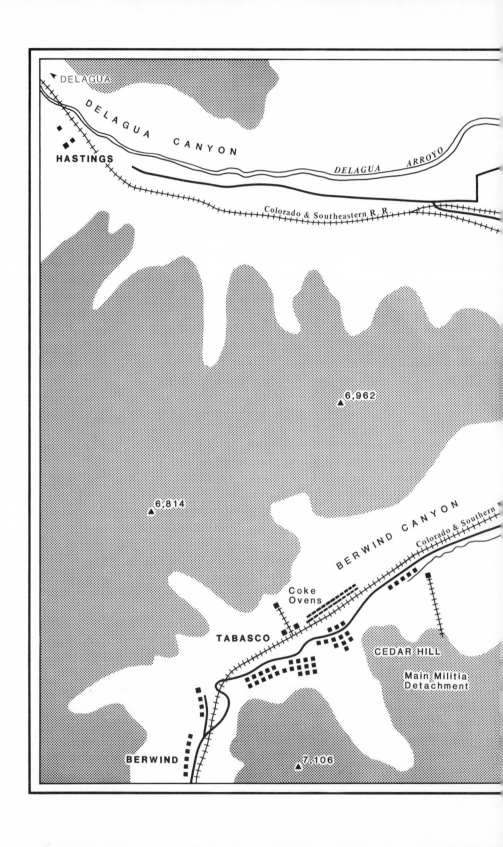

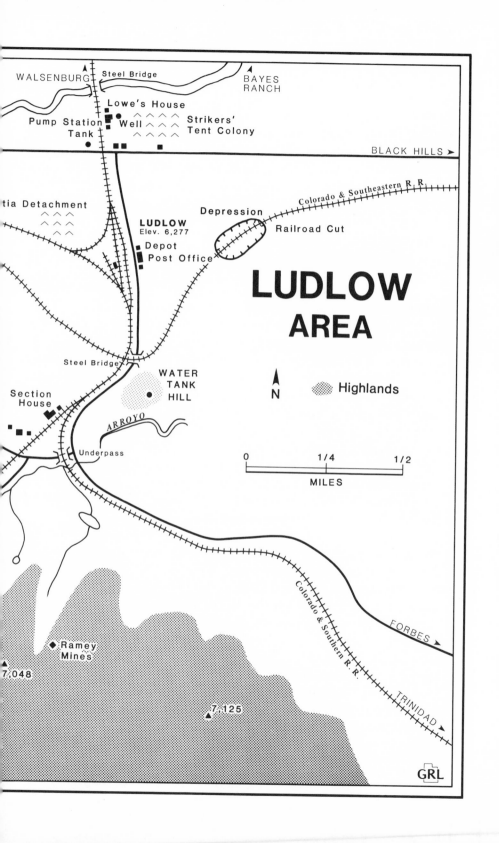

WALSENBURG   Steel Bridge   BAYES
                                              RANCH
                   Lowe's House
Pump Station   Well   ∧∧∧∧   Strikers'
   Tank   ∧∧∧∧   Tent Colony
                                              BLACK HILLS ➤

tia Detachment   Colorado & Southeastern R. R.
    ∧∧∧   Depression
  ∧ ∧∧   LUDLOW   Railroad Cut
  ∧ ∧   Elev. 6,277
              Depot
              Post Office

LUDLOW
AREA

Steel Bridge
              WATER
              TANK   ↑   Highlands
Section   HILL   N
House
       ARROYO
                        0   1/4   1/2
   Underpass
                              MILES

                                        FORBES ➤

                              Colorado & Southern R. R.

◆ Ramey
  Mines
7,048   TRINIDAD ➤

              ▲ 7,125

                                        GRL

painted numbers or out in the ball diamond across the road. In the center of the colony was a public square with a bulletin board and platform for meetings. There was a big tent for dances and cold weather, exercise bars, privies, heaps of coal. When the sun was out, the lines in front of the colony sagged with wash and flags sprouted from the tents, flags of Greece, Italy, the American flag, the proud two-colored banner with the name "Ludlow" stitched to it. More than twenty different languages were spoken in the tents and among the coal piles and lines of flapping wash or were bellowed through the megaphone on the platform.

South of the tents was the railroad junction of Ludlow, with its yards and switches and the lines of coal cars from the mines. There was a Greek bakery, a few saloons, a post office, a couple of stores. The station and its platform would be a point of contention when the strikers tried to stake out their picket lines against the trainloads of scabs. Farther down was a steel bridge which separated the rail lines going up Berwind and Delagua canyons, and a low rise with an abandoned railroad tank they called Water Tank Hill. A little north of the colony was the boxcar home of a railroad man named Lowe and his family, with a vegetable garden and pasture and a deep, abandoned well that led down in tiers to the stagnant water. A few yards beyond the well was a dry arroyo and another steel bridge. If you followed the arroyo east you would come to the Frank Bayes' ranch and beyond to the low, brush-covered slopes of the Black Hills.

The scabs started to come in. Black men brought up from the South, hungry for work. The Ludlow people lined up at the depot to jeer them as they got off the train. They dragged three of the scabs from the Hastings hack, fed them in the colony, then sent them back where they came from. On the fifth of October the Greeks caught a couple of their countrymen who were going to scab at Tabasco under the bridge south of Ludlow, beat them, took one of them hostage to a farm in the Black Hills. The next day, by his own account, Tikas moved into the Ludlow camp.

Then the shooting started. On the seventh Lawson and Mother Jones went to Ludlow and addressed the camp, standing in the back of the union auto. They'd gone on to another meeting in Aguilar but turned in their tracks and made for Ludlow again when they heard that trouble was coming. A couple of strikers from the colony had had a run-in with the guards at the Hastings post office. Lawson and Mother Jones were back in the camp by the time an auto with a C. F. and I. clerk named Larson and the West Virginia gunmen George Belcher and Walter Belk showed up on the road west of the tents. There were some shots from the automobile and the strikers ran for their guns while Lawson tried to hold them back. He told them to keep their guns in their tents, told them they couldn't win that way, but the strikers rushed by him and took up positions behind the strings of railroad cars on the Colorado and Southern tracks and on the steel bridge north of the tents and began firing at the mine guards dug into the brush on the hills half a mile away.

It was a strange kind of battle, almost like some holiday ballgame. The women and children crowded up against the wire fence around the colony, heedless and exposed, while the lead flew. A horse went down on the hill and they cheered. Finally Lawson got them away from the fence and into the tents. He disarmed the men. When the Trinidad branch of the National Guard got in, the strikers had been broken up. Five of the Greeks were arrested for their part in the fight but only Mike Zalaratis was held. Some witness claimed he'd seen him walking around with a Winchester, endeavoring to incite a riot.

That night Lawson met under sheriff Zeke Martin on the Colorado and Southern platform just before the 7:20 train. He asked for help. "Those people, sheriff, are out on the prairie," he said. "They are living in tents and they have no protection. And I want to ask you as sheriff of this county if you are going to protect those people."

Martin told him that the strikers were able to take care of themselves.

"I'm damned glad to know it, sheriff," Lawson said.

The union believed that it was the coal companies' policy to incite the strikers to fight. Early after the killing of Bob Lee, Judge Jesse Northcutt, the C. F. and I. attorney and political operative and owner of a couple of Trinidad newspapers, had been circulating a petition asking for state troops. It was a strategy that had worked for mine operators before. Violence in the strike zone was the wedge that would bring in the militia; as it had in Cripple Creek and in the coalfields in 1904, the state would break the strike with its own troops. But the nearsighted, badgered man in the governor's seat was balking. Ammons was a Democrat, elected with the labor backing of men such as John Lawson and other strike leaders of influence. So, while the governor temporized, the policy of the union leaders in the south was to keep the lid on, to calm their volatile men. Here it was that Louis Tikas had his value. If he could keep the respect of his men, and at the same time hold them, then he would have played his part.

But gunfire came again on the ninth. There had been a few shots fired into a strikers' ball game that morning. Later that day a party of heavily-armed guards rode down to the Ludlow depot to collect a searchlight. The guards trotting across the prairie were as much as an invitation.

About four or four-thirty that afternoon Mrs. Powell and her grandmother were sitting in the yard of their little house south of Ludlow when a group of guards came down from Berwind Canyon. The women had heard shooting and were concerned. Mrs. Powell's husband was a striker, but he had gotten a job herding cattle for the Green ranch and was out with the animals that day. The guards crossed over the steel bridge and got a drink at the cistern. They had white rags tied around their arms. "Was there anybody killed or hurt?" the grandmother asked. "None of our men were killed," one of the guards said, "but we got one of Mr. Green's cowpunchers." Mrs. Powell thought of her husband. "Was he riding a bay horse," she asked. And the man said yes. "Well, if he was riding a bay horse," she said, "I'm afraid it was my husband."

They gave Mack Powell a first-class send-off. It wasn't the last of the long processions of men and women that would wind up the hill to the Trinidad cemetery behind a union coffin.

A few days after Mack Powell's funeral Louis Tikas went north to take care of some unfinished business. On October 13, 1913, he stood up in a Denver courtroom, raised his right hand, and swore to uphold the duties of a citizen of the United States. There had been some delays in granting his final papers. Was he being harassed for his union work, or were the continuances at his own request, and it was just now that he found it important to be out of the Southern Field in order to take the oath? Who knows what he might or might not have been doing while the searchlight detail and the strikers were trading

The C. F. & I. and the Victor–American Fuel Company were in need of men who make a profession of handling a gun against union men, and as the Baldwin–Felts Detective Agency makes a specialty of furnishing these specimens of God's carelessness, these coal companies employed the murder agency to furnish assassins. —Adolph Germer. Mine guards in the "Death Special." Courtesy of the Library, State Historical Society of Colorado, Dold Collection.

shots. He signed his name. His identity as an American—disguise or genuine article or something of both—was complete.

Two days after Tikas became a citizen the guards and the county authorities rounded up fifty strikers in the Southern Field and arrested them for picketing. They marched the men at gunpoint to the Las Animas County jail. Coming down the hill into Trinidad the men began to shout, but they offered no resistance. There were armed men all around them and behind them rolled a grim-looking machine they would come to call the Death Special. G. C. Jones, an organizer for the Western Federation of Miners, tried to get a Kodak of the machine, but was beaten by Belk and A. C. Felts for his efforts. Young Lou Dold did get a picture. You see a boxy, slab-sided vehicle in his photograph, with a spotlight mounted up front and a machine gun poking out the side. Inside a half-dozen Baldwin–Felts men cradle their rifles. Felts had had an automobile shipped in from Denver, tore down the sides and replaced them with three-eighths-inch steel plates made in the C. F. and I. plant in Pueblo. The machine gun, Felts casually admitted later to the House Committee on Mines and Mining, was the same one much worried over by another Congressional investigation, and had had something to do with a steel train and a bullet-riddled strikers' tent colony in West Virginia.

On October seventeenth, at the strikers' colony at Forbes Junction, the gun got its first Colorado work. The next day John Lawson, Louis Tikas and a few others went to Forbes to see the results.

I do not know how much Lawson knew of the Forbes shooting then, but he was angry. The union men were riding in an old spring wagon pulled by a couple of horses. Just before Forbes they came to a railroad cut. The Death Special was standing in the cut. Inside were Felts, Belk, George Belcher, and Jesse Northcutt. Felts had a telescopic sight on his rifle. Judge Northcutt was the only one without a gun. When the wagon stopped the judge came up and said, "How do you do?"

Lawson looked at Northcutt and the gunmen and imagined them sitting in the armored car planning another job on the unprotected tents at Forbes. When Belk asked him what his business was he let him know what he thought. It was Tikas who stopped them. When the young Greek had backed the two off, the union men got back in the wagon and went on. Now they saw what had happened in the camp. Old Man Ure showed them his tent. It had been shot to rags—148 bullet holes in it. He had counted every one. The morning before there had been some shooting in the hills and they all were edgy. The women had moved to the upper colony. The men were on their way up there, too, when the steel automobile pulled up about the same time as a bunch of horsemen. The men in the automobile got out and planted a machine gun across from the tents. One of them came up to the colony gate. He carried a white flag. The man with the flag showed them a union card and took out a bottle and they passed it around. He asked them if they were all strikers and they said they were. "Well," he said, "look out, we are liable to shoot." And he stepped back about five paces toward the colony gate. When he got to the ditch he dropped the flag and ducked for cover and the men in front of the automobile began to fire. Some of the boys in the camp ran for a ditch with their guns. Old Man Ure dived into his tent and scrambled under the bed. Bullets from the machine gun whipped through the canvas, shattered the leg of his stove, plugged his coffee pot, his pails, the bed itself. Outside, in the rain which had started to fall, the gunmen kept shooting. They hit one kid, Marco Zamboni, nine times in the legs as he tried to make it back to a tent. Luca Vahernick they killed outright. The shooting kept up until dusk.

If there is anything that can account for the unconditional hatred the strikers would later show for the guards, for the panic that would sweep through those tents in waves throughout the rest of the strike, it is Forbes. Years later, when Lawson recalled the day he went out there, he remembered how Tikas had stepped between him and Belk, had eased them away from each other in that cool, calm way of his. Maybe it was remembering this that caused him to call Tikas one of the quietest men he ever knew. But there was something more in that almost unearthly calm that seems to surround Louis Tikas until his last day, in that refusal to be provoked. Sensing it might have been why men like Linderfelt and the other gunmen of the strike detested him. For in the letter of justification he would write to the union four months later, Tikas claimed to have been at Forbes during the fight and to have nearly lost his life there. "It was I who sent up people with only seven guns against [the attackers] of our camp who had thirty-five guns and also a machine gun that discharged two hundred fifty shots a second." There is testimony that on the sixteenth of October three strange Greeks with new rifles came into the Forbes colony and that the next day they were joined by six more Greeks with new weapons who went into the hills to do some target shooting. It may be Tikas was one of those Greeks. If he was there, if he *had* led the out-gunned strikers when the shooting started in the colony, his calm the next day is interesting. And it is Greek. Seven hundred years of war and uneasy truce with Venetian and Turk had taught a Cretan something about survival.

With tensions close to breaking Lawson moved into Ludlow. He put up a tent and organized the men into squads, set them to work in a grounds committee, a building committee, a committee on sanitation —anything to employ them—just as later, in jail, he would set up a mock court and give out fines of cigarettes in order to keep his men from exploding. He organized a camp police force and tried to put a man who spoke each of the colony's main languages on every squad to explain things to his countrymen when trouble broke out. It must be the badge of this force that Tikas wears on his coat in the photograph taken of him at this time. The strikers took to wearing red bandanas around their throats to identify themselves. They were called red-necks now by the guards in the hills. The union was buying guns.

There would never be enough guns. It is one of the ironies of this strike that for all the company vilification of the bloodthirsty foreigners in the tents, for all the weapons searches and harassment, the strikers never had enough guns. When they went to fight, many went barehanded, and the wooden rifles they fashioned to drill with or to frighten the company gunmen in the hills became a curiosity, a strangely moving emblem of the struggle.

What they felt now, in the Lulow camp, was their nakedness. They were out on the open plain, caught between the railroad tracks and the fortified camps in the hills. At night the searchlight at Hastings played over the tents. It danced along the paths pointing, dodging, sometimes stopping cold. Once the light followed a union auto going to a meeting on a dark road, picked it out the way a man with an electric torch would hunt a deer. The searchlight shining through the roofs of their tents made them think how thin the canvas was around them, how powerless to stop a bullet. One of the strikers went out and borrowed a high-power rifle from the dentist brother of the union doctor and the guards were a little more careful where they turned their light after that. But always in the camp there was this specter: that the guards would one day come down from the canyons and clean them out. Old union men remembered the strike of 1904 and how they had been rounded up and thrown in railroad cars and dumped on the desert, waterless, without food, beaten and threatened. More ominous was what had just happened at Forbes and in Paint Creek, West Virginia, where not that many months before an armored train had sped by a colony laid out, like Ludlow, along a line of tracks and fired machine gun bursts into the tents of the sleeping strikers. Up in the hills were Felts and Belcher and Belk, the same men who had shot up Forbes. The strikers saw the mine guards riding by on their horses; they heard about their drunken boasts in Baca's saloon. It was as if the history of violence were without imagination, a mindless reiteration of the same few themes. In the colony they dug out cellars under the tent floors for the women and children to hide in, and along the dry ravine they dug rifle pits. The *United Mine Workers Journal* warned that feeling was running high and the strikers were becoming hard to hold. They patrolled the camp now all night long.

The flags bobbed up and down the street. The women and children were singing:

> *The union forever, hurrah boys, hurrah!*
> *Down with the Baldwins and up with the law!*

In the Cardenas Hotel was the governor, down for a firsthand look at the strike, and out on the pavement was Mother Jones with her parade. The marchers' signs read:

WE ARE NOT AFRAID OF YOUR GATLING GUNS, WE HAVE
    TO DIE ANYWAY
GIVE US ANOTHER PATRICK HENRY FOR GOVERNOR
THE DEMOCRATIC PARTY IS ON TRIAL
INSTEAD OF GOING TO SCHOOL WE HAVE TO FEED BLOOD-
    HOUNDS

One law that is not written in the statute. . . . That is the law of humanity and it is the right of one man to be with another and be a citizen and be respected without being bully-ragged. —Ed Doyle. Miners' parade in Walsenburg, 1913. Courtesy of the Library, State Historical Society of Colorado.

DO YOU HEAR THE CHILDREN GROANING, O COLORADO!
HAS THE GOVERNOR ANY RESPECT FOR THE STATE?
LET THE PUBLIC TAKE OVER THE MINES
COLORADO CIVILIZATION TURNS OUT INTO THE RAIN
    MOTHER JONES'S FAMILY
IF UNCLE SAM CAN RUN A POST OFFICE, WHY NOT THE
    MINES?
RAILROAD MEN, DON'T HAUL SCABS TO MAKE SLAVES OUT
    OF OUR LITTLE ONES
WE FURNISH THE SHERIFF WITH A NURSING BOTTLE
COLORADO WOMEN HAVE A VOTE, WHAT ARE THEY DOING
    WITH IT?
WE REPRESENT C. F. & I.'S PROSPERITY SLAVES
YOU CANNOT WHIP US INTO CITIZENSHIP WITH SHERIFFS
    AND GATLING GUNS

A couple of miners' wives showed up in flashy new coats. "And where do you think you're going?" Mother Jones cried. "Get out of my parade! Get out of my parade!"

The governor toured the mines for two days. He saw no violence. Just out of Walsenburg an armed guard at one of the Victor–American mines refused to let his car pass. Someone explained it was the governor in the car. "How the hell do I know?" the guard said. They turned the car around and went back to the main road. "The strike is no Sunday school picnic," Ammons told reporters, "but conditions aren't as bad as I had been led to believe." He did not call out the National Guard. At dawn on the day he left the strike zone, Zeke Martin rode to Forbes with fifty deputies and the Death Special. They surrounded the colony and covered it with four machine guns, then marched the men at gunpoint across the road. The deputies rousted out women and their still-sleeping children, overturned trunks and beds, and tore up the tent floors looking for guns. They arrested four of the strikers for the death of Luke Vahernick, their own man.

Just south of the Colorado line, at the foot of Raton Pass, was a cluster of efficient coal mines being worked by the Phelps–Dodge Corporation. They were nonunion mines, and the strike did not extend as far as New Mexico, but what happened at Dawson that fall would play its own part in the Colorado strike.

On the evening of October twenty-second, Mother Jones was preparing to leave for Washington, D.C., in an effort to pressure Congress into investigating the strike. Not long before she had received a telegram from Dawson asking her to come down and organize the mines. She was just getting ready to go to her train when she got word of the disaster. At three that afternoon a dull rumble had shaken the houses in the Dawson camp. Stag Canyon Number Two had gone up.

The next day Ed Doyle and Ed Wallace, the editor of the *United Mine Workers Journal*, went to Dawson with a thousand dollar check for the women and children of the explosion victims. With them were a volunteer rescue crew made up of Colorado strikers and Louis Tikas.

When the train got to Dawson, Doyle and Wallace went into town. Tikas headed for the mine. He knew there were Greeks trapped underground, as many as a hundred of them; and he knew the company guards were stationed everywhere to keep outsiders from learning to much. Somehow he dodged the guards and got into the weigh boss' shack. On the board were the little numbered brass checks the men of each shift hung on the loaded cars of coal. There were 325 of them. Each stood for a man.

At the station Lou Dold got off the train just as the guards were running a flock of photographers out. He decided to use a little diplomacy. He went to the rescue boss and showed him his press card from the *Denver Post*, asked him if there was anything he didn't want shown. The boss said no, you just go ahead and take what you need. There were representatives from *Collier's* and *Leslie's Illustrated Weekly* at the mine, and he made his deal with them, too, shooting the same scenes he shot for the *Post* but changing the angle a little. The men from *Collier's* and *Leslie's* shipped out his plates in a triple-tiered box and paid him ten dollars a negative on the spot. He was learning there was money to be made off death, more money than he ever got from a Slav funeral.

At the mine portal the rescuers passed through the lines of waiting women who were being held back from the manway by ropes. The women were past wailing now, sobbing dryly, the children whimpering with hunger. At first the rescuers had gone through the bodies below, stopping only to pull out any still breathing. They had brought out twenty-three men alive. There was no hope for the rest. McDermott, the superintendent, was caught down there, and Frank Weitzel, E. H. Weitzel's brother, and the son of one of the big stockholders in the East who had wanted to try his hand at mining, heaped up now among those nameless Greeks and Italians who had filled the shift. The rescuers came up sick with bad air and exhaustion in the two-hour relays the air in their helmets allowed them, filled with the horror of what they had seen below. But now they were bringing up the dead, strapped to skids and pulled out of the nearer entrances by mules. The corpses were wrapped in blankets and tar paper, their faces so charred and mangled they were unrecognizable.

It had been hard, Don MacGregor said, to think of them when they had been alive as men, so many of them, all alike in overalls, black caps, boots, blackened faces. One had begun to think of them as mere bundles of Something. In the mine hospital a stream of men and women came by, lifting the blankets, trying to identify the broken bodies. All at once such scraps as remained became to the survivors valuable—a shirt a woman had washed, a pair of boots she recognized. The corpses filled automobiles and camp wagons and stretchers, lay in piles on the ground. They filled the coal cars coming up from the mine.

They took the bodies into what had once been a company store and was now a temporary morgue, laid them roughly on the single slab, stripped them, and washed them off with a hose. There were hardly enough shrouds for all of them or embalming fluid. Coffins lay stacked where the counters and stands of the store had been, boxcar loads of them. Vic Miller, of Pathé, squinted through the finder of his movie camera and cranked out footage until he could not look into the torn, bruised faces of the victims anymore. Then he shuddered and left the dark morgue and went into the cold sunlight that was flooding the camp. Already the Italian women had started the funeral dirges.

There were no women to keen the *mirologhia* for the Greeks. There was only Louis Tikas, hiding out in the shack of a dead patriot talking to the survivors while the guards searched the camp for him. Between fits of coughing from lungs raw with gas, George Mavroidis told him how he had been working in 13 East when a sudden rush of air had doused his light. Then the gas had come. He'd watched the sixteen men around him wither and drop one by one, and had crawled on his hands and knees to each of them to see if he was dead. Then he too had blacked out. The next morning he had come to in the mine office. Other men told Tikas about the new machines the company had put in, how the fans couldn't handle the increased coal dust. The Greeks counted up their dead. In George Mavroidis' boardinghouse alone there were five empty places at the table. Of the 260 men killed in the disaster, 35 would prove to be Greek. It was the Italians who would suffer the worst loss, leaving 133 of their compatriots dead on that day.

Such disasters can confirm a man in his path. Ten years earlier, one story goes, a young rover with a union card in his pocket named John L. Lewis helped them haul the dead out of the mine at Hanna, Wyoming, and learned what coal mining meant. But Dawson was having no part of union organizers coming down to stir up its men while they heaped up the dead, organizers who could teach men to lay down their tools together in a mine filling up with dust and gas. The Phelps–Dodge guards caught Doyle and a couple of other men, ran them six miles out on the desert and told them to take a walk, and Ed Doyle's union money was no good in Dawson, New Mexico, on that day.

But while Doyle and Tikas and the other union men were trying to duck the guards in Dawson, and filling their minds with dread, in Walsenburg trouble was building. On the twenty-fourth a group of guards and deputy sheriffs was escorting a scab's wife and her furniture into the company stockade. The strikers crowded the alley behind the house she was leaving, shouting and jeering. They followed the wagons down Seventh Street. Some of the children threw clods of dirt. Then, all at once, Shorty Martinez' deputies started shooting. When the firing was over three strikers lay dead. Sheriff Farr barricaded himself in the courthouse with a machine gun and a war of nerves began.

Now panic began to play its role among the Ludlow tents. A kind of incessant, distributed panic that fed on each rumor and each scrap of news. The strikers had seen what had happened at Forbes; then had come the shooting in Walsenburg. In the hills were the guards. Fifty or sixty feet from the tents to the west ran the railroad tracks that could bring out from Walsenburg or Trinidad at any time a trainload of deputies and the machine guns they feared more than anything. On the morning of the twenty-fifth the panic showed itself.

It was Saturday, payday. A cold, blustery day. The men lined up outside the office tent to get their benefits while Lawson and Tikas checked them off. The camp was full of tension. At about one-thirty Adolph Germer telephoned from Walsenburg and said that a train full of deputies was heading south. Lawson sent a gang of Greeks north to stop it. They took up positions near Barnes, but the train sped by them as they fired at it with rifles and six-shooters. There was fighting now along the railroad cut and the steel bridge south of the Ludlow depot between the strikers and the mine guards who had come down from Berwind Canyon. Anna Cameron, the daughter of the Hastings super-intendent, had been in Trinidad. That afternoon she had gotten on the Colorado and Southern coach to go home. When the train got to the Berwind road bridge, three strikers jumped up on the platform between the cars and began shooting at the guards holed up in the section house on the other side of the tracks.

The train pulled into the Ludlow depot but there was no one to meet Anna Cameron and she was afraid. She telephoned Hastings for the hack and the stationmaster went with her to the tent colony. When she got there she saw women and children sticking their heads up from the cellars under the tents. Armed men were going back and forth talking and gesturing. Lawson came up to her. He was dressed in overalls and a miner's jumper. There was a gun holstered on his hip. He picked up her bag and walked her out of the colony to the wait-ing hack.

Back in the camp Lawson loaded food and gear into an old express wagon. They had no horses, so he and some of the men pulled the wagon down to the deep arroyo behind the camp and set up a tent there for the women and children.

In the section house there were twenty mine guards under the command of a case-hardened soldier named Karl Linderfelt. The sec-tion house was vital, for it controlled the railroad line from the south. For the first hour of the fight the firing had been steady. Forty guards and company men had come down from Tabasco to reinforce

Linderfelt's men, but the fire had slacked off and they had retreated back up the canyon. But at 2:00 A.M. the twenty men who remained in the section house telephoned Superintendent O'Neill in Berwind and he told them to come back to Tabasco and take refuge in the powerhouse, where they could keep warm and wait for help. It had started to snow. The guards retreated in the darkness leaving behind the body of one of their men, a drifter named John Nimmo.

They had been followed. At eight in the morning strikers on the hills began shooting from the washer into the hoist house where the guards were bivouacked. By the time the strikers retreated that morning they had killed one more guard, a deputy sheriff named Whitney. On their way back to Ludlow the jubilant Greeks broke into the abandoned section house and dragged away a mattress, a few buckets, an ax, and a side of beef. Then they burned the section house to the ground.

Later that Sunday morning Deputy Attorney Ralston and a Trinidad undertaker went out with a driver to pick up Tom Whitney's body in Tabasco. They had the dead basket propped up in the back of the car and the strikers may have taken it for a machine gun, for when they got to the Berwind road they were fired on. The three men abandoned the car and took refuge under the bridge. Ralston took out a white handkerchief and waved it. After a minute Louis Tikas came down to the bridge and they told him who they were.

Tikas said it was pretty hard. There was nothing but deputies and scabs come under that bridge. He told them to raise a white flag when they were going through that part of the country. One of the strikers nodded in the direction of the hills and the deputies holed up in the mine works: they weren't taking any chances with those sons of bitches. The strikers had torn up the rails north and south of the tent colony, but the Colorado and Southern superintendent had given his word that there were no deputies coming on Number One, so they'd patched up the tracks. Still they waited. When they had loaded the body in Tabasco, Ralston and the undertaker took Louis Tikas' advice and bought a piece of white muslin at the company store to use as a flag on the trip home. They also took the precaution of phoning Bob Uhlich at the tent colony. He told them to wait where they were. There was a trainload of deputies coming from Trinidad and there would be trouble.

Don MacGregor had gotten back to Trinidad from Dawson on the twenty-sixth. He threw himself on a bed without even taking off his clothes. He was exhausted from his work and from what he had seen. But he didn't sleep. Trinidad was filled with rumors that the war between the guards and the strikers was about to break into the open, that the strikers were going up to clean out the canyons. It wasn't long before someone called him on the telephone to tell him that there was a state of the wildest excitement in Ludlow and something was about to happen. He got to the colony and found there was real panic in the air. In the headquarters tent the phone didn't stop ringing. Every ten or fifteen minutes there was a new report that an armored train was about to leave Trinidad and that it was bringing a machine gun. MacGregor telephoned his editor and told him to let the governor know he was carrying a rifle.

People make their reality out of patches. It was words now that crystallized their fears in the tent colony, that guided them. Susan Hollearin, the Ludlow postmistress, overheard a conversation on the phone. She thought she heard someone say the sheriff's orders were to kill everyone they found outside the town. There was talk in the tents of "The Death Special," of an "armored train." The phrases had come out of the Paint Creek, West Virginia, shooting of that February, but they grafted themselves to the Colorado strike and made the terror in the tent colony an object, a weight. Still the train didn't come. They were having trouble finding an engineer to run it. The union train crew refused to transport armed men.

It wasn't until the next day that the steel refrigerator cars in the Trinidad yards were ready to start. Don MacGregor phoned the newsmen hanging around the Columbia Hotel and told them if they wanted to see some action they had better get out to Ludlow. At eleven o'clock the report came in that the train had left Trinidad. Felts had found one of his own detectives who could run a locomotive. The men in the tents swore it would never get there.

In the Ludlow depot MacGregor watched the men running out of the colony. They ran in bunches, scattered, disorganized. Only one or two had weapons in each group. At one thirty he was still in the depot, trying to get through to his office in Denver, when a bullet drove into the Western Union telegraph files beside him from the direction of the steel bridge. He knew the train had arrived. He left the depot at a run heading for the bridge.

Men talk of the hallucinatory slowness of things that sometimes takes place in battle; as MacGregor ran along the line of railroad cars between him and the bridge, odd things popped into his view, stuck there. For about three cars another correspondent named O'Rear ran with him. Then he lost him. He ran beside a striker who had a gun in one hand and a bottle in the other. He asked what was in the bottle and the striker said it was nitroglycerine. MacGregor got away fast. He could hear the whistle of bullets above his head. It occurred to him that it was a machine gun. He recalled that it took awhile to change the level of fire of a machine gun and was not alarmed. Then someone started shooting at him with a rifle, trying to pop him as he ducked among the cars. He hid behind a boxcar for five minutes, then ran on. When he got to the top of the hill he found strikers lying all along its crest. The train was stopped three-quarters of a mile away and there was firing between it and the union men. On top of the bridge stood Vic Miller, cranking his movie camera through the hail of ineffective gunfire and exhorting the strikers not to waste shells. At last the train backed off. The men on the hill gave a cheer. None of them had been hurt. The deputies abandoned the train at Forbes and hiked across to the canyon, taking the machine gun with them.

That had been their destination from the start, the relief of the guards in Tabasco who believed themselves outnumbered and boxed in and who were ready to desert. But in the tent colony the people believed it was they who were in the trap, they who were outgunned. And so they waited for the attack that they felt was inevitable from the guards massed in the hills.

Jim Bicuvaris—Big Jim the Greek—had come down from La Veta on the twenty-sixth. His friend Steve Pappas was in jail again. A month before they'd had poor Steve Pappas in jail on some strike business, caught him with a gun in his pocket when the strikers tried to stop a bunch of scabs going up to Hastings. This was worse. This time they caught him and Mike Puntis with a couple of girls Puntis had brought up from Dawson. They charged the Greeks with statutory rape. So Bicuvaris had come over to see if he could help them out. He did what he could and went home to La Veta. Then he got a call that some fellow was killed over at Ludlow. He broke down his rifle and put it in his suitcase and went back. It was Monday night in Ludlow camp. Bicuvaris says he went to sleep. But he didn't sleep, nor did anyone else in the camp that night. All night long men were coming into the headquarters tent, telling what they had heard, what they were going to do. Four or five autos of armed men had come out to the colony from Trinidad. Searchlights played through the tents. Word was out that the deputies were gathering in the canyons to come down and wipe out the camp. Don MacGregor would say later that he was convinced that what swayed the men in Ludlow was a mixture of terror and a semi-hysterical determination that the deputies would never get near the tent colony with the machine gun.

There was another man in the tents that night who was noting what he saw. His name was Jesse Shaw and he was, or would become, a company spy. He had come out with Bob Uhlich that morning after the train had been turned back and had stayed in the colony all day. Around midnight he witnessed a gathering of the leaders. Bob Uhlich and Mike Livoda and Louis Tikas formed groups to go up the canyon. Then they distributed ammunition.

The moon was out. It gave a little dim light to the men picking their way through the icy boulders under the beams of the searchlights. At daybreak the snow flurries started. Then the first real shooting came. At Tabasco Superintendent O'Neill had gotten together all the hacks and wagons he could find the day before and sent the women and children out of the camp. About six thirty he was having a cup of coffee in the house in which he was baching it with a trio of clerks. Someone must have seen a light. A shot came into the house and O'Neill ran outside and ducked for cover. In Frank Wooten's house they were just getting the children dressed. Wooten's wife had refused to leave with the other women. Now Doctor Lee's hired man ran in to tell them that the strikers had the camp surrounded and they'd better get the family into the cellar. All at once a bullet smashed into the dining room and hit the little girl in the arm. A second shot came through the kitchen and struck the boy in the hip, fracturing it. Somehow they got the children into the cellar and Wooten started to Berwind for the doctor. As he worked his way up the canyon he saw a man come out of the brush behind the powerhouse with something in his hand. The man stood up for a moment and pitched the object down the hill. It was a crude black powder bomb.

Clinton Robinson and eight Hastings guards had waited by the searchlight until it was light enough to travel. Now, in the dawn, they made their way through the fog and flecks of lightly falling snow of Number Four canyon to meet with a party of Berwind men. They were almost to the top of the canyon when they spotted three men pushing through the chest-high scrub oak. The three men had white armbands on. The guards were about a hundred fifty yards away and they called to the three men: "Who are you?" There was a tall man in the brush, the leader it seemed. He called back: "Who are you?" Angus Alexander, one of the Hastings guards, raised his arm to show the white bandage. "Can't you see?" he called. In the brush the tall man held up his own arm, showed he too had a white band. Suddenly the three men across the canyon from the guards started moving. They looked as if they were going to fire. Harry Rinker held up his hand. "Don't shoot, for God's sake," he cried. "We are guards from Hastings."

The tall man opened up from his hip with a saddle gun and Alexander fell. For a moment Robinson just stood there, thinking it was a mistake. Then a bullet hit a log near him and he dropped for cover. The three men in the brush were firing in volleys.

Sometime after midnight the message had come into Ludlow that the governor had called out the National Guard. Now the word went out to the men in the hills and they began straggling into camp, to throw themselves on their cots exhausted. Pete Katsulis came back carrying an extra gun. Big Jim Bicuvaris came down, limping, a handful of men following him. Someone had hit him from behind, maybe one of the Italians. He swore. "I don't see why those fellows can't handle their own men," he said. "I can handle my men." They took him to Doctor Beshoar who patched him up and hid him in a rooming house until Tikas could get him to St. Joseph's in Denver.

Don MacGregor described the men coming in. Many, he said, were still near hysteria and all were touched by despair. The militia was coming, and all they knew was that there would be more men to back up the guards in the companies' canyons, more bullets and machine guns to clean them out.

On the twenty-ninth Lawson was in the Ludlow colony early. He gathered the camp together and told them the governor had promised that the militia would be impartial. It would disarm both guards and strikers and it would not be used to bring in scabs. The men began to turn in their weapons. There were something like two hundred guns rounded up. "The tension in the colony was released that day for the first time in almost a week," MacGregor wrote. "There were laughing and singing and the children played freely." But the next night the terror came again. There were fresh rumors of the guards coming down from the hills, of reinforcements sent out to support them. And now the strikers demanded their guns. They would have torn their leaders apart if they'd been denied. It was a bitterly cold night, but they moved the women and children into the arroyo north of the colony or into Trinidad. And once more MacGregor watched the men go out, "in their usual helpless, aimless way," he wrote, "each nationality going by itself and none with any general plan."

When will the skies clear, when will February come?
So I can take up my rifle, my beautiful patrona
And go down to the plain of Omalo,
So I can make mothers sonless, wives husbandless,
So I can make little children motherless,
Crying in the night for water, in the morning for milk,
And in the early dawn for their sweet mother.

Cretan song

Underneath our starry flag civilize 'em with a Krag
And return us to our own beloved homes.

U.S. Army song of the Philippine Insurrection

7. THE COMING OF THE MILITIA

Let us consider these faces. They sit posed in front of their tents for the enterprising Lou Dold's camera, aware of the impression they are trying to make. They are smiling, a good many of them, no doubt at some joke the young man ducked behind the cloth has just cracked. The smiles perch atop their uniforms like fat and well-satisfied crows on a wash line. These are the officers of the Colorado National Guard. It is rank that those smiles are sitting on, and something more, a kind of holiday spirit: they know, released from their everyday jobs, these lawyers and doctors and businessmen, that war is a game.

Would there ever be another generation so innocent, so eager to go to war?

It was, says Barron Beshoar, son of the union doctor and historian of the strike, a comic book militia—397 officers to 695 men. They were commanded by a Denver opthalmologist and occasional church organist named John Chase, who had earned his spurs in the Cripple Creek strike abusing union men and vying for honor with the posturing ex-Rough Rider Sherman Bell. At Chase's right hand was Major Edward Boughton, an attorney for the Cripple Creek mine owners' association and the militia's legal expert. There was fat, mustachioed

107

Major Pat Hamrock, coach of the state rifle team and owner of a north Denver saloon, who had been a part of the shameful campaign that had crushed Sitting Bull and the Ghost Dancers twenty-three years before and who would be a central figure in the massacre at Ludlow. And there were others like Major Leo Kennedy and Captain Danks and the Denver attorney Philip Van Cise, men of some judgment and fairness, who would treat the strikers with an attempt at understanding. Yet most of them were men of a generation for whom the corpse-heaped battlefields of the Civil War were a thing of books. They took their military tone from men like Colonel Teddy Roosevelt, a fighting Anglo–Saxon who had gone off with flags high to the splendid little war with Spain and who could exult without embarrassment about the fleeing Spaniard he had doubled up like a jackrabbit on Kettle Hill. As president, Roosevelt had displayed a moderation in labor questions few of his background shared.

To the changing America of the late nineteenth and early twentieth centuries, pressed hard by strikes and by the flood of hungry immigrants, foreign adventure was only another form of expression for that strident nativism to which industrial unrest and xenophobia had given birth. In 1884 John Hay, the future secretary of state, published anonymously an ugly little book called *The Bread–Winners* based on the violent railroad strike of 1877. Not one word of *The Bread–Winners* is given to the desperate plight of the striking Baltimore and Ohio workers; and their revolt, which spread to laboring men throughout the United States and was called an insurrection by the secretary of war, is reduced to a row by a mob of idlers and ne'er-do-wells led by a greasy demagogue. Labor troubles in this dreamworld fiction are easily handled by the example of that kindly landlord Captain Farnham, who recruits the small private army which, when all is said and done, has to shoot down only *one* of the almost unarmed strikers in order to disperse them. *The Bread–Winners* was still going through editions as late as 1915. By then its author had kept the Open Door ajar in the Pacific over the bodies of unnumbered Filipinos, had helped create the Republic of Panama for our own convenience, and had made the United States a world power. He had, as his friend Henry Adams put it, "solved nearly every old problem of American statesmanship."

But imperialism is as much an attitude as it is a struggle for bits of ground in far-off lands. In Hay's audience—the businessmen and militarists and politicians who supported him—the psychologies of imperialism and industrialism merged; both the insecurities and appetites for conquest of that audience translated themselves, unhappily, into the language of the industrial world. For these men (when they weren't presenting themselves as enlightened social scientists) had come to consider the nation's mines and mills and factories as nothing more than internal colonies, and the shabby foreigners who manned them as volatile and discontented natives no more able to govern themselves than the Puerto Ricans or the Tagalogs of Luzon. During the Colorado coal strike of 1913–14, ex-Senator Thomas Patterson said it was from the repressive legal code imposed by the United States on the Philippines during the Insurrection that the state militia had gotten its ideas of justice. He may as well have said the code had long been in force in the closed camps of the C. F. and I. The strike had simply shifted enforcement of the code from the superintendent and gun-packing pit boss to the National Guard. The struggle was in the open now, the subjects in revolt. "A state of war exists," Boughton is quoted as saying. "We are in a conquered territory and from the soldier's point of view there is no other law than the supreme will of the Commander in Chief." It had been, after all, only a decade earlier that General Chase had marched his men into a civil court in Cripple Creek, planted a machine gun at the door, and informed the judge that he was now in charge. If it was not war now, the state of mind of the Colorado National Guard would soon make it one.

There were others on the roll of the state militia for whom the psychology of imperialism was not so theoretical: they were the dirty end of the imperialist stick. There was Charles Kennedy, the mine guard who had carried the white flag that day at Forbes (not to be confused with Major Leo Kennedy, Louis Tikas' friend). Kennedy had run away from home at nine, enlisted in the army as a dirty-faced kid of thirteen. He'd served in the Philippines and done a stint in the Dublin Light Infantry in Burma. Although Governor Ammons' orders specifically forbade mine guards from serving in the militia, he was soon to be enlisted, charged with keeping the peace among men whose lives he had tried to take. Later on there would come Captain Edwin

Carson, a vaudeville actor and acrobat who taught gymnastics in a Denver club. He had spent a good part of his life in the British Army and had fought against the Boers and in the Sudan. And there was Karl E. Linderfelt. It is Linderfelt who must concern us now.

In photographs he has the blunt, open face of some Scandinavian farmer—a bull-faced man, he was once described. Stocky, low-hipped, he stands beside his two brothers—officers themselves—or rides through Ludlow at the point of his company full of self-confidence and the power his uniform gives. There is another photograph of him, solitary, disturbing in what we know of him later, wheeling a black horse on a prairie. The shot is leveled slightly lower than the subject, the background blurs. Linderfelt's right hand rides on his hip. His eyes are shaded by his campaign hat. He stares into the camera with the trace of a smile on his wide mouth.

It is as if he is stepping out of a void. I think it is a mistake to think of him that way—as a kind of lone force around whom the violence will somehow gather to a head, as if there was in it all some darker mystery. It is something simpler than that, at once familiar and, for its banality, more terrible. You must will yourself to see him as his fellows did, for always he is surrounded by his messmates, always he is one of them. "Monte" Linderfelt—a man of barracks and drill ground. A professional. He could tell you a story or two about the Philippines or about soldiering across the border for Madero. He had been in southern Colorado since October, scouting the ground for General Chase. When Governor Ammons had made his tour of inspection he had stood in the lobby of the Cardenas Hotel unrecognized by the mine superintendents and the union officers, looking, he said, as common as he could and keeping his own counsel. He had hired on as head of the guards for the C. F. and I. When the strikers attacked the section house on the twenty-fifth of October, it was he who was in command of the mine guards. And, in the early morning hours of the following day, pinned down in Tabasco, it was he who had sent off that series of wires to the governor and General Chase insisting that an attack was imminent, the defenders' ammunition was almost gone, and begging them to call out the state militia. It may be that this had been just his role—to act as a kind of provocateur. It may be that the strikers, in their anger and their eagerness to protect the tents, had

You can not go at it with kid gloves; you have to get results. . . . —K. E. Linderfelt. Courtesy of the Denver Public Library, Western History Department.

played into his hand. With the coming of the state troops to the field Linderfelt would be officially attached to the militia, and the rest of the story of brutality and death will find him always near its center.

He was born in Janesville, Wisconsin, in 1877 of a family of immigrant Scandinavians. He went for a time to Beloit College, then moved west to try his hand at mining. At twenty-one he enlisted in Torrey's Rough Riders to fight in Cuba but spent his service sick with dysentery in Jacksonville and missed out on the glory of battle. But soon he was in the Philippines, a part of the American force sent to put down the nationalist insurgents, and for a time he was in China in the aftermath of the Boxer Rebellion.

In 1901 he was back in the United States. I do not know with what idealism or dreams of military glamour he had gone to the Philippines (as a boy he had served in several cadet corps and a zouave troop), but he came out a brutalized man. He had served nineteen months in an ugly and frustrating war among diseased and degraded men who marched sometimes for weeks hatless, coatless, their shoes rotted off, in sun and rain. He had fought in over twenty-five skirmishes and had learned his soldiering in a war in which the destruction of food stores and the burning of insurgent *barrios* had become unofficial policy. The insurgents were disorganized and poorly armed; sometimes bands of half-naked primitives fought the Krag–Jorgensen rifles of the Americans with spears and bolo knives. Looting and torture and mutilation passed between the Americans and the insurgents in a sort of contagion. To the Americans—even the higher officers —the Filipinos were simply "niggers." The song they sang so insistently that it had to be banned put their attitude succinctly: *Damn, damn, damn the Filipinos.*

Back in the United States, Linderfelt went quartz mining for a time, but he was at Cripple Creek as a company guard and later in the uniform of the state militia when Chase and Peabody and Sherman Bell went out to crush the Western Federation strike. He discovered he had a taste for foreign wars. He went to fight in Mexico with Madero's revolutionaries and narrowly missed arrest and court-martial for looting at Juarez. In 1913 he was back in the militia uniform. Now he faced those insolent, ragged foreigners in the Ludlow tents. He had heard what the Greeks and the Bulgarians had done to each other in the

Balkans—an Apache Indian belonging to the W.C.T.U. couldn't compare with those people, he said. They were rebels who ought to have the old alien sedition laws turned on them. Once one of the officers who had been in the Philippines had defended himself against charges of torturing a prisoner by quoting a West Point textbook: ". . . [guerrillas] are not subject to the authorities of a country, are not restricted by the laws of war, and are generally treated as outlaws and summarily executed if captured." The quote is a chilling one, for this is how Monte Linderfelt would come to look upon the armed Wops and anarchists who opposed him. Hacked at by our little brown brothers in the jungles of North Luzon, at war with Bill Haywood's miners in Cripple Creek and with Diaz' regulars at Juarez, he had learned (as he liked to put it) that you cannot go at it with kid gloves: you have to get results.

On the first of November the people at the Ludlow colony prepared to meet the initial detachments of the Colorado National Guard. They had been calmed by their leaders and told the guard was to be impartial, was to disarm mine guards as well as strikers, and would keep watch against the importation of scabs. As soon as the dust of the cavalry horses was seen, they filed out of camp, fifteen hundred of them, men, women and children, cheering and waving handkerchiefs and flags. As they marched that quarter of a mile down the road to meet the soldiers they went out bravely. Tony Gorci led the way with the camp band tooting out "The Union Forever" and "Marching Through Georgia" on their improvised instruments, a cornet, a few jew's harps, some tin horns. A few of the men were dressed in their Old Country costumes. The rest carried their picks and miner's drills. The children were dressed in white, as if for a Sunday school outing. When he came to write about it later, General Chase would be struck by the picturesque quality of it all.

Outside the camp the strikers piled up what were supposed to be the colony's weapons. There was a heap of twenty-five or thirty old guns. When the crowd saw them they laughed. "Where are the rest?" Lawson asked impatiently. A kid in the crowd came up and gravely dropped a popgun on the pile and Captain Dorn returned it to Lawson with his compliments.

They are ready at any time unless conditions improve to engage in an industrial war and to fight.... —Louis Tikas. Striking miners at Camp San Rafael. Courtesy of the Library, State Historical Society of Colorado.

A state of war exists. We are in a conquered territory and from the soldier's point of view there is no other law than the supreme will of the Commander in Chief. —Major Edward Boughton. Troops preparing for duty in the strike zone. Courtesy of the Library, State Historical Society of Colorado.

It was the beginning of the military occupation of the strike district. It is from this point that Louis Tikas dates his taking over of the Ludlow colony.

So the occupation began as a sort of holiday. Across from the depot and a little south of the Ludlow camp, the brown conical tents of Company K were planted, and soldiers began the work of digging latrines, carrying water, and piling up coal. On the train coming down to the strike district Captain Van Cise had stood up on a seat in the coach and made a speech to his men. "Do nothing rash," he said, "and do not act without orders. Wait for commands, but when you get them, obey implicitly and promptly. You are on serious business. There are 1,000 Greeks, veterans of the Balkan war, in the strike district. They are trained soldiers and they are heavily armed, armed to the teeth. We are not to provoke trouble. We are to preserve peace. But if you have to shoot, don't shoot over their heads. Don't waste ammunition. If you have to shoot, shoot to kill." For a time the warning seemed hardly necessary. By the third of the month strikers and militiamen were playing football together and the Ludlow band was tuning up in the big tent for the first dance.

Linderfelt said that he was ordered at one time to gather information on the militia for General Chase. The men were twenty-two years old, nineteen, twenty-one. He said Tikas and Rubino were licked by a bunch of kids. In photographs the soldiers do have the look of kids. Cleaning pistols and rifles in the armory, horsing around in front of a field gun, they have the clean-shaven, innocent faces of boys just off the farm or out of school, a look far different from the ragged ferocity of the armed young strikers in their red neckerchiefs and looped cartridge bandoliers. In fact, Van Cise's Company K soon got to be called the College Company, and, indeed, in ranks made up largely of young professional men it did number a couple of seventeen-year-old college students. But if strike duty began as a holiday for such men as Van Cise ("A society boy," his critics called him), for the poorly fed and clothed and often unpaid troops who did the mundane fetching and carrying of the camp and went out on the routine patrols it soon came to be something worse than tedium. It was the militia's responsibility to keep union men and mine guards and scabs apart, to inspect the trains to make sure strikebreakers were not being sent in from across state lines, and to collect the guns.

Under Van Cise the searches for guns were carried on in a way that was not abrasive. He had the good sense to keep Company B, stationed in Berwind Canyon, outside the perimeters of the Ludlow colony during the searches. For if Van Cise's College Company and the Ludlow sector's ranking officer, Major Leo Kennedy, were respected by the strikers, Company B was despised. At its head was Karl Linderfelt, now wearing the insignia of a lieutenant of the Colorado National Guard.

On the fourth of November Van Cise and Major Kennedy raided the Ludlow colony and the arroyo behind it looking for arms. According to the *Denver Express* all was good spirits and nothing was broken into without the owner's permission. There were jokes and banter. For the first time the militia searched the town of Ludlow itself. They looked into the shop of an Italian butcher and found a thousand rounds of ammunition and a Winchester hidden in the freezer. Then they went into the bakery of a Greek named Nomis. They tore up the floorboards and discovered another thousand rounds of ammunition and in the loft three or four rifles and about the same number of revolvers. Most of the revolvers were new and what Van Cise called high class.

It was the guns that got the Greeks into trouble. They were married to them. They would not, could not give them up. The Greeks lived apart in their own section of the camp in one or two big tents. They held themselves tense against the world, for in their self-importance was their manhood, their self-respect. Now, with the battles of late October and the coming of the militia, a myth began to grow around the Greeks—the myth of them forming a little Balkan army among the strikers in the tents, armed, efficient, and ruthless. No doubt their own view of themselves, their own sense of being men in the world coincided at some point with that myth growing outside them. It was like the flash point of two charged wires. Much violence would be blamed on the Greeks and much trouble. Most of it would hover around the guns.

The myth was not slow in starting. On November fourth, the *Trinidad Chronicle-News* warned of "a band of warlike Greeks who have been carrying on guerrilla warfare in the hills for weeks and

I was also ordered to turn in to the Commanding General some information in regard to the average age of these imported gunmen and they averaged twenty-two years, nineteen and twenty-one years all along. So Tikas and Rubino were licked by a bunch of kids. . . . —K. E. Linderfelt. Militiamen in the 1913–14 strike. Courtesy of the Library, State Historical Society of Colorado.

who have repeatedly declined to obey the orders of the strike leaders."
A week later, Tikas himself made an appearance in Judge Northcutt's paper.

> "Louie the Greek" leader of three hundred of his countrymen—
> striking miners at the Ludlow tent colony, is perhaps the most con-
> spicuous figure in the industrial war in southern Colorado. "Louie
> the Greek" is shrewd and fearless—a veteran of the Balkan war, and
> he controls the Greeks at the tent colony with a spoken word, a lift
> of the eye brows or a gesture of his hand.

None of it was true. Tikas was no Balkan veteran. He did not control
the Greeks with a spoken word or a lift of the eyebrows, nor did
anyone else. "Every man is a leader for himself," Pete Katsulis put it,
"every man just the same." If the Greeks had any special regard for
Tikas it was more as a spokesman than as a commander. He was an
interpreter, a link between the Greeks in the tents and the union
hierarchy. And if he controlled his young countrymen, he did it with
the strength of his own argument, with their respect, not with any
military authority. For anyone who—unlike that dreamer reporting for
the *Chronicle-News*—knows anything of the Greeks (and he would
have only to look as far as his high school Homer) knows that those
tents were a stew of wrangling and argument and of jealousies which
would, in the course of the strike, come near to ripping the Greek camp
apart. But that is not the issue. The issue is what the men of the
militia and the men who ran the mines believed.

What that was can be seen in the apocryphal joke that was just
then making the rounds of the Denver clubs. The *Pueblo Chieftain* had
reported, it seemed, that six big Greeks had walked into a meeting of
the coal operators and asked to be reinstated in their jobs. The Greeks
said that Frank Hayes and other strike leaders had told them that the
Balkan war had been transferred to this country and that the men on
the other side were all Bulgarians. Once they found out it wasn't true,
they wanted to go back to work. Meanwhile, at his headquarters
outside of Trinidad, General Chase was adding his own bit of lore to
the myth of the Greeks for the benefit of the press.

He had been advised, he reported in his portentous military style,
that a certain Greek was known to be recruiting his countrymen from
all parts of the state (and, indeed, from outside the state) to come and

join forces with the strikers. Chase was even able to quote this fiery
Hellene: "The miners' Union is greater than the United States Government. And when the Union gives the word to fire upon the soldiers,
we will obey the order."

And so the myth. It is hard to believe it wasn't willed by men
like John Chase, eager to transform a grubby and frustrating police
duty into a patriotic adventure. It is hard to believe they didn't will
that handful of ragged, undisciplined men who still held to their guns
into a dangerous, ordered force. It was the great tragedy of the strike
that the myth of Chase and the others would impinge on that of the
Greeks themselves. There *were* men in the Greek tents who had come
back from the Balkans, though never the thousand cutthroats the militia
liked to imagine—a handful, perhaps, but they had brought with them
some military skills and a residue of glory and respect. And it was at
just this moment (and how much it would cost them!) that the Greek
sense of patriotism and military potency was at its peak. In a few
short months of hard fighting the Greeks had almost doubled the size
of their country. They had annexed Crete, taken Salonica, and were on
the threshold of the holy city of Constantinople itself. Coursing through
them in their miserable tents in backward Colorado, the thrill of all
this, of the achievement of the Great Idea of Byzantium reclaimed, and
of their pride in the Greek Premier Eleutherios Venizelos—a Cretan,
as most of them were—must have blended and confused itself with
the progress of the strike. They were young. Jim Bicuvaris, a leader,
was in his early thirties. Tikas was twenty-seven. There were other
men, maybe a good part of them, still in their teens. There were no
wives or children for them to worry about, no elders to cool them off.
Despite their hard experience in the mines and their bullet-filled
cartridge belts, like the guardsmen of Linderfelt's census, they themselves were no more than a bunch of kids.

But the militia and the Greeks were not alone in their addiction
to martial fantasy. In Ludlow Don MacGregor was doing his best in
his own right to pump up the military myth. Soon after the encamp-
ment of the National Guard he wrote of a Greek veteran of the Balkans
coming up to Captain Dorn and asking him if he might drill with the
militiamen. The Greek shows the soldiers a stunt. Cocks his rifle and
holds it at the ready, then, miraculously, without seeming to move a

muscle, throws himself flat on his stomach, his rifle set to fire. "That way," he says, "you get first shot when enemy shows up."

A soldier asks the athletic Greek how he prefers to meet the enemy, marching toward him in a body or scattered out. "Damn fool march on him all together," said the Greek promptly. "Scatter; get line on one man; kill him; then go after 'nother; get him too; keep self out of sight all time."

Such bloody dreams. On the eleventh of November, Louis Tikas shows up himself in MacGregor's prose. Again the subject is war. It seems the Mexican imbroglio is much in the minds of the striking Greeks. A delegation of patriots from Glenwood Springs comes down to ask Tikas what course they should follow should war be declared. Tikas goes to Major Kennedy and says he doesn't know what to do with his boys. They're all talking war with Mexico and want to enlist under Kennedy if it comes.

> "Fine," snapped the major. "Bring 'em over."
> "But they can't enlist until this . . . ," Tikas waved his hands toward the Hastings and Berwind canyons, where the mines sent up their dark smoke—"is over."
> The major grunted.
> "Right," he said. "Let's hope it is soon over."
> A moment later he himself gazed off into the canyons.
> "I wish war would come," he said. "I wish it would come soon. Then we would be relieved of this duty. There's none of us like it. I never did fancy being a policeman myself."

Did they speak this way, crusty soldier, melodramatic Greek? Or was MacGregor putting words into their mouths? But something was at work, for all the tinny rhetoric. MacGregor, the Greeks, Major Kennedy, General Chase—there at the end of one era and the beginning of another they were living out the heroic lie. It was the lie of imperial America, the lie of Byzantium reborn.

And there was Tikas. Surely he was part of the lie. Lawson attested to his mildness; Van Cise called him the single greatest force for peace in the strike. But perhaps the strangest testimony to his pacifism comes from the man who would, eventually, kill him. For it was Linderfelt who said of Tikas that "he knew more in five minutes than Lawson or anyone else knew about handling the foreigners in that tent colony." And yet there were those militant letters, there were the times he took his gun and went down to the bridge with the others. Was it his pacifism he reined in, then, or was it his wildness? I think he was a man who was playing a double role: among the militant young Greeks he must act the part of the *leventis*, the dashing young warrior, and act it well if he was to hold them; but to the colony, and to the militia, he must be peace incarnate. As for his own motives, there are only guesses. To Senator Helen Ring Robinson he had "the look of a man who cared more for ideas than for bread." It was a tribute colored, perhaps, by his martyrdom. And yet it is not easy to see in his acts, or in those few words he has left behind, only some narrow opportunism. Once he spoke to Professor Brewster, a union supporter. He said—and it may be the closest we will ever get to discovering what it was he was after—that his mission was to "raise the Greeks."

For a few days in the middle of November the dream of violence showed itself for what it was. Sitting in the darkness of a Walsenburg movie palace, strikers and mine guards watched themselves cast up on a screen, transformed. There were the men with the rifles, crouched beside the steel bridge, there was the steel train. Cut away from them and set spinning into that silence which is at the center of all films, their actions had acquired a monstrous significance: they were watching themselves become their own history.

It could be those actions still exist, frozen and coiled in some airless canister on a forgotten archive shelf. It is strange for me to think what it would be like to see those men with whom I have lived so long on the page suddenly lurching across a movie screen, to watch the kick of their rifles, the dust spurting up. Would they seem to me any more real? Or would those flickering images be only another kind of fiction? It is unlikely I will ever have a chance to know. On November seventeenth General Chase confiscated a thousand feet of Vic Miller's film; if any copies survived it is probable that they have long ago been melted down for their silver, and those momentous, shadowy gestures returned to the metal out of which they came.

On the twentieth of November, a little after seven thirty in the evening, George Belcher and another Baldwin–Felts gunman stepped out of Hausman's drugstore in Trinidad. Belcher stopped to light a cigar. Just then someone coming out of the blur of the crowd behind him began firing a soft-nosed .38 bullet into the back of his head. In the eerie light of the undertaker's parlor a young boy, the son of Doctor Beshoar, watched them strip the West Virginia man who lay on the slab. He did not forget what he saw, for when they got off Belcher's shirt they found wrapped around him an armor casing of plate steel. The shot had been well informed.

General Chase ordered Trinidad sealed off. An Italian named Zancanelli was arrested for the murder. The same day they ran in a gang of strikers for singing "The Union Forever" in a saloon. Belcher had not been much admired in Trinidad. There were few who melted away with the crowd at the fatal shot who would admit to seeing anything, but the killing of Belcher set off another stage of the military occupation, for now the wholesale arrests began. The next day, the twenty-first, Jim Bicuvaris was arrested in St. Joseph's Hospital in Denver and charged with the murder of Angus Alexander. They pulled in another Italian named Zeni for the Trinidad killing and kept him and Zancanelli tormented and sleepless in the county jail. And while they were working over Big Jim and the two Italians in Trinidad, in Welch, West Virginia, they were burying George Belcher.

Strange where the uses of art and violence meet. Before the body of the dead gunman had fairly cooled the local poet was already composing a tribute.

> Under the wide and starry skies
> They dug the grave wherein he lies,
> But long he lives in our hearts who dies
> As he, in doing his duty well.
> And this be the verse ye have impressed
> On the marble shaft on Belcher's crest,
> "Home is the mountain child, home from the West,
> Asleep in his native hill."

On November the twenty-fifth Zancanelli confessed. He implicated a couple of union organizers named McGary and Carter in the plot to kill Belcher. That night General Chase ordered Van Cise to surround the Ludlow colony and let no one escape.

There was great excitement in the camp. The men left their tents and held meetings. There were threats. It looked very bad. Charlie

Costa and his wife Cedelina came back from town, tried to get into camp, but were turned back by the militiamen, whom they cursed wildly. Van Cise went to the colony leaders and told them he would permit no more threats. He singled out Louis Tikas for doing effective work in quieting down the men. The next morning, at ten thirty, the soldiers lined up the thirteen hundred men, women, and children of the colony and scrutinized each face. They searched some of the tents but found no arms. In the camp itself they made no arrests, but in Segundo they picked up Bob Uhlich and Ed Doyle. A letter had turned up addressed to one of the men being hunted as an accessory to Belcher's murder and it had Doyle's signature on it. The next day was Thanksgiving. Doyle was released from custody on order of the governor. Uhlich they kept. And in the San Rafael camp outside of Trinidad the ragged and chafed militiamen burned the state auditor in effigy while the band played "There'll Be A Hot Time In The Old Town Tonight." A union man himself, the auditor had managed to hold up their pay. The next night Mike Livoda, Tom Perrett, and Louis Tikas were arrested on the outskirts of Trinidad. They were taken to the Las Animas County jail.

Sports shade off from the basis of hostile combat,
through skill, to cunning and chicanery, without its
being possible to draw a line at any point.

Thorstein Veblen

I was early taught to work as well as play;
My life has been one long, happy holiday.
Full of work, full of play—
I dropped the worry on the way
And God was good to me every day.

John D. Rockefeller

8. A GAME OF GOLF

In spite of the drizzle, the writer Elbert Hubbard noted that the estate
was beautiful. Once through the gate there were woods on woods.
Birds were everywhere, squirrels leapt through the branches of the
trees, and now and then a cottontail rabbit scampered across the road.
Once they had to slow for a brace of pheasants that ran ahead of the
Packard up the wet, curving drive. At the edge of the golf links they
stopped. Their host arrived just then. He was pedaling a new bicycle.

"On schedule, boys, on schedule! That's the thing!" said John D.
Rockefeller. He sprang lightly off the bicycle.

Doctor Bustard pointed to the machine. "Been wasting some of
your hard-earned money, I see."

"Yes, I am getting extravagant," said the old man. "That wheel
cost me just fifteen dollars. I saw them advertised and sent one of my
boys down with the money. Twenty-five years ago that wheel would
have cost you one hundred dollars. And yet they talk about the high
cost of living."

Since his retirement the old man had been devoting himself to
golf. He had come to the game late, and like everything he did in his
life, he approached it with system and with a restrained, but ferocious,
passion. In order to keep his feet from moving when he swung, he had
at first driven croquet wickets around them. He had hired a boy to

125

shout out to him on every tee, "Hold your head down! Hold your head down!" He was now seventy-four years old.

So they played a game of golf. Bustard is not of great interest. ". . . Rosy, smiling, tall, athletic, intellectual, kindly, friendly," Hubbard wrote of him, leaving little to the imagination. A live-wire sort of clergyman, at ease among the Rotarians of this world. At Brown he had played a wonderful third base. Elbert Hubbard is more complex— think of him between the millionaire and the man of God, bending over to tee up his ball—a sort of rich man's William Morris, up there with his Roycrofters in East Aurora, New York, practicing—trying to prac- tice—a little pious capitalism of his own (he had once written an article entitled "The Divinity of Business"), which largely consisted of making leather bookmarks and publishing *The Fra*, a magazine devoted to the praises of the industrious. In the winter of 1913, when the *Cleveland Leader* photographer memorialized this golf match, his hair had not yet reached the silken lengths of the kept bohemian it would attain a few years later. He had written that sensationally popular pæn to duty called *A Message to Garcia* in which a businessman tries without success to get his lazy or argumentative or incompetent hired help to write up a brief memorandum of the life of Correggio. It is never explained why the businessman needs a memorandum on the life of Correggio. Now the three of them, the retired millionaire, the live-wire minister, and the writer, manipulate the ritual sticks and balls in those ceremonies of place that congratulate them for being who they are.

Pock! A ball flies off the tee, arcing away till it becomes a pin- prick against the soft line of hardwoods rising out of the mist. They joked. Bustard told one about a preacher and a tramp. John D. Rockefeller punned on the minister's loud, worn golf trousers: "Bustard wears 'em because he thinks I am very fond of checks."

How wonderful are the really comfortable—to wear patched trousers to a millionaire's golf match!

They talked about road building, the old man's passion. Rocke- feller said he wanted to live just fifty years longer. Things were moving so fast and they were moving in the right direction. He wanted to stay and see what a beautiful place the civilized world would be when businessmen awoke to their opportunities.

In the photographs of that day Rockefeller's large, gaunt head perches precariously on his thin shoulders. He seems somehow mummified, like a long-dead pharaoh, very old and very frail.

I do not imagine they spoke much of the people slowly starving in their tents in Colorado on that drizzly winter day. The old man was now inactive in his enterprises. He held about forty percent of the Colorado Fuel and Iron Company common stock, that was all. Over there, in the tents, there was only some vast and barely comprehensible natural law working itself out, of which he was only the passive agent. It was a law which might seem as arbitrary and capricious as the rules of golf, yet its rules were the only ones conceivable, as awesome as thunder, and as heedless of the lives of individual men.

He had built his own fortune on the daring use of other people's money, and he'd played the Great Game boldly. It was only just that he keep his chips. The prophet of business combination saw only self-destruction in the combination of labor. "I have watched and studied the trade unions for many years," he told W. O. Inglis. "It is hard to understand why men will organize to destroy the very firms or companies that are giving them the chance to live and thrive; but they do. . . . Soon the real object of their organizing shows itself—to do as little as possible for the greatest possible pay." That very summer of 1913 he had refused to give his gardeners Labor Day off. "Instead of spending money on amusements, my employees will have an opportunity to add to their savings." As a child he had said of checkers, "You don't think I'm playing to get beaten, do you?"

Elbert Hubbard poises himself, bends intently over the tiny white ball. Interestingly enough, he detests the game of golf.

"We have recently been hearing much maudlin sympathy expressed for the 'downtrodden denizen of the sweat-shop' and the 'homeless wanderer searching for honest employment,' " he had written in the famous *Message*, "Nothing is said about the employer who grows old before his time in a vain attempt to get frowsy ne'er-do-wells to do intelligent work."

He takes a short practice stroke, measuring his swing.

"Let us drop a tear, too, for the men who are striving to carry on a great enterprise, whose working hours are not limited by the whistle, and whose hair is fast turning white through the struggle to hold in

line dowdy indifference, slipshod imbecility, and the heartless ingrati-
tude, which, but for their enterprise, would be both hungry and
homeless."

Whack! The ball sails off. Fra Elbertus smiles under his tweed cap.

"Have I put the matter too strongly?" he asks rhetorically. "Possibly I have; but when all the world has gone a-slumming I wish to
speak a word of sympathy for the man who succeeds—the man who,
against great odds, has directed the efforts of others, and having succeeded, finds there's nothing in it; nothing but bare board and clothes."

Very carefully, and with deference, John D. Rockefeller lifts
Hubbard's ball out of a particularly bad lie and places it in perfect
position on the fairway. "You know this is winter golf," he explains
in the gentlest way possible. "All rules are off after November first."

After Hubbard putts out on the last hole the old man fishes an
envelope from one of his pockets and puts the writer's ball into it.
He gives it back to him with a bow. "As a souvenir of a very happy
occasion!" he says. He has beaten Hubbard and Bustard by six strokes.

There were photographs taken and Bustard and Hubbard stayed
on to play a final hole to break their tie. When they started home
in the Packard they saw, at a bend in the drive, the old man. He had
gotten off his bicycle and was working with three Italian laborers on
the road. "I am just showing these boys how to distribute gravel,"
he said. "See this?"

He took up a shovelful of rock and gave it a dexterous flip. "I have
not forgotten how—have I?" the old man said. The rock fanned out
across the road.

Throughout the fall, L. M. Bowers had been keeping John D.
Rockefeller, Jr., informed of the progress of the strike. Rockefeller
had not been in Colorado since 1904. At the age of thirty-nine, his
father retired, the responsibility of the strike was his. He is a hard man
to assess. That silence, that mask which was in the father a blind for
so much suspicion, for so much vigilance and cunning, was in the son a
deep and abiding modesty, a diffidence toward the world. He had
learned to put it to good use. It was a hedge against the greed of all
those unknown outsiders and the sycophants who threatened to surround him. He had learned another thing about silence—that it

You know this is winter golf. All rules are off after November first. —John D.
Rockefeller. From left to right, Elbert Hubbard, John D. Rockefeller, Reverend
W. W. Bustard. Winter, 1913. Courtesy of the San Francisco Public Library.

allowed him to pass on responsibility to his subordinates. He learned to suggest, rather than command. He was his father's son. His silence gave him that distance from the world he may have craved, yet there was a spiritual shrewdness in it too; without formulating it in so many words he knew that it was silence that permitted him to be a Christian. And so we will never precisely know what he thought of the news he received of the Colorado strike, of old Bowers' fulminations against Colorado's ineffectual "little cowboy governor" or the labor agitators or the bloodthirsty Greeks or all those "cheap college professors and cheaper writers in muck-raking magazines" or the lot of "milk-and-water preachers" who were assaulting the businessmen who had made the country what it was. He read Bowers' letters, and no doubt he believed them. Like all men of little imagination, he was compelled to take his image of the world from the rhetoric of others. Eighteen hundred miles away from his mines, buffered by the insulation of his office in New York, for Rockefeller the strike would take on the merits of the kind of moral battle he could understand.

On the twentieth of November Secretary of Labor W. B. Wilson had wired him asking if he would use his influence to get the coal operators to sit down with the union and settle the strike. He replied by return wire in one of those precisely worded statements over which he took such pains.

> So far as the Colorado Fuel & Iron Co. is concerned the matter is entirely in the hands of its executive officers in Colorado. They have always been quite as solicitous for the well-being of the employees as for the interests of the stockholders. The men who have brought about this strike are not representatives of our miners, as only a small percentage of our men are members of unions, and all but an inconsiderable fraction of those who are have protested against the strike. The action of our officers in refusing to meet the strike leaders is quite as much in the interest of our employees as of any other element in the company. Their position meets with our cordial approval, and we shall support them to the end. The failure of our men to remain at work is due simply to their fear of assault and assassination. The governor of Colorado has only to protect the lives of the bona fide miners to bring the strike to a speedy termination.

In the office at 26 Broadway the thin ribbon of the ticker tape clicked away underneath its glass dome, then disappeared in coils into the wastebaskets. It was a tenuous link to the outside world. Stock prices. Fluctuations in grain and oil. The stark flecks of news moving between the figures, then falling away . . . And in the cocoon of silence in which he had surrounded himself, the messages Rockefeller received from his mines in Colorado created a fiction which, as it was right-minded, he must believe in. The crusade for the Open Shop became for him the strike's nerve and sinew.

All his training had shaped him for crusading. There were the mornings at Forest Hill which began with family prayer. By the time he was ten years old he was recording in a careful hand the one-cent debts of the "delinquents"—their fines for being late. On Sunday, after tea, there were children's prayer meetings. Each of the children selected a besetting sin to fight and pray against during the week and report upon at the next meeting. Already he was keeping accounts of his charities. There were trips—a trip west in a private railroad car with Doctor Biggar and a clergyman or two. The house was filled with clergymen. Apart from church, there were no friends, no social life. At thirteen he described himself as "shy, ill-adjusted, not very robust." College would bring him out. He became business manager of the Brown football team (he made it a paying operation), overcame the prejudices of his stricter relatives and learned to dance. He made Phi Beta Kappa. When he entered his father's business he was for a time adrift. He lost a million dollars to a Wall Street sharper. He took to carrying a four-foot folding ruler to measure things for himself. A friend characterized him in a letter as a grumpy, morose, and gloomy young man.

It was the immense wealth that weighed on him. "I never had the satisfaction of earning my way," he wrote, and always the shadow of his father loomed over him and filled him with a sense of over-whelming gratitude, a gratitude that could sap a man of any sense of self. He wrote that he was always glad to black his father's shoes or pack his bags. Between them there was none of the common banter of father and son, no confrontation, no argument. They shared a silence which was, for them, all the more profound. When the younger Rockefeller spoke it could have the circumlocutory and abstracted quality of a man walking through a drawing room spread with tacks in his bare feet, not wishing to disturb the other guests.

He found himself, John D. Rockefeller, Jr., in charity. He discovered he had a will. Will was not for him some dark streak in the blood; it was a kind of moral gymnastics, something to be cultivated, built up. He discovered he liked cutting logs.

It was to the newly-established Foundation that he gave his best efforts. Born to great wealth, the wealth itself was not a gift, but a charge. To distribute it, not lavishly, not as a spendthrift might, but in a regular, ordered way—this was his clear duty. Even charity, like the great industries, must be made to conform to the harsh and immutable laws that governed the world. "It is a great power to give," the elder Rockefeller would say, "It may be equally virtuous to withhold." The son agreed. Early on, John D. Rockefeller, Jr., had defended the corporation to one of his Sunday school classes. "The growth of a large business is merely a survival of the fittest," he had said, following the lead of the Social Darwinists. "The American Beauty rose can be produced in the splendor and fragrance which bring cheer to its beholder only by sacrificing the early buds which grow up around it. This is not an evil tendency in business. It is merely the working out of a law of nature and a law of God." Poverty, inequity, disease— what were these more than the canker on the rose? The object of true charity was not to reward them, but to eradicate them, as the Foundation was eradicating hookworm in the South. He fell to the work with a will. At the Foundation he was in a different world from any he had known, surrounded by men of real gifts, doctors and professors and social scientists. In time he came to give up almost all of his corporate directorships. Of the few he kept was one in a company that had ceased paying dividends, one his father was convinced was not worthwhile: the Colorado Fuel and Iron Company. The younger Rockefeller's education, his Christian principles, had made him a liberal.

In 1913 he founded the Bureau of Social Hygiene. Its purpose was to study and alleviate prostitution. Given that airless, closed room in which he lived, hemmed in as he was by the conservatives in his office, by the sycophants and churchmen, to move one glacial inch in such a direction must have been an overwhelming and exhausting thing. Once Rockefeller had to issue a letter to the press: "My attention has been called to the fact that moving picture shows dealing with Vice have been advertised as 'based on the Rockefeller report . . .'" It was a hard line for a man so shy, so fastidious, so deeply moral to tread. There was no bland and accommodating philanthropy here, but a kind of heroics. Anthony Comstock said the findings of the Bureau should not be published. Rockefeller stood by his work.

So he became a social technician. He studied the world as a problem that could be solved with science, with goodwill. He read. Biographies of other rich men, reports on alcoholism and prostitution. In his library there was a copy of *Das Kapital* annotated in his own hand. And yet what reading he did, his study, only had the effect of broadening the prejudices he had begun with, after all. It was as if for Doctor Biggar's simple homeopathy he had merely substituted the massive inoculations of the Foundation and the harsh dynamics of Social Darwinism as a societal cure. In the aftermath of the strike in Colorado he would send off to his publicity man Ivy Lee an article by a New York University professor which he considered "one of the soundest, clearest, most forcible pronouncements" he had ever read:

> One is told that in each year 200,000 women in our land are compelled to sell their bodies to procure the necessities of life, and that each year sees 700,000 children perish because their parents had insufficient nourishment. . . . If it be true . . . one must concede that their deaths are a blessing to themselves and to the community. Such children should not have been born. . . . Unskilled labor is merely animated machinery for rough work and adds very little value to the final product. One E. H. Harriman is of more lasting service to a nation than would be 100,000 unskilled laborers. Without a Harriman they would be a menace.

Samuel Gompers well understood this language, the language of the social technician. Reading Rockefeller's testimony on the Colorado strike he pointed out how often Rockefeller used the words "capital" and "labor." "Note the abstract terms with the effect of isolating the problem from the human beings concerned," Gompers acidly remarked. But that was Rockefeller's way. If the philanthropist had ever talked to any immigrant workers at length they were probably the smiling Italian gardeners of Pocantico or Forest Hill whom his father would pick up coming back from his afternoon drive. He had managed to make his report on vice without talking to a single prostitute.

So he did not go to Colorado. He was far too sensible to believe a personal tour of the strike zone would allow him to get the facts. He kept in touch through his officers in the Colorado Fuel and Iron Company. And he worried about them. On the twenty-fourth of November he wrote Bowers that he and Welborn were frequently "in our minds." "At the same time we have the utmost sympathy for the unfortunate employees of the company, who are suffering so severely directly and indirectly, as a result of this conflict of labor which has been forced upon them much against their wills." On the eighth of December, while Louis Tikas and fifteen other military prisoners lay freezing in the Trinidad jail, Rockefeller worried about Bowers' health: "You are fighting a good fight," he wrote, "which is not only in the interest of your own company but of other companies of Colorado and of the business interests of the entire country and of the laboring classes quite as much. I feel hopeful the worst is over and that the situation will improve daily. Take care of yourself, and as soon as it is possible, get a little let-up and rest."

Louis Tikas had had no charges put up against him; he and the other militia prisoners in the Trinidad jail were held under some vague and sweeping quasi-military authority, and in fact it never would be determined if martial law had been declared in the strike zone. Nor would it have made any difference to Chase and his officers. The men held by the militia had seen no one but their guards and their fellow prisoners since their arrests, and they did not have counsel now. It was very cold. The steam heat in the jail had been cut off when the first of the military prisoners had been brought in. The floors were covered with crawling things and there were no covers on the bunks. A man spent a good deal of time standing up against the iron bars. Louis King, the black striker accused of shooting the Wooten children at Tabasco, told what he was given to eat at the two meals they allowed him: four biscuits the size of a half dollar, a teaspoonful of molasses, a thin strip of bacon, half a cup of coffee. That was breakfast. At dinner there were three little slivers of coarse bread, a tablespoonful of beans, a little salt pork, the teaspoon of molasses, the half cup of coffee.

The militia began calling up the prisoners for examination. Major Boughton, the chief legal officer, lead the proceedings. He was later to say that it was a matter of indifference to General Chase whether the men held in jail by his commission were guilty or innocent. It was clear that the militia's task was to break the strike. The officers of the commission sat heavy, conscious of their dignity, laden with the decorations of their rank. From their belts hung sidearms and dress sabers.

Not all that went on in that room in the Columbia Hotel will ever be known. The men were grilled, asked endless questions. Mike Livoda said they asked him everything about himself from the day he was born. He couldn't tell them anything they wanted to know. They turned him and Tom Perrett loose. On December first they called up Tikas and Bob Uhlich. Uhlich was intractable. He refused to testify, saying only the civil court had any jurisdiction. The commission declared him to be a "dangerous and undesirable alien." Tikas they tried to bargain with. They promised to release him from jail on condition that he go to Ludlow and persuade the Greeks to give up the strike and go back to work. They may have hinted things would go well with him if he implicated higher union officials in the October violence. What he answered may be inferred: they sent him back to jail where he spent the next two weeks.

How he occupied himself in those two long, freezing weeks it would be interesting to learn. "You know," Mike Livoda said, after they let him go, "when a fellow is fighting for something good he doesn't mind, even if they send him to jail. That is how I felt while I was in that dark, stuffy cell, and I was so happy I just kept singing union songs all the time." Livoda sang, Uhlich, the dangerous "anarchist," read: *The Pickwick Papers*; *The Three Musketeers*; *Les Misérables*. As for Tikas, who knows? It was jail that turned Gene Debs into a socialist and Dostoevski into a mystic and Cervantes into a novelist, and now Louis Tikas—did he gnaw his guts or did he think? Some vision, Uhlich's vision, or the vision of socialists like Adolph Germer or Frank Hayes, or the more pragmatic one of trade unionists like Lawson—did it begin to form for him? Hayes, Lawson, Uhlich, these were the leaders who surrounded Louis Tikas, that quick and aspiring man. He may have admired some of them, looked up to them. And so I wonder what went through him in that cell in the Trinidad jail. One thing is certain; when he speaks of his jailing in his letter to the union two months later, he refers to it with pride. "Our people will tell you that I am the man who was arrested on November twenty-eighth and who remained in jail until the nineteenth of December 1913," he wrote, "because I preferred to go to jail myself rather than allow any of your people to be deprived of their liberty."

On the fourth of December it snowed. It was the worst storm Colorado had experienced in thirty years. Forty-two inches of snow fell in Denver. At Ludlow Victor Bazanelle woke up with the tent sagging down and three feet of snow on top of him. He pushed the tent up, rolled over, and slowly got out. The whole tent had collapsed. There were others down all over the camp. It was a good thing the miners were handy with a shovel.

That night they arrested Adolph Germer. C. F. and I. President Jesse Welborn wrote to a company director that the storm ought to make a good many of the strikers leave the tents for "the comfortable houses and employment at the mines." But he was wrong. In the Trinidad jail sleet drifted through the broken windows. Tikas and the fifteen other prisoners of Chase's army slept on bunks covered with three inches of snow.

And while the militia prisoners paced up and down in the Trinidad jail, the scabs had begun to arrive in droves. On the thirtieth of November, Van Cise was awakened in his tent before dawn by Bernardo Verdi, the leader of the Ludlow Italians. Verdi was in a highly agitated state. There was a train coming with strikebreakers on it and if they got out at Ludlow, Verdi said, the strikers would kill them. If the soldiers tried to protect the scabs, they would kill them too. Van Cise explained that the governor's orders were that no strikebreakers would be allowed to come into the district and Verdi left—but with a threat. Half an hour before train time a sergeant phoned Van Cise from the depot. Almost the entire colony was down there, spoiling for trouble. When Van Cise got to the depot it looked to him as if every man and woman in the tents was out. They were swarming over the tracks and the depot grounds. The women were armed with clubs—baseball bats, boards covered with spikes, tree limbs with sharpened branches. Some had collected little piles of rocks. Van Cise had a detail fix bayonets and they cleared the tracks. The strikers lined up again on the road east of the depot. The women stood in front with their clubs, the men behind them. Van Cise collared the three leaders, Verdi, Jones, Gus Weinberg, and told them they would have to take their people back to the tents. They refused. Then Van Cise told them he would hold them responsible for the actions of the strikers and ordered one of his sergeants to draw a pistol. He told the sergeant if anything happened to shoot all three of them. The strikers began to disperse. By the time the train came in most of them had gone back to the colony. In the coaches Van Cise found five or six strikebreakers and sent them back to Trinidad on the same train. Then the snow began to fall. It was during that time, when the men and women of the colonies were busy digging out their tents, that Governor Ammons rescinded his order: strike-breakers would now be allowed to come into the district.

His English was not very good, but his choice of language was good although his pronunciation was poor. He said that his purpose was to try to raise the men of his nationality.

Professor James H. Brewster

9. HIS VOICE

Winter had hit hard at the people in the camps. They had begun the strike thinking they would be out a month; it had been three months now and there was no sign of a settlement. At Ludlow the paths worn between the tents and the privies or the coal piles or Snodgrass' little tin-sided store turned slushy between the drifts of dirty snow or slicked over with ice. Water froze in the barrels outside the tents. When it stormed, gangs of men pulled the snow off the sagging tent roofs to keep them from crashing down. The men still went out with shovels and picks and a loop of wire looking for rabbits, but there were thirteen hundred mouths to feed in Ludlow alone and the game was getting pushed back deeper and deeper into the hills. The strike benefits never stretched far enough to fill the strikers' bellies. They were hungry in the camps, and they began to wear on one another. The women spent days huddled under their blankets with the children in the biting cold. Their clothing was wearing out, coats and overalls getting shabby. At the store or at the depot the militiamen ragged the women about their "union shoes." There were rumors the union was broke.

Horace Hawkins, the union attorney, had started working on habeas corpus proceedings in the cases of Tikas and Uhlich and several of the other men. Uhlich would not be out on bail until September of the next year, but on the fifteenth of December the militia released Tikas from the Trinidad jail. There is a letter Tikas sent to the editor of the *Trinidad Free Press* upon his release that tells of his reception in the colony. It is a moving thing. "Dear Sir," he wrote, "In regards to calling you up by phone I have changed my mind, so I will write you

139

a few lines of information. I arrived at Ludlow about 3 P.M. The most people of the tent colony were waiting for me, and after visiting the colony tent by tent and shaking hands with most the people, I find out that all was glad to see me back."

Tikas went on to deny a story in the *Trinidad Advertiser* that ninety strikers from Ludlow had gone back to work at Delagua, then he talked about the change of feeling between the militia and the union people since his jailing, of the anger building up in the colony because of the insults and searches and the harassment. He concludes:

> I am leaving tonight for Denver to attend the state Federation of Labor convention and believe that I will be called to state before the delegates of the convention anything that I know concerning the militia in the southern field. While I stay a few days at Denver I will return to Ludlow again.

LOUIS TIKAS
Ludlow, Colorado

There were speeches in Denver's Eagle's Hall. And there was outrage. The day before the State Federation of Labor convention began the Vulcan mine in Garfield County had blown up. Thirty-seven men had been killed, scabs, most of them, in a mine the union had been calling a death trap months before. By way of compensation the owner, E. E. Shumway, who had been one of J. P. Morgan's Men and Religion Forward luminaries, had offered the families of the dead seventy-five dollars to pay for the funerals. It might have been only justice that Shumway himself would die a few weeks later from gas inhaled in his own mine.

On the sixteenth of December a march was organized. Two thousand men and women tramped through the snowy streets of Denver behind Mother Jones. In the photographs taken on that day it is Tikas who stands at the old woman's side, carrying the banner of Ludlow. The marchers came into the statehouse and confronted the governor, but as in most such confrontations there were only words, and they went back to Eagle's Hall. They issued a long resolution. "The working people of Colorado are peaceful and law abiding," it said in part, "but if a working man is ever tried and executed by a military commission when the courts are open and unimpeded, then other lynching parties are liable to be formed. If this be treason, let the coal operators

And old Mother Jones thought there was nobody like him. He called her mother, too. —Mary Thomas O'Neal. Mother Jones and Louis Tikas on the right. Denver, December, 1913. Courtesy of the Library, State Historical Society of Colorado.

It's going to be the happiest Christmas ever for some of the kiddies, for many of them, born in the dingy coal mining towns, have never had a single Christmas present. —Denver Express. Children at the Walsenburg tent colony, Christmas, 1913. Courtesy of the Library, State Historical Society of Colorado.

make the most of it!" Then they appointed an investigating committee and the strikers went home.

Tikas returned to Ludlow something of a hero. His name had appeared prominently in the *United Mine Workers Journal* during his confinement. He had been called a "conservative, cool-headed man," and his work of preserving order "even under the most provoking circumstances" had been praised. He said, in the letter he wrote to the International seven weeks later, that the people in the camp spoke of him with love.

At Christmas the union put up a big tree at Ludlow. Louis was there, distributing gifts, apples and nuts, shoes for the kids. You can see the children at the camp in Walsenburg standing outside their tents in the snow, the boys all holding up the identical slate they had been given, the girls with their new dolls. The *Denver Express* claimed it was the first Christmas many of those children had seen. Anyone who knows those struggling coal camp families is inclined to believe it.

Dusk. I go out to photograph Louis' coffeehouse on Market Street. It is still a district of transient hotels and labor agencies and saloons as it was in 1911, the year Louis Tikas was first listed in the *Denver City Directory*. In the photographs of that era Market Street is crowded with people; teams and wagons fill the pavement. Now there is only a terrible emptiness, as if the city is simply retreating from its past, leaving only wreckage behind. The building that housed the coffeehouse is still standing, re-plastered, anonymous. I hadn't bothered to photograph it the last time I was in Denver. Over on Curtis Street the address Tikas gave as his residence when he went into district court to petition for naturalization in 1913 is gone. I had taken a few shots of that building, the Paxton Hotel. Now it is plowed up, an asphalt blank at the edge of the hard new high-rise buildings that Denver imagines are the future. The coffeehouse itself would be gone the next year.

I think of Utah Phillips' song about Larimer Street, a block or so over:

You knocked down my flophouse, you knocked down my bars
And you black-topped it over to park all your cars . . .

The song goes on to tell how Denver is giving way to

suit-and-tie restaurants that's all owned by Greeks
and counterfeit hippies and their plastic boutiques . . .

But the Greeks I am looking for down here owned no suit-and-tie restaurants. Across the street from Louis' coffeehouse still stand the hotel where the police broke up that nest of Greek cardsharks in 1909 and the row of seedy turn-of-the-century brick warrens where Skliris kept his employment office. There is still an employment agency in that row, but it has no jobs in mines or mills or on the railroad, only notices put up on a chalkboard by ranchers hoping to pick up a stray hand or two for the haying from among the derelicts who wait in the doorways or inside the missions—if they are lucky enough to find any they can sober up. Now and then some cowboy or wino shambles by. A whore comes out of a bar and asks me what I'm doing. She's drunk. A young black woman with a beat-up, still-pretty face. I tell her I'm taking pictures.

"How about this one?" She bends over and flips her dress above her head. Straightens up, laughing. I take a few pictures of her mugging for the camera. Then I start for my car. She tries one more time.

"I can give it to you every which way," she says.

Little by little I had begun, I thought, to understand him. It was strange. Sometimes, as I worked, he was like a presence in the room. And yet, of course, that was illusion. What I knew of him was only fragments, particles held together by my own imagination. That sense of his presence was only some fiction that had grown up in my mind. And so I traveled during my summers, hoping to catch a glimpse of Louis Tikas passing momentarily across the memory of one or another of those who had known him. In Denver I hung around Nick Frangos' Congress Lounge. There was a tip from his brother, the doctor, that sent me to Oak Creek where I interviewed Gus Papadakis and John Tsanakatsis. I talked to Mike Livoda. And there was old Mike Lingos in Price, Utah. Then in Chicago, Peter Louloudakis. It was only accident that led me from one man to another. My picture of Louis Tikas was made up of chance meetings, words dropped sometimes almost by mistake, those random flecks of memory that were, it seemed, detached from the events that gave them birth, floating free. It was as if the history I was trying to write were a kind of dream, one of those dreams in which the story rewinds crazily to take up some new event —a phone ringing in the next room, a car backfiring on the street— then starts up again but is never solid, never real. Working late one night in the Denver Public Library I came across a photograph of the man I had always known as Louis Tikas lying dead in the Trinidad mortuary. But the photograph was labeled "Charlie Costa." Beside it was a photograph I had never seen before. It was of another corpse, and its face was smashed and bloody and I thought, all at once, was this Tikas' face? But my mind would not accept it. Without warning that edifice I had created of the past had suddenly collapsed, swirled dizzily into some broken place in time. Later on I discovered that the photographs had been mislabeled, but I had learned that there was no solid ground to what I was doing. I thought of Tikas in all the roles in which I had imagined him, some opportunist pulled out of a Denver coffeehouse, graduate of Athens University, young man waiting for a picture bride, scab—one by one the roles had hardened around him in my mind, had spun out some plausible story from their core, and one by one each had fallen, had given way to some later image, solid as the previous one had seemed. Imagination itself was the destroyer, anarchic, self-devouring. I was clinging to the fragile accidents of discovery.

The old men were dying, and Louis Tikas was dying with them. I could do nothing to hold back that rush of death. I was, in a sense, an accomplice. For there was a fatal lethargy in me which at times left me numb and immobile. In the fascination of that dream of history I had watched a line being drawn across the past over which, somehow, I was not permitted to pass. I put things off, did not follow up on what clues I had. It took me two years to try to discover if Mary Thomas was still alive. I very nearly missed Mike Lingos. I saw Louis Tikas fading away from me, and I was almost glad. As if something in my own dying had been vindicated.

"On December 30th, most all day I spent my time with Dr. Harvey and Dr. Jolly, Major of the Military, vaccinate the people in the Ludlow tent colony. About four o'clock P.M. I was with the doctor and some fellows come in and they called me out, and they told me that some nigger shot another nigger in tent number 38, and they wanted me to go after him. . . ."

Coming through the page, it is the same thickly accented immigrant voice Professor Brewster of the State Federation of Labor Committee described. And it is as unexpected as the dash of cold water at the end of a dive. Leaping across sixty years of stillness, I am listening to Louis Tikas himself.

Louis goes on, telling the committee what had happened the day before. The stenographer takes it all down. Tikas tells how the crowd tried to stop him from going after the murderer, how they warned him the man had a gun.

"I didn't stop at all, but I been after him and I grab him," Tikas continues. "I asked him if he killed the other man and he told me he did. Also I asked him if he carried a six shooter and he told me yes, sir. And I take the six shooter away from him and I take him from tent number 42, and I brought him over to the guard tent, and I called up Major Kennedy in the Military camp stationed at Ludlow for a detail."

On December 30, 1913, George Shepard Wilson killed Kid Morgan at the Ludlow camp over twenty-five dollars and a shotgun, and Louis Tikas went after him. The Greek was brave, no doubt, cool as he tended to be in emergencies. Yet something else is happening here. Preserved in the cracks of the past is a dead man's voice. Of all the devastations of history, the most terrible, it may be, is to rob a man of that, to leave him beached and mute, some small figure in an equation or last little buzz in a circuit of cause and effect. But here, for a moment, among these sheaves of brittle affidavits on a library table, a voice I had never expected to hear escapes the past. It leaps across the years and collapses them. And after a time, it recedes once more into the silence.

So Lawson and Brewster and the other committee members stand around him and Louis Tikas tells his story. At about 7:00 P.M. he started out from the camp to meet the number two train from the north. He had an electric torch with him. About fifty yards from the depot he came across three or four soldiers with a team of mules trying to pull a stranded automobile from the snow. They turned him back to the colony, swearing at him. A cavalry man with a drawn rifle rode behind him as he walked, shouting at him to get back where he belonged. Tikas went to the office tent and called Major Kennedy. They had known each other from Denver, had developed a mutual trust. Kennedy said, "They have no right to stop you, Louie." Tikas set out once more for the train.

In the depot they were bringing in a militiaman who had been thrown when his horse tripped on a strand of barbed wire buried in the snow. He had been one of the detail going to pull out the auto. They put him on a bench and rushed out for the doctor from the military camp. Pretty soon the doctor came back and examined him. The man had a slight concussion and was badly shaken.

After a while Linderfelt stormed into the station. He asked what had happened and someone told him Cuthbertson's horse had tripped over a wire pulled across the road. Linderfelt turned to the militiamen. "Have you got a pair of wire nippers?" he asked. One of them said he had. "You go down and cut every goddamn wire around there. If a man comes to stop you, you kill him dead." At that moment Tikas and a boy came into the depot.

Look at the two through Linderfelt's eyes. A couple of little foreigners defying him, tripping his men. Louie the Greek going up to the window as if he owned the place. There had probably been bad blood between the two men before this. Linderfelt would remember Tikas well after the massacre, a brainy, shrewd man, so unlike himself. Louis and the Greeks would follow him on the streets of Trinidad, rag him. You couldn't tell Linderfelt they were coal miners. As far as he could see they were a bunch of bootblacks down from Denver, fighting men living off the union dole in the colony. He remembered twice, in particular, when he was in the picture show Louis had stood up in his seat pointing and he could hear their remarks and Louis had said, "There is that Linderfelt now." Once he ran into Tikas in town and the Greek threw up his fingers in a certain way and said "someday" and smiled. Linderfelt knew what that "someday" meant. It became a greeting for them. The Greeks would say it on the cars going into Trinidad when they saw him—"someday"—and Linderfelt would say, "Let her come." And it didn't help his disposition any, all this continual picking. He was not used to that kind of scrapping; he didn't quite understand it, and it wore on a man, and possibly he did get short-tempered. So now he had a man down and the two foreigners in front of him. He asked the soldiers who had stretched the wire and one of them pointed to the kid and said "that fellow."

The kid didn't know much English. He just kept saying yes, yes, yes, over and over again and Linderfelt cursed him, didn't give him a chance to explain. He grabbed the kid and pulled him outside. The people in the depot could hear him out there, going at the boy. When the boy came in he had his hat on and someone said Linderfelt had hit him and split his head open.

Then Linderfelt went after Tikas. The kid had said Louis knew him and at first the Greek had denied it. But when the kid told him who he was, what tent, then Louis said yes, he was acquainted with him. Linderfelt told him he was lying about the boy and now he was lying about that wire.

Tikas never answered him. But when Lieutenant Lamberton explained to him what had gone on, he said he didn't know anything about it. It was the first time he had heard about the wire. Then Linderfelt boiled over. He grabbed the Greek by the collar with both hands and dragged him outside the depot, then spun him around a couple of times and knocked him back against the wall and held him while Sergeant McDonald made a show of pulling out his gun. In a moment Linderfelt has his own gun out, holding Tikas with one hand while he tried to beat him over the head with the weapon until Lieutenant Doll, from Company K, grabbed the six-shooter and pushed him back.

They took Louis back into the depot and once more Linderfelt drew his gun. To Susan Hollearin, the postmistress, it seemed as if Linderfelt was deliberately trying to provoke Tikas, to force him to retaliate. Linderfelt swore at Tikas, told him he was running this neck of the woods, not a lot of Dagoes down in the tent colony. He had a bunch of soldiers and they were just back from Old Mexico and they were going to clean out every goddamn striker and Dago in the country. He knew Tikas was a friend of Major Kennedy's. He didn't give a damn for Major Kennedy or anybody else.

Linderfelt turned to McDonald and told him to place Tikas and the boy under arrest. Doll began to argue with him but Linderfelt prevailed. "Turn these men over to the depot guard," Linderfelt said, "and I will put charges against them in the morning."

They took Louis and the boy to the militia camp and Major Kennedy examined them. After a while Linderfelt called up to ask if Tikas was under arrest. Kennedy told Doll to tell him he was going to take care of Louis. "What kind of care?" Linderfelt asked. Kennedy said it wasn't any of his business. A couple of militiamen took Tikas back to the tent colony. About eleven thirty Kennedy called him and said he'd talked to General Chase and Chase had said to release him. "I want to fight this case, Louis," Kennedy said over the telephone, "and I want you to help me." And Tikas answered, "I tell you, you know Major, I stand on my word."

We will not hear Louis Tikas' voice this clearly again. From now on it will come in fragments, strained through the memories of others, revised by the people he got to write his letters and by the processes of myth. The story he told of that encounter with Linderfelt, rehearsing it word by word for the commission stenographer, had contained, although he did not know it, a foreshadowing of his own death. Major Kennedy sat in his tent listening to that thick-accented, earnest voice coming over the wire. Then he said, "I know, I know Louis." And he hung up the phone.

The next day General Chase ordered Ludlow searched for arms. Linderfelt's men, the "yellow bands" from Berwind Canyon, formed a cordon with their horses around the camp while the other companies went through the tents. Mike Sikoria, an Old Country miner who had seen a good deal in his fifty-six years, came out of the colony and went up to the little rise beyond the depot they called Water Tank Hill. Under the shadow of the tank was the man who had cut the wire and thrown it down the colony well the night before. He was sitting on a seat beside a machine gun, just like a bird on a fence. "I like to have Kennedy tell me to push once—kill all of them," Sikoria remembered him saying. "If he can, let me go; I kill all the men and children in this house. Just once let me go with the machine gun." Linderfelt too was on the hill with the gun. He was still smarting from his run-in with Tikas in the depot and Kennedy's rebuke. Kennedy, Van Cise, Doll—what did any of them know of military affairs? They worked with the strikers, did everything they possibly could for them, and then tried to throw all the blame for anything that went wrong on him. When Professor Brewster went up, he showed him with a glee that shook the old man to the bone how the machine gun could sweep the colony.

Sometime during the search the militiamen brought a seventeen-year-old kid named Brian Orf up the hill. Orf lived at the Ludlow pump station. He had given the Berwind men some trouble about swearing at him in front of his cousin when he tried to take her through the line. Half of the soldiers looked so drunk Orf thought they couldn't sit a horse. Linderfelt himself acted drunk or crazy or both. "I would not blame that fellow if he had taken the butt of his gun and hit you in the jaw with it," he said to Orf when the kid complained of the treatment one of the men had given him. "That is the only way we could teach you ignorant people anything. I am Jesus Christ and all these men on horses are Jesus Christ and we have got to be obeyed. You want to know that. You people are getting too goddamn chesty around here."

He asked Orf if he wanted to go to the depot and Orf said yes.

"You turn around and beat it for home," Linderfelt answered.

"You move goddamn quick about it," someone else said.

"Bastard. Goddamn little son of a bitch," said Linderfelt.

The militiamen searched Mike Sikoria's tent three times. The officer in charge said they'd have to search again. This time they would pull up the floor. Sikoria got mad and walked away. "Take the whole tent," he said. "Take the whole tent." He was to remember later searches whose object was, it seemed, solely to harass people, to steal from them, drive them outside in the snow. The people sang union songs while the militiamen robbed the tents of watches, money, knives, combs, razors, anything. In the colony Van Cise's men found thirty-five rifles hidden under the tent floors or outside in the ash pits. Most of them were in the section inhabited by the Greeks.

Lawson and the committee from the State Federation of Labor wired the governor. They had reason to believe it was Linderfelt's deliberate policy to provoke the strikers to bloodshed. He had threatened to kill Louis Tikas. But nothing would come of their demand to remove Monte Linderfelt, and nothing would come of it when Linderfelt's fellow officers privately suggested to General Chase that he take the same step. The people of the tent colony begged Tikas to get out. They told him Linderfelt would kill him. He stayed. The committee continued its investigation.

Leaf by leaf the affidavits piled up, the telling of incidents which seem, sixty-five years later, sometimes horrible, sometimes almost trivial. They were real. They happened to the people of those camps. A man remembered what the militia had done to him, how they caught poor, ignorant foreigners and forced them to dig what they told them were their graves (they were privy vaults), then laughed at them when they dictated their goodbyes to their wives. He remembered the drunken soldiers coming into the tents at night and the women pushed out of the depot and into the cold and what they had done to his buddy when they caught him picketing and what they had called his wife. The anger seeped into the heart a drop at a time. In the colony they remembered the constant searches and that swaggering bunch of Jesus Christs down from Berwind with the yellow bands around their hats; Monte Linderfelt and his men remembered the Dagoes who defied them. There were scores to be paid.

Kostas Markos lay dying. He had been living in a house in Walsenburg with Gus Papadakis and twenty-five or so other Greeks. He was older than the others—thirty-two—with a wife and a couple of kids in the Old Country. When the strike broke out he'd been mining at the Ravenwood pit. He was unwell even then. The young Greeks had taken pity on him and brought him into the house. They made him the house cook while they scrounged for food or kept their eyes open for strikebreakers. One day they caught a couple of Greeks at the Walsenburg depot coming in to scab. They brought them to the house, cooked for them, convinced them to get behind the union. On the twenty-sixth of November Markos took them out to see the town. The militia caught him with a gun in his pocket on Sixth Street. They beat him and threw him in jail. The two scabs were forced into a mine.

The Greeks in the Walsenburg house tried desperately to get a lawyer to Kostas Markos but the militia let no one see him. He lay shivering on the damp cement floor of a cell in the basement of the courthouse for twenty-two days with only a couple of thin blankets to cover him. He was suffering terribly from rheumatism in his legs.

Finally the militiamen took him to their tent hospital. There they saw what was wrong with Kostas Markos and let him go to a room in the Oxford Hotel.

On the third of January the investigating committee came to the hotel. Tikas interpreted. Lawson asked Markos what his nationality was, asked him if he was married. Markos told how he had lain freezing in the jail those twenty-two days, how they fed him just enough to live on, wouldn't let him have a bath. The county officers would come in, call him a son of a bitch, call him a cocksucker. They told him the Greeks were bad people, always in trouble. If the strike was lost, they wouldn't allow the Greeks to work in the mines anymore. Then they told him they'd turn him loose if he'd go back to work. He refused. When he was arrested he had a silver watch from the Old Country and one dime in his pockets. They took the watch away from him, but let him keep the dime.

"Ask him this, Louis," Lawson said. "Ask him if any doctor, any military doctor, or any other doctor ever came to see him while he was in jail, to see if he was sick."

Tikas asked him and Gus Markos said no.

When Doctor Nur examined him in the hotel, he told Markos he was going to die.

Big Jim Bicuvaris too was in jail. Two days later they interviewed him in Trinidad. Tikas was the interpreter, but Bicuvaris spoke fair English and answered most of the questions himself. He told them how he'd been arrested on the twenty-first of November by five men in civilian clothes at St. Joseph's Hospital in Denver, where he was still recuperating from the wound in his thigh. The men had had no warrant. They'd taken him to the county hospital and chained him to a bed by his left leg and the next night a detail of militiamen came and put him on a train for Trinidad. He sat up all night on the train between two soldiers, so cold he couldn't sleep. In Trinidad they kept him in the military camp twenty-four hours sitting on a horse blanket. The next day they took him to the Las Animas County jail.

The guards wouldn't let him sleep, threw water in his face. After the second night Bicuvaris just curled up on the floor and didn't move, even when one of them prodded him in the neck with a bayonet.

Louis broke in: "After they punched him he got mad and he walked up and grabbed one bucket he have right in his cell and he throwed it at him, you know. He can't come out."

"What was in the bucket?" someone asked.

"Piss."

The soldiers took away Big Jim's crutches and the bucket and kept them two days. Then they walked him over to the Columbia Hotel and kept him up three days and nights while the military court interrogated him. They brought him back to jail. He said to the lieutenant, "If you keep me awake here and don't allow me to sleep some more, I feel lots better take me out and shoot me." After a while they moved him to the city jail and didn't bother him. He was thirty-two years old, six-foot five. Before they threw him in jail he'd weighed maybe two hundred pounds; now he was down to a hundred seventy five. In his cramped cell he'd taken an old belt and tied his head up in a sling against the bars so he could stretch out his leg.

On the fifth of January Kostas Markos died in Walsenburg.

The committee finished its report. Weary, provoked, Governor Ammons commented only that the testimony the State Federation had gathered in its 760 pages had not been sworn.

And all this time the coal companies were bringing in scabs. By January, according to Jesse Welborn, the C. F. and I. had imported 1,400 of them, 200 or so being sent to other mines. With the ban against importing strikebreakers lifted and the militia standing by to see them off the trains, there was little the union people could do but line up and jeer them at the depots. Most of the scabs didn't know what they were getting into. Sometime toward the end of January, while the Tabasco guards drank in a saloon, 50 Bulgarians fled into the snow and made their way down the canyon to the Ludlow colony. They had been brought from the Pennsylvania coalfields and promised work in a mine near Denver, where they were assured no strike was going on. The company paid them a dollar a day at Tabasco, they said, and deducted ninety-three cents of it for board. The other seven cents went to pay for their transportation. A few months before the countrymen of these frightened miners were exchanging lead and atrocities with the Greeks in the hills of Macedonia. Now, in the tents of

Ludlow, it was the Greek Louis Tikas who took them in and fed them and parleyed with their chief.

There are other stories. Some of them are told in the testimony given the Congressional Investigating Committee of that winter. They are sad, some of them strangely affecting. One group of scabs was recruited in Pittsburgh around the thirteenth and fourteenth of December. They heard about work in Colorado in the saloons or through ads in immigrant newspapers, and they crowded into an employment agency where an Italian most of them knew only as Dominic signed them up. When the train was loaded in the Pittsburgh yards there were still several hundred men trying desperately to get on. A coal miner named Yansenski remembered how all the Poles got drunk that first night on the train. They'd give the Italian a quarter and he'd give them a little bottle of whiskey. Some of the Italians were singing and dancing in the aisles. They had a guitar and an accordion. The next morning when the whiskey was gone they looked at the contracts they had been made to sign in such a hurry. Then they realized a strike was on. "It was all done so fast we did not have time to do more than just sign our names. The agent said when we came there that evening, 'Quick, write your name' and then we went on the train." They tried to get off the train, but it wasn't allowed. Dominic stood by the door and said everything would be all right, the strike would be settled. Outside of Chicago the doors were locked. Some of the men climbed through the toilet window and got away. About fifteen miles out of Trinidad the train stopped and a detachment of soldiers got on with fixed bayonets. The scabs were given another paper to sign that said they had been informed a strike was on. Dominic went through the train pulling down the blinds. The Italians asked him, "Are you going to take us to a slaughter house, you son of a bitch?"

The scabs were as afraid of violence as they were driven by their hunger. And there may have been some who were so raw to the industrial world that they scarcely knew what sort of war they had found themselves in the middle of. Vittorio Troio was on that train. He had been in America only ten months. He couldn't read. They had brought him to Colorado to work but he didn't know what a strike was. Semoni Quantino thought a strike was a union, that a union was another thing, another job. Ubaldo Morelli had never been in a strike before; he knew it was something in regard to a union, but he didn't know what. He didn't know why men went on strike. They may have been feigning ignorance, these poor men with their native suspicion of courts and laws—it is hard to say. The translator for the Congressional Committee believed that the concepts of industrial struggle had hardly begun to penetrate the languages many of the scabs spoke. Beyond the English one, he said, there was no word in Slavonian or Polish or Croatian for strike.

At the mines the scabs tried to get away. The superintendents told them they had to stay, had to pay off their board and their railroad fares. At Tercio they took away their shoes at night to keep them from walking out. Still they drifted off. They would pretend to need a pass to visit a friend at another mine, or bribe a guard with five dollars or a bottle of whiskey or wait until the guards or militiamen were drinking as the Bulgarians had and sneak away, cutting a broad detour around the closed camps through the hip-high snow. They had been told that the union men would kill them if they caught them, but they made their way into the Ludlow colony nevertheless, exhausted, hungry, scared. There Tikas and the other leaders took them in, fed them, and brought them to the union attorneys in Trinidad to make affidavits. One couple, a man and woman named Brockett, are particularly associated with Tikas, who took them to the Packer Building to tell their story. They were not poor immigrants, but part of a group of about thirty men and their families lured out from Joplin, Missouri, to work in the mines in a fraudulent land deal. For them it wasn't American dollars, but that old dream of an independent homestead in the West that had brought them into an industrial war.

According to the census the union took that winter there were 22,000 men, women, and children on its relief rolls in Colorado in January of 1914. By the middle of the month there had been 16 babies born in the camps according to Lawson, all of them boys. If there were any in those tents who thought these children would enjoy even a few days of peace in the new year they were deceived. By the end of the month there would be more turmoil, this time on the streets of Trinidad, and it would come near to setting off a full-scale battle. But there was to be something of perhaps greater significance still: on the first of February Major Leo Kennedy would be sent to take charge of the

Representative Byrnes: *Is he the man who swears he took that out of the well?* Lawson: *Yes. He would swear it was taken out.* —House of Representatives, *Conditions in the Coal Mines of Colorado.* Louis Tikas showing barbed wire thrown in the Ludlow well by the state militia. Winter, 1913–14. Courtesy of the Bancroft Library.

Fremont County district, where there had been trouble. It is a temptation to speculate on what the loss of this fair-minded officer would mean for the people in the tents at Ludlow and for the warlike Greeks who respected him and for Louis Tikas, his friend.

There is a final relic from this hard winter that remains to talk about. It is a photograph of Louis Tikas standing by the Ludlow well and holding in his hand the tangle of barbed wire the militia had thrown down the well shaft after the tripping incident. In the photograph Tikas looks thin, hardly like himself in his other pictures, as if already he is retreating out of the light, becoming blurred and specter-like. But he is wearing the puttees the people of the camp remember him in and a slouch-brimmed hat. A pair of field glasses is strapped over his shoulder. Except for the hat, this is how he will dress on the day he is killed. A month later Lawson will refer to this photograph in the Congressional Committee hearing. Between the image I keep in my mind and Lawson's words there is a strange sort of hollow.

"Who is that?" a committee man asks.

Lawson answers, "I don't know his name. The other is Louis Tikas. He was of Ludlow tent colony at one time."

"Is he the man who swears he took that out of the well?"

"Yes. He would swear it was taken out."

It was the last photograph of Louis Tikas alive.

God Almighty made the women and the Rockefeller gang of thieves made the ladies.

Mother Jones

10. THE WOMEN

"He always dressed very smart. Wore puttees. But he was well educated. And he was always a gentleman. And old Mother Jones thought there was nobody like him. He called her mother, too."

So, sixty years later, sitting in the Tick Tock Restaurant in Hollywood, what Mary Thomas remembered of Louis Tikas were those puttees. It was as if in some strange way that was all that need be said, and that random detail, rising up fresh from memory, had called up for a moment that young Greek she used to know, the camp, the strike itself. And she remembered Mother Jones. As she spoke I could hear still the faint trace of Wales in her voice. Surviving in a word, a phrase, like Louis' puttees, it was a warrant of that past, as if old Mother Jones herself had been brought before me. "She'd always have me start the singing, make all the children sing. And she'd say, 'Now Mary, start singing here. They're in there right now. I want them to hear it.' And she'd holler up to the mining bosses, 'Now, what are you doin'? Why, I've got the people right here that want to talk to you!' That's how she was. Oh, she was tough."

Mary Thomas, scarcely topping five feet, with her picture hat and her animated hands and her intemperate Welsh twang and her memories of Colorado—she must have been something then. I imagined her a girl of twenty-two standing at the Trinidad depot with her two small daughters beside her and that deep red hair she had been so proud of falling down her back, still wearing her Old Country leg-o'-mutton blouse and a sailor hat stuck on the back of her head with an elastic band, her wedding presents packed carefully in the trunks at her

159

feet, the silver tea service her Society had given her, her gold baptismal bracelet, her beautiful Bible. She had come to Colorado looking for her errant husband. She found him in Delagua, digging coal, but it was a stormy marriage and it wouldn't outlast the strike. While she stayed in Delagua she had come to know some of her neighbors—Charlie and Cedi Costa, Tony Gorci who played the fiddle and had an Italian band. They prized her for her singing voice and she called them her friends. When the strike came on and word went out from the union to vacate the company houses, she moved with the rest of them to the Ludlow colony. She considered herself as much of a striker as anyone.

There is a change in the women of the camps with the coming of the strike. I see them in an old photograph as they sit in the meeting hall at Starkville with their men, many of them still wearing the Old Country kerchiefs. How deeply had life changed for the immigrants among them even before the strike. Those small opportunities, those almost insignificant changes in habit and custom America had given them—how remarkable they would seem to a woman brought up in medieval Calabria. Women have power in Southern European cultures, and in some their ascendancy in the home is almost mystical, but almost always confronting the outside world was the place of the men. Now these women were sitting in a meeting beside their husbands, no longer excluded, a part of the great affairs of the world, relied upon, needed to win this strike. Up on the stage Mother Jones was haranguing them in her high-pitched Irish voice, stabbing at them with her finger. Maybe what the old woman was saying was somehow coming through, a part of it, a flavor. It was not new to the women of Ireland or Scotland or Wales. It was not new to the Americans or any of them who had watched their men go out in the strike of 1903. But to those women of the closed villages of the Italian south, where only now such ideas were slowly beginning to be heard, the awakening after the long sleep was all the more sudden, all the more profound . . . *This earth was made for you, was it not? And it was here a long time before the C. F. & I. came upon it. When the C. F. & I. came upon this earth, they did not get a mortgage on it, did they? No, they did not. The earth was here long before they came, and it will be here when their rotten carcasses burn up in hell* . . . And she spoke of them, spoke of their sacrifices. She looked at them with her sharp blue eyes and asked all of them who had gone to the seashore to raise their hands. She said if she was in an audience of C. F. and I. women and asked if they had gone to the seashore every one of them would raise their hands. And she touched on something more, their humiliations. *Did Jack ever tell you, "Say, Mary, you go down and scrub the floor for the superintendent's wife or the boss's wife and then I will get a good room."* They applauded then. *I have known women to do that, poor fools. I have known them to go down and scrub floors like a dog, while their own floors were dirty. . . .* And then the old woman held out a promise: *You will be free. Poverty and misery will be unknown. We will turn the jails into playgrounds for the children. We will build homes, and not log kennels and shacks as you have them now. There will be no civilization as long as such conditions as that abound, and now you men and women will have to stand the fight.*

They did fight. And often it was the women who took the lead. At Sopris, according to the *United Mine Workers Journal* of October sixteenth, it was the women who were most militant, and it was with great difficulty that they were prevented from "cleaning up" the scabs. And when the scabs came into Ludlow on November thirtieth, it was the women who were in the fore of the mob, brandishing ball bats, clubs studded with spikes, jeering. It was the women who railed most at giving up the guns at Ludlow, and it was they who gathered there along with wire fence beside the tracks to teach their children to curse the militia Tin Willies. "We are not a charity organization," Mother Jones had told them. "This is a fight to the finish."

Crowded into the tents of the union colonies, their world had perceptibly altered. They pose a bit self-consciously for photographs in the union commissary, preparing a meal, young women, many of them, experiencing for the first time that heady sense of power the first whiff of revolution brings. Working in a group, each felt course through her a more than personal current of purpose and strength. Mary Thomas remembered dimly being put on a table to sing at a Welsh strike benefit as a child; when she sang now there were thirteen hundred voices singing with her. Free of the narrow routines of the company towns, human sympathies found in the strike at its best an expansion, a generosity. For the first time, in lives hardened by labor, these miners' women had a chance simply to be together, to relax.

An army of strong mining women makes a wonderfully spectacular picture. —Mother Jones. Miners' wives preparing food for strikers. Courtesy of the Denver Public Library, Western History Department.

You will be free. Poverty and misery will be unknown. . . . We will build homes, and not log kennels and shacks as you have them now. There will be no civilization as long as such conditions as that abound, and now you men and women will have to stand the fight. —Mother Jones. Strikers at the Forbes tent colony. Courtesy of the Library, State Historical Society of Colorado.

It was an important thing. When Senator Helen Ring Robinson visited the camps, she noted the feeling of cooperation that had spread among the women of various nationalities. What must that cooperation be for women who had been bred to distrust so thoroughly even those who lived beyond the sound of the village bell—the narrow *campanilisimo* of the Italian south? And now they were challenging not only their own pasts, and their cramped rituals, but the very structure of the industrial world itself. In the sudden opportunities of the strike, in its chances for action and voice, these women had more, it may be, to win than their men.

In a certain subtle but elemental way, the course of the strike had changed the real nature of the relations of women and men. For the strike now comes down to waiting. And the women are good at that. With the men idle, their daily tasks take on a new significance, their routine becomes the emotional core of the strike. It is they who must hold the strike together.

And so each pair of overalls patched, each bucket of coal saved, each meal skimped out of the three-dollars-a-week benefit, the fifty cents they give for each child, eats into the hearts of the mine owners, pushes the strike that much further on. It is not the demonstrations or the violence or the speeches that will win this strike, if it is to be won, but the simple continuity of feeding and washing and cleaning that goes on between those canvas walls, those trips along the muddy paths between the wash lines and the coal piles and the store. And if the women give up one day on that scrimping and hoarding and patching and say they've had enough, then the strike is lost.

In the resolve of the women on strike that winter, Mother Jones was a catalyst. She was already eighty-three at the time of the strike. Her energy and determination—and her sense of theater—would stay with her until her death at the age of one hundred. She had been born in Cork, Ireland, in 1830 and had immigrated young to Toronto. She taught school for a while, then turned to dressmaking because, as she said, she preferred sewing to bossing little children. This affection for children stayed with her all her life. She said she always had a bit of candy for them somewhere about her and often she is surrounded by children in photographs, with an insistence that seems to go beyond the uses of publicity. Perhaps they reminded her of those four children of her own she had watched die with their father in the Memphis yellow fever epidemic of 1867. With the end of her family she went to Chicago and opened a dress shop. In her autobiography she tells of sewing for the rich matrons of Lakeshore Drive while watching the jobless and hungry walk along the frozen lakefront. It was the time of the Haymarket riot and the first national railroad strike, and she learned much from the labor radicals of the day. Her husband had himself been a working man, and when he died it was his local of the Iron Molders International Union that had buried him. In 1871 her dress shop was destroyed in the great Chicago fire. But by 1880, she says, she was wholly engrossed in the labor movement. It was coal that most absorbed her.

"The story of coal is always the same," she wrote. "It is a dark story. For a second's more sunlight men must fight like tigers. . . . That life may have something of decency, something of beauty—a picture, a new dress, a bit of cheap lace fluttering in the window—for this men who work down in the mines must struggle and lose, struggle and win."

In 1903 she came to Colorado. She got into an old calico dress and a sunbonnet, put together some pins and needles, elastic and tape and went down to the closed camps of the south disguised as a peddler, living in the miners' houses, probing them, discovering how willing they were for a strike. The 1903–4 strike failed, but in 1913 she was back. What she could use, she knew, were the women. She could use them indirectly, to shame the men into the fight, telling the miners, as she did on the plains outside of Walsenburg in 1913, that if they were too cowardly to stand up against the coal operators and the Baldwin–Felts thugs there were enough women in the country to beat the hell out of them. And she could use them directly. If the men were browbeaten, afraid, in danger of being arrested or killed, the women had a certain immunity from the worst violence. It was an immunity that could be put to work. In 1899 she had organized a mob of women in Arnot, Pennsylvania; they routed the scabs coming out of a struck mine with mops and brooms and howled and beat on dishpans to stampede the mules. "An army of strong mining women makes a wonderfully spectacular picture," Mother Jones wrote.

She detested a woman who wouldn't fight and she detested the fashionable causes that kept the women of the upper classes filled with

We are not a charity organization. This is a fight to the finish. —Mother Jones. Mother Jones leading a parade in Trinidad. Fall, 1913. Courtesy of the Library, State Historical Society of Colorado.

meretricious zeal when the real fight was elsewhere. "Organized labor should organize its women along *industrial lines*. Politics is only the servant of industry. The plutocrats have organized their women. They keep them busy with suffrage and prohibition and charity." She pointed out that she didn't need a vote to raise hell.

Profane, contentious, almost independent of the union leadership (how many times had she struck out on her own, against their strategy and their wishes?)—eloquent. She wrote of the sound of the machines falling on the ears of the children working in the mills "like iron rain." She had a kind of foulmouthed eloquence for other occasions. In West Virginia they remember how she told a gang of company gunmen "I've sat on a bumper inhaling mule farts and it smelled better than you sons of bitches." Of such language she said, "That is the way we ignorant working people pray." Her militant rhetoric was both the glory and the despair of the union officials. It could make her invaluable in an organization drive or the first stages of a strike, but she could come close to wrecking any chance for compromise or negotiation with her intemperance, and she could be a major problem in heading off violence. In the bad days of October, when the shooting began at Ludlow and Lawson was desperately trying to disarm the strikers, Mother Jones had argued with him, demanding that the strikers keep their weapons. They remember her in Colorado to this day passing out rifles: "Here you go. I hope you use it."

She was an actress. And like all good actresses she had a fine sense of her own presence—sense enough of it and of the irony of her diminutive appearance to slip through the ranks of strikebreaking soldiers without them noticing who she was—"just an old woman going to a missionary meeting to knit mittens for the heathen of Africa." And like an actress she could be misled by the chance to play a good scene—misled, it seemed at times, almost into betraying her cause. But in 1913 she had the shrewdness to realize that at eighty-three she was more valuable to the union as a symbol than as anything else; and infinitely more valuable, once the strike began, in jail than on the street.

Since mid-December she had impatiently awaited a call from the union to go down to the strike zone. "And it can't come too soon," she told a reporter. "Chase will throw me in jail. I would bet on that.

He'll do it because he doesn't know any better, because he doesn't know that persecution always helps instead of hinders any battle. And let him do it. Let him have his men disgracing their uniforms, shoot me. I'm prepared for that too. I wish they would. It would mean a wave of feeling over this country that would crush Chase and everybody like him. It would mean certain victory, and it would mean the end of state troops serving men with dollars."

She tossed back her head, laughed. "But I don't expect they'll shoot me. I guess even Chase knows better than that. They'll throw me in jail and before they get me out they'll wish they'd never done it. It was the same in West Virginia. They threw me in and then they didn't know how to get me out."

On the fourth of January, at eight in the morning, she was arrested by the militia at the Trinidad depot. An hour and a half later she was put on the Denver-bound train with a detail of soldiers to make sure she kept going. But on the eleventh of January she was back. In her autobiography she tells how she slipped by the detectives watching her Denver hotel and made her way to the railroad station. It was an hour before the train was scheduled to leave for the south. She walked out to the yards where they were making up the coaches and slipped a porter a couple of dollars. She asked him to tell the conductor that Mother Jones was on the train and to let her get off before they got to the Santa Fe crossing in Trinidad. She was asleep in her berth by the time the train pulled up to the platform to board the passengers for the south. While she napped, detectives were searching every face. Early that morning the porter awakened her and the train came to a brief stop on the outskirts of Trinidad. The conductor helped her off.

"Are you doing business, Mother?" he asked.

"I am indeed," she said.

As the train pulled away the conductor waved to her. Then she walked into Trinidad and checked into the Toltec Hotel. While the militia searched the depot she ate her breakfast and went up to her room. It was there she was arrested three hours later by General Chase himself. They took her to the Mount San Rafael Hospital and confined her in a room under guard. Chase had been forced to play into her hands.

The Greeks lived a little removed in the Ludlow colony, near the ball diamond. They had their own big tent about half a mile from the one Mary Thomas was living in. They were a proud lot, as Mary remembers them. And apart. When she thought of it, the way they acted was very much like the Welsh—very distant, unless they knew you. They were bachelors, all of them, and they were young. They were living in close quarters with people they'd never cared to have much to do with, the *xeni*—the "foreigners" as they habitually called anyone who wasn't Greek, forgetting, of course, that *they* were the foreigners, they were the ones who stuck out like sore thumbs. They were wary, clannish, and they bore their reputations as fighters with heroic exaggeration. Once, at least, they took on the role of self-appointed moral police and slapped a curfew on a couple of girls from the camp who had gone over to the tents of the militia. They wanted no scandal to attach itself to the colony. And sometimes they danced.

Changed now from the dingy overalls that made every miner the same, they appeared in their Old Country costumes, the boots and black pantaloons of the Cretans, the dashing white kilts of the Mainland. Athletic, strenuous, each man in turn took the lead in the dance while some *lyra* player sawed away, leaping, spinning, whirling on one heel —"like flying through the air" Mary Thomas remembered it. What must they have seemed, these swaggering young Greeks with the cigarettes cocked behind one ear, to the young women of the camp, whose lives knew only the pinched, drab world of the company town? And to those exotics themselves, the Greeks, how must these *xeni* women have seemed—women so different from their own, who went to town unchaperoned and wore hats . . . They were all of them caught up in a revolutionary moment, and in the rush of change old moralities fell, old customs. To the Greeks who had curfewed the wandering camp girls it was the *appearance* of scandal that was the terrible thing; scandal itself was interesting. They had come from a world with an almost schizophrenic sexuality. For all those passionate *amanes* with their endless catalogs of dark eyes and honey lips, the practice of love was smothered for the Greeks under arranged marriages and haggled dowries and impossible standards of modesty. Yet now they were away from all that; and there, within arms' reach, were those bold *Americanidhes*:

I wish I was a little bar of soap, my girl
Tied to your bath with a string,
I'd slide from you slowly and you'd catch me again,
And you'd put me wherever you like . . .

So the great Harilaos would sing, his fingers flying up and down the
neck of the *lyra*. Harilaos who himself married an *Americanidha* and
taught her to dance as well as any Cretan girl . . .

I'd wash your sweet little body, my girl,
and foam from all my passion . . .

The Greeks sat in their tent arguing among themselves, dealing
out endless hands of cards, mending their threadbare clothes; and on
those freezing nights when they stood picket outside the camp or lay
sleepless in their cots they must have thought of the young American
women separated from them by something as thin as the canvas walls
of a tent, met on the snowy paths, or sometimes framed in silhouette
against an open door. Old Gus Papadakis, who liked to insist on the
strict propriety of the Ludlow Greeks, caught once off guard, laughed
and said he stayed away from the tempting young *Americanidhes* in
the tents—"not like Louis and them." "Women with tits, men with
whiskers," my grandfather used to say.

And there was Louis Tikas in his motoring hat, his puttees, of all
the Greeks the most progressive, the quickest to catch on. He had
moved by this time from the Greek tent into a tent of his own in order
to have a phone. As camp boss it was necessary to have the telephone
near him and it was just as necessary, I think, to move himself away
from his fellow Greeks, with their quarrels, their rivalries and their
hair-trigger suspicions. He prided himself on his scrupulous fairness to
all the people of the camp. No doubt, too, he prided himself on his
calm. And so he found it sometimes wise to carry on camp business
away from the rumors and instant hysteria of the tents. He told Major
Hamrock once that he preferred to meet him away from the camp
where there weren't so many people listening in. He was taking his
meals now at the tent of a miner's wife named Pearl Jolly.

"She forced herself in on everybody. One of that kind. I believe
that he would have been alive today. . . . These soldiers, she'd been

flirtin' with them too, and I think there was a lot of jealousy there. And that's why they took such revenge on him. And killed him. . . ."

Sift through the jealousies and rumors of that closed little tent colony. The calumnies of the militiamen who had their own axes to grind. It is impossible. What is left is simply rumor still, and voices. ". . . Pearl Jolly. And he couldn't get rid of her. Hung on and hung on. And they went to dances, he and her. Went to dances in another little town. These soldiers, they used to go there too. And anybody could see she was playing the field, see. Nobody knew much about that, and I never told on her. Oh, she's the one that caused his death. He was a perfect gentleman. A perfect gentleman. Everybody loved him and they hated this woman who was ruining him. . . ."

She'd been married less than a year to a Scot who'd come to the United States as a child. She mentions him, briefly, when she appears before the Walsh Commission in May of 1914. He testifies for Bob Uhlich after the strike, another time he is listed among those arrested for picketing on Water Tank Hill. We know a little more about Pearl. She'd been born in a C. F. and I. shack in the Southern Field. Her father had been killed in a mine accident and she remembered bitterly the way the company had treated her family after that. For a time she'd gone to work as a nurse in the Minnequa Hospital in Pueblo. Perhaps, as in Tikas, there was something of the opportunist in her. It may be the strike was a chance for her to break away from old restraints. Like Tikas she was a figure in the tents—camp nurse, a leader of the jeering against the scabs and the militiamen. Mary Thomas said that it was Pearl who had been dressed down for wearing a fur coat to Mother Jones' parade. And in something I find nowhere else but in Mary's memory, there is the claim that in the months before the Ludlow massacre Tikas was brutally beaten by militiamen on Pearl's account. At the court-martial of the guardsmen when Ludlow had been burned to the ground and Tikas was dead, one of the militiamen joked about the closeness of the tents of the Greek and the miner's wife, and said the two of them had been spotted together in Trinidad's red-light district. I think of Louis Tikas and Pearl Jolly, young, in high spirits, sneaking off to dance those fast new steps, the tango, the Hesitation Waltz. Tikas must have been a man of some attraction, and not only to the twenty-year-old wife of a coal miner. Senator Helen Ring

Robinson remembered his idealism and his courage. And more than sixty years after she had visited Ludlow as a young and privileged woman interested in social justice, Josephine Roche recalled Louis Tikas as "a lovely person." As for Pearl Jolly, whoever or whatever she was, she proved a woman of courage, and for most of Louis Tikas' last hours on earth, amid the gunfire and panic of the tents, she was with him.

At the Mount San Rafael Hospital Mother Jones had been kept incommunicado for over a week. The union would have a holiday with the image of that frail old woman trapped behind locked doors, a bayonet-wielding guard pacing back and forth outside her cell. Very soon her legend would transcend even the exaggerations of the union propagandists and enter the purer realm of industrial folklore (*In front of these brave soldiers loomed a sight you seldom see/A white-haired rebel woman whose age was eighty-three....*) But now she joked with her guards and bent her mind to smuggling out a letter.

On the twenty-second of January, the women from the tent colonies massed in Trinidad to demonstrate against her jailing. It was their show, their parade. They marched up Commerical Street, over a thousand of them, carrying banners and flags. People stood against the buildings enjoying the spectacle. At Main the women turned. Then, all at once, they hesitated. At the end of the block, near the post office, waited the mounted soldiers of the National Guard. General Chase himself was there, running his horse nervously back and forth through the ranks. He called out to the women to stop, to go back. But the women's hesitation lasted only a moment. They had been confronted with a symbol, and symbols stop only those who let them. There was a shout and they kept on marching.

Watching the women as they passed triumphantly between the files of mounted men was a sixteen-year-old girl named Sarah Slator. Chase rushed by her on his horse, yelling at her to get back. Stunned, she didn't move. Chase kicked at her with his stirruped foot. Then, startled by his motion or by the crowd, his horse shied, ran into a horse and buggy at the side of the street and the General fell to the pavement. The spectators screamed and laughed. The Slator girl didn't hear the order he gave as he got up, but she heard him shout, "Ride down the women," and, "Make them get back." And suddenly the horsemen were rushing through the crowd, slapping at the marchers with the flats of their swords, trying to wrench away the flags and banners the enraged women swung at them. A militiaman on a horse whipped his sword at Sarah Slator but she ducked behind a telephone pole and it hit the wood with a smack. "Break your sword, I don't care," she cried, and he swung at her twice more. In front of Zimmerman's she saw four militiamen taking two women off to jail. "Shame on you," she yelled. "Take four men to take two women—how many does it take to take a man?" One of the soldiers brought the butt of his rifle down on her foot. Then they grabbed her and took her off to jail. They threw her in a filthy cell with another woman. After a while they brought in Mary Thomas.

Mary Thomas had not marched in the parade that day but had watched from the sidewalk. When the scramble started, a militiaman had ordered her to move and she'd taunted him—"You go on and go wash your dirty clothes you have on before you order me off of the sidewalk." He'd started to pull her by her fur piece and she'd fought back, scratching and clawing at him, while the people around her cried "shame" to the soldier. The militia had taken her off to jail. While they were booking her they asked what they should put down for the color of her hair and she told them to put down pale blue. Then she telephoned Louis Tikas at the colony and told him she was under arrest.

What had happened in the streets of Trinidad was magnified with bad communication and with anger. Lawson, outraged, unclear on the facts, wired the union in Indianapolis that Chase had ordered his men to shoot to kill, that women with babes in arms had been jabbed in the back with bayonets and trampled under the feet of the horses. The state militia called it a riot and would maintain that the women had turned from their route to march on the San Rafael Hospital and liberate Mother Jones. But it was Chase who had brought on the confrontation, it was the militia that had rioted. The day after the parade the women of the tent colonies crowded into Trinidad's Castle Hall for an indignation meeting.

There was an outsider at that meeting who wrote a derisive account of the proceedings for the *Trinidad Chronicle-News*. But through the sarcasm and condescension of that anonymous eyewitness report, we see something happening that is remarkable. One after another these "poor, misguided women" got up to have their say. First came the chair of the meeting, a Mrs. Walker, then came a Polish woman from Walsenburg: "She stepped to the front of the stage, rolled up her sleeves and from her build and actions one was not sure whether she was just preparing for the wash tub or to enter the prize ring." She spoke in Polish, then in broken English. But the epithets she used came through and were plain. A Slavic housewife stood up, a matronly woman who spoke in her own tongue. Then an Italian woman said a few words in her language. Then came a woman who'd lived in Walsenburg, an American. "I have always wanted to be a hero and be in front at the battle," she said, "and I have had my wish today. I hate men. I can only talk revolutionary, keep things stirring all the time, keep the pot boiling. You women, elect your class, come to the front with ballots, instead of bullets. We will learn these men something. . . ." They were speaking not through their husbands, not through their mute labor, but in their own voices. Their very awkwardness, that brutal ineloquence, was the sign of their transformation. Mother Jones would have been proud.

While the women shouted and cheered in Castle Hall, Mary Thomas sat in her narrow cell at the county jail. Her daughters were with her now, one three years old, the other four. She let them tear up the bathroom and throw whatever was loose out the broken window. When Mary was tense she would either scream or sing. Now she sang. She sang arías from the operas she remembered and when a crowd gathered in the alley outside her cell she began to sing "The Union Forever" and motioned them to join in, although she couldn't see them. Then the men held in the jail began to sing with her and the police moved into the alley and drove the crowds away. As they left, the people threw rocks at the jailhouse windows. When Mary's husband came to see her, the jailer said he must listen to their conversation. They spoke in Welsh.

In the days after the attack on the parade the union leaders desperately tried to quiet their outraged men. In Walsenburg the strikers demanded that Adolph Germer tell them where the union guns were concealed. He resisted with difficulty and would have to spend a good deal of time defending himself against charges of cowardice after the strike. The pleas of officials like Germer moved some of the men, but not all of them. One night bands of strikers quietly took up positions on the rooftops of Trinidad. They were armed and they were waiting only for an excuse to open up on Chase's headquarters in the Columbia Hotel. In the piñon pines above the tents of the military camp outside the San Rafael Hospital another group of armed men waited. These were the Greeks.

Again we see Louis Tikas. This time it is in the pages of Barron Beshoar's book on the strike, *Out of the Depths*. Already he is half-myth. He is armed, with a gunnysack filled with food and ammunition slung over his shoulder. He is just going to the field when John Lawson intercepts him and tells him to call in his men. The Congressional investigation of the strike that had been so long promised and so long stalled would at last be held.

It is my desire to state to you, as concisely as the matter will permit, the services I have performed for the United Mine Workers of America during the fifteen months that I have been engaged in the work of that organization.

Louis Tikas

11. THE INVESTIGATION

If Lawson and Louis Tikas met that night, if it was their meeting that averted a full-scale battle, I do not know. The strikers were angry and they were armed, but they were always disorganized and, as for the Greeks, with their independence and that dark streak of jealousy that seems to run through the race, they took orders from no one—not Tikas, not anyone else. They melted back from their positions on the rooftops and in the piñons and no shot was fired. There was work to be done. The night before word of the Congressional investigation had come, a violent windstorm had knocked down seventy of the Ludlow tents.

On the fourth of February Judge Northcutt's *Trinidad Chronicle-News* ran a rather crude sort of spoof, a page of a paper called "The Ludlow Lyre." "Lon Jawson" is listed as Editor, "Hank J. Frays" Manager, and one "Louie Pikus" City Editor. Among the items is a notice stating that the daily target practice of the Balkan War veterans has been postponed for two weeks "on account of no ammunition." But the satire, so far as Louis Tikas was concerned, had been misplaced. Four days after the "Lyre" was printed he left the Ludlow colony, no longer head man, no longer an organizer, no longer, it seems, a part of the struggle. The next day the strikers' newspaper, the *Trinidad Free Press*, printed what was intended to be Tikas' union obituary.

Louis Tikas, better known as "Louis the Greek," who had been the leader, mayor and guardian angel of the little tented colony at Lud-

175

low, has been succeeded by P. E. Quinn, international organizer for
the United Mines Workers of America. Quinn took charge today.

The *Free Press* account went on to praise Tikas as "one of the leading
counselors in the affairs of the union miners," and told how he took a
prominent part in the battle of Ludlow and had distributed gifts to the
colonists at Christmas. The article said he would leave that night to
testify before the Congressional Committee in Denver.

Tikas never was called to testify. A day after the hearing began,
on February tenth, he wrote a letter to the International Officers of the
United Mine Workers. It was his vindication. Dictated to some
American, or rewritten from his notes, it gave a synopsis of his first days
in the union since the walkout at the Frederick slope mine. But even
through its careful phrases his anger seethed.

> Upon my release from military custody, mention of my name
> occurred time and time again in the newspapers; the people spoke of
> me with respect and love. For some unaccountable reason—presum-
> ably petty jealousy at my success—certain people known as National
> Organizers, (I do not care to mention specific names unless called
> upon to do so) began to plot and connive against me. These men,
> seated around a large table in comfortable chairs in the Trinidad
> office, smoking their good fifteen cent cigars, riding in automobiles
> at the expense of the organization and their work limited to the
> making of a few speeches, presumably thought that I desired their
> soft lap and that I would oust them from their jobs, so they, instead
> of working in the interests of your people, plotted to discredit me
> with the people and this is how they hoped and worked to do it. . . .

Louis continued his letter, told how these anonymous organizers displaced his name from the newspapers (though he cared but little for
newspaper notoriety), sought to undermine his authority with the
people in the tents, who would look to other leadership when they saw
he could not get them the supplies they desperately needed. He remembered one day when he had an angry set-to in the Trinidad union
office during a blizzard. It must have been the windstorm of January
twenty-sixth, which flattened the Ludlow tents. He had gone after
coal to keep his people from freezing. The reply he got in the Trinidad
office was, "You can go to hell." The supplies he ordered to relieve the
suffering of the people, the lumber and blankets and stovepipes and
shoes, he never received. It was the shoes especially that preyed on

him. Three or four times he called up William Diamond about those shoes, and his answer was that he would not send them because Tikas failed to recognize him as head man.

Even before the confrontation during the storm there had been friction between the two men. On the tenth of January Diamond had written to Ed Doyle asking him outright if he wanted him to remain as head of the Trinidad office: "I am either in charge of this office or I am not in charge. In either case I want to know it." He wanted an immediate reply. Money was scarce and there had been large expenses —the newspaper, the union auto. The District Office was pressuring Diamond; he bristled at talk about his books. Early in the strike he'd wired Doyle that he was broke and for a time had found it advisable to stay out of the office in order to dodge his creditors. And now the fieldworkers were contracting debts without going through him. "In fact we are not consulted by some of the district men down here. They don't seem to recognize that this office is in existence."

It wasn't until the end of the month that Doyle replied. If any of the district workers would not toe the line Diamond was to contact the Denver office at once and steps would be taken to remove the man. Doyle, too, was being pressed. He went on to say that International Secretary Green had instructed him to have all branches dispense with any organizers or fieldworkers it was possible to do without. It was the opening Diamond had been looking for.

But the confrontation between Tikas and the ambitious young Diamond had more to it than dollars and cents and the chain of command. It had taken on the character of a personal struggle. According to Tikas, Diamond had openly boasted that the people in the tents would receive nothing until the Greek had been deposed as head of the Ludlow colony. "I ask you," Tikas wrote, "how can I recognize as head man one who refuses the necessities of life to those under my charge? . . ." There was something else Tikas suspected was behind it all: that he was a Greek. He only hinted at this in his letter, but the Greeks thought themselves mistrusted and disliked by the union hierarchy, and it is easy to see that the union might feel itself well rid of that handful of intractable, hot-tempered young Hellenes in the Ludlow tents. Tikas contented himself with asking why, when every other nationality in the union had one representative to every 200 men, he was the only organizer among the 547 Greek miners in Colorado, among the 3,000 Greeks in the unorganized mines of Alabama, New Mexico, and Utah and the 13,000 Greeks in the union fields.

In fact, in his struggle with Diamond, he had overstepped his bounds. He was an immigrant, a "no-nameovich," and whatever the make-up of its membership, the United Mine Workers was run—would continue to be run—by Anglo–Saxons. The recent biographers of John L. Lewis—that politician who better than anyone knew the uses of the immigrant vote in union power struggles—put it this way: "In the world of union politics, new immigrants deferred to English-speaking leaders, who, in turn, appointed the immigrants to UMW positions they might never have won in contested elections." If a man like Tikas was to rise to prominence he would get there by the patronage of his betters, not by sticking out his neck. But pride or impatience or simple loyalty to the people in the tents—there was something that would not permit Louis Tikas to defer to the hail-fellow young Michigan organizer in the Trinidad headquarters. Tikas was the greenhorn, the outsider. He watched them in that warm office laying their plans—Diamond, his crony Bob Bolton, the corpulent E. M. Snyder who had gotten so drunk the night of the October twenty-seventh battle he couldn't lead his men—they were building their soft jobs on the backs of those people out there shivering in the tents. And he despised them.

Yet there were others who were after Louis' job that winter; they were his own Greeks.

There was living in the tents of Ludlow a Greek named Pete Katsulis—Little Pete—a wily man, an ambitious man. Perhaps even then he was jealous of Louis job, as Bill Pappas and others were jealous. Because even then he was working against him.

Katsulis had come over from the Mainland in 1906 or 1907. He'd been a section boss on the Rio Grande at Durango, then had set up as a labor agent, bringing in fifty or sixty Greeks to work at the Frederick mine in the Southern Field. In Van Houten, New Mexico, he was run out of town because the bosses thought he was trying to organize, but it wasn't until the strike broke out in 1913 that he joined the union. He thought Louis Tikas was a fool. Tikas was getting a hundred a month, paying his own expenses. Pete Katsulis knew the job could be worked for more than that, a hundred twenty-five, a hundred fifty. Fool like Louis was, he never did get enough.

It was in the summer of 1914 that Katsulis would say all this, testifying before the grand jury sitting in Trinidad, dodging and maneuvering, trying to avoid his own indictment. Louis didn't trust him because he was an outsider, from a different part of Greece. He didn't like Louis' system. Louis was always trying to keep people excited all the time, keep them ready for something. He told Louis it wasn't right. When Lawson came out he talked to him about it, about how Louis was stirring up the people. That's why they put Tikas out of the camp . . . The indictment came nevertheless. Katsulis had bragged about killing a guard at Tabasco the previous fall, had even written to the Greek newspapers about his leadership in the fight. Bitter at the union hierarchy, desperately trying to proclaim his innocence before the grand jury, he tried to shift the blame to a dead man. But sixty-five years later it is himself he betrays. It is as if the flap of the Greek tent at Ludlow is raised for a moment and we see them there. Anyone who has read Kolokotronis or the memoirs of the great Makriyiannis or Byron's letters from Missolonghi would recognize those voices, the same vanity and injured ego, the same contention and note of self-pity that simmered through the councils of the chieftains in the wars against the Turks. There were turncoats and informers in '21 and they were to be found among the tents of Ludlow now.

So they talked about Tikas in the Greek camp. Talked about the American woman he was running around with and how he had been a scab in the Northern Field. Then there was Louis' job itself. Talking with the union big shots, interpreting. What the hell, some of them said, I could do that job myself. Organizer's pay and a ride in the car with the big shots was better than starving out there on the prairie on three dollars a week. In the photograph which exists of Pete Katsulis in those days, cocky in his red neckerchief and tipped-back cap, his toothy mouth opens up in a grin that engages his whole face. We will never have so good a picture of Tikas, who always seems to be retreating from the lens, blurred slightly, never quite there.

On February fifth Diamond wrote Ed Doyle to assure him that any changes the Trinidad office made in its executive workers would not be made without Doyle's consent. He told him of the damage done by the windstorm and detailed the work of shoring up the tents. Then he wrote that he would as much as possible cut down on expenses in order to harmonize with the advice from Secretary Green. "We have let four men off during the past week and will probably let one or two more off just as soon as we have made arrangements to handle the work they are now doing," he said. One of these men was Louis Tikas. It was Diamond's vindictiveness or the machinations of Greeks like Pete Katsulis or perhaps something of both that had cost him his job. Or it might have been something else. For when the Congressional Committee began its hearings into the strike in Denver on the ninth of February Tikas sat in the audience silent. Nine days later the Committee moved to Trinidad, and he followed.

In the Opera House the miners crowded the aisles, the balcony, their faces thrust dimly out of the half-light. Lit up against a blood-red curtain the stage was laid out with the tables of the hearing's participants. At the Committee's table the chairman, Doctor Foster, listened, ready to intervene. Young Jimmy Byrnes of South Carolina, conspicuous in his blue serge suit, sat chewing gum. Evans of Montana was taking notes. Now and then the harsh electric light caught the glint of C. F. and I. attorney Fred Herrington's bald head or Captain Danks' pompadour. Sometimes a baby cried. But the audience was silent except for a cough here or there or the shuffling of feet. Sometimes one of them would stand up to try to catch what some person on the witness stand was saying, and then they would all get up, straining to hear.

They were interrogating Jesse Shaw. He was Northcutt's protégé.

"You have heard of the fight on the 27th have you?" Northcutt asked.

"Yes, sir."

"Was it over when you got there?"

"Yes, sir."

"Did you go into the Ludlow tent colony?"

"Yes, sir."

"How long did you stay there?"

"Stayed until morning of the 28th."

"Did anything unusual take place during the night?"

"There was quite a bit of talk and flurry during the night."

"Tell the Committee about it."

"On the night of the 27th, about 12 o'clock, they formed a body of men to go out and take Hastings. . . ."

Costigan, the union attorney, was on his feet objecting. Doctor Foster let Shaw go on. They had run Shaw out of the union, accused him of spying, embezzling his local's funds. Now he was spilling everything.

"Well, on the night of the 27th, about 12 o'clock, there was some of the leaders there—Louis the Greek—I see he hiked out as soon as I took the chair—and another man they called . . ."

It is as if the air was all at once sucked out of the room. Suddenly Louis is gone, before I'd even known he was there, drawing a hush from the atmosphere around him. As so often, it is his absence, that hollow place in the activity that surrounds him, that is the most solid thing about him. So it is with the hearing.

Jesse Shaw continued. He told how Tikas, Uhlich, and Mike Livoda talked about the attack and gave out guns. Told how Jim the Greek had come limping down from the hills with a wound in his thigh, and how he and A. C. Felts had gone to Denver to identify him. That November somebody had blown up Shaw's house to reward him for the job he'd been doing for the C. F. and I.

The union called its own witnesses. Men and women who testified to the conditions in the closed camps, the beatings, the harassment by the militiamen and the company guards. On the platform E. H. Weitzel sat half a dozen feet away, smiling and taking notes, while men whose work depended on him talked of shortweight and brutal pit bosses and explosive shafts. For the reporters in the audience the voices of the witnesses fell one upon the other, resolved themselves into a drone, like the humming of bees.

They brought up Marco Zamboni and he told how he lay in the rain at Forbes for three hours while the guards shot at him with the machine gun. Andy Colnar told them how the militia had set him to work digging a latrine they told him was his own grave . . . still Tikas was not called. It may be that for all he could tell of the abuses of the guards and the militiamen, it was what he could tell of the Greeks that would be most damaging. The union might have doubted his loyalty now that he'd been fired. Or he may have been fired precisely because of the kind of questions Fred Herrington and Jesse Northcutt could have put to him. Tikas might have told us much, had he talked to the Committee, or nothing at all. Instead he sat in the audience mute, as dark and unformed as those shadowy faces beyond the light.

Jim Fyler, the secretary of the Ludlow local, came up to the stand. He told how a few days before the militia had caught a bunch of them on Water Tank Hill and marched them up to Tabasco. Linderfelt had stood them against a wall with a cannon pointing at them and some of them were beaten. He didn't think it was any way to treat an old man. Fyler was forty-four years old.

"And you call yourself an old man?" a committee member asked.

"Well, I don't know," Fyler said. "If some of youse had put in thirty-five years digging coal, you would begin to think you was pretty old."

Judge Northcutt asked Fyler if he had ever been hazed at college.

Diamond, too, took the stand.

His testimony is disappointing. He told how he'd mined coal in Michigan, had gotten elected to the International Board. How he was run out of West Virginia by the Baldwin–Felts. He had been at Ludlow on the twenty-seventh of October and ready to take charge of the men if necessary, but he'd given no orders. He didn't think the men would have obeyed him if he did. As he sat there, watching this man Diamond on the stand, there was a rumor that Louis Tikas may have thought about: it is possible Diamond was a company spy.

The evidence against Diamond is fragmentary, and it is intriguing. One or two stray notes in the Lawson and Doyle collections in the Denver Public Library and the two men's recollections of the strike suggest Diamond, along with other union men, was a traitor. A traitor to whom? To the union or to Doyle and Lawson? With the strike broken, the bitterness of the abandoned officers of District 15 may have cast a retrospective suspicion on men like Diamond, who, for a time, survived the wreckage. Yet even while the strike was being fought he was mistrusted. In the fall of 1913 he had ordered a shipment of guns from the East without consulting the policy committee. When the guns were seized outside of Clayton, New Mexico, there was talk that Diamond himself had tipped the authorities off. To judge from Doyle's correspondence there were questions, too, about where relief supplies were going and how Diamond kept his books. (There is a story going around in Colorado even now that he embezzled the improbable sum of $92,000 from the union and skipped off with it to Hawaii!)

Affable, cigar-smoking Billy Diamond—was he in fact playing both sides? If he was, then his firing of Tikas would make another sort of sense, for it would deprive the Ludlow colony of a man they loved and cut the Greeks off from their only effective leader and their coolest head. In the confusion of those days no one was above suspicion. Before the strike C. F. and I. Chief of Detectives Billy Reno had hatched a plot against Mike Livoda, circulating a forgery among the Slavs in order to discredit their most active organizer. The taint of that forgery still clung to Livoda in spite of his dedication. Lawson and Doyle knew their movement was riddled with spies, but how did you get rid of them? In times like those a man scrambled as best he could. And Billy Diamond was ambitious.

In March of 1914 Diamond was pumped in the *United Mine Workers Journal*'s "Run of the Mine" column:

> Always calm, good-natured, he never hesitates when the necessity arises to take a determined position. Splendid judgment, great fortitude in trying circumstances, ability, all the requirements of a leader has the hardy, little Michigander. He is "the right man in the right place."

In August, with the strike virtually broken, a large photograph of the smiling Diamond appeared in the *Journal*. He looks like the horse that *Journal* editor Wallace was backing in the union derby. By the summer of 1916 Diamond had moved up to a new position, that of union statistician, but in February of the next year he was replaced by another ambitious young man, whose dark face, even then, betrayed something harder and more demanding than did the well-fed cheeks of smiling Billy. It was John L. Lewis and he would make the statistician's post into something more than the sinecure it had been. In June of 1918 Diamond's name appeared in the *Journal* for what was probably the final time, listed as president of the small, reactivated Maryland District 16. He had served there as an officer on and off since

Lewis had taken over as statistician. By then John L. Lewis had gone to Colorado to gut the torn and bankrupt District 15. He had moved up to the vice presidency of the union and kept a strong hand on the *Journal* as its manager, while his friends kept Frank Hayes, president of the union in name only, awash with alcohol and his own sentimental poetry in some or another hotel. And Diamond simply disappears. Like his old rival Louis Tikas he becomes a little grain chipped off history and floating loose, who knows where. He'd had a few moments of glory and tasted a little power and had been talked about as a spy and if he was probably no one will ever know.

The Committee hearings moved to Walsenburg then back to Denver. In the Greek tent the strains of the strike were beginning to tell. Factions were forming. The Cretans were trying to push Katsulis out, Bill Pappas was talking about taking over Louis Tikas' job. Their money was down to nothing. Conductors on the trains got to know young Gus Papadakis, riding from Walsenburg to Ludlow when anything was up. The ticket cost a dollar. Somehow the conductors never saw him get on the train. Yet the Greeks remained militant. Lying idle in the tent or in the house in Walsenburg, grown sick of arguments and cards, one of them would all at once jump up and say, "Let's go shoot up the goddamn scabs!" And they would file out to lie low in the hills and fire the nuisance rounds they hoped to scare the strikebreakers away with. It was on one of those midnight expeditions that they stopped the auto of a badly scared Walsenburg hardware merchant named E. L. Neelly. The merchant's fright was not misplaced. Early in the strike an auto full of guards had been ambushed outside of La Veta. But Neelly was lucky. He recognized some of the men he'd been secretly supplying with guns. They took him to a tent colony nearby and turned him loose and did not forget him that summer when he ran for sheriff against Jeff Farr.

The Greeks had other allies—some as unlikely as the girls in the Walsenburg whorehouses, who would tip them off when a bunch of scabs were enjoying themselves in the rooms. Then the Greeks would go down and clean the scabs out and there would be torn knuckles, bloody heads and a few arrests. This was the way the working girl showed her solidarity with the working man. Toward the end of February an incident occurred that the Greeks would remember bitterly.

About that time a Cretan by the name of Galanis had come into Trinidad from Gunnison. He had tried to ingratiate himself with the company men and in retaliation the Slav and Italian strikers had wrecked his shoe shop. Now Galanis sent a friend to the Greek camp with a petition demanding restitution. But the Greeks were wary. They did not know the final purpose of the paper Galanis wanted them to sign; they thought it might damage them. In the tents with them was Galanis' cousin. Unsure of Galanis' motives, of what he would do now that they refused to sign, they kept the cousin hostage. They held him a week, then they took pity on him and let him go. When the boy left them, he wept. He had become one of them. And now the hardest thing of all came to the Greeks. For Galanis took a job with the C. F. and I. and undertook to break the strike. The scabs he brought in were their own countrymen.

And so they came, Greeks to break a Greek strike. The number I have heard is about a thousand, although this is certainly high. But there were enough. They were recruited from Bingham Canyon, Utah. So tenuous was their loyalty—or so sharp their hunger—that they had forgotten the Cretans' struggle against Utah Copper and the padrone Skliris in 1912. It would be important to know how many of them had in fact gone out in that strike and been blacklisted for it. One of them, a boy named George Paterakis, had sat with murder in his heart toward the padrone one night in 1912, not knowing it was Skliris himself, seated in an automobile disguised as a woman, he had just waved through the rifles of the strikers' blockade.

On the twenty-seventh of February, Governor Ammons signed an order recalling all but two hundred troops from the south. The militia had very nearly bankrupted the state. Those who remained, and the company-subsidized force of volunteers soon to be collected from among the mine guards and the toughs of the Trinidad streets, would do damage enough.

That winter Lou Dold had been making good money selling postcards of the strike. He sold them like newspapers just as soon as he made them. Shots of the Death Special, the strikers in front of their tents, the militiamen—people were eager to buy them. There was a fellow named Hainlon who had been hanging around him and the two had become pretty close. During the Mother Jones parade that fall Hainlon had been there, running the photographic plates Lou took back to the studio. Now he helped Lou when he went out to shoot, ran out for coffee and sandwiches, helped peddle the postcards on the street. He never took anything for it, was just interested, giving Lou a hand. Once he fixed the two of them up with a couple of married women. He was helpful that way. Lou thought he was working for the union.

On the tenth of March the Trinidad office of the United Mine Workers got a tip that something was up at Forbes. They got Lou Dold and Hainlon and a few of them drove out to the tent colony in the Red Special. A scab had been found dead on the Colorado and Southern embankment outside Suffield. The railroad crew who found him said he'd been drinking and had staggered blindly into the moving train, but the coroner's jury said he'd been beaten to death by the strikers. Sheriff Gresham's men pushed a pair of dogs into the tent colony at Forbes and said that's where the scent had led. Chase had wanted the Forbes colony broken up for months. He acted now.

In the tents at Forbes was a young woman named Emma Zanatell. She'd been born in the Old Country, but among her earliest memories was being carried out of her house in Sopris in her mother's arms while the house went up in a dynamite blast behind her. And she remembered her father being beaten and jailed. The labor wars of the '90s and the strike of 1903–4 had left her no stranger to coal camp justice. She'd married young—her husband was a Swiss–American pit boss at Forbes. When they brought a gang of black strikebreakers to his mine, her husband had quit and the two of them had moved into the tent colony. They'd lived in that tent since September. On hot days the sun poured through the canvas, and the air was stifling, motionless. Now it was bitter cold. Emma was pregnant. Her time came two months early, and there was trouble. She was carrying twins, and they would not come out right. They phoned the camp doctor at Forbes but he refused to come down. Then they called the union doctor, Ben Beshoar. They waited, the women running in and out of the tent, scared, not knowing what to do. It was hours before Doctor Beshoar arrived from Trinidad. When he got there he was soaking wet. The deputies had shot up his car and he'd had to abandon it and crawl up the creek bed. When the babies came, they were dead.

The next day the people of the Forbes colony went to Trinidad to bury the stillborn twins. They left Emma and a woman to sit with her in the tents. It was then the militia came down out of the hills. They stormed into one of the abandoned tents, broke open a cupboard and made themselves a breakfast of ham, eggs, bread—the kind of meal they had not eaten in a while. Then they set to work cutting the guy lines of the tents and scattering the goods. One of the soldiers came into Emma's tent and asked who she was and what she was doing there. She told him about the twins and he said that in that case they weren't going to tear her tent down, they'd just light a match to it. Just then another militiaman stepped in. "I'll kill you before you hurt her," he said. "She's there sick in bed and they're burying her twins. You're not going to hurt her." Emma always remembered that boy. For a long time she said prayers for him.

Up in the hills Lou Dold was watching it all. He had a view camera with a telescopic lens and every time he took a picture he'd hand the plate to Hainlon to put away. Later they went into the colony. They posed the people outside the ruined tents, standing in the snow. Among them was their neighbor, Old Man Johnson, a bearded veteran of the Civil War who had survived Andersonville only to look on this spiteful little operation in Colorado. In the photographs the men stand with their hands in the pockets of their coats, cold, looking mutely at the wreckage. Amid the tangle of bedding and broken goods a couple of kids chew numbly on sandwiches. That day the sheriff arrested sixteen of the Forbes men for the murder of the scab. Subsequently, three more would be jailed. Among those they brought in was old John Ure, who had lain under his bed that October while the machine gun bullets of the Death Special riddled his tent.

There is a sort of irony that backs up in the throat, as if the events themselves wished to mock their telling. In the night, while the people of Forbes desperately tried to find some shelter from the March snow, the militia had its final Grand Ball in the Cardenas Hotel. You can read of the ball in *The Great Coalfield War*, George

Now, they had some tents here in Forbes . . . and they had just set up their tents and it was cold—I think it was snowing. . . . They come rushin' down here and tore the whole tent colony down. And I was right here by it with my camera. I made these pictures. —Lou Dold. Forbes tent colony, destroyed by the state militia. Courtesy of the Library, State Historical Society of Colorado, Dold Collection.

McGovern and Leonard Guttridge's account of the strike. After the bugle calls, the pomp and the pageantry, the band played the last song. It was "Home Sweet Home." Then the musicians put their instruments into their cases and the officers escorted their ladies out of the darkening hall.

On the nineteenth of March Billy Diamond led a union group to Forbes to put up the tents. Linderfelt stopped them. Five days later Lawson went out with another group, and he too was prevented from rebuilding the camp. To make sure the union got the point the militia left a detachment of men camped on the spot. There are photographs of the attempts to rebuild the colony. You see in them militiamen standing in front of the half-raised tents with fixed bayonets, pushing people back. While the militia went about its work Lou Dold snapped away from the back seat of a touring car. One of the soldiers came up to him and asked him what he was doing. Dold had his view camera and the Graflex hidden in the car. He kept a Kodak on top of the seat as a blind—if they were going to take anything, let them take the Kodak, it didn't amount to much. "We'll get you too," the soldier said. Dold went back to Trinidad with Hainlon and developed the shots and sold them as he always did. It was only when the strike was nearing its end and the federal troops had replaced the militia in the south that he got a letter saying that his friend Hainlon, who was always so helpful, so ready to run for a cup of coffee or sell his prints, had been a spotter for the C. F. and I.

On the fifteenth of March Mother Jones was released from the San Rafael Hospital. The union had not ceased its clamor in her behalf, filing writs and exploiting her confinement in its propaganda. Doctor Beshoar had tried to see her, was refused as he knew he would be, and overnight garish cartoons blossomed on union pages. Once Pearl Jolly had taken a room next to the old woman in the hospital in what the militia insisted was an attempt to smuggle her out. Mother Jones had become a profound embarrassment to the officers of the National Guard. They sent her to Denver under escort with orders not to return to the strike zone. But on the twenty-first she was on her way back and was arrested outside Walsenburg on the train she had shared with detective Billy Reno all the way from Denver. They took her to the courthouse and threw her into a cell. It was the same basement room from which they'd taken Kostas Markos that January to die.

In her autobiography Mother Jones writes of that dank, freezing jail. She tells how she fought off the sewer rats with a beer bottle and how she watched the feet of the people passing on the street above her through the cellar window; miners' feet in old shoes, soldiers' feet in government leather, the shoes of women, heels run down, the dilapidated shoes of children, boys with their feet bare. The children would scrooch down and wave to her, but the soldiers would run them off. She stayed until the sixteenth of April. She had managed to smuggle out an incendiary letter, had given endless copy to union propagandists, and had raised a legal storm that was on the verge of blowing her into the state Supreme Court. General Chase had had his belly full of her. There was little more she could do.

In the meantime Louis Tikas had come back to Ludlow. Pete Katsulis says he had stayed out four or five days; it was probably longer. Now Tikas' skills as a peacemaker were badly needed in the tattered camp. For the remnants of the militia were even more bent on driving the hungry and ragged strikers from their tents than before. On the twelfth of March, General Chase issued an order stating that 450 militiamen still in the field would not be sent home "because a clash between the militia and the strikers is expected." The expectation, it seems, was manufactured by the militia itself. That same day twenty-odd cavalrymen took up skirmish positions just over the rise on the Ludlow plain. When the westbound train pulled into the depot, three of them rode their horses down and charged up on the platform, knocking people about, trying to provoke them into retaliating. On the twenty-eighth of March they were back again. Race tensions between the black strikebreakers and the bullying company gunmen had finally boiled over in Hastings. A scab had emptied his revolver into Marshal Clint Robinson and the militia had used the excuse to search the Ludlow camp, pushing people out of the tents, breaking open their trunks and floors. Lawson and Fyler and Louis Tikas worked desperately to hold their people back. It was about this time that John D. Rockefeller, Jr., was preparing to testify before Doctor Foster's committee in Washington.

To the younger Rockefeller it was a test. His father, he thought, had been the best business witness there had been. He too must prove himself. This was not a battle between businessmen and their employees—he had no stomach for that. It was something finer and more essential: the fight for *the sacred right of an American citizen to decide for whom and on what conditions he will work.* So he went to Washington and sat before the Committee, bland, self-assured, answering their questions. He was well prepared. His father had been a master of the art of scrupulous silence; the son was ready to speak out. And when they asked him if he would stand by his decision not to unionize the camps even if it cost him all his property and killed all his employees he replied, "It is a great principle." He had done his duty as best he knew how, and would do it again in the same way. His conscience acquitted him. His father celebrated his testimony by giving him ten thousand shares of C. F. and I. common.

On April fourteenth John D. Rockefeller, Jr., sent a note to L. M. Bowers forwarding a pamphlet from the Industrial Department of the Y.M.C.A. He wrote, "It may be that it would be worth while to consider the establishment, in connection with the steel mills, if not of the mining camps, of a Young Men's Christian Association under the management of the Industrial Department." It was the first suggestion on the conduct of the Colorado Fuel and Iron Company during the strike he had yet made. It was during this same mid-April period that he turned down a request by Frank Hayes to meet personally that would be his last chance to settle the strike before the bloodshed to come.

While Bowers was considering what he should reply to his boss' thoughts on industrial Christianity, the last of the militia to be sent home was leaving the Southern Field in one final, drunken, mutinous spree. That same afternoon, April seventeenth, sixty gunmen from Segundo and Valdez marched along Commercial Street to the Trinidad armory, where Monte Linderfelt swore them into the newly-formed, company-subsidized volunteer force—Troop A. Linderfelt's own company, too, had been left behind to keep the peace—the most despised of all the military units, Company B, the yellow bands of Berwind Canyon.

> *Heraclitus somewhere says that all things are in pro-*
> *cess and nothing stays still, and likening existing*
> *things to the stream of a river, he says you would not*
> *step twice into the same river.*
>
> *Plato*, Cratylus

12. THE MEMORIAL WHEAT

Past Colorado Springs the land changes. The green, watered pastures and lush fields begin to give way to sagebrush and the dry, empty clarity of desert. You come to Pueblo, a snake of off ramps and signs advertising motels and the stacks of the steel plant releasing their smoke into the still air, and then it is desert once more, the endless monody of sagebrush and dry ravines and the mesas coming up one after the other out of the emptiness like drifting ships.

There is a memory I always carry with me on these desert journeys of those long rides of childhood through country such as this. It is in me like some oddly valuable box, which is both empty and a gift.

So I remember those long rides back. The family captive in the heavy car, myself roasting sullenly in the back seat beside my sister while the vacant landscape sped by; miles of parched sage and empty plateau, with here and there a few stunted cedars or piñon pines, a patch of stiff, cloudless sky above the crenelated bluffs, the shadow of the car hanging motionless from the wheels. In my mind these endless rides of childhood never have any destination, but end because finally they must, on the baked, drab main street of Price or Helper or Bingham Canyon. The towns were all the same. We sat in dark houses with linoleum floors and lowered blinds and the damp, heavy smells of cooking over everything. In these houses we were served preserves, a glass of iron-bitter water in which a spoon drifted. They spoke in Greek, a language of family secrets and the drone of the Orthodox service and the dull buzzing of old women in black. I fidgeted in dark

193

rooms where the thin, burnt odors of Sunday rose from the wicks floating in their tumblers before the dark icons.

Often the visits were part of the rituals of a death. Then we were
given the traditional spoonful of boiled wheat sprinkled with raisins
and powdered sugar and pomegranate seeds. In my parents' childhoods
the memorial wheat had been heaped up and decorated with silver shot
in the form of cypress trees and crosses. Now the wheat came back
from church sealed in little cellophane packets. Once, in the car going
home, I opened the packet and tasted the wheat. It was glutinous,
overpoweringly sweet. I never tasted it again.

We left the towns. When we did there was always in me, like the
taste of that bitter water, the thin taste of disappointment. As if there
had been something to read in those stifling parlors or behind the faces
of those empty false-front main streets, some revelation in those incessant returns. Whatever was to be read never came. We drove out the
same road we had come in on, down that same stunted main street with
its plate-glass windows that reflected only their own vacancy, the barren
false-front stores that were never romantic, as they were in the movies,
only shabby and poor, that pervasive sense that everything had stopped
there, that it was always Sunday. In Magna, Utah, under the drifting
smoke of the copper mill, there was a battered movie house marquee
that hung over Main Street and read, as long as I could remember,
CLOSED FOR THE SUMMER   BUY BONDS.

But whatever it was I was looking for could never be found on
those narrow main streets as they were, but only as they existed in
my mind. For there were names before there were towns. Price,
Helper, Bingham Canyon, Rock Springs—long before I knew the
faces of the towns themselves or could place them on a map, the names
had collected around them like an aureole the stories I heard at the
family table—my grandfather's terse and usually grim ones, my father's
wonderful arabesques, the accurate ones my mother was even then
collecting. It was all there, the history of my tribe, George Zeese and
Mike Papanikolas and Tsambasi the horse trader and Leonidas Skliris
and Big Nose Pete. The names of the towns held the stories down to
earth, kept them in order, like a necessary punctuation. Thirty years
later those names would be a passport. I would trace them with old
men whose lives had led them through one of the towns after another

in search of work or a place to settle down. But then, between the names, so full of meaning, so charged, and the towns themselves there was only a terrible disjunction, and in that gap, without my recognizing it, there was growing a mute and rootless nostalgia. There could never be, for me, some Proustian torrent of return. For the emptiness of those desert towns could only speak itself; it had no secrets to give up. After all, it wasn't to *my* streets I was returning.

Out of Walsenburg it started to cloud over. The summer thunderheads began to roll up over the mesas and send their shadows running darkly across the ground. When I pulled off the road at Aguilar the first cracks of thunder started. I went into a bar, had a beer, and asked around. "You must mean George," somebody said. "He's the only Greek around here." I looked up the name in a phone book and called him up.

He was a Euboean. His father had been well off, but there was trouble at home, and so he had come to America with his brothers in 1910. He'd been run out of Gallup, New Mexico, because he'd been suspected of being in the union. He'd come to Colorado after that. His wife was an American woman. Her father had kept a store in Aguilar and she remembered having to leave the town when the strikers had burned down the Empire mine after the Ludlow massacre. We sat on their front porch talking while the soft, cool rain pattered down. The old man's pale gray-blue eyes seemed dim and far away. He didn't know if he could help me.

"The first strike that was up here in Colorado was 1913," he said. "It was some time in November, I don't understand exactly, October, November, some time like that. Yes, I joined the union. I was down in New Mexico and I come to Trinidad. I was preparing to go to Florida. I was going to work in the sponges. I was a pretty good diver when I was young. So I was thinking of going there, but when I come to Trinidad there was about five hundred Greeks there in Trinidad. I meet another guy who stops us there, tells all about the strike, about the mines. We're going to win, going to make a lot more money. Go sooner back to the Old Country. So we stop there."

The rain fell. Now and then there was the distant boom of thunder. "I've forgotten a lot," the old man said. "Sometimes I can't even tell you what I had to eat last night."

The woman sympathized with me. She was shy, delicate. She must have been pretty as a girl.

"Sometimes," she said, "he goes on a jag and can tell you all kinds of things."

I asked about Louis Tikas.

"Yes, I remember. Well, he was a pretty good guy, good organizer. Was always rushing here and there to help the people. Especially the children, when there was the strike here at Ludlow. They burned two times the camps . . . When they start the shooting down here in Ludlow we was with a bunch of Greeks that was up in Walsenburg, and we went up to the camp—it was a camp town and it was called Big Fork . . . And down here there was fighting in Ludlow. That's where they killed Louis Tikas. There he went to protect the women and children and then they killed him."

We talked a while longer about the strike and the mines and how he had missed the Hastings explosion in 1917. The rain let up. I put my tape recorder away and he looked at me and asked what I would do with the tape and I told him about the book I hoped to write. Then he said, "Are you a good man?"

Driving toward Trinidad, I thought of the awful sameness of these interviews. It was as if the laceration of the past had simply broadened, and I knew nothing more, a few more facts, a name or two. I thought of all I could have asked the old man in Aguilar, but had not remembered to bring up. Maybe it didn't matter. In what little I was learning about Louis Tikas, it might have been that he was receding ever farther away from me. The road was still slick from the downpour. To the south the clouds loomed up black and moving. Except for the few sprinkles that now and then dashed across the windshield of the car, the rain had stopped. There would be more showers toward dusk, brief, sudden, drenching the sage and the piñon in the hills.

I turned off the highway at the Ludlow exit and drove down the gravel road to the monument. There was a picket fence around it and a few desert trees. On the gate someone had hung one of the dried-up wreaths from the Ludlow Day ceremony. This time I found the monument both ugly and touching. The miner shielding his wife and child looked like no coal digger who ever lived, a lump of stone carved to represent someone's idea, and empty as are all such ideas. I walked around to the remains of the pit where the women and children had suffocated and lifted the metal door that covered it. Then I walked down the few cement steps to the bottom. The air was stale, damp. I went back up into the light. Across the dirt road a windmill all at once started whirling wildly. A flock of mourning doves broke from the dry grass along the tracks, their wings whistling like shotgun pellets. The wind kicked up the smell of wet dust that meant the rain was coming again. And suddenly it was falling, the drops hard, big as marbles. The door of the pit fell shut behind me with a heavy clang. I took refuge in my car.

The rain stopped. I walked north along the tracks. Opposite the monument I could see a little depression in the grass where a water tank had once been. This is where Tikas and Fyler and the Italian were killed, running toward the colony across the road. Steam rose from the sagebrush, the smell thick and acrid. The sun was out, burning hot through the humid air the storm had left behind it. Grasshoppers sizzled in and out of the weeds like sparks. Behind a barbed wire fence was the shack that stood over the pump house and the deep well the women had hidden in the day of the massacre. It was boarded up, sealed. The young jackrabbits along the tracks were so shy they didn't even run when I flushed them. Someone remembered that after the tents had been set afire in 1914 the rabbits had started from their burrows and stood transfixed while the field burned around them.

I sat beside the concrete stanchions of the railroad bridge. It was sundown and the light was cutting through the gap of Delagua Canyon like a blade. I tried to imagine the women and children running up the arroyo in 1914, with the tents in flame and the bullets falling around them. But there was something shrunken and dry about this landscape that did not fit the landscape I had in my mind, that would not join with it. It was like the concrete stumps and broken shells of the coke ovens that were all that remained of the mines at Hastings and Tabasco and Berwind, a bare scratching on the surface of my imagination, that was all.

All at once there was the blast of a train horn. I scrambled down the cinders of the embankment. The engine had its light on, driving toward me and on to Walsenburg and Denver. As it passed it cut across the shaft of light coming down Delagua Canyon. The broken light rifled through the gaps between the cars and fell on the embankment and the waving grass like the blades of a reaper. Then the train was past. Only a trembling was left on the ground. It was perfectly hot and still. The blades of the windmill hung dead. A farm dog was up on his forelegs underneath it, lapping water from the trough.

I got in my car again and drove on. It was almost dusk. Once more I thought of the old man in Aguilar. And I thought of the empty landscape I had just left behind. The failure, I thought, was in myself, in my own weakness or faltering imagination or simple inability. In my notebook I had written down a dream I once had. In the dream I had gone to interview an old Greek. His house was covered by a strange sort of haze, as if it was shrouded in something like mosquito netting or thin muslin. A fine light, like powder, was falling over the porch and its white pillars. Inside the house there were many objects on the dark wooden tables, old photographs, memorabilia. I was aware that the old man had a secret. The secret seemed to fill the house. It pressed against the walls of the dream. Yet it did not reveal itself, and I was too awkward, too clumsy to extract it. The objects on the tables fell at my touch.

It was a long time before I understood that in the dream the old man was dead, and that while I dreamed I too was dead. That was the secret. My muteness was coming from my own grave.

As if in death he was more solid, more real, somehow, than he had ever been in life, his wounds were the most definite thing about him. When Bob Bolton went down to fill out the death certificate he listed Louis Tikas' occupation as miner, his birthplace Greece. He thought he was thirty-five years old. He did not know the name of his mother or of his father or their birthplaces. So Tikas lay there dead, without a parentage or a history, shorn of his real name, a body on a slab. Only the wounds were left.

One of the bullets had entered below the scapula between the third and fourth ribs. It had passed the left lung and the base of the heart and torn open all the vessels of the right lung and come out through the chest on the right side. The second had entered his right hip and had fractured a vertebra, then passed through the stomach and the right lobe of the diaphragm and out just in front of the seventh rib.

The third bullet, too, had entered through the right hip. It had lodged in the second costal cartilage, just below the skin. His chin was bruised and there was a contusion on his left hand, which he had raised to ward off the blow from Linderfelt's rifle stock. On the side of his head there was a scalp wound an inch and a half long, caused by a blunt object, which had laid bare the bone. He had died of internal hemorrhage.

Detached from the man himself, the wounds floated free. I did not even know where the man was buried, as if there was not even some final dust to cover his broken remains with. I squatted in the basement of the funeral home going through the old ledgers. Maybe in burying Louis Tikas I could give him what in his life he had not had for me—a sense of solidity, a purchase on history. On page 107 of one of the ledgers I found the entry:

No. 191_____   Louie Tikas

	Ludlow
street address	city or town

Age 30 yrs_____ mths_____ ds.	Date of Death April 21, 1914	occupation coal miner
Place of Burial Trinidad, Colo.	Date of Burial April 27, 1914	Cemetery K. of P.
Time of Funeral 10 a.m.	Place of Funeral chapel	Clergyman Greek Priest
ordered by		Charged to U.M.W. of A.

Now that I'd found what I'd come looking for, the thin elation of discovery gave way to a sort of disgust. In the room there was a narrow bed shoved against the wall and an old table with a plastic cover. I wondered who it was who slept on that poor bed and ate on the table. Some absent watchman of the dead who could not see me here pillaging his account books. On the shelf above the ledgers were old bottles, dusty faintly obscene. One had a label on it: "tissue rebuilder."

Here, in this morgue, that image I had carried so long in my mind of that lifeless young Greek was turned into something foul by the dress of death. It was as if history was some species of necrophilia: I was scavenging in his remains. And yet there was a fascination in taking everything in the ledgers down, and something necessary, too, as if this very banality was what had to be swallowed . . .

Casket	size	30.00
Grave vault		5.00
Embalming		. . . . .
Cemetery		10.00
Cemetery expense		5.00
Hearse	color	10.00
Carriages	3 at	15.00
Bearer's coach		. . . . .
Suit		5.00
Dress underwear		1.50
Clergyman		. . . . .
Services		10.00
Flowers		. . . . .
Candles		. . . . .
Gloves		1.15
Extras		. . . . . $40.00 Deductions
Total		
		92.75
		Headboard __✔__

That was the final indignity of death, that gross materiality, those columns of figures that didn't add up. Stamped over the bottom of the ledger was a final entry:

	MDSE	42.75
	Cemetery	13.00
(Sexton)	Services	10.00
	H.	8.00
	Livery	15.00
	Expenses	88.75
	Sundries	. . . . .

I copied down the figures and went out of the mortuary blinking in the sunlight. On the front porch I shook hands with the owner, who was running for county coroner and wondered how many others would grasp that bony hand in the course of the campaign. I felt relieved I was only a tourist. I carried my notebook to the car like a dog making off with a bone.

Mrs. Gertrude Bebout had a program. She repeated the phrase, since I hadn't understood it the first time. "I have," she said, "a program." Then she explained it was a television program she meant, some continuing series of domestic heartbreaks and bad news which she and her friend watched daily, religiously. I stood over her dining room table while she spread out the cemetery records. A large woman, full of sass. She had inherited the keeping of the cemetery after her husband died. The Knights of Pythias, she informed me, had let the place go to hell. It was called (was the name of her own invention?) the Sheltering Pines now.

She got out the plot map and together we looked at the record of the dead and their narrow real estate, those little rectangles of ground inked in with their plot numbers and their names. Foreigners, most of them—Slavs, Greeks, Orientals—who had probably left behind little more than that few feet of earth and their names in Mrs. Bebout's book. Some hadn't left even that. One complete row was marked in the record only "Jap, Jap, Jap."

After Mrs. Bebout's program was over I returned and we went to the Sheltering Pines, following part of the route the funeral cortege must have taken on the April morning of Louis Tikas' burial. We passed the tracks and the thin, muddy trickle of the Purgatoire, then drove out to the ridge and the little patch of grass up against the raw dirt of the mesa. When I got out of the car Mrs. Bebout warned me away from the weeds at the edge of the cemetery where she'd heard rattlesnakes chattering a few days before. At Block 3 – 39 E ½ Lot 42 there was only a flat stretch of smooth grass. I had not expected anything else. If Louis Tikas ever had a marker it was some temporary cross that had long since disappeared. Somewhere below me his bones lay, that was all I knew.

In the Sheltering Pines the corpses were crowded together in their little districts of the dead as in life they had crowded together under the tipple or the mill in their Greek Towns and Bohunk Towns and

Little Tokyos. I walked among the graves, spelling out, letter by letter, the names of the handful of Greeks. There was a date of birth, a date of death, maybe the name of some district in Greece from which they'd come. Some of the other stones, the ones carved in the Cyrillic alphabet of the Bulgarians and the Slavs or the characters of the Japanese, told me even less. I came to a row of stones that must have lain over South Slavs. I could tell by the identical dates of death that these were men who had been killed in the Hastings explosion of 1917.

Mrs. Bebout talked about the strike. She'd been just a girl, but she remembered the strikers who'd been burnt out of Ludlow living in temporary shelters near the tracks. There was one family who had a dog they couldn't keep and they gave it to her. It was a yellow St. Bernard puppy. She loved that dog, and it had come out of the Ludlow massacre. She remembered the militia, too. There were all kinds of stories about them. "Do you want to hear rape stories?" she asked.

That night I lay in bed in the Oasis Motel in Raton, New Mexico, watching without much interest the House Judiciary Committee arguing the articles of impeachment on an ancient black and white *Airline* television set. Above the set was a cheap tapestry the dark Italians who owned the Oasis must have put there. In the tapestry John Kennedy was looking past the flag flying in the nubby blue sky above the White House to the dome of the Capitol. I thought of that other president whose fate was being debated in the crackling static of the set, and of those dull, petty men who surrounded him—they were less real to me than Mrs. Bebout's soap opera. The faces of the Committee swam up to the television screen, dim and gaping, like fish bumping against the sides of an aquarium. It was as if they were trying to nose dumbly into history.

History—the word itself was slippery. Was it those earnest, gaping faces in the murky waters of the television set or the endless repetitions of some soap opera or the frozen sentiment of the Italians' tapestry on the wall? Or it might be some empty model of a past tricked out in charts and graphs floating off in the airless prison of a library reading room. But for me the terrible fear was that, after all, it was only a specialized form of nostalgia; that under the flimsy partition of the past it was only the meaningless and empty present gnawing into consciousness like a blind rat chewing in a wall. Lying there, I knew that what had come on me was a kind of accidental misjudgment: I had turned back once, and now, in the darkness, I was trying to find my way out.

When I got back to Denver I called up Mike Livoda. I remembered the first time I'd met him he'd been on the phone bawling out the president of his local. Now he was recovering from an eye operation. I spoke into the receiver wondering how much of him was there to hear me. "Hey Mike," I said, "I hear they can't keep a good man down." He said he'd heard that before himself and guessed it was true. He was out of bed shaving himself the day after they'd opened him up. I told him I'd been to Trinidad and he said he'd been down there not long ago himself, burying his sister-in-law. He too had tried to find Louis Tikas' grave, but had come up empty. "What the hell kind of cemetery you run here?" he'd said to Mrs. Gertrude Bebout.

I buried myself in the library. I was not even sure what I wanted. Surely it wasn't some balanced and general view of the strike, or even, exactly, a sense of the role of Louis and the Greeks. I listened to those spectral voices on my tape recorder, straining to hear if out of those faint lines of static there might emerge some word, some hint. And I was forced to face something I had not wanted to think about: that in the fading memories of those old men I might miss some shred of information, some vital word, and that would make all the difference.

"Tonight I learned an interesting thing," I wrote in my notebook. "This history will not exist until I write it. Until then it is a blank, a zero. And if all those old men die before I record their words, their memories of Louis Tikas, then Tikas himself will not exist—except in a few dry words in the textbooks and those photographs." But it wasn't history in any sense I could name that I meant by that word, nor was it the linked pieces of a life, Louis Tikas' life, laid out whole from beginning to end like some fish on a plate. There would never be enough pieces for that, I knew, nor would that be important. The old men were dying. With each mouthful of breath, with each gesture of the hand, they were receding from their lives, moving off into the ranks of the dead, who were nothing but their stories. The thing I was searching for was in those dying voices; it may be in their very halting.

It welled up in the silence of those few poor photographs Louis Tikas had left behind.

And yet, now and then, I did catch a glimpse of it. I found it in those odd, ephemeral details which popped up at random in the words of those who had lived through the strike, details whose very insignificance put them out of the reach of dissolution—Louis Tikas' puttees, the way Mike Livoda had squatted over the stock of his rifle, Mary Thomas' nickname "Goldie"—all this time, which pounded everything else down into mere chronology, could not account for; nor could myth, with its terrible appetite for stasis, devour. The details existed in two moments, the moment of their happening and the moment of their rediscovery. Between those two moments, like flecks of energy for an instant passing by each other on the spiral of history, some necessary spark had gapped, the moments had merged and fulfilled themselves. And that was beyond mere nostalgia. One night, preserved somehow in a sixty-year-old document, I found mention of a yellow St. Bernard running terrified among the embers while the tents of Ludlow burned. I had swum into the disaster of history and come back with Mrs. Bebout's dog.

The old ceremonies fall away. My children will never know the towns of my childhood returns, or the taste of the spoon in the preserves, or of that iron-hard tap water or the taste—too sweet to bear—of the memorial wheat. Such things may not be passed on. It is as if memory was some thin and endless book, whose first leaves were always falling away for each new reader, or some Heraclitian river constantly bearing itself away from you, even as you flowed away from yourself. I think of the young Greeks in their tent at Ludlow at the end of the hard winter. Between us there is only the faint connection of a few moments of shared ritual, of the few dim tastes and familiar smells of nights such as those when I, like they, had waited for the ceremony of the Resurrection.

On Good Friday they had washed and cleaned their poor clothes. Perhaps some had fasted, though in that long winter there had been enough of fasting. Women would have kept them to the tradition, but here there were none of their own women, so each man must have done what he thought fit. Some of them may have gone by train to Pueblo or Denver to make the sign of the cross in front of the flower-covered bier and take the communion wine and bread. Here there was no church. And so they waited. They lay in the tents drifting off between sleep and memory, thinking of the bier, of the wine and bread, of what they knew. There were other things, hardly registered, yet marking them as well—the feel of a flap of canvas against an arm, the creak of a man's cot as he turned in his sleep—paltry things, yet history was weaving itself from such textures for them, from the things most ready to hand.

Would there be chanting in the morning? What about the lamb? Thinking of them there, I think of myself, and how as a child I stood under the dome of a Byzantine church on that same Great Saturday night, dizzy with the smells of incense and burning wax, an unlit candle in my hand. I, too, had left school on Good Friday to stand in a half-empty church under the cool, distant face of Christ Pantokrator painted in the dome, so different from the soft, womanly Jesus of the Americans. I, too, had crawled under the tomb with the other children. Now I waited for the instant when that single light would glimmer in the darkness of the Holy Gate and Christ would be risen. It is at this moment that I am nearest to those dead, anonymous men sleeping in the tent at Ludlow. But the moment cuts me away from them like a knife. The chants give themselves over, the light is lit. And from the sanctuary comes the cry: *Christ is risen from the dead. By Death trampling Death and upon those in the tomb bestowing life* . . . yet there is something in me too proud to bend or too bitter for consolation. One after another, the candles of the people are lit. They lift the empty winding-sheet above them and carry it in triumph around the church while the anthem of the Resurrection swells. And thirty years later, with the sharpness of the fast still souring my tongue, I know that it is just this moment that I long for, and for the taste of the memorial wheat and for all those childhood returns—of all that is intransmissible about history, of all I might have shared with those men asleep in the tents.

Let them sleep. Their breath expands in the air. There, on the edge of death, they are cleansed, forgiven. History is the surface of my skin.

But weeping he leaves them, goes apart,
And his heart was in chains, because he was a champion.
And when he came to his village, his eyes filled with tears
To see the houses still burning.

The Song of Daskaloyiannis

13. LUDLOW

Once again I am looking through the photographs. Fragments passing
in front of me, shreds of time caught and held as on a wire. A flag
flutters from a staff above a tent. Somewhere a birdhouse perches on a
pole. Improvised bleachers, exercise bars at the edge of the camp,
a washtub leaning against a tent door. The people of the colony are
here, too, posed beside the canvas walls of their temporary homes or at
their tasks: a couple of greasy immigrants clowning for the camera,
carving up meat in the commissary, someone heaving a shot put, outside of one of the tents, a black man with his seven kids, a baby lying
in a rubber-tired buggy. Scribbled in pencil on the back of one photograph, in Lawson's hand, "Sent to HQ for report on camp conditions."

Now tintypes of the big storm. Ghostly figures lifting their arms
above the drifts. Stovepipes covered by the snow. A package of
Kodak shots. Men building a human pyramid, posing on the ball
diamond. Do I see Louis Tikas in this picture, standing in the midst of
a group of men, his hat off, hair parted in the middle? Another group
of men—are they playing *boccie?*

Around the photographs, unseen, there stretches a mental topog-
raphy, all the camera hasn't captured. The railroad tracks and the
county road that separate the colony from the conical tents of the
militia, behind the colony the deep arroyo and the steel bridge. The
pump station and the Lowe's little boxcar house, the deep, covered
well with the rickety steps leading down in stages to the foul-smelling
water. East of the Lowe's, Frank Bayes' ranch. South now to Ludlow
station with its depot and the few false-front stores and rows of cars.

It was at this commanding point, the Cross-Roads, that the Ludlow tent colony was located. —Ludlow: Being the Report of the Special Board of Officers. . . .

Ludlow tent colony. Courtesy of the Library, State Historical Society of Colorado, Dold Collection.

Then the little rise of Water Tank Hill and curving away the tracks of the Colorado and Southern and the overhead bridge. To the west the flat mesa of Cedar Hill, Hastings Canyon, Delagua . . . I come to a shot of Ludlow colony. The camera hovers above the camp as if mounted on a railroad car or a water tank. People are standing in little groups among the tents. There are a few patches of snow. The shot is labeled April 20, 1914. The heart catches.

On the eighth of April Helen Ring Robinson came down to the Southern Field. She was a handsome woman, something of a celebrity, the only female state senator in the country. She had come down to investigate the strike situation and to work up an article for Hearst's *New York American*. She talked to one of Governor Ammon's appointees who had been sickened by what he'd seen of the militia's brutality and told her he wished he had a few dozen well-done bombs to throw at the right people. In Pueblo she talked to C. F. and I. manager Weitzel, a man who impressed her with his fine courtesy and high ideals—in certain directions, she was quick to point out. She went through Trinidad's red-light district on West Main. And as she toured the dreary camps and bleak collieries, she kept thinking about that earnest young man in the East who had just testified to the Congressional Committee. She didn't see a bathhouse or a recreation center or a dance hall in the camps. Only the company saloon and the burning piles of slack and the workings of the mines. And she thought how blandly Rockefeller had said he had done nothing to end the strike, how he had left everything to his officers. One phrase in particular stuck in her mind. He had said his conscience entirely acquitted him in the case.

She went out to some of the tent colonies. She found the people pretty comfortable and, it seemed to her, rather happy. Spring was coming on, and, so she later reminded the Walsh commission, it came on very beautifully in the mountains of Colorado. She found in the camps, among the women, but especially among the children, that the long winter had brought the twenty-two nationalities of the tents together in a rather remarkable way. But there were other things moving below this surface harmony. There were many in the camps, she discovered, who still remembered bitterly the 1903 strike with its brutalities and forced deportations. When the militiamen came by, the angelic children of the tents would turn instantly into little fiends, shouting at them, calling them scab-herders, Tin Willies. Senator Robinson had planned to spend a week in the South, yet she could not get over the idea that the whole thing was being staged for her particular benefit by the strikers, by the operators, by everyone. She left after two days, still uneasy and feeling she hadn't gotten an impartial look.

But still she could not get over her need to know the truth. A week later she was back, and this time told no one she was coming but a friend in Walsenburg. She went out to the colonies again and what she found she could only describe as an atmosphere of dread. She talked to Fyler and Tikas. The men did not say much to her, but the women told her they thought something was going to happen. They took her into the tents and showed her the pits where they were going to hide in case of an attack by the militia. She could not say why, but the feeling was present that an attack was imminent. It all seemed to center around Troop A. Troop A—that hastily-assembled collection of mine guards and pit bosses armed and paid by the companies—which had been formed to take up the slack left by the removal of most of the militia. There were one hundred and thirty men or more, unorganized, without uniforms, scarcely drilled. Doctor Ed Curry was one of them, who in the bad days of the past October had boasted drunkenly in Baca's saloon that the company guards were coming down the canyon to wipe out the tent colonies. So was E. J. Welch, editor of one of Judge Northcutt's labor-baiting newspapers. The troop was under the leadership of an English soldier of fortune and music hall acrobat named Edwin Carson, who would later admit that he could not hold his riffraff command to any sort of discipline. And in Berwind Canyon there were still the thirty-four men of Linderfelt's Company B —the hated yellow bands. Linderfelt himself had been relieved and was to be sent out of the strike zone "recruiting." But he had stayed on in the South, nursing his anger at his superiors and the ragged foreigners in the tents.

It was Saturday, April eighteenth. At Pocantico Hills the elder Rockefeller was practicing his putting and whacking drives for the amusement of his grandchildren. He called to one of his workmen and told him to stop what he was doing and put on a uniform to caddie for him. In the tent colonies it was payday. That morning, while Louis Tikas was in Trinidad, the militia had booted a striker off the platform at the Ludlow depot. A crowd swarmed out of the tent colony, excited and angry. Jim Bernardo and Gus Weinberg and some of the other leaders stood on the platform stirring them up. Bernardo said they would show Rockerfellow and a few others that they were not dead presently. In Walsenburg Senator Robinson was given a reception by the Democratic committee. The atmosphere was desperate. She talked to young men, sympathizers of the strikers, who had been turned down for service in Troop A. She understood something— no one said what—was going to happen about Thursday.

Now it was Sunday, April nineteenth. What was foremost in the minds of most Americans was not the ugly little standoff between mine owners and half-starved immigrants in Colorado. For days the newspapers had been filled with the posturings of diplomats and politicians around the insults offered to our pride in revolutionary Mexico. Woodrow Wilson had given the dictator Huerta an ultimatum that he must order a salute to the flag fired by 6:00 P.M. that evening or face reprisals. And so the country waited, quick with anticipation that flowed like a current through a naked wire. And in that ragged little cluster of tents flecking the prairie at Ludlow the Greeks were having their Easter.

The Greeks had been determined to have a better Easter than the Catholics. They had planned their celebration with care. Gus Papadakis came down from Walsenburg for the day. He remembers they put a lamb on the fire, bought a couple of barrels of beer. And they had come up with a present for the women—something so outlandishly American that it wildly amused these oriental bachelors: gym bloomers. So that morning, while the country perched on the edge of war and the lamb roasted over the coals, there was a ball game at the Ludlow colony. It was the women who played, dressed in their new bloomers, while the men hooted and razzed them. At about one they all went over to the Greeks' for dinner. No doubt the lamb was stretched pretty thin on those plates, but it was Easter dinner nonetheless, and after they ate, Louis Tikas, dressed in his Cretan *vrakes*, took pictures of the women in their bloomers—five different ways, as they remembered it.

Then they went back to the diamond and played another game of ball and this time the men played the women, and it was the men's turn to get hooted; what did they know about baseball, this bunch of Wops?

It was then that four militiamen came up, Patton, Martin, Finn, and Zimmer. One of them was mounted. They had their rifles with them. The soldiers had often come to the ball games before, but they had never brought their guns. Maggie Dominiske thought to herself, "They are going to try to start trouble."

They started to jaw each other, and the women started in on the soldiers. A man in a straw hat and overalls went up to Martin and Zimmer and stretched out his arms. "If you want to shoot me, shoot me now," he said. "This is the best chance you will get at me." Everyone roared. And then the women started up again. Pearl Jolly said, "If we women would start after you with BB guns you'd drop your rifles and run." Maggie Dominiske turned around, laughing, and Patton, the man on the horse, looked at her. "Never mind, girlie," he said. "You have your big Sunday today and tomorrow we'll get the roast." Maggie laughed again and the man on the horse said, "It would only take me and my four men to clean out this bunch." Then Corporal Patton said it was stable time and they went off.

That night there was a dance in the big tent. The camp band fiddled away and some of the more adventurous strikers tried out the rag dances that were just then being denounced from serious pulpits. Did they dance then, the Greeks, flying through the air as Mary Thomas remembers them? I like to think so. As for Louis Tikas, he was busy with other things than dancing that night. The militiamen who had tried to break up the ball game had come back. They hung around the tents, moving back into the shadows when any of the colony officers tried to approach them. Someone heard a rumor that they were trying to blow up the camp.

Joe Dominiske came to the dance and told Maggie she and the children had better go home. They set out the camp guards. At the depot Zimmer and Martin and the others found the fight they'd been looking for all day and beat up a few of the strikers. Martin, at least, would be remembered for that on the morrow. Sixty years later Mary Thomas remembered a man beaten at Ludlow that night. She said it was Louis Tikas and that it was because of Pearl Jolly that the soldiers attacked him. But I think her memory misled her. For if Tikas was beaten that night surely there would be other mention of it. There is another story, too, of Tikas on that Easter evening, passed on from mouth to mouth until it has become distorted like the whisper in the children's game. Years later it was said that on that night Louis Tikas sat down to write a letter to the woman he was bringing from Greece as his bride. That there was a marriage on his mind was true, and it may be he did sit down to write a letter. But the wedding he wrote about—if he did—was not his own. His last night alive is as obscure as anything about him. And if he watched that night, or lay alone, it was hidden behind the canvas of his tent, which kept its own secrets.

Because there had been the dance the night before and they had been up late, Maggie Dominiske let the children sleep longer than usual on the morning of the twentieth. She got dressed and then thought she would wash, since it was Monday, so she put her water on the stove to heat. While it was heating she went to Mrs. Jolly's tent to get some postcards of the Easter they'd had in the camp the week before.

She found Louis Tikas in Pearl Jolly's tent. The three of them sat there awhile looking over the picture postcards of the American holiday. Over at the diamond a few of the kids were playing ball. The Greeks were still savoring the Resurrection, celebrating. Then someone came to the tent door and told Tikas there were four militiamen who wanted to see him.

He went outside and the women followed him. Corporal Patton and the three other men who had been in the camp the night before were waiting for him. They had a paper with the name of a man on it whom they said the strikers were holding in the tent colony. They wanted him now. Tikas looked at the name. He said he had no such man on his books.

Tikas asked him who gave him the authority to get this man— he understood the military authority in Las Animas County was no longer in commission. Patton was in no mood to argue. He told Tikas if he didn't produce the man by that afternoon the militia would search the colony. The Greek seemed nervous to Patton. He kept trying to get a look at the paper Patton hid in his hand. Tikas asked him if Hamrock was at the military camp and when Patton said yes, the Greek said he would like to speak to him. The four men of the detail turned back to the militia tents. Patton said roughly as they went, "All right. We'll be back again."

On the way back to Pearl Jolly's the women asked Tikas if there would be any trouble and he said no, everything would be all right.

At the military camp Major Pat Hamrock rang up Louis Tikas. Hamrock had been in command at Ludlow for only three days. He sat now in his tent with an old woman who did not speak any English and who didn't know anything except that she wanted her husband. Hamrock got Tikas on the wire and asked him if this man, Carindo Tuttoilmando, was in the colony. He said he was aware that the man wasn't on Louis' books for pay, but he wanted to see Louis if he wasn't busy. The two men had been on good terms. Hamrock trusted Tikas and took him at his word. But there was something agitated in the Greek's voice. Tikas said he didn't want to go to the militia camp, that he was afraid to go there. Hamrock told him he didn't need to be afraid today any more than any other day. And he ended with a threat. "You had better come over," he said, "or I will send someone to bring you over." Tikas hung up the phone.

Hamrock looked over at the Ludlow colony. There was a real flurry coming on. Someone was out there making a speech. Large groups of men were circling around him. He telephoned Linderfelt at Cedar Hill. He told Linderfelt that Tikas had refused to give up a man and that he'd sent for the Greek and might need some help. He told him to bring down his troop for drill. They would search the colony and see if the man was there. At the strikers' tents the crowd seemed to be very busy now. They broke and men ran from one tent to another. Hamrock called Cedar Hill again. This time he got Lieutenant Lawrence. He told Lawrence he'd better put the baby in its buggy and bring it along. The troop on the hill had just finished saddling up. Someone told Linderfelt that Hamrock wanted the machine gun. He hitched up a couple of mules to a wagon and they loaded the gun and ammunition. A few seconds after Hamrock got through talking to Cedar Hill Tikas rang him up. He said, "I will meet you at the depot if you want to see me." Hamrock said very well. He went off, taking the old woman with him.

What happens now has a logic of its own, and it is beyond the logic of those who participated in it and beyond their attempts, in the aftermath, to explain. So in the days afterwards, in commissions and investigations and documents, they would try to fix the blame. The people in the tents would ask why it was that Linderfelt was at Cedar Hill on that day and why he had put off leaving on the morning train. They would remember the threats in the saloons and in the camps and how Forbes had been destroyed and they would remember that ball game on Greek Easter and the omens of what would happen the next day. And the militia would remember too: the farmer who had moved his family out just before the fight, the Greeks who had warned their brother scabbing at the Ramey mine there would be an attack, and how the striker Snyder had said in the Ludlow depot that it was the Greeks who started it all, that they had planned it for Easter but got too drunk and put it off . . . But the memories were only partial, they canceled themselves, contradicted their own logic, and they did not add up to the event. Would the Greeks have told a man like Snyder, an American, who didn't even own a gun, if they had been planning something? And could he be held to what he blurted out in his anguish with his dead boy in his arms at the Ludlow depot? Linderfelt, too, would justify himself: had he been planning the fight, he, a professional soldier, veteran of so many skirmishes and battles, would he have waited all morning and not have had his guns in place to attack at dawn? Would he have had his wife with him at Cedar Hill? Or let the Greeks take up positions before he fired at them? Would he have exposed his men to such danger? And why were his men off tending horses that morning instead of mounted and ready to go? And the strikers: if it was their plan to start something why were the women and children in camp when the shooting began? Why did they not bottle up the militia in the canyons? Why did they give them a chance to send for reinforcements? But the violence was beyond such argument. Since the tents had been set out naked on the plain that fall there had been growing in the minds of the strikers and the mine guards and the militia like the germ inside the wheat an image of them in flames. It was as if, once having been thought, that image could not be pushed back down under consciousness. The strikers feared it and the guards and the militiamen wanted it with a violent urgency.

It entered even their speech without them willing it: *tomorrow we'll get the roast*. It was the logic of a dream trying to achieve itself. The tents had weathered and soaked all winter long. Now they hung dry as tinder from their skeletons.

There remains the question of that harried, nervous foreigner's voice coming over Hamrock's wire. Tikas, that cool man, that leader—now he was afraid. The men had seen their tents torn up again and again, their weapons confiscated, their small keepsakes stolen, their women insulted. They had vowed never to permit another search. Now they heard the militia was again coming and they were angry. Was it of this he was afraid—that he would not be able to hold his Greeks this time, that this time they would get away from him? Or was it something else, something he'd heard on a tapped line? The letter might have been a trap, some bait to lure him into the soldiers' camp and hold him. He had not been able to get a good look at the steel bridge south of the depot. And he wanted to see if the reports his men were bringing him about it were true. He got the Greeks together and told them he would meet Hamrock at the neutral ground of the depot and made them promise to do nothing until his return. Then he set out.

Hamrock and the old woman were waiting at the depot when he got there. Tikas recognized the woman and said he had had her husband in the colony Saturday night. He was a cripple, no good to the strikers and no good to the companies and he didn't want him in there. Next time he came through he'd kick him out. It was very Greek, this cruelty to the maimed. But Tikas was thinking quickly too: he did not want the colony searched. Hamrock was sitting on an upturned breadbasket while the Greek stood by a post explaining about the crippled man. Susan Hollearin, the postmistress, called across two or three times to Hamrock and asked if there was going to be trouble. Hamrock just looked at her. People going by the depot had told her about something that worried her. It was what Louis Tikas had observed for himself walking up to the depot and what Marion Derr was just now seeing.

Mrs. Derr had been washing her hair in her little house near the station when her husband came into the kitchen and told her to come to him and come quick. He wanted to show her something. He pointed up the Colorado and Southeastern tracks south of the depot and to the left of the steel bridge. When she looked she saw two machine guns near Water Tank Hill commanding the station and the tent colony, and soldiers hurriedly fixing breastworks around them. All down the tracks stood men with rifles. Two militiamen on horseback came galloping by from the direction of the steel bridge. They met another group of men, then all of them turned around and started back toward the bridge. As they passed, one of them, a Mexican, shouted, "Good, we're off."

Back at the depot Hamrock and Tikas continued to talk. Then suddenly Lieutenant Lawrence burst in, out of breath from a gallop across the tracks. "Major, my God," he said, "look at all those men with guns going over to the hill. We are in for it." Hamrock went out and looked around the corner of the depot. He saw a line of men running out of the tent colony to the east. They were armed. Already Tikas had started toward the camp. "I will stop them," he said. "Go ahead, Louis," Hamrock cried. "You have got to get busy." Someone coming up the tracks heard Tikas say as he ran, "What damned fools."

For the Greeks had seen the machine guns too. They gathered together and talked in a panic. There was a kid with them named Mike Lingos. He had been a mule driver in one of the mines and had smashed his fingers badly and been let go. He was still bandaged and would go out to fight that day firing his rifle with one hand. It was this moment he remembered. There were three of the Greeks who had been in the Balkan War. Now one of them, a tall Cretan, spoke up. "Listen boys," he said, "I just came back from the wars in Macedonia and I know how to fight. I know something about strategy. Don't face them directly. They'll turn their machine guns on us. Your plans aren't good. Let's go by the corner. We'll throw a few bullets over here at the corner to divert their attention . . ." They stood arguing desperately while the machine guns were being planted. They were afraid of the guns they could see and of something they only imagined: poison gas. "I'll shoot off my guns to attract the guards while you take the women and children away," the tall Cretan said. "Don't worry about me. I'll protect myself."

The Greeks set out for the railroad cut east of the colony where there was good cover in the weeds growing out of the sandbanks. There were maybe thirty-five of them, running, exposed. As they ran

Linderfelt's men on Water Tank Hill watched them. And they begged
Linderfelt for the order to fire.

After Tikas had gone to the depot Maggie Dominiske had returned
to her own tent with the postcards. She put the postcards in an envelope and sat down to address them. Her children were just out of bed
and weren't all dressed. She heard music outside and looked through
the window in the end of her tent. It was some of the Greeks still
celebrating their Easter. They had a mandolin, a flute, some kind of
violin. She had just gotten the envelope addressed and ready to send
when somebody called, "Look out for trouble! The militia is coming!"
She ran out to see what was going on. She met Mary Thomas who told
her they had better take their children to the pump station. Maggie
didn't think there would be trouble, but she told Mary to take her
children anyway and if anything did happen they would be out of the
way. Then she went to the front of the colony where the people were
standing. Mrs. Fyler was there with her husband, who was looking
through a pair of field glasses. Mrs. Fyler asked her husband if he had
seen their boy and he said he hadn't Then they saw Louis Tikas running toward them down the road. He was waving a couple of white
handkerchiefs above his head, signaling them. He hadn't reached them
when the first bomb was fired in the military camp. Now he was closer.
They heard him yelling at them to get back.

The bombs were a signal to the militiamen at Berwind and
Delagua. When Tikas got to the camp the second bomb was fired and
then the gunfire started. The people ran for it. Women rushed around,
grabbing their children, not knowing where to go. They ran out of the
camp, then turned in confusion and headed back to the tents. Some of
them kept going for the arroyo or the pump house. From the depot
Susan Hollearin watched a Slav who worked for her father ride off
on a wildly bucking colt. Charlie Costa ran by Maggie Dominiske
and she called out, "Charlie, be careful. The soldiers are all around
those hills." The Italian said they had to lead the fight away from the
tents or the machine guns would kill every woman and child in the
camp. Tikas waved his handkerchief at Maggie and Mrs. Fyler. "Good-
bye," he said. "I will never see you any more." Then Maggie's husband told her to run to her children and she did. She would hide in

the barn by the pump house all day while Mary Thomas and other refugees from the colony huddled on the stages of the deep well, pinned down by the militia's gunfire. It would be almost dark before the freight from Pueblo would pass between them and the militia, giving them a chance to escape to Bayes' ranch, pulling their terrified children up the arroyo while the militia's bullets fell around them.

Not all of them made it out of the camp immediately. John Bartolotti ran back to his tent to warn his wife and children of the militia. Husband and wife left the breakfast burning on the stove and dragged the bed out of the tent so they could get the children into the pit under the floor. There were two families in the pit, Mrs. Fyler and Virginia Bartolotti and their children. When the shooting started the bullets shattered the oatmeal pot on the stove and the big Fyler girl fainted so that John Bartolotti had to bring her to with sugar and wine. Then Mrs. Fyler said this was no place for them and the women and children ran to the pump station, ducking down the cover of the arroyo behind the tents. The Snyders kept to their tent. Snyder had no gun and for most of the day would hide cowering under his tent floor. Clorinda Padilla and Juanita Hernandez had only time to get into a cellar with their children when the signal bombs went off. So did Mrs. Tonner and Maria Czekovitch. There was another woman who remained behind. This was Pearl Jolly. Tikas found her and said if she wasn't afraid he wanted her to stay in the camp and take care of the women and children. Then he went to join his men.

From the militia camp Corporal Benedict watched him run into a tent and come out with a rifle and field glass. Then, through his own glasses, Benedict saw the Greek wave his hand toward the north and start off in the same direction at a run. Hamrock, too, was back in the militia camp where he was trying to get a message through to General Chase. As he waited for his telephone connection he watched the people running from the colony. It reminded him of a picnic party, everyone carrying baskets and blankets, running as if they were trying to catch a train.

Where the first shot had come from would never be known. It may have been from the Greeks running along the Colorado and Southeastern tracks or from the militia or from that lone Cretan who had gone off to draw the soldiers' fire, for someone near the bridge behind the tent colony was peppering the military camp, forcing Hamrock to duck behind the cover of a string of railroad cars and causing a couple of soldiers watering horses in the pasture to turn their animals loose and run. But it was east of the Ludlow depot that the battle claimed its first casualty. The Greeks had tried to flank the machine guns on Water Tank Hill. Now they had taken up a position in the weeds of the railroad cut facing the militiamen strung out among the little knolls opposite them. Lieutenant Lawrence lay on his belly watching the strikers move along the tracks, directing his men's fire. He had just told them to watch their ammunition when behind him Private Martin called out that he was hit. Lawrence turned and saw Martin lying flat on his back with blood flowing from his neck. He stuck his thumb into the wound to stop the blood and dressed it as best he could. "Why are my feet in the air?" Martin asked. Lawrence told him they weren't in the air. "I would be all right if I could just move my fingers," Martin said. He told Lawrence not to make the bandage so tight, the bullet was choking him. Then he gagged as though he was trying to get his breath and said his feet were in the air and he could not move his fingers. There was a burst of gunfire from the cut and Lawrence's men were driven back. It wasn't until nine that night that Martin's body was recovered. Lieutenant Lawrence shined a flashlight on him and saw that both his arms had been broken and there were powder stains on his mouth. His face had been caved in by a rifle butt. When they tried to undress him his belt buckle was so stiff with blood they had to cut his trousers away with a knife.

In the colony Pearl Jolly had gone from tent to tent, looking to the women and children who hid in the cellars. The gunfire was coming irregularly now, a kind of sharp-shooting. The women asked her to put on a white dress with her red cross emblems on it and she was afraid, but she did it, pinning the crosses to her chest and arms. When she got out of her tent the militia took them for a target. She started to run. A bullet ripped off the heel of her shoe and at first she thought it had shot her foot off, but she kept going. When she got back to her tent she found four men lying on the floor—Louis Tikas, Joe Dominiske, Jim Fyler, and Jim Bernardo. They had gotten the telephone out of Louis' tent and were calling Trinidad, trying to get reinforcements. They asked Pearl if she would make some sandwiches. The militia must have caught her reflection in the big dresser mirror near the door when she went into the kitchen, for they started firing into the tent. She lay down, thinking they might imagine she was dead and stop shooting. The mirror shattered with rifle shot. After a while she got up and finished the sandwiches. She took them to the other side of the tent and again the militia spotted her and started shooting. "For God's sake stay away from here," the men cried. "You are a hoo-doo." They told her to take the crosses off her dress so she wouldn't be such a mark.

It was about eleven o'clock when John Lawson got to the battle. John Barulich, the automobile driver, the union paymaster Peter Gorman, and Mike Livoda started out with him. They had gotten Tikas' message. "We're coming, Louis," was their answer. At Suffield they let Livoda out to warn the little tent colony there then continued north. Outside of Ludlow the bullets were falling fast. Lawson heard them popping all around him but didn't see any dust kicking up. He ordered Barulich to stop the car and they all got out and lay down on the prairie. Lawson tossed a white handkerchief in front of him and the shooting got heavier. He saw he could not get to the tents so they got back into the car and turned around, then started for Bayes' ranch. They stopped at Bayes' and Lawson headed down the arroyo in the direction of the tents.

In the tents Tikas, too, had heard the explosive snap of the bullets. He had wasted a couple of hours with Fyler and Jim Bernardo running from tent to tent trying to find the damn fool who was shooting at the militia with a six-gun and drawing their fire—but it was no six-gun; the bullets coming from the machine gun were themselves explosive, crackling in the air as they sped through the camp.

When Lawson got down the arroyo in back of the colony he found his own men lined up behind the protection of the bank and stretched out in the rifle pits. He watched a group of women and children making their way up the arroyo to Bayes' ranch. They told him there were more in the colony but that they were safe in the cellars. Tikas came out of the colony and they talked. Then Tikas said he was going back to the tents. The two men embraced.

Somewhere in the colony a man was hit. Pearl Jolly tried to get to the dispensary but the militia's guns picked her out and she had to turn back. They decided that if Tikas could go ahead of her and unlock the door quickly she could get in and out with the dressings before the soldiers spotted her. But they got caught between the tents. They dodged behind a coal pile hardly big enough to hide one of them while the machine gun raked the ground a foot behind them. They lay pinned there for what seemed an hour. Then Snyder made his way up to them. He told them his boy was killed. The machine gun picked him up and chased him, and Tikas and Pearl were able to get away. About three o'clock the firing began to get heavier. The militia was shooting dogs and chickens—anything that moved.

By four o'clock the militia's reinforcements had arrived from Trinidad. There were eighteen or twenty mine guards and militiamen from Troop A, some other men from Segundo. They had no uniforms, were hardly under command. They got out of their train at Rameyville and commandeered an automobile to carry their machine gun. While they were loading the gun one of the men in the automobile heard Linderfelt order his men to fire at everything they saw. George Titsworth, Sr., the Segundo mine guard, asked him, "Do you want us to set fire to the tents?" "Yes, whenever you get to them," Linderfelt said. They moved the machine gun down to Water Tank Hill and planted it. Someone overheard one of the officers—Hamrock or Carson—say they had forty minutes yet before dark to take and burn the tent colony.

Some of the men from Trinidad worked their way up the tracks and began to move along the arroyo to the steel bridge. Captain Edwin Carson saw thirteen men run out of the tent colony and take a position farther along the wash. He called to them: "Don't fire, you damn fools, or I will fire back at you." He heard some foreigner yell back, "Oh you go to hell." Then the strikers began to shoot. Carson yelled again and the foreigner called back a filthy epithet and the shooting began in earnest. The Englishman could see other men beyond the horizontal bars returning his shots from a breastwork near the big tent.

About seven the first of the tents caught fire. The militia had gotten into the colony and driven off the defenders from the steel bridge. Linderfelt had come into the camp with an automobile and was busy loading it with ammunition from Lawson's headquarters tent. In her cellar Mrs. Tonner lay with her five children, heavy now with a sixth. She heard Cedi Costa crying, praying to Santa Maria, and begging Linderfelt not to kill her and her little children. She heard Linderfelt say, "There is no use in your crying and carrying on. We have orders to do this and we are going to do it, no mercy on any of you." A militiaman tore down the tent next to Mrs. Tonner's, then set a broom on fire with coal oil and touched it to her own tent. Gusta Radlich helped her get out. They grabbed the children and ran to another tent farther down. Tikas was there and he helped her into the pit underneath it. He threw water in her face to keep her from fainting.

Tikas and Pearl Jolly and the few men who had stayed in the camp had gone through the tents dodging bullets and searching from cellar to cellar. They had rounded up about fifty women and children and were trying to get them up the arroyo. They heard screams coming from one of the cellars and someone said there were still people in tent Number One. "You people had better hit it for that ranch over to Bayes," Tikas said. He told them he would go after the people in Number One.

There were five or six tents burning near the blacksmith shop. The militiamen had fallen back from the steel bridge and a handful of strikers hidden in the arroyo made a rush into the colony to put out the fire. But the militia drove them back with the machine guns. Now the gunfire from the militia became insuperable. Bullets exploded wherever they struck, going off like bunches of firecrackers, chewing the canvas sides of the tents to lace. The militiamen were operating the machine guns like hoses, swinging them back and forth in swaths.

In tent Number One Mary Petrucci was crouched with her three children in the cellar. The bullets had come so fast that she had shut the cellar door, but now she raised it and saw the fire moving like a stream across the opening. The tent was all ablaze. She clutched the baby to her and dragged the two year old by the hand while the four year old ran behind. Outside the tent she saw the militiamen by the water tank across the tracks. She was hollering and they hollered back and then they started shooting. Just in back of her tent was Number

58. She ran into it and saw the door of a cellar open and she hurried
the children down the earth steps.

Huddled together in the narrow cellar were eleven people—
Cedi Costa, Patria Valdez, Alcarita Pedragon, their children. Cedi Costa
and Patria Valdez were pregnant. Mary Petrucci said they were burning the tents and they'd better get out. Cedi Costa told her she had
better stay because it was safer in the pit and they could not burn.
The smoke began filling the tent. The children were coughing and
crying now. Cedi Costa pulled a cover over her and her two children
and Mary Petrucci asked her to give her some of it. Cedi Costa said
there was not enough for herself.

Now in the colony everything was in confusion. Militiamen
moved among the tents, spreading the fire, taking what they could.
Some of the tents were lifted off their foundations with explosions.
Snyder was hiding under his tent floor when the militia ripped open
the canvas and set it on fire. They pulled out his wife and daughter
and then the girl said something and they heard him under the boards.
One of them said, "You son of a bitch, get out of there and get out
God damn quick." He asked them to help carry the dead boy to the
depot and they swore at him again and asked if he wasn't big enough
himself. As he stumbled off with the boy on his shoulder and the girl
on the other arm George Titsworth, Sr., threw a gun on him and said,
"God damn you, you have fired as many shots as anybody, you red neck
son of a bitch. I have a notion to kill you right now." Carson and
Lieutenant Connor and Linderfelt went through the tents pulling what
women and children they found from the cellars. The women were
screaming, begging the militia not to kill them. Carson found himself
dragging a couple of kids away from the fire. A little boy was hanging
to his cartridge belt and wailing that he was not going to go, that he
had prickers in his feet. One of the boy's shoes was off. When Carson
stopped to bandage the prickers the boy let out a yell. His right foot
had just then been shattered by a bullet. And all the time the undisciplined troops were looting, clinging to that strange, useless junk that
in their excitement they scoured the colony for. Carson tried to make
them drop it. Most of them ignored him. He saw someone run off with
a suitcase, another with a suit of clothes. Somebody with an umbrella.

They gathered the cheap watches and jewelry from the tents. One of them wheeled off a bicycle. There was a big yellow and white St. Bernard dog circling the camp in confusion. Its head had been creased by a bullet and it was trying to pick things up from the ground. Finally it picked up a big piece of burning timber in its mouth and trotted off with the rest of the militia.

It was about this time that Tikas started back toward the colony. He had been with his men in the arroyo. They were almost out of ammunition and had decided to retreat to the Black Hills. Later on the strikers would say that Tikas had gone back to beg the militia to stop the shooting so they could put out the fire and save the camp. He was unarmed.

He was coming from the direction of the arroyo and the tent colony. Came up in that direction. It was dusk and I could not see him very plainly until he was fairly close . . . I waited until he came around the corner of the pump house and I told him to put up his hands.

Lieutenant Connor

R. J. McDonald, a military stenographer, and E. J. Welch, the editor of the *Trinidad Advertiser*, were walking back from the steel bridge. They had seen enough of the shooting that day and of the burning tents. Across from the colony, near the water tank, they heard a commotion and then someone came up out of the darkness and said that Louis the Greek had been captured and they wanted to hang him. McDonald said, "They don't need to hang him. Why don't they just take him prisoner?" Welch said it was none of their business. Linderfelt and Hamrock were coming up the tracks toward them. Welch told them about Tikas. Linderfelt was carrying a broken gun over his shoulder by the barrel. He said he hadn't let them kill Tikas or hang him, but that he'd spoiled an awful good rifle.

About twenty feet farther on the two men heard a fusillade go off and they dived over the railroad bank. Then they got up and started to walk back down the track to the depot.

In the Ludlow depot the militiamen stood around or lay on the floor joshing each other and bragging about what they'd done. They'd broken into the Snodgrass store and were eating oranges out of a crate. One of them said he knew he'd killed one red-neck at the bridge and would have to go down at daylight and try to get another one. They thought they had done a pretty fair day's work. Snyder was there, his dead son wrapped in a gunnysack, trying to comfort his weeping wife. Farber, the stationmaster, started to take up a collection for him. Juanita Hernandez and Ciorinda Padilla had been in the pit under their tent all day. The soldiers had dragged them out and taken them to the depot and now one of the soldiers was playing the accordion the women had seen him take from the tents. Someone else brought in a violin, a bunch of blankets. One man told about three dogs he had cut loose. Another came in from the colony with an American flag. He said he couldn't let it be burnt up. Some of the women were cursing the Greeks, saying they were the cause of the fight, that their husbands didn't want to go out. Snyder started to tell Linderfelt that the Greeks had planned the attack for their Easter but put it off, that they wanted to trap Hamrock while he was talking to Tikas in the depot . . . A man turned to him. "Snyder," he said, "I want to tell you something. It just depends who is present what kind of a statement you make." The Greeks had given the children in the colony a treat on their Easter. Susan Hollearin had helped take it up to the camp. Now she watched the militiamen coming back from the tents with their pockets bulging with it. After a time someone came in and said Louie the Greek had been shot. He knew it was Louie because he had a pair of leggings on and a pair of field glasses.

Charges and Specifications preferred against Karl E. Linderfelt, 1st Lieutenant, 2nd Infantry, National Guard of Colorado.

Article 58

Charge 1: Arson, in violation of the fifty-eighth (58) Article of War.

Specification 1, in that Karl E. Linderfelt, 1st Lieutenant, 2nd Infantry, National Guard of Colorado, did willfully and maliciously burn, or cause to be burned, certain tents or tent houses located in the county of Las Animas, State of Colorado, in what is commonly known as the Ludlow Tent Colony, said tents and tent houses being then and there used as dwellings, storehouses and offices in said

Ludlow tent colony, situate aforesaid, and being the property of sundry and diverse persons, being then and there engaged in a strike in said county of Las Animas and State of Colorado, said tents and tent houses being the property of other persons than that of the said Karl E. Linderfelt.

This at Ludlow, in the County of Las Animas, State of Colorado, on the 20th Day of April, A.D. 1914.

Charge 2: Murder in Violation of the fifty-eighth (58) Article of War . . . and that in consequence of said burning as aforesaid the life of Cedelina Costa was lost, the said Cedeline Costa being then and there a human being, living in one of the tents or tent houses, used for habitation, as aforesaid, in the aforesaid tent colony, situate at Ludlow, in the County of Las Animas, State of Colorado. . . .

(And of: Patria Valdez
And: Elvira Valdez
Mary Valdez
Eulala Valdez
Rudolph Valdez
Frank Petrucci
Lucy Petrucci
Cloriva Pedragon
Rogerlo Pedragon
Lucy Costa
Onafrio Costa
These last were children.)

Specification 15: that in the Ludlow Tent Colony on the 20th day of April, A.D. 1914, unlawfully, willfully, feloniously, premeditatedly and of malice aforethought, one Frank W. Snyder, a human being, did kill and slay

(And also: one Frank Rubino
one James Fyler
one John Bartolotti
one Carlo Costa
strikers.)

Specification 25: In that Karl E. Linderfelt, 1st Lieutenant, 2nd Infantry, National Guard of Colorado, at, to-wit; the Ludlow Tent Colony in the County of Las Animas, State of Colorado, unlawfully, willfully, feloniously, premeditatedly and of malice aforethought one Louie Tikas, a human being, did kill and slay.

Article 62

Charge 4:   Larceny, in violation of the 62nd Article of War.
Specification 1:   In that Karl E. Linderfelt . . . did feloniously take, steal and carry away three hundred and fifty (350) dollars of the value of 350.00 Dollars, the property of one Luis Tikas contrary to the statutes in such cases made and provided against the peace and Dignity of the State of Colorado and to the prejudice of good order and military discipline.

Charge 6:   Assault with a deadly weapon with intent to do great bodily harm.

Specification 1:   In that Karl E. Linderfelt . . . at, to-wit, Ludlow tent colony . . . having then and there a certain deadly weapon, to-wit; a U.S. Springfield Rifle, did then and there with said deadly weapon, with said rifle, unlawfully and feloniously commit an assault upon and against one Luis Tikas with intent then and there to commit to and upon the person of said Luis Tikas great bodily harm.

It appears that the civil authorities have preferred no charges against Lieutenant Karl E. Linderfelt and have taken no steps with a view of taking jurisdiction in this matter.

Lieutenant Linderfelt, you have heard the charges and specifications read—
Q. How do you plead to the 1st specification, 1st charge?
A. Not guilty.
Q. 2nd specification, 1st charge?
A. Not guilty. . . .
The accused, Karl E. Linderfelt, 1st Lieutenant, 2nd Infantry, pleads "not guilty" to all the specifications and all charges. . . .

They sat at the rifle range at Golden in late May 1914, Linderfelt, Hamrock, Cullen, Pacheco, the rest, giving their story to the Court-Martial.

Q. What was Tikas doing when you first saw him?
A. Approaching the pump house slowly and looking all around there, evidently reconnoitering.
Q. Have a flag with him?
A. No sir.
Q. Any emblem of peace on him?

A. No, sir. He evidently didn't know that our men were occupying the pump house and probably didn't know we were at the steel bridge.

Q. You never ordered at any time for your men to fire at him?

A. No sir. . . .

Q. Could you tell whether he had any arms or not?

A. No sir. I merely saw the silhouette against the burning tents.

Q. Make a good mark to shoot at?

A. Splendid.

Captain T. C. Linderfelt

When I got down to the road crossing, I hollowed "I have got Louie the Greek."

Q. Then what happened?

A. The crowd all rushed up to him.

Q. How many would you say were there?

A. Thirty or forty of them. . . . Monte asked this fellow where his guns were and he told him that he did not have any.

Sergeant Davis

I was down below south of the junction of the railroad and the road when someone hollered away up ahead they had Louis Tikas, and I immediately jumped up as did others lying along the track and we went up there and around Louis Tikas. I don't remember who had him in charge, but he had been captured near the steel bridge.

Q. Did you say anything to him?

A. Yes, sir, I talked with him. I said to Louis, I said, "I thought you were going to stop this. . . ." And Louis said something, I don't recall just what he said, and I turned away and the men were coming up . . . and the blaze from the tent colony was shining right on them, and . . . Louis said, "Well, we'll get all you scabs before morning." And I whirled on him and struck him with my rifle and he threw his arm up this way, and I caught him across here and the stock snapped off. I struck him too short. . . .

Q. Did you talk to him after that?

A. Yes sir.

Q. What was said?

A. I started to say, I said, "Yes, I heard that line of talk long enough, Louis," and he said, "Well, it was my fault," and the minute he said that all these men closed right in and they used about the same expression he used at me, and they were going to hang him, lynch him, shoot him, and started to, and I knocked up quite a number of guns and knocked one man down, and finally I went away . . .

but I will say about striking the man then, it was not fifteen minutes before I had heard from the extreme right they had got Martin's body and heard that from a wounded man as he was left he was found with his face turned up, his face beaten in with rifles and I heard it worse than that. . . .

Q. Why do you remember Cullen?

A. Because I turned Tikas over to Cullen.

Q. What condition was Tikas in when turned over?

A. What condition?

Q. Yes sir.

A. Standing up talking.

Q. A prisoner?

A. Yes, sir, a prisoner.

Q. Did you so inform Cullen?

A. Yes, sir.

Q. What instructions did you give him?

A. I told him to look out for the man, that I turned him over to him and that he was responsible for him. . . .

Q. What would be the duty of a soldier under these conditions if his prisoner attempted to flee?

A. Follow the instructions of a soldier.

Q. What are they?

A. Halt him and if he won't stop fire on him.

Linderfelt

We went probably fifty yards or more, would not know the exact distance from the cross road going towards the depot and the firing started again. It seemed as though it was coming from where it had been to the east, to the south and east of the colony. We jumped behind the track again, where we had been previous on the west side of the track. I looked around and saw nothing of the soldiers or prisoners, so I jumped behind the west side of the track and I started back to where they had been towards the cross road, a little to the rear of me, probably 20 feet the last time I had turned around, and as I came up on the track I saw three figures running towards the colony in the glare of the burning tents.

Sergeant Cullen

Q. Was it evident that Tikas was trying to escape?

A. Sure he was making that effort.

Q. Running pretty fast?

A. Yes sir, he was doing his best.

Q. You are positive he had gotten past the corrugated iron building?

A. Yes sir. He was near the telephone post to the right of the building.

Sergeant Davis

I saw two of them fall simultaneously and the third one a few seconds afterwards. He was up towards the store in the southwest corner of the tent colony. . . .

Sergeant Cullen

Q. I will ask you, Major, from your experience and your knowledge of rifles, what force would it take to break the stock of a Springfield?

A. It depends a great deal on the grain of the stock. How the grain runs. I have known Springfields to break when giving the order "arms."

Colonel Verdeckburg: Look at this rifle and tell us whether it would break readily or not?

A. It looks to me like there was a fault in that. I don't think it would take much of a blow to break that.

Q. Is that a knot, Major Hamrock, in the end there?

A. It looks to me like that stock had been cracked and it had been cracked for some time. You can see how the oil has worked in there from the oil through the stock. You can see that it is not a fresh break. . . .

Major Hamrock, recalled

And therefore after consideration of all the testimony introduced in the hearing of this case, the court finds the accused, Karl E. Linderfelt, 1st Lieutenant, 2nd Infantry, National Guard of Colorado of the

1st specification, 1st charge	Not guilty
2nd specification, 1st charge	Not guilty
1st specification, 2nd charge	Not guilty
2nd specification, 2nd charge	Not guilty
3rd specification, 3rd charge	Not guilty

. . . 1st specification, 6th charge—the Court finds the accused, Karl E. Linderfelt, 1st Lieutenant, 2nd Infantry, National Guard of Colorado, guilty of the facts so charged—that is to say, that part of Specification one (1) charge six (6) reading as follows:

"* * * having then and there a certain deadly weapon, to-wit, a U.S. Springfield Rifle, did then and there, with said weapon, with said rifle . . . commit an assault upon and against one Luis Tikas. . . ."

But attaches no criminality thereto. . . .
AND THE COURT does therefore ACQUIT HIM the said Karl E. Linderfelt, 1st Lieutenant, 2nd Infantry, National Guard of Colorado, upon
all the specifications and all the charges.

3:30 P.M. adjourned.

For three days the bodies lay near the tracks. The colony was in
ashes. Where the tents had been were only charred frames and twisted
bedsteads and the coils of springs, the dark forms of the heavy cast-iron
stoves. The day after the battle Frank Bayes and Pete Mellis had
climbed Bayes' windmill and watched through a pair of field glasses
while the militiamen went among the tents still standing and doused
them with coal oil then set them afire. The dead wagons had come out
from town but the militia had driven them off with machine gun fire.
It would be a while before they found the contorted bodies of the
two women and the eleven children suffocated in the pit under tent
Number 58. The railroad tracks were littered with shell casings and
the whiskey bottles left by the militia.

At the depot the militia was holding George Churchill and his
brother and a frightened Italian rancher who had come down in a
buggy and had tried to help them get away. The Churchills had been
playing ball in the big field when the fight started and had taken
cover in the cellar of the Snodgrass store. The militiamen forced the
Churchills and the Italian and a Greek they'd captured named Mike
Pappas to lug ammunition to the soldiers near the pump house. They
told the prisoners they wanted the cartridges to kill their Wop friends
with. The four men passed the charred remnants of the camp. Wash
was still lying in tubs or hanging from the lines. There was food in the
kettles on the stoves. The burnt frames of baby carriages were standing where they had been left the morning of the fight. Here and there
a flock of chickens was roosting in the embers. The camp dogs cowered
in the pits. George Churchill had a little water spaniel he was fond of
and it came up to him singed and burnt around the eyes but the soldiers
wouldn't let him keep it. They were shooting the dogs as nuisances.

They saw the bodies of Tikas and Bartolotti lying by the road.
The militiamen told them Louis the Greek came out of the colony the
night of the battle and begged for his life. They said at first they were
going to hang him but they told him to run and then they shot him.

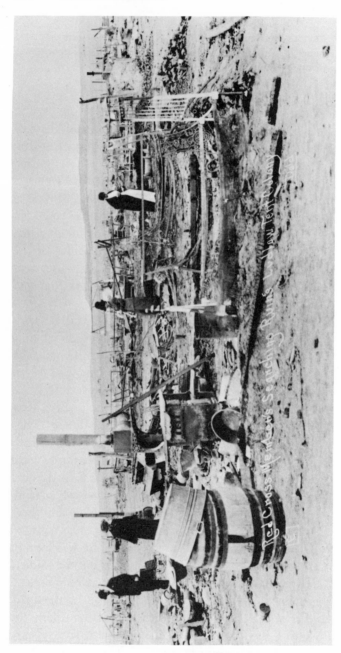

The tent colony, or where the tent colony had been, was a great square of ghostly ruins. Stoves, pots and pans still half full of food that had been cooked that terrible morning, baby-carriages, piles of half-burned clothes, children's toys all riddled with bullets, the scorched mouths of the tent cellars . . . this was all that remained of the entire worldly possessions of 1,200 poor people. —John Reed. Ludlow after the massacre. Courtesy of the Library, State Historical Society of Colorado.

They bragged that they'd shot Mrs. Jolly in the arm and someone showed them Fyler's watch and said Fyler had come out of the camp with a bag of money and a gun and they'd got him too. The four prisoners went back to the military camp and the soldiers made them haul coal and water, wash dishes, cook. They worked the Greek harder than any of them. They kept him up all one night and the next day without sleep. District 15 President John McLennan was there too, a prisoner. He'd been arrested when he tried to get into the camp after the battle. The militia told George Churchill not to talk to him but he looked so downhearted George Churchill did anyway when he thought they couldn't see him.

How Louis Tikas had met his death cannot be known. There are accounts by some who said they saw it—accounts other than those given out by the militia—but they are garbled, unlikely in their details. Deeply troubled, Philip Van Cise came down after the massacre to start his own investigation. The evidence he took was suppressed. In the report of the National Guard's special board of officers, Danks and Boughton and Van Cise agreed only that the evidence as to whether Tikas and Fyler and Bartolotti were shot trying to escape or after they had been made to run was conflicting. A year later, at the secret court of inquiry established by the new governor of Colorado to investigate charges against the militia, Van Cise testified that he had obtained a sworn affidavit from John Davis, a sergeant in Company B, stating that after Linderfelt had broken the stock of his rifle over Tikas' head, he had wanted them to hang the Greek but had been dissuaded. Then Linderfelt had started to walk away, but had turned and called out to his men "shoot the prisoners." And then the prisoners were pushed over the track against their wills and shot in the back. If Davis was telling the truth, or was simply working to save himself, was never put to trial.

Tikas had gone toward the burning tents knowing he would be captured. He had not taken his gun. His men had retreated up the arroyo to the Black Hills, and he knew that beyond the pump house there would be only the men of the state militia. Perhaps he thought he would find Hamrock there, that he could bargain with him, offer himself as a hostage to save the camp. He found Linderfelt instead and for the first time this cool-headed man lost his temper. It may have

Some one came in and said that Louie had been shot; he said he knew it was Louie because he had a pair of red leggings on and a pair of field glasses. —R. J. McDonald. Bodies of Tikas, in the foreground, and James Fyler at Ludlow. Courtesy of the Bancroft Library.

cost him his life. And yet I think even before he set off down the arroyo to the tents, in some manner he must have known he was going to his death.

Even in the photograph showing Tikas lying dead on the Ludlow plain there is something indefinite. He lies with his feet toward the camera while a handful of militiamen look from the ruins of the tents. You cannot see his head. Beyond him is the corpse of another man. The man is wearing overalls and one leg is doubled up under him as if he was shot down in the act of running. But the photograph has been so heavily retouched that it is impossible to tell if the figures were ever really there at all, if they were not simply painted over a blank space on the plate. And so the last clear image of Louis Tikas at Ludlow comes through the eyes of the man who might have killed him. Up on Cedar Hill Linderfelt looked at the dead wagon as it made ready to turn back to town. There were six bodies heaped up on it, five dead strikers and the mutilated Private Martin. He saw Tikas' feet sticking out of the back of the wagon still wrapped in their leather leggings, the shoes on.

> *Lord, give rest to the soul of Thy departed servant,*
> *Louis, in a place of brightness, a place of verdure, a*
> *place of repose, whence all sickness, sorrow and sigh-*
> *ing have fled away.*
>
> The Order for the Burial of the Dead

14. SURVIVORS

They packed the union hall in Trinidad, sleeping in improvised beds, going from the hall to the morgue and back again, asking news of their kin. Pedro Valdez had ridden the rods of the first freight he could catch out of El Paso when he heard something had happened in Colorado. He had come back to find them all dead—his wife, his children, all of them. It wasn't until she was in Trinidad that Mrs. Fyler learned from Mrs. Bartolotti that her husband was killed. In a window-less shabby corner of a Trinidad rooming house, Alcarita Pedragon lay on a dirty bed, still hacking from the smoke and trying to tell Evans of the *Denver Express* what had happened. It was hard for her to talk, but she told him how they had crouched in the pit and how, when the tent had caught fire, the children had coughed and cried and the women had tried to pray. The bigger children had tried to climb out of the cellar. They had taken hold of the burning floor, but their fingers were singed and they fell back on the rest of them. When the fire had died down she and Mrs. Petrucci had tried to drag their children out of the pit but the gunmen were shooting at them and they ran to the station. She had felt more like cursing than praying in that pit. She wished she had died with her little babies.

In a dark back room of the union hall the strike leaders were meeting—Lawson, Diamond, Bolton. The air was rancid with tobacco smoke. None of them had slept for more than an hour in the past two days and their tempers were on edge. Now they talked about a truce with Chase and the militia. The strikers had not waited for Lawson's "Call to Arms" to be published to fight back after Ludlow. At dawn on the twenty-second of April they had attacked Delagua and, moving

239

swiftly through the flakes of a spring storm, had burned the Empire mine outside Aguilar, driving thirty-five people into the shaft. The news of Tikas' murder had sped from coffeehouse to coffeehouse in the West. Thirty armed Greeks had marched over Raton Pass from New Mexico with flour sacks full of food and ammunition slung over their shoulders. In El Paso County two hundred men quit the mines. Seventeen of the Greeks there picked up their rifles and bought tickets to Trinidad. Frank Mancini of *Il Risveglio* had raised a company of a hundred Denver Italians and was ready to send them south. New York's Greek-language *Atlantis* received a telegraphed appeal for donations to the union from Stergios Mavroidis. Mavroidis said the strikers had been battling for three days in the mountains without food against the armed guards of the coal companies. On the streets of Trinidad knots of men stood about or sat on the curbs, unshaven, red bandanas around their throats, talking among themselves in their own languages while haggard women and children moved among them. There had been impromptu parades and much singing of the union song and vows to remember Ludlow. At the old San Rafael militia camp outside of Trinidad, companies of dark men in cartridge bandoliers were drilling on the parade ground, using wooden guns if they had no others. The Greeks had flown their blue and white flag from Castle Hall. When they moved their ammunition in, there was very nearly a riot. Through Hamrock's field glasses at his camp at Ludlow reporters could see the strikers in the Black Hills digging trenches.

At MacMahon's mortuary Lou Dold set up a camera. In the garish light of the magnesium flash he caught the bodies of Tikas and Fyler and Bartolotti and the Snyder boy propped up on boards. Cleaned now, the face of Frank Snyder showed only a bruise above his eye where the bullet had entered but the back of his skull had been blown away. Dold took a close-up of Louis Tikas showing what the union people said were heel prints on his face. A rumor was going around that the militiamen had cut off the Greek's penis and stuffed it into his mouth.

On the twenty-fifth of April they buried the women and children taken from the pit. While the bells of the Catholic church rang, Vic Bazanelle watched them loading the hay wagons with the caskets of the children and then he got his gun and went looking for General Chase. Two days later they buried Louis Tikas.

His coffin, covered with flowers, had headed the procession for the dead women and children. Then it was brought back to the mortuary to await the arrival of Father Paschopoulos from Denver. In the hall beside it were the bodies of two other Orthodox strikers, Nick Loupiakes and a Slav named Nick Tommich, who had been killed in the fighting outside the Empire mine. Frances Wayne, of the *Denver Post*, watched the ragged, weary men file by Tikas' body all day, their eyes glassy from lack of sleep. They touched Louis' forehead, then crossed themselves and muttered a prayer. Then they went off to the camp at San Rafael. On the twenty-seventh Father Paschopoulos, gray bearded, in a white robe shot through with silver and gold, prepared to chant the service for the dead. Frances Wayne wrote that before the service began four Greeks came into the mortuary and pounded four times with the butts of their rifles on the floor and vowed to avenge Louis Tikas. I have not heard that story repeated by any Greek and perhaps it is part of the legend that now, in death, began to harden around the man. Father Paschopoulos started the cermony. A Greek in overalls and corduroy coat chanted and swung the censer in front of the improvised altar. In some accounts, it was Tikas' rival, Pete Katsulis, who led the responses. Standing bareheaded in the cramped hall of the mortuary there were mostly men, a handful of women. They carried scented tapers in their hands.

There is a special pathos in all of this. Tikas had died unmarried. He had fathered no children to live after him, had continued no line. In the Greeks' eyes, he had died unfulfilled. Had this been the Old Country they would have buried him in the bridal crown and regalia of a groom, for Death was his bride now, the tomb his marriage bed. The laments the women would keen would be filled with these images of loss. And yet the death of Louis Tikas had been, in its way, a fortunate one, and the chants that rose up from that crowded hall were filled with the joy of rebirth. For Louis Tikas had gone to his death cleansed. He had died during the Bright Week of the Resurrection and, the tradition had it, even if he had not given satisfaction for his sins, in falling then he still had been granted pardon.

The priest anointed Louis' forehead and sprinkled a pinch of dust on it and kissed his cheeks. Then the congregation said "Christ is Risen" and the benediction was given. And they went out of the mortuary.

They filed up Main and into Commercial Street in a double line, almost five hundred Greeks following the dusty plumes nodding above the horses pulling the funeral coach, behind them two thousand others, men and women, silently marching. They passed the spires of the Catholic Church, the brewery, the *News* building. People watched from the windows and the sidewalks as the procession moved by. Some took off their hats for the flag, which was draped in black crepe. At a side street an automobile stood idling. A wagon waited for the procession to pass. In the photographs taken of this day the tranquil smoke of the brewery fades into a sky which is as hard and still as if it had been stretched on a frame.

At Camp San Rafael a couple of dozen men gathered in a ragged line and pulled off their caps as the hearse creaked by. The procession climbed the hill to the Knights of Pythias cemetery and then the marchers stopped and lowered the coffins into the red dirt of the freshly dug graves.

"Open O Earth and receive that which was made from thee," Father Paschopoulos chanted. He took a handful of dust and cast it over the coffins. Then he poured oil from the shrine lamp and scattered the ashes from the censer and the graves were filled up and the final hymns were sung.

Now, according to the Greeks, for two days the soul of Louis Tikas would wander over the earth with the Angels sent to accompany it. And since the soul had loved the body, it would hover over the place in which it parted from the flesh. So it haunts the site of the Ludlow camp, wanders like a bird which seeks a nesting place but finds none among those burnt cellars and scorched remains. On the third day the soul is brought to do reverence to God and is shown the fair abodes of the Saints and the beauty of Paradise. And after six days, Christ-like, it is taken down to Hell to view the torments of the damned. On the fortieth day it is brought to judgment.

The aftermath of the strike comes to me in fragments: mules shot down as they ran from the burning stable at Forbes, Greeks retreating

Balkan-style from the Rocky Mountain pit, Lou Dold telling the red-necks where they could find a bunker full of company explosives, the Japanese scabs burned to death in their shack, a striker banging wildly on a piano pulled up and down the streets of Aguilar on a dray while what was left of the Empire mine smouldered behind him, shattered tipples and twisted flues and dynamited tracks. And on the Hogback above Walsenburg a handful of strikers dug in among the rocks and holding off Colonel Verdeckburg's whole force.

I had talked to some of the men who had been there. Mike Livoda remembered Don MacGregor, who had seen all he needed to turn him striker, in top boots and bandoliers (drunk, some said), directing his men. And Gus Papadakis had showed me with his cane how they aimed the homemade mortar some red-neck had put together out of a length of pipe. He remembered standing over Major Pliny Lester's corpse. "I kicked his butt," he said. On the thirtieth of April the federal troops arrived and the fighting was over. And all that was left of the strike were the survivors.

They took the union women on tour. Pearl Jolly, Mary Thomas, Mary Petrucci, still barely coherent, stunned by the death of her children in the cellar. There were speaking engagements, rallies, long rides from city to city in Pullman cars. The liberal and radical presses ran long articles on Ludlow. There was a blistering account of the massacre in *The Metropolitan* by John Reed, grim cartoons in *The Masses*. In Chicago the union women met Jane Addams. At the White House the President dandled one of Mary Thomas' daughters on his knees while Mary told him of the horrors of Ludlow. The newspapers were full of naval displays and crack regiments, the brutality of Huerta. To the public at large, caught up in the thrill of a Mexican war, it was as if the butchery of a dozen starving people in Colorado were superfluous, an irritant to the conscience. At 26 Broadway Mrs. Upton Sinclair took the women up an elevator and into Rockefeller's office. They sat in the reception room, unannounced, waiting. No one asked them who they were. Mary Thomas' two girls played on the floor. After an hour they undid the lunches they had brought with them and began to eat. Men kept coming in and out of the reception room, looking at them nervously, pretending to go through the file cabinets. A sad-looking man came out and smiled at the children. Then he went back inside.

The police came up and escorted the women and the two girls away. The sad man had been John D. Rockefeller, Jr.

He had stood in that same office a month before watching the news of Ludlow come in toneless shreds of information over the ribbon of the ticker. In the airless little room he had built for himself, in his isolation, no one will know what he felt, if he felt anything at all for the dead in those burning tents half a continent away. "Telegram received . . . ," he had wired to Bowers the day after the massacre. "We profoundly regret this further outbreak of lawlessness with accompanying loss of life." That January Rockefeller would undergo days of increasingly hostile questioning by Frank Walsh of the United States Commission on Industrial Relations. Throughout it he would maintain his innocence of conditions in Colorado, his lack of firsthand knowledge, his willingness to learn. Impressed, Mother Jones would spend over an hour in his private office giving him a maternal talking-to about Colorado and unionism. John Lawson was not so easily convinced. He sat in the Commission hearing listening to Rockefeller read off the list of his new Foundation's accomplishments—the Belgian relief mission, the bird sanctuary, university training for the elect. When it was his turn to testify, he said that a wave of horror had swept over him while he'd listened to that catalogue of good works. For him it was only a willful attempt to substitute philanthropy for justice. "There are thousands of Mr. Rockefeller's ex-employees in Colorado today," he said bitterly, "who wish to God they were in Belgium to be fed, or birds to be cared for tenderly."

The union had given up on the first of December 1914. "We recognize no surrender and shall continue to propagate the principles of our humanitarian movement throughout the coal fields of Colorado," the statement read. "We advise all men to seek their former places in the mines and those who are refused employment we shall render assistance to the best of our ability and shall provide every legal protection to those of our members who are being persecuted by the hirelings of organized greed."

And so the poor Greeks wandered through the Southern Field, trying to get a job. They were despised by the mine owners and pit bosses, distrusted even by their own union. They had no money and no clothes. Gus Papadakis, George Koutsales, Spiro Cadeles, three friends, searched every mine for work. Finally they got put on, Gus Papadakis at the Lester mine, the other two men at Rouse. But Galanis, the Greek whose store had been wrecked and whose petition the Greek strikers had refused to sign, now worked for the C. F. and I. He got a tip they were mining and had them all fired. Then the three broke up. "We spred never see one nother and all the gang must miss one to nother," Papadakis wrote sixty-four years later. As for Pete Katsulis, Tikas' rival, he had fed the Grand Jury just enough information on John Lawson to bring in an indictment. Diamond had kept him on as an interpreter after Tikas' death, at ten dollars a week, but he'd wanted the organizer's job, and that Lawson had not given him. Then the C. F. and I. gave him a job in one of its mines. Bill Pappas, another of Tikas' rivals, was talking, it was said to a Denver detective agency about his fellow Greeks.

In September 1915, eighteen months after the Ludlow massacre, John D. Rockefeller, Jr.,was in Colorado touring mines with his new advisor, the Canadian sociologist and politician Mackenzie King. While John Lawson lay in the Trinidad jail awaiting trial for the killing of John Nimmo, Rockefeller ate a meal at a company boarding-house ("These beans are bully"), danced the Hesitation Waltz with miners' wives, worried about a mule's harness gall, and put on a suit of overalls so new the creases squeaked to descend into a mine and hack away at a coal seam for ten minutes with a pick. "We are partners," he said to the miners. He would sell out his interest in the Colorado properties in the 1940s. His response to Ludlow was the company union, a blend of Mackenzie King's brand of industrial paternalism and the public relations ideas of publicity agent Ivy Lee. For all their suffering, the miners had gotten only this: some recognition of their grievance, some shallow acknowledgment that they might have something to say about their work and their lives. There would be more strikes ahead in Colorado and bloodshed, and it would not be until the New Deal that the union would be able to establish itself in the state.

In February of 1917 John L. Lewis came to Colorado to declare District 15 bankrupt, purge it of its militants, and move its offices to Pueblo. John Lawson was out on bail. There was a new administration in the Colorado State House and his indictment for murder was soon to be reversed by the state high court, but he had been driven out of the union hierarchy and was digging coal in a mine in the Northern Field. Doyle, too, was no longer important. At the union convention of 1916 he had run on too long in denouncing the national organization, was silenced from the speaker's chair by John L. Lewis, and his speech expunged from the records. The Colorado strike had been a costly one, and the union was beginning a long period of retrenchment. Even the *United Mine Workers Journal* had lost its old seriousness and fire. There were sections now in Italian, Polish, and Slavic (managing editor of the paper, as well as union statistician, Lewis was just learning the importance of the immigrant vote), an occasional melodramatic poem by the alcohol-sodden Frank Hayes. But the long articles on socialism and debates on the theory of the general strike were gone, and the covers were no longer the crude, militant cartoons of earlier days but sentimental photographs of June brides and barefoot children and soon they would themselves give way to the get-out-the-coal propaganda of the war. Three years after the massacre, Ludlow was hardening into the gestures of ritual. On the anniversary of the killings the crowds gathered at the site, speeches were made, a band played, and Lawson or someone else dropped a bunch of flowers into the death pit. Already Louis Tikas had become little more than a fiction, as remote and frozen as the carved figures they were planning for the Ludlow monument.

> Who knows what deeds on ancient days
>   Gave impulse, yearnings, tendencies?
> Who knows what blood flowed in his veins?
>   Perhaps the blood of Pericles. . . .
>
> Oh, Louis Tikas, gallant soul,
>   Defender of the helpless, weak;
> Knight of humanity, you were
>   More than American or Greek. . . .

And so Tikas becomes that bloodless and hollow thing, a martyr. There is something touching in all this bad poetry, but it tells us more of the living than the dead. And in the hundreds of words written on him that would follow the massacre it would be as if Louis Tikas' soul never would find its rest, but was destined to flutter ceaselessly between the sentimental tributes of the left and that parody of an anarchist imagined by the corporate propagandists. A week after the 1917 Ludlow Day ceremony the Hastings mine exploded and again the bodies piled up, 121 of them. John Lawson ran into Gus Papadakis in Walsenburg. He remembered the young Greek's face. "What are you doing?" Lawson said. "Come on." And Papadakis worked feverishly for two days with Lawson and the helmet crews, pulling the corpses of his buddies out of the mine.

At last the war came. Elbert Hubbard had been dropping an occasional sycophantic note to the junior Rockefeller ("I had a delightful game of golf with your father on Saturday. How fine and brown and well and strong he is") suggesting that Rockefeller might very well wish to circulate a number of copies of *The Fra* with a write-up of Colorado at two hundred dollars a thousand. Hubbard got his articles written, the sort of thing you might imagine. The last came out in January of 1915. Four months later he went down with the *Lusitania* on his way to give the Kaiser a piece of his mind. He was traveling first class.

And then we were in it. They drafted Gus Papadakis. Put him into what he called his "killing" uniform and sent him to France, where he got into a few skirmishes. But by then he had grown callous to bullets whistling over his head. Boughton, too, went to war and became Pershing's expert on International Law. Danks and Van Cise went, as did Pat Hamrock. During the first months of the war fever there is a minor incident reported in the Denver papers that sets off some curious reverberations. One night in August of 1917 a Greek candy store owner on Curtis and 18th chased a gang of soldiers out of his shop for causing a nuisance. The next night fifty uniformed men were back. They armed themselves with rocks, formed a line, and marched by the shop at the double-quick, heaving the rocks through the windows. At Camp Baldwin the commanding officer denied his men had anything to do with the matter but said he would investigate anyway. It would be interesting to know the results of that investigation. The C.O.'s name was Lieutenant Colonel Karl Linderfelt. After his acquittal by the National Guard court-martial he had gone to look things over in Mexico, but apparently had not stayed long if he ever did cross the border. According to the *United Mine Workers Journal*, he was soon hauled into police court in Denver for attempted rape. Then, with the coming of the war, he had joined the regular army. He too went overseas. And so did Lou Dold.

When the war was over, Lou Dold came home. All his life he would carry a whiff of gas from the trenches in the bottom of his lungs and the scars of his wounds, and he would remember the week he spent AWOL in Paris. He had been through five major battles. He had been made and broken a half-dozen times, and he'd been court-martialed, too. When they mustered him out he said yes to everything. He was just tired of the army.

Somewhere along the line he married, but it soon broke up and he went to Leadville where his father was running a mine, and then down to Gallup to work for a photographer, but he couldn't get his price. So he set to wandering with no money and no destination. He followed the Santa Fe tracks into the Indian country and got a job at a trading post on the Zuni reservation. He stayed there five months. Then he set out again. One night he was walking along the tracks in the desert. He was tired and he wanted to lie down but there was something moving beside him in the darkness. He thought it might be coyotes. After a time he saw what it was: giant tortoises. He kept walking. Up on the bluffs a light appeared. It blinked a moment, then went out. When he got near enough, he saw the light was coming from a shed into which people kept coming and going. He went inside the shed and saw they were all Mexicans. Propped up on a trestle against a pile of harness was a corpse laid out in a coffin. The Mexicans were trying to pin a cross to the coffin but the pins kept falling out. Lou Dold asked them for something to eat but they pretended they couldn't understand him. After a while he couldn't stand watching the Mexicans fumbling with the pins and the cross any longer and stuck them to the coffin himself. All at once the Mexicans understood him and got him some food and coffee and a place to sleep. He had grown familiar with death on the Meuse–Argonne drive—more familiar than he ever had been squinting through the ground glass of a camera. He wandered a few weeks more then hopped a freight and ended up broke and hungry in Raton. He talked his way into a meal at a restaurant and bumped into a friend from Trinidad on the street. The friend told him he'd see him a little later, then flipped him a silver dollar. "Play with this a while," he said. Lou Dold was back home.

Sooner or later they all came home. Arrived at some sort of stopping place, some ending. Ed Doyle became a traveling auditor for a railroad brotherhood. Lawson went on to a position of comfort and success running Josephine Roche's mines. No one deserved that ease more. A military hierarchy that placed more of a premium on loyalty than competence would make Pat Hamrock adjutant general of the Colorado Guard in his own right. He would see out yet another bitter strike. And once more Karl Linderfelt's name comes up in the Denver papers in language that has a grim familiarity. On September 8, 1920, the *Denver Post* reported that he had been selected to head a new volunteer "municipal protective force." The force would consist of 150 to 200 picked men, who would be expert rifle and pistol shots and familiar with the handling of machine guns and other anti-riot military apparatus. I do not know if the force was ever gathered. According to reports, Linderfelt went off, after a time, to Oklahoma and ended up in San Diego. Perhaps his violence had run its course. Pearl Jolly, too, seems to drop out of history after her brief moment of public glory. She ended up with her husband in the dreary coal and railroad town of Rock Springs, Wyoming, and they were, Mike Livoda says, very respectable people. Livoda himself kept working, as an officer of District 15, ran a CCC camp in the Depression. His Denver apartment became a haunt for anyone who wanted to know about the great coal strike of 1913–14, and he would take down his union rifle and tell you just how it was.

And all the time John D. Rockefeller was lurching into the American mythology. Having outlived his ferocious appetites, the machinery of his corporations grinding on without him, he was troubled by bad digestion. Who could guess that he was consumed by the fear that he would die in the poorhouse? He became a ghost flickering through the Pathè newsreels, a revenant from another age, "Neighbor John" in the name he had given himself, a cadaverous figure in knickers and cap, swinging a golf club or handing out dimes, something to be booed in the darkness of the Trinidad movie palaces by the children of the strike.

For a time the coffeehouse at 1746 Market Street seemed to have a life of its own. Old John Tsanakatsis remembered it well, surviving prohibitionists and reformers, until Greek Town dried up around it. Every morning one of the Greeks would make the pilgrimage downtown to hand the cop on the beat the daily bribe so the games of poker and *skampili* and *barbout* could continue undisturbed. And now that imperious man Louis Tikas had watched going into his employment agency across Market Street was coming to his own bitter end. Shorn of his power at Utah Copper, sliding into ruin, Skliris, the padrone, too, enters into a kind of myth.

He shows up again in Colorado, almost a figure of pity. Comes to Pueblo trying to peddle mining stocks, hangs around a few days, then disappears. Someone said he clerked for a Greek farm in California, took a job as a mine guard in Arizona. It was there Gus Papadakis ran into him when the Cretan was looking for work at the Morenci copper mine. Skliris seemed to be doing all right, had plenty of money to spend. Someone said to Papadakis, "He's just as poor as you are. He doesn't have a goddamned dime." Skliris, who once spent more than a coal miner made in a year entertaining a lieutenant and his bride in the Hotel Utah with wine and food and musicians brought in from New York, broke now, finished. In Arizona he bumped into the man who'd stopped him in the car the time he'd sneaked into Bingham Canyon dressed as a woman. Skliris offered to make him superintendent of his mine in Naco for a couple of thousand dollars. One afternoon I sat in a Greek coal miner's house in Walsenburg while the old man told me how Skliris had come to his ruin. In the old man's mind it had become a kind of nightmare, the sort you will wake up from cold and sweating. He told me how after the strike at Utah Copper Skliris had gone off to drill for oil with old John Dee himself. There were the two of them, partners, the billionaire and the Czar of the Greeks. Skliris kept putting his money into the ground and Rockefeller kept telling him the holes were coming up dry; the more money the Greek put in, the drier the holes became, until old John Dee had broken the Czar of the Greeks. Before I left the house I caught one last glimpse of Skliris. It was in Grand Junction, Colorado, in 1919, and Skliris was running the icehouse. The old man had been one of Skliris' workers. There was an argument, and the Greek had squared off against the overseer of the Mexican laborers. Skliris came out of the office and told the Greek not to fight, that the Mexican would beat him . . . As the old man told me this, I imagined the shafts of light coming through the slats of the ice plant, the men waiting in a circle, standing in pools of water and sawdust.

They fought and the Greek knocked the Mexican down. Skliris came over to the Greek and told him to get dressed. "I'll give you the rest of the shift," he said. It was the kind of irrational, impetuous generosity that was, in its own way, as chilling as any of his cruelties. The two of them went off and for an hour Skliris, that man who would hardly deign to speak with a laborer, made much of the young Greek, fawning on him and warning him not to go back to the plant. The story was over. For a moment Skliris was standing in the gloom of the icehouse with the machinery throbbing and the afternoon poised on a knife-edge and the ring of men waiting for the fight. And in my mind Skliris was smiling.

So they survived.
Co-lum-bus discovered America . . .
The song went, rattling in my head
. . . in four-teen nine-tee twoooo.
Then came the English, and the Dutch, the Frenchman and the
*   Joooo . . .*
Some vaudeville patter song coming out all bass drums and fruity horns and squeaky soprano over a scratched Victrola disc.
Then came the Swede and the Irishman, who helped the country
*   grow.*
Still they keep a-coming and now everywhere you go-o-o . . .
ka-boom and a thump on the drums announces the moral:
There's the Argentines and the Portuguese, the Armenians and
*   the Greeks . . .*
One sells you papers, one shines your shoes, another shaves the
*   whiskers off your cheeks.*
When you ride again, in the subway train, notice who have all the
*   seats . . .*
And you'll find they are held by the Argentines and the Portu-
*   guese and the Greeks. . . .*

There it was, the story of my race. Luck and Pluck. Savings and Sweat. They clawed their way up that Social–Darwinian ladder to the top. I remember a story my grandfather told me about his first days in this country, digging a sewer trench in Oklahoma City. It was almost a grotesque diagram of the way things were supposed to work. There was the Irishman up on top and underneath him the Pole and then came the Wop. On the lowest platform was the black man. And down in the bottom of the trench, up to his knees in the freezing muck, was the new man, the Greek. My grandfather wondered why the black man always turned his shovel a certain way to drip the ice-cold water down the Greek's back, but the next day the Greek had changed places with him and by the end of the week there the Greek was, up on top. Well, it was a little crude, but that was *to systema*—the system—as the Greeks liked to say, and they were good at the system.

But like a stuck record I kept going back. I choked on the system. I thought of my grandfather in the bottom of that trench with the water trickling down his neck and how he'd really washed dishes in the Ritz Hotel—not lounged around with the Argentines and the Portuguese, as the song had it. And I wondered if old John Tsanakatsis ever got a seat on the subway he built ("What did you do when you got to New York?" "Work on them railroad tunnels. You know? You ever seen them tunnels?") Under the allegory of success there was a darker story, and somehow it had to do with those who failed, with those who left no issue and no name, whose lives were holes in the webs of history. I thought of that night under the Chicago El in 1910 when George Zeese stood staring into a stick-up man's gun and everything hung on a hair. When he pulled his own gun the black man holding the pistol on him smiled and moved back into the shadows. "Oh," he said. "I didn't know you was one of us."

One night I sat in a workingman's cafe in Canea on the Island of Crete watching Gus Papadakis draw with his finger a diagram of a two-hundred-foot room in a mine. I had come to Crete with the name of a village outside of Rethymnon where I thought I might find some memory of Louis Tikas, but all I'd found was the community secretary of Mesi, who sat in his undershirt scanning a village register whose pages, as far as I was concerned, were blank. So now I sat with Gus Papadakis while the crowds poured by in the ritual evening stroll. We were talking about Colorado. Already he was restless, thinking of going back. I had seen in his small room at his nephew's house the old trunk he'd shown me in Oak Creek. He had come back to Crete to die.

Gus finished his diagram and told me how they'd drilled the holes, he and Dave. He remembered some of those rotten rooms. "I never buy a foreman a cigar in my life," he said proudly. "Or a drink."

That was what it came down to, the years of wandering, looking for a job, landing one, moving on: never to own a house or a piece of ground or sit down at your own table—it was always some boardinghouse where you'd pass the food from hand to hand and yell to the kitchen when you needed more. And all the time there were the jobs they'd run him out of, the strikes he refused to scab. Two years later I would find him in a Denver hotel room listening to the ball game. He had gone back. Even the trunk was gone. There was only a suitcase and a few clothes and those little threads of pneumoconiosis that had seized up his lungs. He talked about being cremated when he died. Everything he had fought for he'd pared down to a phrase: I eat, you starve—it wasn't right.

That summer on Crete we took a little trip over the spine of the White Mountains to the desolate coast of Sphakia where the old man was born. The old man had a habit of pretending not to be Greek. He'd go into a dingy restaurant and shout in English to the startled waiter, "Hey, what the hell's going on here? We gonna get any service?" It was his kind of humor. We went up to Anopolis, Daskaloyiannis' village, and sat in the barren square an hour. Everyone thought we were crazy.

One day we walked up to the monument above Chora Sphakia. Through the steamy plate of glass at the base of the stele we looked at the skulls of the dead patriots massacred by the Germans in World War II. Gus pointed to the barren limestone crags that rose above the town. "You come from these rocks and go over to mine coal—what the hell did we know?"

A few days later I came back to Sphakia. I was alone. I had hungered for the place's pitiless kind of beauty. At night in the taverna below my hotel room, the old men started to sing. Sporadically, drunkenly, they were singing a snatch or two of one of the old heroic songs about Digenis who wrestled with death or Daskaloyiannis or the fighting in '41. I awoke out of a dead sleep to hear them, but in my drowsiness I could not force myself to rise. Nor could I make out more than a few words, and I fell back asleep.

And that was all. The old-timers, who had taken so little from the world, would simply disappear. That winter John Tsanakatsis had died in Las Vegas. I was left with a dim memory of a sporty cap and a marvelous Cretan laugh. And as for Louis Tikas—it was as if he were destined to remain suspended between that past, which could never be fully recovered, and that posterity I could not, finally, create for him. Try to imagine him a survivor, coming back from his errand somehow on that night when the Ludlow tents were all ablaze and the machine guns ripped through the camp. Imagine him going on in the union, stripped of his power like Lawson and Doyle, growing bitter and hard. Or a businessman, perhaps, wiping a counter with a greasy rag, fathering children, going to AHEPA conventions in a white linen suit. Or living on a bachelor, returning to his native island forever stamped as "the American." Could I imagine him idling out the rest of his days playing cards in some coffeehouse? It is all this history forbids you to ask. One final image remains: an old man standing beside me at the edge of a caved-in street in an eastern Utah mining town watching the water pour in a torrent through a ruptured main. He had gone out to fight at Ludlow carrying his rifle in his one good hand and he remembered a tall Cretan who had stood up and told them their plans were all wrong when the shooting began. Now he sat in his house picking at the cluttered contents of his table with his coal miner's hands —pieces of string, a union pension book, bits of broken things. His logic had gone when his wife had died, he said. Between the past and memory the gap was as real and as final as the one between us and that future it had been forbidden us to question. We stood looking at the water pouring hopelessly out of the chasm in the summer rain and he had forgotten the street that would take him home.

But I knew I would go back to Greece. It was only there that I could in some way make my peace with this story, and with Louis Tikas—or what remained of him. There had been a custom in the back country of the Greece of Tikas' childhood, and it was at once both primitive and revealing. Seven years after the burial of a man the villagers would dig up his bones and wash the dirt from them. If the bones were clean, then the dead man's soul had been liberated from the agony of this world and had entered the realm of Death. But sometimes it happened that a few shreds of flesh still clung to the bone, and this was a sign borne by those killed by violence, the unavenged. The ghosts of these corpses were driven to haunt the living, themselves neither living nor dead, until the last shreds of flesh had been stripped away. I kept remembering how Mary Thomas had stood at the elevator of her hotel and told me she often dreamed about Ludlow. Dreamed about it yet. And then, with the thin edge of the actress she had always aspired to be rising in her voice, she said, "If you go to Greece again, tell them from me that they can be proud of the Greeks we had there. That every one was a hero. I have tears coming to me. That's the way I feel about that." Then she said, "You write this and take it to the Greeks, because they had a pretty good man there in Louis." It had been that seven years and more since I'd first come across Louis Tikas' name in the library basement. I had dug what I could of him out of America.

The past can be seized only as an image which flashes up at the instant when it can be recognized and is never seen again.

Walter Benjamin

15. LOUTRA

It lies among the endless olive groves which spread out beneath Psiloritis' western slope, a speck on the road leading east from Rethymnon. At the beginning of the village there is a new coffeehouse with a high ceiling and an echoing terrazzo floor, the property of the mayor. The old town still stands, a place of red tile roofs and narrow lanes undulating along the sides of the hill. The whitewashed stone houses are built one against the other, as if for comfort or protection. Now and then there is a wall and an old Turkish arch, or a mud oven standing in a courtyard. The olive trees shimmer silver-green when the breeze blows through them.

"I am called Emmanuel Marangoudakis," the letter read, "living in the village of Loutra (10 kilometers east of the city of Rethymnon). I have just heard on March 2, 1975, of your letter. With great pleasure I will attempt to the best of my ability to help in your writing on the book of the brother of my mother, Ilias Anastasios Spantidakis (the true name of Louis Tikas)...."

There is a necessary fatuousness in writing history: the illusion that you alone have come this way, pored over the words in this old volume, made the map of this forgotten country. It is never true, as necessary as it is to be thought. Loutra has always existed. These streets, these lights and shades, these stones—they have been here all along. It was you yourself who were missing. And so it was I found myself walking down these quiet lanes two years after I had left Crete thinking I would never find this place, talking to this kind man, Emmanuel Marangoudakis, while his young son pranced like a gazelle along the cobblestones and my wife took pictures. How nearly it was that I did not find Loutra. For years the name Tikas had stood like a wall between me and his birthplace, cutting off any chance that I might trace his origins beyond that fiction he had covered himself in, his American persona. There was only one clue, that small note on his citizenship papers that said he had come from a place six miles from Rethymnon. In a kind of futile stab I put a compass on a map of Crete and drew a circle with a fifteen-mile radius around that cramped town and sent a letter to the mayor of each of the sixty and more villages within its arc saying that I was looking for a man whose Greek name I did not know, who had been killed in America sixty years before. One reply had come back. It was chance, I realized, a simple accident that had restored this place. But I walked through the village of Loutra and all at once Ilias Spantidakis' beginnings, like a fabric on a loom, were pulling themselves into a whole with the naturalness of something I had always known.

The house itself was still standing. Unwhitewashed, the stones bare, it jutted out in the narrow wedge where two lanes met. Across the way was the house of his mother's clan, the Toutountzidakis, and the cousin who would grow up to be Ilias' great friend. The Spantidakis house still had the stumps of the beams which had supported a balcony on one side. In the cellar was a mill and a press for olives. During the harvest a mule or horse would turn the mill and extract the oil, which the villagers sold to the traders in Rethymnon. This is what Ilias Spantidakis knew of the industrial world when he took ship for America. There was one more feature of the house. At exactly the point where the two lanes merged there was a small terrace, no bigger than a good-sized bed. Here it was that Ilias Spantidakis' father kept a little coffeehouse.

It was the coffeehouse that must have given Ilias his first education. What he overheard, a boy serving those bearded and turbaned veterans of the disaster that was Cretan history, would be his earliest definition of the world. His father was already old by the time he was born. If the village reckoning can be trusted, he was sixty-four, an elder, with a few olive trees, a few sheep, the mill, and the coffeehouse. The administrator of the villages of Loutra, Aghia Triada, and Mesi was located in Mesi, yet Anastasios Spantidakis is remembered as a sort of unofficial mayor for the whole Arkadhious district with its sixteen villages. He was called the *proestos*—the first citizen, and it was to him the villagers came with their problems of land, their disputes (for the mayor in those days served also as a jurist), to drink a drop of raki, and to discuss that terrible thing that lay on them like a curse, the Turks.

In Loutra the Christians lived side by side with the Turks, sharing the narrow alleys and the groves, washing at the same stream. Turks they called them, but they were in fact probably almost all ethnic Greeks, descendants of those converts to Mohammedanism who had existed on Crete since the Ottomans replaced the Venetians as masters in 1669. They spoke Greek and prayed facing Mecca, respected the Christian saints and celebrated Ramadan (as did their Orthodox neighbors), and they waited for the periodic revolts that would leave the island washed in blood and the houses of the village locked against each other. In Loutra they remember it as a time when the Christians dared not hold up their heads.

All these things the boy Ilias Spantidakis learned. At night he would have heard them at the table on the terrace of the house repeating by rote the long, impossible romance of Erotokritos, who loved a king's daughter, or trading love-couplets under the gravid moon.

> My girl, if I had my youth again
> I'd love you—and one or two others. . . .

He would have heard, too, those darker songs of the table, the songs of the heroes, of Digenis, the warden of the border, who wrestled with Death on the threshing floor, and of Daskaloyiannis of Sphakia, who had given himself as a hostage to save his people, and whom the Turks had flayed alive. He came to know, like all Cretans, that history was not a page in a book, but something held in memory and in the blood. His father had already come to manhood when Arkadhi had been blown up; his great-uncle had died in the fighting in the hills.

He had been three years old when he got his first taste of the tragic history of the island. I do not imagine the outbreak of the summer and fall of 1889 left him with more than confused and fragmentary thoughts of the flight of villagers and the shooting. In Iráklion, forty miles east, the six-year-old Nikos Kazantzakis was taken by the hand, terrified and sick, to kiss the feet of three Greeks dangling from nooses under a plane tree in the town square.

In 1896 the terror began again. What started as a reform movement had become a revolt. By June Greeks and Moslems were burning each other's villages. The Turkish troops brought in from Zeitun bragged openly about the massacre of the Armenians. There were stories that they were selling earrings from the victims with the severed ears still attached. By August 11,000 Moslem refugees were crowded into Rethymnon, starving, living in filth. A strange quiet had come over all of the Rethymnon district. There was little left to pillage. In Pyghi, the village in which Ilias got whatever schooling he had, five churches had been destroyed. He may have watched the burning of groves he knew well, of his own school. He was ten years old.

I do not know how the residents of Loutra survived that starving winter of 1897, when snow from Psiloritis blanketed the area and the Turks burned the olive trees for charcoal. Whether they went off to some safer part of the island where there was shelter and still a little food or took ship to mainland Greece with other refugees or somehow stayed on is impossible to know. But they did survive. When the sharp fighting broke out around the district late that winter and in the early spring, the men went off with their rifles. They fought a day or two, then came back to put in what they could of their crops. In September 1898, the most terrible atrocity of the struggle took place. Again it was in Iráklion. There the Turks massacred five hundred Christians and looted and burned much of the city. But in the fighting a few British sailors had been killed and at last, in the agonizing saraband which Europe and the Sultan had been dancing over the island for two hundred years, the Great Powers were forced to act. An ultimatum was presented to the Sultan, Prince George of Greece was chosen high commissioner of an autonomous Crete, and the island was rid of the Turkish grip.

On the morning of May 18, 1899, Prince George arrived in the harbor at Rethymnon on board the Russian cruiser *Donetz* in order to attend the celebration of the czar's birthday. He went to a series of religious ceremonies, lunched with the Russian officers, and set out on a four-day tour of the district, followed by an escort of Russian military men and mounted country people. There was great rejoicing, and the villages through which the Prince passed had been festooned with garlands. At the foot of Mount Ida, which the Cretans called Psiloritis, near the monastery of The Incorporeal One, there was a torchlight procession. I wonder if young Ilias Spantidakis was one of those who stood in the dust of the road or held a lighted brand in the flickering shadows, breathless to see this Greek prince, who was all Hellenism in himself, and all freedom. A few months before Kazantzakis had witnessed Prince George's arrival on the Island. "The whole of my inner breast is adorned, like all Crete on that day, with myrtles and laurels," he wrote. It was out of such moments that came the wild nationalism that would mark a whole generation of Greeks, and which only the 1921 disaster in Asia Minor would begin to tame.

And so Ilias Spantidakis had had what was no doubt his first coherent experience with the sound of battle and with both the fiery patriotism and the hatred that had split Crete in two since Venetian times. He had learned something of survival from all this, that first instinct of the Greek race, and he had learned something of the cunning that tells you when to keep silence and when to take up the gun. He was thirteen years old, already with the quick mind and avid spirit that the cramped village, that little world of olive grove and narrow street, was stifling.

"Ilias' hobby was to make the wild tame. For example, he would take wild rabbits and train them to play with dogs, wild birds played with cats. He would call them and they would sit on his shoulders. Ilias was a courteous man, he liked amusement."

He went to Rethymnon, a town of minarets and old Venetian fountains, where the houses were built right up to the waves. He walked along the quay where ships from all the world lay at anchor, strolled among the Venetian houses with their shuttered balconies. With his friends he sat in the coffeehouses watching the young swells in western clothes go by, the Russian officers in their smart uniforms, the merchants in their European suits and straw hats, wives and daughters marching primly behind them. Going home at dusk he watched the lighters skimming to the ships in the bay, a lantern bobbing in the prow. He passed by the public square where the letter writers sat with their inkstands and pens tucked into their sashes, waiting for clients. Perhaps he stopped to look in on one of those marvelous cafes the

Rethymniote Prevelakis has described, where the Turkish storyteller sat cross-legged on a little dais spinning out his endless tales while the smoke of the hookahs swirled languidly around him. And in Rethymnon he no doubt visited other places less respectable, as his contemporary on the opposite coast, the penniless Sphakiote Papadakis was doing just then, to do "whatever bums did" in town.

He was a courteous man, he liked amusements. He went about the neighborhood entertaining his friends with the tricks that strange patience of his had allowed him to teach the small animals he caught. When he went to Arkadhi they pointed out the remains of the powder magazine the Cretans had fired and the table in the refectory still marked with the grooves of the yataghans where the slaughter of the Christians had taken place. Someone may have shown him, in the hills above the monastery, the place his great-uncle had fallen. Perhaps he visited the cave of Melidhoni where, among the stalactites, the burnt bones of the martyrs of 1824 were still visible. He may have gone to Perivolia on that holy day when they brought out the perfumed skulls of the four martyrs hanged by the Turks in 1866 and walked in sacred procession with them to Rethymnon. The Cretans had learned to celebrate such grim occasions with singing and festival. Like Digenis, they drank a toast to Death in the skulls of their ancestors.

In 1905 the ambitious attorney Eleutherios Venizelos staged his abortive revolt against the Powers. This time the battle cry was *enosis* —union with Greece. Once more there was musket fire in the hills and along the coast. Ilias Spantidakis had just turned nineteen. At Kasteli, on the coast, at Platania, at Atsipopoulo, the Cretans of the Rethymnon district met the Russians. It was here, if anywhere, that Ilias would get his first taste of gunpowder and earn his village reputation as a guerrilla fighter. The Venizelos revolt failed, and Crete would not achieve union with the mainland until 1913, but young Spantidakis was not to be caught up for long in Cretan politics. Something else had taken his energy now, and his imagination.

"He finished the lower school and instead of heeding the wishes of his father to continue his studies—he was very bright and a good student—he lost his head from the instigation of acquaintances and they left for America in 1906. . . ." He was eager, full of fire. The thought of those tedious days in school, of the long walk to Rethymnon and back every day to continue his education, weighed on him. His signature would remain forever frozen in the uncertain traceries of a grade school boy—no one who ever saw it would confuse him with a graduate of Athens University. Instead of the desk and the Rethymniote master, he fell in with a group of young men like himself, and all of them were crazy for emigration. Some were going to Germany. Ilias decided on America.

He was the oldest man in the village and his eyes had the milky-blue cast of the blind. He said he was "ninety and past"—he had the villager's habitual contempt for exact dates—and he sat on the edge of his bed diminutive, almost doll-like, wearing much-patched khaki riding breeches of the kind that supplanted the black *vrakes* as the dress of the Cretan patriots. His name was Demetrios Kalergis. Underneath his bed, standing neatly side by side, were his high-topped boots. Later on my wife would tell me she noticed a cobweb had grown between them.

"Ilias," he said, "was a good man, he didn't harm anyone. He loved the birds. He was a *leventis* . . ." The word *leventis*— it meant a young man with dash, a champion.

Kalergis reached under the bed for his cigarettes, waved Mr. Marangoudakis away when he offered a light. The old man found his matches and lit his cigarette ceremoniously, smoked. What he knew of Ilias Spantidakis was now simply a few tatters, a few rags of information. His false teeth lay on the window ledge in a kind of disembodied parody of speech. Swallows had roosted in the eaves of his room. Mr. Marangoudakis' boy noticed it and watched with delight as the birds flew in and out of the house.

They talked some more about Ilias. Mr. Marangoudakis rushed the old man on. He had warned me Kalergis had little to tell. They remembered the stories, the two of them, about how Ilias went to America with a pair of other young men from the village, Evangelis Katsikas and Karalis. Katsikas worked for Ilias in the coffeehouse in Denver. When Katsikas came back to Loutra he told them how all the exiled Cretans knew Ilias would sympathize with the poor, with those in need. "If any of the *andartes* come to my coffeehouse," Ilias would say, "all you have to do is show them my picture." Mr.

Marangoudakis paused a moment to explain the word for fighting man: "*Andarte*," he said. "It's like we see in the movies." The old man remarked that he hadn't heard Ilias and Katsikas went together to America.

"You told me that," Mr. Marangoudakis said.

We continued our walk through the village. At each house we visited there was the obligatory thimbleful of raki, perhaps a sweet. In the house of Toutountzidakis' daughter we heard again how the news of Ilias Spantidakis' death in America had come on the very day that his sister Argyro, Marangoudakis' mother, was to be betrothed. They had called it a bad omen in the village. How strangely that need to make sense of a life had twisted things into the shape of legend. It must have been to his sister that Ilias was writing the night before he died. It must have been her betrothal, not his own, that the letter was about. Mr. Marangoudakis talked on, words I only half caught between his Cretan accent and my poor Greek. Was I hearing this? Was he saying he would have avenged the death of his uncle, but that he was trapped, had a family to take care of, had no way to get to America?

At least in memory the ghosts of the old religion of fate and blood retribution still haunted Loutra. Perhaps in another generation they too would be forgotten, as the old songs were being forgotten and the heroes, like their guns, put away in a world that was becoming wider and less difficult and less cruel, yet lacking somehow a denseness, a heroic grace. We walked up to the graveyard above the village. The tombs rose out of the ground, bare vaults of concrete and stone. On some the vigil lights were still burning. The old bones had long ago been dispersed. Ilias' father, the patriarch, lived to be a hundred and five and died in 1927—lived long enough to hear of the violent death of one of his sons, but spared that of the other. Mr. Marangoudakis told me how it was in the war. Konstantinos Spantidakis, the son who remained, was killed by the Germans during the occupation, as was his nephew, Eleni Vavadaki's boy, the strongest man in the village. Toutountzidakis, Ilias' cousin and great friend—poor Toutountzidakis—he too had gone to America and as soon as he came back they grabbed him for the army. He was killed by the Germans in '41, dragged out of his bed in the night and shot. I think of Ilias

Spantidakis—had he survived America to return, his fate might have been only postponed.

When the occupation ended, civil war came to Greece. The propaganda of the Left and the Right had torn the village in two. Mr. Marangoudakis had been a member of ELAS—the Left resistance movement. He'd had no politics, no deep ideas. He just wanted to fight the Germans. Then the propaganda came and the nights when he slept with a gun in his pocket. "And it wasn't outsiders," he said. "It was your own people." The Loutrans had turned upon themselves in the struggle. They had become their own Turks.

We went back to the village. The evening light was just touching the houses rising above the little stream, turning them golden. I wondered if this was how Ilias Spantidakis would have remembered it, in just this light, with the little stream where the women had laid out the clothes to wash glinting in the foliage and the water spilling out of the fountain where the Turks had walled up the spring which had given its name to the place. The fountain was still there, a stone dam with a spigot sticking out of it and a graceful Turkish or Arabic inscription across its top. The Moslems were gone in the 1923 population exchange after the Greek disaster in Asia Minor. Loutra was wholly Greek. This fountain and the memories of the atrocities were all that remained. But by then Ilias Spantidakis—or Louis Tikas—or Louie the Greek—was dead.

It was dark now and we sat on the terrace of the house of the mayor's brother, eating, drinking raki. Upstairs my wife slept, worn out with Crete and with what we would discover were the first stirrings of our child. Out on the flagstones of the little terrace Marangoudakis' boy and the daughter of the house chased each other through the shadows. The citrus trees of the garden were banded in white lime. There were neat rows of shrubs and vines, chickens roosting in their coop. Everything was in its place. And so we toasted each other, and Crete. The accident of my method had brought me here, a letter flung out on the wind, and I had found out not really very much, after all, but it was enough. I had restored Louis Tikas, or that ghost of him I had borne with me so long, to his home and his name. And in a sense I had freed us both. I could learn little more. But I think if I were to choose, I would have had the search end in just this way, in fragments, in small pieces of a life caught and held for a moment, and then released. And perhaps seeing Louis Tikas in such glimpses was somehow truer than the artifice of continuity you made of a life—your own life even. In the dark stream of existence there was no stopping and no purchase. And from where would you step if you could? So Louis Tikas' life rose up, moment by moment, now in Loutra, now in Colorado, in fragments miraculously intact, fragments crystallized in the stream like those bits of pollen and seed from vanished forests accidentally preserved in beads of amber.

There was a photograph Mr. Marangoudakis had sent me of his uncle Ilias Spantidakis, the young Louis Tikas, taken just before he left for America. I have it by me now. He stands there on that day in 1906 when he went with his friends to the festival of Moni Arseniou and posed for a traveling photographer against a painted backdrop. Beside him, just peeking out from under the edge of the piece of paper the photographer has taped over the negative, is the tip of the white evzone kilt Toutountzidakis is wearing—in those bold days of 1906, with the idea of *enosis* blazing in the air, it was a fine thing to dress in the mainland skirt and pose beside a man, like Ilias Spantidakis, wearing the black breeches of Crete. So there is Ilias, young, with his black fez and his embroidered vest and the beginnings of that mustache he would shave off at Ludlow, a late sacrifice to America. It is the same costume he would wear among the Ludlow tents on holidays and which would perish with him in the battle. He is nineteen years old. In his sash he carries a pistol, a flintlock as it happens. On his left wrist is a bracelet with an oval stone in it. For a long time I puzzled over that bracelet and what it might mean. Then I realized it was a link with a past more distant even than that of the gun or the fez or the black pantaloons: it was the guard some great-great grandfather had worn Idomeneus-like against the snap of the string of his Cretan bow.

He stands there poised on the edge of the abyss the flash of light has made between himself and the future. Proud, a young *palikar*. All a photograph can tell you, really, is the present. Maybe it is only our overmastering hunger for something more that makes us fill that moment with our own terrible nostalgia, our myths of history or of ourselves. And yet it is just here, in this little seed of light, that we become that future the actors are posing for, that we become their

Ilias Anastasios Spantidakis (the true name of Louis Tikas). . . . —Emmanuel Marangoudakis. Louis Tikas just before his departure for America in 1906. Courtesy of Emmanuel Marangoudakis.

posterity. Outside the festival goes on; they are turning in the broken circle of one of the island dances. The young girls are looking at the *leventes* as they leap and strut while the *lyra* saws. Standing there, on the brink of a new world and a new name, Ilias Spantidakis looks without fear at his own reflection. It is at this moment that he overcomes death.

It was late. We drove back to Rethymnon. The lights of the car caught the white, painted trunks of the olive trees along the roadside as we rushed by them in the dark night.

APPENDIX:

A NOTE ON GREEK ORAL POETRY AND HISTORY

Toward the conclusion of the eighteenth-century Cretan epic poem *Daskaloyi-annis*, the singer gives a picture of a land devastated by the Turks and laments that never again will there be "white-haired old men to sit by the table, to eat and drink, to sing with strong voices, and tell of heroic deeds, and the woes of war, and the table to echo from one side to the other." Yet the tradition of the epic song did survive in Crete, and well into our present century researchers have had no trouble collecting examples of epic verse going back to the song cycles of the legendary Byzantine hero Digenis Akrites. Nor has the making of new songs ended. The late Professor James A. Notopoulos, author of the article on *Daskaloyiannis* from which much of the information in this note has been derived,[1] was able to record in the late 1950s not only performances of that epic, and recitations of the seventeenth-century literary epic *Erotokritos* (see p. 20 and Reference Notes), but a song composed in the traditional style lamenting the German occupation of World War II. For the young Cretans who would find themselves in the mines of southern Colorado in 1914, the epic tradition had not only been a bridge to the past but an active shaper of character: "The mother sings lullabies to her baby to have him grow up into a *palikari* (hero); she sings to him the brave deeds of Cretan heroes; the grandmother imbues the growing child by the evening fire with the many heroic revolts of Crete and the grandfather sings to the child on his knees the epic glory of Crete." It would have been just such songs that Louis Tikas would have heard sung around the

---

1. James A. Notopoulos, "Homer and Cretan Heroic Poetry: A Study in Comparative Oral Poetry," *American Journal of Philology* 73, no. 3 (July 1952). For quoted material see pp. 237, 227–28, 240. A synopsis of *Daskaloyiannis* is found on pp. 244–49. Another essay by Notopoulos and examples of Greek epic songs are found in "Modern Greek Heroic Oral Poetry," Folkways Recording FE 4468. For a summary of the history behind *Daskoloyiannis* see Xan Fielding, *The Stronghold: An Account of the Four Seasons in the White Mountains of Crete* (London, 1953), pp. 204–9.

table of his father's coffeehouse, and in fact in Loutra in 1978 I just missed the chance of hearing a Sphakian who had married into Tikas' clan sing part of the song of Daskaloyiannis composed very nearly two hundred years before.

The lesson of such heroic songs is pride in manliness and warrior courage and tragic dignity in defeat. Both implicitly, in techniques of composition and performance handed down through generations, and explicitly, in their reiteration of events often long in the past, the songs express historical continuity. Yet if they celebrate history, they also distort it. The singer, as Notopoulos puts it, "plastically shapes a plot in obedience with the dictates of artistic illusion in an oral recitation and not with standards of historical truth." Thus history is compressed in song, and complex issues are assimilated to the differing complexities of art and lose both historical depth and accuracy of focus in the "eternal present" of the epic mode. Eighteen years after the revolt of Daskaloyiannis reached its tragic end the tangled motives and events of the uprising are dramatically recast as a series of starkly foreshortened confrontations between Daskaloyiannis and his companions and Daskaloyiannis and the Turkish pasha. When in his *Memoirs* the Roumeliote hero Makriyiannis is forced to come to grips with the destructive politics of the post-revolutionary period of mainland Greece and explain his own role in them, he finds himself resorting to prophetic dreams, and, in a remarkable passage combining the Homeric journey to the land of the dead with the wisdom of the folktale, we are taken to Hades to hear the great warrior Napoleon, whom Death has killed "without a gun or sword," lecturing Czar Alexander on the evils of flattery and the machinations of the European powers. The nakedness of the two autocrats, stripped now of their honors and decorations, is contrasted to the glorious raiment of the great figures of the Greek past: Napoleon's only covering is his winding-sheet. "All the world was not space enough for him, all the wealth of men didn't satisfy him, nine lengths of cloth were enough, and even some left over."[2]

That this tendency to recast history in the terms of folklore and folk poetry is not only the province of bards and warrior-poets like Makriyiannis can be seen in an anecdote recorded by anthropologist G. James Patterson in the late 1960s from a habitué of a Greek coffeehouse in Denver. An important episode in the convoluted political and military maneuvers of the Balkan War of 1912–13 is compressed into a few lines of epic simplicity and the Cretan premier of Greece, Eleutherios Venizelos, working with Odyssean guile, *personally* tricks the Bulgarians into abandoning Thessaloniki and leaving it for the Greeks.[3]

---

2. *General Makriyiannis' Memoirs {Apomnimonevmata}*, introduction by Spiron I. Asdraha, (Athens, n.d.), pp. 333–34, 437–39. See also J. A. Notopoulos, "The Warrior as an Oral Poet: A Case History," *Classical Weekly* 46, no. 2 (17 November 1952). It is unlikely that Makriyiannis, who was nearly illiterate until the age of thirty, would have got these epic motifs from reading Homer.

3. G. James Patterson, "Greek Men in a Coffee House in Denver: Five Life Histories," *Journal of the Hellenic Diaspora* 3 (April 1976): 32–33.

So far was one Greek survivor of the Ludlow Massacre from understanding the real complexities of absentee ownership in the dynamics of the Colorado strike of 1913–14 that he insisted that John D. Rockefeller, Jr., had had the armor-plated "Death Special" (see p. 90 and Reference Notes) built for his own protection. Faulty history, if vivid poetry. Rockefeller's first visit to his mines came ten years before the strike began; he would not see them again unil a year after the conclusion of the strike.[4]

Myths, Lévi–Strauss tells us, are "machines for the suppression of time." The very conventions of epic poetry, by turning history into myth, have in a sense made history static, unable to do more than repeat itself in the tragic continuity of an epic present. In order to understand the Greeks of Louis Tikas' generation—and probably the South Italians and South Slavs as well[5]—we must see them against the background of a culture that measured time in the primitive cyclical rhythms of the farmer's or shepherd's year and history by the tragic alternation of epic victory and epic defeat. Overnight these men were thrust into a world where time was measured by the whistles of the mine and labor by the ton of coal. In their war with industrial America they had to do battle not only with the present, but with their own conception of the past. If they were to triumph they would have to learn to see history—the history which they were now making—not as a value or a theater or a ritual or a myth, but as a complex process where the impersonal forces of economic and social pressures interacted with and sometimes overwhelmed the personal. They would have to learn to measure their victories and their defeats not according to the standards of an epic past, with its immemorial themes of armed conflict and personal honor and Homeric wrath, but according to the drier but more realistic standards of the industrial world. They would have to learn to substitute for the ideal of total participation in a glorious epic tradition a sense of partial participation in that historical *future* for which the union, with its progressive goals, was educating them. They were men in transition. A gauge of the incompleteness of that transition may be read in the role the Greeks would play in the gunfire at Ludlow. Louis Tikas, the Greek interpreter who stood between those two worlds, the epic and the modern, may well have been a sacrifice to both.

---

4. Mike Lingos, taped interview.

5. Both South Slavs and South Italians in the Colorado coalfields in the years before World War I were heirs to a strong heroic tradition. For the South Italian tradition of heroic banditry see E. J. Hobsbawm, *Primitive Rebels: Studies in Archaic Forms of Social Movement in the 19th and 20th Centuries* (New York, 1965), pp. 13–56, and Carlo Levi, *Christ Stopped At Eboli: The Story of a Year*, tr. Frances Frenaye (New York, 1976), pp. 135–45. Levi's description of the operation of myth and history in the psychology of the Lucanian peasants is exceptionally rewarding. The classic work on South Slavic epic song and its Homeric parallels is A. B. Lord, *The Singer of Tales* (New York, 1965).

REFERENCE NOTES

A word on names and quotations in this book: some of the immigrant names which appear here are, sadly, no more than guesses. A number of them are dependent upon the memories of people speaking of events sixty years in the past and on the writer's luck in transcription; others have come down from the work of court stenographers and newspaper reporters whose standards of accuracy, when it came to hard Greek and Italian and Polish names, were sometimes loose. I have wanted to write of the events in this book as much as possible as they were experienced by the men and women who lived through them, and so I have relied heavily on quotation. All of the quotation comes from directly transcribed testimony, tape recorded and written interviews, and other first-person accounts, and is, of course, only as accurate as the memories of those who were there to remember. And if they remembered things a little differently on separate occasions, I've simply had to choose. Indirect quotations in the book are also taken from such sources, albeit compressed and rearranged. Any researcher who has gone out with notebook and tape recorder to try to capture the past knows that now and then the most interesting response from an informant comes after the book and the machine have been put away. This has been especially true of some of the material given to me by Lou Dold and Gus Papadakis, and therefore I have made a distinction in these notes between the dated and more formal tape-recorded and occasionally written *interviews* and those undated and informal *conversations* in which, during the course of a dinner or a walk, some fresh memory of the great strike of 1913–14 might surface, to be jotted down on a napkin or the back of an envelope and later transferred to my notebooks before it disappeared.

A final note: readers checking the sources given in the reference notes against the texts may find in a very few cases the two differing slightly in detail. In attempting to draw scenes in the book as vividly as possible I have worked

273

from multiple sources, and not wishing to burden the notes needlessly, in some places I have cited only the major or representative references.

ABBREVIATIONS

Autobiography	Mary Harris Jones, *The Autobiography of Mother Jones*, 3d ed. (Chicago, 1974).
CCMC	U.S. Congress, House, *Conditions in the Coal Mines of Colorado, Hearings before a Subcommittee of the Committee on Mines and Mining*, 63rd Cong., 2d sess., 1914, pursuant to H. Res. 387, in 2 vols.
CIR	U.S. Congress, Senate, *Industrial Relations: Final Report and Testimony Submitted to Congress by the Commission on Industrial Relations, Created by the Act of August 23, 1912*, 64th Cong., 1st sess., 1916, Doc. 415, vols. 7–9.
Coalfield War	George S. McGovern and Leonard F. Guttridge, *The Great Coalfield War* (Boston, 1972).
Depths	Barron B. Beshoar, *Out of the Depths: The Story of John R. Lawson, A Labor Leader* (Denver, 1942).
DC	Edward L. Doyle Collection, Denver Public Library, Western History Department, Denver, Colo.
DE	*Denver Express*, Denver, Colo.
DP	*Denver Post*, Denver, Colo.
DT	*Denver Times*, Denver, Colo.
Farrar	Frederick M. Farrar Papers, Denver Public Library, Western History Department, Denver, Colo.
Foreigners	Mary Thomas O'Neal, *Those Damn Foreigners* (Hollywood, 1971).
LC	John R. Lawson Collection, Denver Public Library, Western History Department, Denver, Colo.
TCN	*Trinidad Chronicle–News*, Trinidad, Colo.
Tikas to the UMW	United Mine Workers of American District 15 Correspondence, UMW National Headquarters, Washington, D.C.
UMWJ	*United Mine Workers Journal.*
Special Convention, 1913	"Proceedings of the Special Convention of District 15, United Mine Workers of America Held in Trinidad, Colorado, September 16, 1913." Edward L. Doyle Collec-

tion, Denver Public Library, Western History Department, Denver, Colo.

UMW Proceedings   *Proceedings of the . . . Biennial Convention of the United Mine Workers of America . . .*, 1914, 1916 (Indianapolis, 1914–16).

CHAPTER 1—BEGINNINGS

1 JOHN TSANAKATSIS AND GUS PAPADAKIS: interviews and conversations, 29 August 1973.

7 MANY . . . RETURNED TO THEIR NATIVE LANDS: Theodore Saloutos, *They Remember America: The Story of the Repatriated Greek–Americans* (Berkeley and Los Angeles, 1956), p. 29, gives the figure for the Greeks as roughly forty percent by 1931. See also the table he reproduces on p. 30 for comparison of the Greeks leaving the United States between 1908–31 with other immigrant groups.

7 THE GREEKS . . . WERE EXTRAVAGANTLY HISTORICAL: see Appendix.

CHAPTER 2—1746 MARKET STREET

9–11 GEORGE ZEESE IN COLORADO: interview and subsequent conversations.

11 TIKAS . . . IN COLORADO: from Tikas' petition for naturalization, 1 April 1913, Records of the U.S. District Court, Denver, Colo.

12 WITH HIM WERE OTHERS FROM HIS VILLAGE: Emmanuel Marangoudakis to the author, 8 June 1976.

12 "ALL THESE HAVE LEFT THEIR BELOVED FATHERLAND": Seraphim G. Canoutos, *Hellenikos Emporikos Hodegos* [Greek–American Guide] (New York, 1911), quoted in Thomas Burgess, *Greeks in America* (Boston, 1913), p. 43.

12 GREEK SUGAR BEET WORKERS: Alvin T. Steinel, *History of Agriculture in Colorado* (Fort Collins, Colo., 1926), p. 408.

12 WORKED FOR AN INSURANCE AGENCY, KEPT A SALOON: CIR, vol. 7, p. 6355.

12 HEAD OF A SYNDICATE OF BOOTBLACKS: Ibid., p. 6364. Sam N. Soter of Salt Lake City recalled in 1981 that the prominent Utah Greeks Louis and George Demopoulos received their American name—Strike—from this Denver incident.

12 TIKAS' DECLARATION OF INTENTION: 1 April 1910, Records of the U.S. District Court, Denver, Colo. Slightly abbreviated in the text.

16 GEORGE ALLISON: *Rocky Mountain News*, 2 May 1935.

16 FIFTEEN GREEKS TO GRECO–TURKISH WAR: Ibid., 23 April 1897.

16 RUSH OF GREEK IMMIGRATION: Theodore Saloutos, *The Greeks in the United States* (Cambridge, Mass., 1964), pp. 16, 44–45. Saloutos discusses the questionableness of such early immigration figures when applied to the Greeks, who tended to classify themselves on ethnic rather than national lines, while United States officials usually classified Greeks emigrating from Turkey or Bulgaria as Turks and Bulgarians, etc. A Greek view puts the number of Greeks leaving Europe and Asia Minor between 1899 and 1911 as 253,983. Theodore Saloutos, *They Remember America: The Story of the Repatriated Greek–Americans* (Berkeley and Los Angeles, 1956), p. 10.

16 ENTIRE PROVINCES . . . DESERTED: Saloutos, *The Greeks in the United States*, p. 31.

17 SMELTER OPERATORS . . . FIRING "WHITE MEN": *DT*, 25 June 1902.

17 SIXTY–SIX GREEKS . . . LEAVING TRINIDAD: Ibid., 28 February 1901.

17 GEANAKOS AND KARAKATSEANES: Ibid., 20 July 1901.

17 ROW IN THE COLONY: Ibid., 4 February 1901.

19 240 GREEKS: Department of Commerce, Bureau of the Census, *13th Census of the United States Taken in the Year 1910, Report by State Supplement, Statistics for Colorado* (Washington, D.C., 1914), p. 592.

19 "MODERN APOLLOS": *Denver Republican*, 29 December 1908.

20 VICTOR–AMERICAN EXPLOSION AT DELAGUA, 1910: Colorado State Inspector of Coal Mines, *Fourteenth Biennial Report* 1909–1910 (Denver, n.d.), pp. 154–64; Peter Loulos, interview.

20 WORDS: for other representative Greek proverbs see B. J. Marketos, ed., and Ann Arpajoglu, tr., *A Proverb For It* (New York, 1945).

20 EROTOKRITOS: Seventeenth-century Cretan epic by Vincenzo Kornaros.

20 AMANES: from the characteristic sigh in love couplets.

21 LEFT THE COFFEEHOUSE TO LOUIS: John Tsanakatsis, interview and conversation.

21–23 LOULOUDAKIS: Peter Loulos, interview.

22 THE LETTER: from Peter Loulos to George Terezakis, editor of *Kriti* [Crete], 2 November 1973.

22–23 LOULOUDAKIS AND ORA WILLIAMS: Peter Loulos, interview and conversation. Their marriage certificate is still on file with the Jefferson County Clerk and Recorder in Golden, Colo.

23–24 GREEK TOWN IN 1911: Ballenger and Richards, *Thirty–Ninth Annual Denver City Directory for 1911* (Denver, 1911), and John Rougas, interview. Rougas recalled Kutsofas as Tikas' partner in 1910.

24 GEORGE ALLISON'S CANDY STORE: *Rocky Mountain News*, 2 May 1935.

24 SOUTH OMAHA RIOTS OF 1909: Saloutos, *The Greeks in the United States*, pp. 66–69.

24–29 LEONIDAS SKLIRIS: see Helen Zeese Papanikolas, "Life and Labor Among the Immigrants of Bingham Canyon," *Utah Historical Quarterly* 33 (Fall 1979): 294–303, and "Greek Workers in the Intermountain West: The Early Twentieth Century," *Byzantine and Modern Greek Studies* 5 (1965): 192–95, 204–7. Skliris' employment agency is listed as 1715 Market Street in Ballenger and Richards, *Thirty-ninth Annual Denver City Directory for 1911*. For Skliris' gouging of Colorado railroad workers see CCMC, vol. 1, pp. 80–81. Cf. also U.S. Congress, Senate, *Abstracts of the Reports of the Immigration Commission*, 2, "The Greek Padrone System in the United States," 61st Cong., 3d sess., 747, pp. 391–408.

24 A CORINTHIAN: John Rougas, interview.

25 PHOTOGRAPH OF SKLIRIS: Salt Lake City *O Ergatis* [The Worker], 25 March 1908.

27 STOWED AWAY ON A LINER: *Price* (Utah) *Sun*, 9 April 1915, quoted in Allen Kent Powell, "A History of Labor Union Activity in the Eastern Utah Coal Fields: 1900–1934," Ph.D. diss., University of Utah, 1976, p. 203.

27 DENVER TIMES: 16 May 1900.

28 SKLIRIS WOUNDED: Louis James Cononelos, "Greek Immigrant Labor," M.A. thesis, University of Utah, 1979, pp. 260–61; see pp. 252–54 for Greek workers' views of Skliris and other labor agents.

28 SOMEONE BEGINS TO SING: see Appendix.

CHAPTER 3—A LESSON IN ECONOMICS

31–34 THE TOWNS: Helen Ring Robinson, *New York American*, 12 April 1914; *Foreigners*, pp. 63–64. According to Colorado Fuel and Iron Company President Jesse Welborn, in 1914 the C. F. and I., which owned 300,000 acres of Las Animas County, produced thirty-five percent of the coal mined in Colorado, while the rival Rocky Mountain Fuel Company and the Victor–American Fuel Company produced thirteen and fifteen percent respectively. CCMC, vol. 1, p. 532, vol. 2, p. 2494.

34 HARD QUESTIONS: CIR, vol. 7, p. 6955.

34 A SALOON FOR EVERY SEVENTEEN MEN: Ibid., vol. 9, p. 8917.

34–36 A YOUNG GREEK: Gus Papadakis, interviews and conversations.

35–36 THE MINE: Gus Papadakis, conversations; Joseph Husband, *A Year in a Coal Mine* (Boston and New York, 1911), pp. 20–26, 29–35, 44–48; Stephen Crane, "In the Depths of a Coal Mine," *University of Virginia*

Edition of the Works of Stephen Crane, ed. Fredson Bowers, vol. 8, pp. 593–600. For a description of mines and mining in southern Colorado from the operators' point of view see F. W. Whiteside, "The Trinidad District in Colorado," *Coal Age*, 24 February, 2 March 1912.

36 INDEPENDENT CONTRACTORS: CCMC, vol. 1, p. 401.

37 "HOW MANY MULES?": *Autobiography*, p. 200; Robinson, *New York American*, 12 April 1914. UMWJ, 9 January 1913, gives a Wyoming version.

37 BREAK EACH OTHER'S STRIKES: CIR, vol. 9, p. 8947. Union officials also had reason to believe it was the deliberate policy of coal companies to employ men speaking different languages in the same mine in order to impede organizing. CIR, vol. 7, pp. 6499, 6531. See also *Report of the* [United States] *Industrial Commission*, vol. 15 (Washington, D.C., 1901), pp. 405–7.

37 UNDERCUT A WAGE: CCMC, vol. 1, p. 717; CIR, vol. 9, p. 8081. The 1910 "Dillingham" report of the United States Immigration Commission found that while the floods of immigrants from southern and eastern Europe were not as a rule engaged at lower rates of pay in the unskilled work they sought, "they were content to accept wages and conditions which the native Americans and immigrants of the older class had come to regard as unsatisfactory." In the coalfields of western Pennsylvania, where the new immigrants had largely displaced the older immigrants and native-born Americans, the average wage of the bituminous coal worker was forty-two cents a day below the average wage paid in the coal mines of the Middle West and Southwest, where the older class of miners still predominated. *Abstracts of Reports of the Immigration Commission*, vol. 1 (Washington, D.C., 1910), pp. 37–38. See also *Report of the Industrial Commission*, vol. 12, pp. LXXX–LXXXI, CXLVII–CXLIX.

37 MINE ACCIDENTS 1910–13: Colorado State Inspector of Coal Mines, *Biennial and Annual Reports, 1909–1914*.

37 HASTINGS MINE EXPLOSION OF 1912: UMWJ, 27 June 1912.

38 COMPANY-CONTROLLED CORONERS' JURIES: CIR, vol. 7, pp. 6784, 6786, vol. 8, pp. 7265–96. One coroner's report had only this notation: "Accident; fall of rock in mine; internal injuries; pelvic region; no relatives and damn few friends." CCMC, vol. 2, p. 1831.

38 AVERAGE DEATH BENEFIT: CIR, vol. 8, p. 7805.

38 TWENTY-DOLLAR COFFIN: CCMC, vol. 2, p. 1874.

38 "DAGOES ARE CHEAPER THAN PROPS": Ibid., vol. 2, p. 2630.

38 CAMP AND PLANT: the Colorado Fuel and Iron Company magazine published between 1901–4 in Denver and Pueblo, Colo.

38 PROFESSOR KEATING'S LECTURE: *Camp and Plant* 1 (Jan. 18, 1902): 82.

38 A CITY OF PAPER: for circulars sent to their subordinates in the field by E. H. Weitzel, manager of the C. F. and I. fuel department, and W. J. Murray, vice president and general manager of the Victor–American Fuel Company, see respectively CIR, vol. 7, pp. 6738–50, and vol. 8, pp. 7350–57.

38 NONINTERFERENCE IN POLITICS: CCMC, vol. 1, p. 514.

38 ADHERENCE TO LAWS: John Lawson gave the dates of Colorado laws regulating working conditions in the coalfields, yet largely unenforced by the time of the 1913–14 coal strike: abolition of scrip, 1899; right to organize, 1897–1911; right to checkweighmen, 1897. CCMC, vol. 1, p. 1308. For the complex history of the eight-hour movement in Colorado, see G. P. West, United States Commission on Industrial Relations, *Report on the Colorado Strike*, (Washington, D.C., 1915), pp. 62–63.

38 CHECKWEIGHMEN: CCMC, vol. 1, pp. 500–501, 544.

38 CIRCULARS STOPPED SHORT: T. James, a miner from Indiana, had this to say about such circulars: "Circular says: 'Arrange proper shelter holes.' 'Arrange to have trolley wires guarded, etc.' 'Install signalling apparatus, etc, etc, etc,' Oh, its so easy to say arrange this and that, but get your wings off and come down to earth.

"In the first place, the foreman is a working man, second, he holds down his position by getting the coal out cheaper than any one else; third, if he gets it out cheaper, he gets a premium; fourth, if he doesn't get it out cheap, he gets 'canned,' and someone gets the job who can get it out cheaper. . . .

"The stock holders are clamoring for dividends. Dividends, dividends, give us more dividends. To hell with the miner, he's only a common laborer anyway. Insure him and if he gets killed the insurance company will pay damages or beat his wife and kiddies out of it through court juggling. . . ." In the socialist James' view ultimately it is not even the stockholders who are to blame, but workingmen foolish enough to vote against their class interests. UMWJ, 20 February 1913.

38 "WE DON'T CARE WHETHER YOU ARE A MEMBER OR NOT": CIR, vol. 8, pp. 7014–15.

38 A PETITION: CCMC, vol. 1, p. 1105. For more on the coal miners' grievances in southern Colorado see CIR, vol. 8, pp. 7025–31, and Special Convention, 1913.

39 PICTURE OF WILLIAM A. PINKERTON: *Coalfield War*, p. 63.

39 BILLY RENO AND JEFF FARR: *Coalfield War*, pp. 80–81; 30–32.

39 BOB LEE: CIR, vol. 7, p. 6782. See also Reference Notes to Chapter 6, p. 80 OF THE LEE FAMILY.

39 CHARLIE O'NEILL: CCMC, vol. 1, p. 1097; CIR, vol. 9, p. 8488.

39 OSGOOD . . . FOUNDED THE C. F. AND I.: for the early history of the C. F. and I. see H. Lee Scamehorn, *Pioneer Steelmaker in the West* (Boulder, Co., 1976) and *Coalfield War*, pp. 6–18.

39 CHARGES: information about the charges at the mines and camps is sprinkled throughout the major studies of the 1913–14 strike. See Special Convention, 1913, and CIR, vol. 9, p. 8494, for representative information.

39 OVERALLS: CCMC, vol. 2, p. 2010.

39 "WHAT A MAN EARNS IN COLORADO": CIR, vol. 9, p. 8037.

39 SCRIP: CCMC, vol. 2, p. 1893; CIR, vol. 7, p. 6517.

39 BAZANELLE: from interview transcripts for *The Life of the Western Coal Miner* project video tapes.

39–40 "A POOR MAN HAS GOT NO LAW": CCMC, vol. 1, p. 691. Cf. a Welsh miner in southern Colorado in 1914: "Out in this country . . . we have neither got laws nor nothing else. We are 'rupted.' " CCMC, vol. 1, p. 1008.

40 THE DREAM DID NOT DIE: two years after the conclusion of the 1913–14 strike, C. F. and I. manager E. H. Weitzel inadvertently suggested that there was more to industrial paternalism than simple altruism. In a letter to John D. Rockefeller, Jr., he defended the closed camp as necessary to protect the workers, especially the childlike foreigners, from sellers of patent medicine and cheap jewelry, "blue-sky" salesmen, solicitors for unsound insurance companies and gold mining stocks, labor organizers, and other "fakirs." "With a free hand these people [union organizers] could in a few months enroll practically all our foreigners. . . ." By the time he got the letter, Rockefeller had repudiated such overt paternalism and let Weitzel know it. Raymond B. Fosdick, *John D. Rockefeller, Jr.: A Portrait* (New York, 1956), p. 165.

40 SOPRIS IN 1903: *Camp and Plant* 1 (14 December 1901): 67.

40 WOP TOWN: CIR, vol. 9, p. 8931.

40 TYPHUS: Ibid., p. 8499.

40 C. F. AND I. HAD LOOKED AT ITS CAMPS: quoted in William James Ghent, *Our Benevolent Feudalism*, 3d ed. (New York, 1903), pp. 60–61. For a description of C. F. and I. welfare work see *The Survey* (3 February 1912), pp. 1706–20.

40 STRIKE OF 1903–4: *Coalfield War*, pp. 41–50, and Philip F. Notarianni, "Italian Involvement in the 1903–04 Coal Miners' Strike in Southern Colorado and Utah," in *Pane E Lavoro: The Italian American Working Class*, ed. George E. Pozzetta (Toronto, 1980).

40 THOUGHT OF THEM AS THEIR HOMES: how pervasive the hold of the coal company was on the imaginations of its workers was vividly brought home to me during an interview with an old Greek in Raton, New Mexico, who found it important to insist that when Louis Tikas was killed in 1914 *it wasn't even on Company land!*

40 IMMIGRANTS HAD HEARD OF ROCKEFELLER: CIR, vol. 9, p. 8486.

41 IDA TARBELL ON ROCKEFELLER: quoted in Allan Nevins, *John D. Rockefeller: The Heroic Age of American Enterprise* (New York, 1940), vol. 1, p. 111.

41 GOOD FELLOWSHIP; NEVER HAD A CRAVING; WAKEN OUT OF A NIGHT-MARE; RAISE A FLAG: Nevins, *John D. Rockefeller*, vol. 1, pp. 111, 103, 100.

41 LEDGER A: a page of the ledger is reproduced in Allan Nevins, *Study in Power: John D. Rockefeller, Industrialist and Philanthropist* (New York and London, 1953), vol. 1, p. 17.

41 QUARTER OF A BILLION DOLLARS TO . . . BENEFACTIONS: CIR, vol. 8, p. 7850.

41 GOD GAVE HIM HIS MONEY: Nevins, *Study in Power*, vol. 2, p. 194.

41 COMBINATION: Ibid., vol. 1, pp. 96–99.

42 "A LABORER IS WORTHY": John D. Rockefeller, *Random Reminiscences of Men and Events* (New York, 1909), p. 74. The italics are mine. When asked how workers might participate in the profits of the C. F. and I., the senior Rockefeller answered that they could buy shares. CIR, vol. 9, p. 8303. (In 1914 a share of C. F. and I. common stock sold for around $33, putting it somewhat out of the range of the average Colorado miner. CCMC, vol. 1, p. 534.)

42 COMMENDED HENRY FRICK: George Harvey, *Henry Clay Frick, The Man* (New York and London, 1928), p. 264.

42 $696 IN WAGES: *Coalfield War*, p. 22. The figure comes from the coal operators. State Labor Commissioner Edwin Brake gave the average wage per man at five Colorado mines in 1912 as $640.70. Colorado Bureau of Labor Statistics, *Fourteenth Biennial Report, 1913–1914* (Denver, 1914), pp. 163–64.

42 A DOLLAR IN DIVIDENDS: CIR, vol. 7, p. 6703.

42 ROCKEFELLER IN COMPIEGNE: Nevins, *John D. Rockefeller*, vol. 2, p. 565.

CHAPTER 4—THE NORTHERN FIELD:
THE MAKING OF AN ORGANIZER

43 THE TWENTY-FIFTH OF OCTOBER 1912: *DT*, 26 October 1912.

43 EMOTIONAL MEETING: *DT*, 21 October 1912.

44–45 UTAH COPPER STRIKE: see Helen Zeese Papanikolas, "Greek Workers in the Intermountain West: The Early Twentieth Century," *Byzantine and Modern Greek Studies* 5 (1979): 204–7; "Life and Labor Among the Immigrants of Bingham Canyon," *Utah Historical Quarterly* 33 (Fall 1965): 294–307; Russell R. Elliott, *Radical Labor in the Nevada Mining Booms 1900–1920* (Reno, Nev., 1961), pp. 52–59; and Louis James Cononelos, "Greek Immigrant Labor," M.A. thesis, University of Utah, 1979, pp. 200–12. Skliris had survived a spontaneous strike by 300 Greeks at Bingham Canyon in 1909. According to the Western Federation of Miners *Miners' Magazine* of 4 November 1909, Skliris' attempt to get the men back to work failed. "Notwithstanding the presence of twenty-five armed deputies the striking Greeks commanded him [Skliris] to leave the town at once and made the superintendent understand that they will never have anything to do with such a scoundrel scab herder and grafter, and they proceeded to carry out their command by taking him by the arm and leading him down the road with jeers." An indication of how narrow were the Greeks' views of the larger issues of the 1912 Utah Copper Company strike was their offer, at first, to go back to work at the *current* pay scale if only Skliris were removed. For a further discussion of the primitive level of Greek workers' social ideologies in this era, and an indication of possible changes, see Reference Notes to Chapter 6, p. 81 GREEKS UNTOUCHED BY SOCIAL IDEALS.

45 SKLIRIS DRESSED AS A WOMAN: George Paterakis, interview notes.

45 CARTOON: *DT*, 29 October 1912. The badges were given out by the Chamber of Commerce.

45 FAMILY DUTY: see Chapter 15.

46 "A SCAB": cf. CIR, vol. 8, pp. 7022–23.

46 THE NORTHERN FIELD: UMWJ, 13 February 1913. For accounts of the strike in the Northern Field see *Coalfield War*, pp. 75–77, and *Depths*, pp. 18–30. For a description of the mines see R. A. Pierce, "The Lignite Fields of Colorado," *Coal Age* (3 February 1912), pp. 534–48.

46 DUG THEM OUT OF THE MINE: CCMC, vol. 1, p. 93.

46 STOCKADES: for a description see Ibid., vol. 2, p. 2405.

46 CHARLES SNYDER: affidavit reprinted in UMWJ, 13 February 1913. Another version of his story appears in CIR, vol. 8, pp. 7055–58. Snyder would later testify against John Lawson in Lawson's trial for the killing of John Nimmo. See *Depths*, pp. 274–75, and Snyder's testimony in *People of the State of Colorado* v. *John R. Lawson et al. . . . ,* Farrar, vol. 21.

47 ELI GROSS: CCMC, vol. 1, pp. 49–53.

47 WALKOUT AT THE ALPHA PIT: UMWJ, 11 January 1912.

48 SCABS AT THE FREDERICK MINE: Adolph Germer, UMWJ, 5, 12 December 1912. The description of conditions in the Northern Field mines is from an account of the Golden Ash mine, which saw ten men walk out four days after the scabs at the adjacent Frederick mine put down their tools. Germer said conditions at the Golden Ash were "a fair example of the conditions in other scab mines." See also CCMC, vol. 2, p. 2563. The number of strikebreakers varies. See p. 48 TIKAS' LETTER, cited below.

48 RALLY'S TELEGRAM: DP, 18 November 1912.

48 TIKAS' LETTER: Tikas to the UMW, 10 February 1914.

48 WALKOUT AT THE FREDERICK MINE: UMWJ, 5 December 1912; DE, 19 November 1912. In the latter John Lawson says the walkout was unsolicited.

49 FIRE: UMWJ, 5 December 1912.

50 TROUBLE ON THE TWENTY-FIRST OF NOVEMBER: UMWJ, 5, 12 December 1912; DE, 22 November 1912.

51 TRIAL WAS A FARCE: UMWJ, 12 December 1912.

51 DOYLE'S ACCOUNT BOOK: Doyle to UMW President John P. White, 22 April 1913, DC.

51 NOT THE FIRST GREEK UNION MAN: see DP, 7 July 1911, for a Greek striker's view of the controversial Whitford injunction.

51 DOYLE'S FIRST MEETING WITH TIKAS: CIR, vol. 8, pp. 7022–23.

51 WHITE IN THE NORTHERN FIELD: UMWJ, 9 January 1913.

52 "HE RUN FROM THE BACK DOOR": John Tsanakatsis, interview and conversation.

52 "THEY SHOOT HIM": Ibid.

52 LETTER DICTATED BY TIKAS: Tikas to the UMW, 10 February 1914.

52–53 FIRST NOTES: for examples of stories showing Tikas as a graduate of Athens University and a descendant of famous Greek leaders see CIR, vol. 9, p. 8121, vol. 7, p. 6645; and John Reed, "The Colorado War," Metropolitan 40, no. 3 (July 1914): 68. The notions that Tikas was a Rethymniote and was waiting for a picture bride, or was writing to a picture bride the night he was killed, were coffeehouse hearsay in Carbon County, Utah.

53 A PAMPHLET: Ludlow: Being the Report of the Special Board of Officers Appointed by the Governor . . . (Denver, n.d.).

CHAPTER 5—ORGANIZING: THE SOUTHERN FIELD

61 LOUIS R. DOLD: Louis R. Dold, interviews and conversations.

64 MIKE LIVODA: see also CIR, vol. 8, pp. 7042–43.

66 BEATING OF LIVODA: see also CIR, vol. 8, pp. 7042–43.

67 A LIST . . . ED DOYLE KEPT: Ibid., vol. 7, pp. 6951–52.

67 JOHN LAWSON: Ibid., vol. 8, p. 7187, vol. 9, pp. 8020, 8034–35; CCMC, vol. 2, pp. 2379–80.

67 DOYLE: CIR, vol. 7, pp. 6925–34, 6987. Doyle gives the date of the Spring Valley shooting as 1892. Other accounts of the event say the miners were rioting.

67 DOYLE'S RECORD: Ibid., vol. 8, p. 6996.

67 JOHN McLENNAN: Ibid., vol. 7, pp. 6509–10.

67 ROBERT UHLICH: TCN, 3 December 1913.

67 ADOLPH GERMER: Coalfield War, p. 85. Germer had also been in the mines as a boy.

67 WILLIAM DIAMOND: See Chapter 11 and Reference Notes.

68 FRANK HAYES: CIR, vol. 8, pp.7189–90; Coalfield War, p. 88. Hayes was to serve a term as lieutenant governor of Colorado in 1937 in the administration of Teller Ammons, son of Governor Elias Ammons.

68 CRANE VISITED A BREAKER IN PENNSYLVANIA: Stephen Crane, "In the Depths of a Coal Mine," University of Virginia Edition of the Works of Stephen Crane, ed. Fredson Bowers, vol. 8, pp. 591–92. For more on boys in mines see John Spargo, The Bitter Cry of the Children (New York and London, 1906), pp. 163–64.

68 LAWSON'S FIRST STRIKE: Winnifred Banner, "Struggle Without End," typed and incomplete ms., LC, pp. 1–2. "This institution [the breaker and its boy slate pickers] might well be called the cradle of industrial unionism" (ibid., p. 2).

68 AN ACTIVE AND PASSIVE ORGANIZER; DUMMY REAL ESTATE FIRM: Anonymous, "Doyle Notes," LC; Depths, pp. 49–50, 57.

69 WALTER BELK; ALBERT FELTS: Coalfield War, p. 88.

69 FELTS' DEATH: The American Labor Year Book 1921–1922, vol. 4, ed. Alexander Trachtenberg and Benjamin Glassberg (New York, n.d.), p. 197; Dale Fetherling, Mother Jones, The Miners' Angel (Carbondale and Edwardsville, Ill., 1974, 1979), p. 194.

69 SEVENTY-FIVE BALDWIN-FELTS MEN: Coalfield War, p. 88.

69 DOVER HOTEL: UMWJ, 25 September 1913.

69 258 DEPUTY SHERIFFS: Ibid., 9 October 1913.

69 RED-HANDED MURDERERS: CIR, vol. 8, p. 7820.

69 GAME WARDENS: "Doyle Notes," LC.

69 GUNS WERE BEING IMPORTED: CIR, vol. 7, pp. 6562–63.

69 "SPOTTERS"AT BOWEN: CCMC, vol. 2, p. 2567.

70 BEST RIFLES MONEY COULD BUY: CIR, vol. 8, pp. 7262–63.

70 NUMBER 52 WROTE FROM TIOGA: Ibid., p. 7063.

70 DELAGUA . . . NO PLACE FOR AN AMERICAN: Ibid., p. 7062.

70 DOYLE'S MINUTES: DC, p. 2.

71 MORE THAN TWENTY-EIGHT AFFIDAVITS: Tikas to the UMW, 10 February 1914. Examples of affidavits from Greeks in the Northern Field probably collected by Tikas are reproduced in CIR, vol. 8, pp. 7040–41, 7043.

71 PIKE VIEW STRIKE: DE, 1 April 1913.

71 FINAL CITIZENSHIP PAPERS: see dates on Tikas' petition for naturalization, Records of the U.S. District Court, Denver, Colo.

71 COLORADO SPRINGS PAPERS: the Pike View strike was covered in the Colorado Springs Gazette, 2, 3, 6 April 1913, and the Colorado Springs Evening Telegraph, 1 April 1913.

71 NUMBER 52 . . . TRYING TO QUELL A PREMATURE STRIKE: CIR, vol. 8, p. 7064.

71 STILL ORGANIZING ON HIS OWN TIME: Tikas to the UMW, 10 February 1914.

71 CURIOUS STORY: Milton Karavites, interview, conversation.

71 NICK MATSOUKAS' ACCOUNT: National Greek Press (Chicago) [Ellenikos Typos], 9 July 1976.

72 TWO LETTERS BY TIKAS: Tikas to the UMW, 10 February 1914, 28 August 1913.

73 FREDERICK MINE: this mine is in the Southern Field.

73 ALREADY IN SEGUNDO: proceedings of the Las Animas County, Hearings of the Grand Jury 1914, Farrar, vol. 5, pp. 2254–55.

74 IN DELAGUA . . . THE GREEKS WERE ANGRY: CCMC, vol. 1, p. 1203.

74 KOSTAS PAPADAKIS: Gus Papadakis, interviews and conversations. Papadakis had been fired for being a troublemaker at the Hastings mine and was working at the Oakview mine just before the 1913 strike call.

74 DAVE . . . TOLD HIM ABOUT THE UNION: blacks had been important in the United Mine Workers since its earliest days. A valuable study could be made of the strong parallels—with key differences—betwen black and immigrant experience in the UMW. See Herbert G. Gutman, Work, Culture and Society in Industrializing America (New York, 1976), Chapter 3, "The Negro and the United Mine Workers of America."

74 STRIKE CLAIMED ITS FIRST DEATH: UMWJ, 21, 28 August 1913.

75 BURIED GERALD LIPPIATT: Ibid., 28 August 1913.

75 TIKAS WAS BACK IN DENVER: the date comes from Tikas to the UMW, 28 August 1913.

75 AMMONS' NEGOTIATION ATTEMPTS: CIR, vol. 8, pp. 6409–10.

75 OPERATORS OPPOSED TO NEGOTIATING: Committee of Coal Mine Managers, *Facts Concerning the Struggle in Colorado for Industrial Freedom*, Series 1, Bulletin No. 6 (Denver, 1914), p. 38: "The mine managers offered to submit to Governor Ammons or to any arbitration board named by him, every demand made except that of recognition of the Union, but they would not treat in any way, directly or indirectly, with the organization known as the United Mine Workers of America." Victor–American Fuel Company chairman John Osgood's speech to a meeting of Colorado newspaper editors on 13 November 1913 is revealing: the mine owners refuse to arbitrate with the union, among other reasons, "because their [the union's] sole purpose and only demand before the strike was called, as well as now, was that we should enter into a contract with them, practically giving them control of our business. . . . Because the United Mine Workers of America is an unincorporated, irresponsible and purely voluntary association without any standing in the financial world. . . . Because of the men they claim to represent, a large number have been guilty of violence and other unlawful acts. . . . Because the officers of the United Mine Workers have instigated a reign of terror in the coal fields of the state for the purpose of intimidating our men who are working. . . ." Reproduced in the Colorado Bureau of Labor Statistics, *Fourteenth Biennial Report 1913–1914* (Denver, 1914), pp. 153–54. The aversion of industrialists to negotiating with unions in this period has been accurately termed "pathological."

75 BOWERS' LETTER: CIR, vol. 9, p. 8413.

75 FIFTY–FOUR DOLLARS RELIEF: DC.

75 BACK IN EL PASO COUNTY: UMWJ, 25 September 1913.

76 CONVENTION ROLL: Special Convention, 1913.

76 MOTHER JONES' SPEECH: CCMC, vol. 2, pp. 2630–35.

76 LIST OF DEMANDS: CIR, vol. 8, pp. 7035–36.

76 SCABS OF 1903: Professor James Brewster, union attorney: "The scabs of 10 years ago have found that they must be the union strikers of today," CCMC, vol. 1, p. 93.

77 DOYLE HAD LEASED GROUND: *Depths*, p. 57.

77 TENTS HAD BEEN ORDERED: Utah coalfield tradition has it that some of the tents came from the Carbon County district.

77 AT COAL CREEK: *Coalfield War*, p. 104.

77 DR. SCHWEGEL: DE, 24 September 1913. After a letter of protest by the Austro–Hungarians of Colorado, Dr. Schwegel was called back to Vienna. UMWJ, 9 April 1914.

CHAPTER 6—THE STRIKE BEGINS

79 DON MACGREGOR'S ACCOUNT OF THE EXODUS: *DE*, 24 September 1913.

80 LAWSON . . . RALLYING THE STRIKERS: *Depths*, p. 62; *Foreigners*, pp. 99–100.

80 RAILROADS DELAYED THE TENTS: CIR, vol. 1, p. 212.

80 GREEKS CAMPED OUT: *Depths*, p. 63.

80 TROUBLE IN SEGUNDO: *DE*, 25 September 1913.

80 "OF THE LEE FAMILY": Inis Weed, "The Colorado Strike," typed ms. in the Commission on Industrial Relations Colorado Strike Reports, National Archives, p. 15. Jesse Welborn of the C. F. and I. was still sentimentalizing gunmen like Lee after the Ludlow massacre: "The marshal is often the one man in the camp to whom the employees tell their troubles, both real and imaginary." Committee of Coal Mine Managers, *Facts Concerning the Struggle in Colorado for Industrial Freedom*, Series 1, Bulletin No. 15 (Denver, 4 September 1914), p. 70.

80 A KENTUCKIAN: 25 September 1913. MacGregor gives a colorful account of the Lee ranch near Springer as a haven for outlaws and of the Lee brothers' depredations in New Mexico in this report. See also CIR, vol. 7, p. 6782, and Weed, "The Colorado Strike," pp. 13–14, for other accounts of Lee.

81 LEE HAD BEATEN UP . . . SEGUNDO GREEKS: CCMC, vol. 1, p. 537.

81 SEEN PLOTTING AGAINST HIM: *TCN*, 25 September 1913.

81 MOST ABUSED OF THE CAMP WORKERS: Las Animas Grand Jury, Farrar, vol. 5, pp. 2254–55.

81 ITALIANS OF THE SOUTHERN FIELD: Philip F. Notarianni, "Italian Involvement in the 1903–04 Coal Miners' Strike in Southern Colorado and Utah," in *Pane E Lavoro: The Italian American Working Class*, ed. George E. Pozzetta (Toronto, 1980).

81 "THE 29TH OF JULY": M. McCuster, "Reports on Colorado Situation," typed ms. in the Commission on Industrial Relations Colorado Strike Reports, National Archives, p. 21; CCMC, vol. 1, p. 424.

81 GREEKS . . . UNTOUCHED BY SOCIAL IDEALS: Greek involvement in American labor movements and leftist politics has been, for the most part, insufficiently studied. But it seems likely that in the Rocky Mountains the Greeks participated in strikes led by militant unions for pragmatic or emotional reasons, not for ideological ones. Their role was to be foot soldiers and occasional victims in the struggle, such as Nick Spanudhakis, who was one of the I.W.W. pickets killed by Colorado State police outside Lafayette in 1927, or the other Greek casualties in the Utah and Nevada copper strikes of 1912 and the Colorado strike of 1913–14. Individualistic, innately conservative, and with the villager's

usual distrust of new ideas, Greek workers in the Mountain West saw themselves as only temporary residents in this country, with little incentive to bear the weight of a strike for economic or social gains that would only appear in the long term. They had brought no tradition of progressive ideology from their industrially backward homeland, where the first socialist deputies would appear in parliament only in 1910. None of the Greeks who were in the Mountain West before the First World War interviewed by me ever mentioned knowing what a labor union was in the Old Country, though, like George Zeese, they may have had faint recollections of brotherhoods of typographers and stevedores in the few large cities. Louis Tikas may have been familiar with the craft guilds of Rethymnon. See Pandelis Prevelakis, *The Tale of a Town*, tr. Kenneth Johnstone (London and Athens, 1976), p. 110. According to S. Victor Papacosma, "The Greek Press in America," *Journal of the Hellenic Disaspora* 5, no. 4 (Winter 1979): 55, the Greeks in America had relatively few radical newspapers and journals compared with other ethnic groups and these seem to have come into being only at the outset of World War I. The two most important book-length studies of Greeks in America written at the peak of Greek immigration found Greek participation in leftist politics and the union movement in this country negligible. "Socialism finds no followers among the people of this [Greek] race in the United States. . . . Greeks are apparently not inclined to join trade unions, partly because there are comparatively few of them who are laborers in unionized trades, partly because they prefer their own organizations, and partly because they are not wanted by the unions." (Henry Pratt Fairchild, *Greek Immigration to the United States* [New Haven, 1911] pp. 209–10.) "In regard to strikes the Greeks differ from other nationalities. To be sure, in Lowell and elsewhere the Greeks sometimes walk out with, or even without, the other textile employees, but they do it in their own exclusive way. Being thoroughly organized and sufficient unto themselves, they care naught for labor unions nor the I. W. W." (Thomas Burgess, *Greeks in America* [Boston, 1913] p. 154.) The major instance of Greek labor radicalism would probably not come until the mid-1920s–30s with the forming by New York City Greeks of a militant local of union furriers. See Theodore Saloutos, *The Greeks in the United States* (Cambridge, Mass., 1964), pp. 332–33, and esp. Philip S. Foner, *The Fur and Leather Workers Union* (Newark, N.J., 1950), pp. 160–62, 490–94, 520.

But there were exceptions to this lack of ideological commitment to their strikes by the first Greek immigrants. Stergios Mavroidis, who wired the *Atlantis* after the Ludlow massacre, was remembered by Colorado Greeks as rooting openly for the Wobblies and supported efforts to form a dual union of Colorado coal miners in 1918. Chapter 14, Reference Notes, p. 240 MAVROIDIS' TELEGRAM; pp. 245–46 LAWSON AND DOYLE. Louis Theos was remembered by the Greeks of Bingham, Utah, as an officer in the I.W.W. See Helen Zeese Papanikolas "Life and Labor Among the Immigrants of Bingham Canyon," *Utah Historical Quarterly* 33 (Fall 1965): 293. And one would like to know if that Anastasios Papas writing on "Greek Workers in America" in *The International Socialist Review* 15, no. 2 (August, 1914): 112–13, who described himself as a "class-conscious working man," was speaking only for himself or for other (and how many?) less articulate Greek laborers in America, men who, as Papas puts it, "never saw a mine, factory, railroad or other modern industry before coming to America," and never heard of a labor union or a strike or heard the word "scab." Traveling to Salt Lake City, Papas learned of Leonidas Skliris' success in hiring Greeks as scabs and how Greeks had been used to break a strike in the smelters around the city. ". . . For you must remember that these workers did not understand the English language. All they knew was that they had to get a job." Papas continues his analysis, telling, in the familiar leftist language of the day, how these same scabs get five to ten years of experience in "wage slavery" and "capitalist oppression" and with capitalism as their tutor revolt against their unbearable conditions and make "some noble fighters in the class conflict." He ends his brief article with a vivid denunciation of the Ludlow massacre: "Woe to the hands that shed this costly blood! Over the bodies of these martyrs do I prophesy that this foul deed will some day be avenged! And the spirit of Louis Tikas shall lead them on. . . ."

81 VENDETTA: J. K. Campbell, *Honour, Family and Patronage: A Study of Institutions and Moral Values in a Greek Mountain Community* (Oxford, 1964), esp. pp. 193–98, 268–73. In a country as rough as the American West of the 1900s, where bushwhacking and other forms of lawlessness cut across cultural and social lines, the ethnic component of strike violence should not be overstressed. Still Campbell's superb study of the nomad Sarakatsani gives important insights into the state of mind of preindustrial Greeks. Cf. also Herbert G. Gutman, *Work, Culture, and Society in Industrializing America,* (New York, 1976), pp. 55–66, for examples of the violent reactions of preindustrial Americans to industrialization, including many examples of how immigrants channeled their responses through the rituals of their own cultures. Gutman cites the particularly gruesome case of the crucifixion of a Pennsylvania mine boss by Slavic miners in 1910 (p. 578).

81–82 SHOOTING OF BOB LEE: *TCN*, 24, 25 September 1913; *DT*, 25 September 1913.

82 ABERCROMBIE: *Depths*, p. 66.

82 THREE GREEK BAKERS: UMWJ, 2 October 1913.

82–83 ANGELO ZIKOS: "Transcript of Statements of Witnesses Appearing Before the Investigating Committee Appointed by John McLennan, President State Federation of Labor, Investigating Conduct of State Militia
in the Southern Colorado Coal Fields," LC, pp. 259–67.

83 CAMP AT LUDLOW: CCMC, vol. 1, p. 216; Foreigners, pp. 108–9.

85 TWENTY DIFFERENT LANGUAGES: CCMC, vol. 1, p. 546. The number
of languages varies in different sources. There were about fourteen
important tent colonies in Colorado during the strike. Lawson trial,
Farrar, vol. 21, p. 1590. John McLennan claimed 11,232 men were on
strike. CIR, vol. 7, p. 6518.

85 LOWE HOME: see Chapter 13.

85 BAYES' RANCH: see Chapter 13.

85 SCABS STARTED TO COME IN: TCN, 7 October 1913.

85 SENT THEM BACK: Depths, pp. 67–68; CIR, vol. 8, p. 7151.

85 CAUGHT A COUPLE OF THEIR COUNTRYMEN: CCMC, vol. 2, pp. 1738–
43; TCN, 6, 7, October 1913.

85 SHOOTING STARTED: CIR, vol. 8, pp. 7151–52.

85 LAWSON AND MOTHER JONES' SPEECH: Lawson trial, Farrar, vol. 21,
pp. 1593, 1595–96.

87 RUN-IN WITH THE GUARDS: CCMC, vol. 1, pp. 214–15, 314–15; UMW
Proceedings, 1916, vol. 2, pp. 957–58.

87 BELCHER AND BELK: CCMC, vol. 2, pp. 2478–82.

87 LAWSON TRIED TO HOLD THEM BACK: James Fyler, Jr., affidavit, LC.

87 STRANGE KIND OF BATTLE: Depths, pp. 68–69; TCN, 8, 9 October
1913.

87 MIKE ZALARATIS: TCN, 16 October 1913.

87 LAWSON MET ZEKE MARTIN: CCMC, vol. 1, p. 215.

87 COAL COMPANIES' POLICY: Colorado Bureau of Labor Statistics, Biennial Report 1913–1914 (Denver, 1914), p. 185.

87 NORTHCUTT'S PETITION: Coalfield War, p. 113. UMWJ, 16 October
1913, reported that Sheriff Farr requested the state to send aid because
"Greeks and Italians are dangerous anarchists."

88 AMMONS ELECTED WITH LABOR BACKING: Coalfield War, p. 93.

88 GUNFIRE . . . ON THE NINTH: Depths, p. 69; Coalfield War, pp.
116–17.

88 MRS. POWELL'S STORY: CCMC, vol. 2, p. 1913.

88 MACK POWELL'S FUNERAL: UMWJ, 23 October 1913.

88 FINAL PAPERS: Tikas' petition for naturalization, 1 April–13 October
1913, Records of the U.S. District Court, Denver, Colo.

90 STRIKERS . . . ARRESTED FOR PICKETING: *TCN*, 16 October 1913.

90 DEATH SPECIAL: UMWJ, 23 October 1913.

90 FELTS HAD AN AUTOMOBILE: CCMC, vol. 1, pp. 216, 339.

90 MACHINE GUN IN WEST VIRGINIA: Ibid., pp. 343–44.

90 LAWSON AND TIKAS GO TO FORBES: Ibid., pp. 295–96; Winnifred Banner, "Struggle without End," typed and incomplete ms., LC, pp. 31–32.

91 FORBES SHOOTING: UMWJ, 30 October 1913; CCMC, vol. 1, pp. 217–18, 790–93, 913–14.

91 ONE OF THE QUIETEST MEN: Court Martials, Farrar, vol. 20, p. 50. Lawson's description of Tikas: "Tikas was: medium sized, 155 pounds, dark, full, pleasant face, educated, member of Hellenic society, good disposition, courageous" LC.

91 TIKAS' LETTER: Tikas to the UMW, 10 February 1914. Tikas probably means the gun could fire 250 shots a minute. The number of shots is variously given. Cf. CCMC, vol. 2, p. 2483.

92 THREE STRANGE GREEKS: CCMC, vol. 2, pp. 1634–35.

92 LAWSON MOVED INTO LUDLOW: Ibid., vol. 1, p. 219; Lawson trial, Farrar, vol. 21, pp. 1639–40. Lawson gives the date of the organization of the squads as October 11, 1913. For Lawson in jail see *Depths*, p. 313.

92 TIKAS' BADGE: this might also be Tikas' game warden's badge. See Chapter 5 Reference Notes, p. 69 GAME WARDENS, and CCMC, vol. 2, p. 2835.

92 RED BANDANAS: *Depths*, p. 74:

92 UNION WAS BUYING GUNS: CCMC, vol. 1, p. 323, vol. 2, p. 1599.

92 WOODEN RIFLES: CIR, vol. 9, p. 8762; McCuster, "Reports on Colorado Situation," p. 16.

92 SEARCHLIGHT: UMWJ, 16 October 1913.

93 STRIKER BORROWED A HIGH-POWER RIFLE: *Depths*, pp. x-xi.

93 BELK: CCMC, vol. 2, p. 2482. He was under indictment for the murder of an Italian in a West Virginia "riot."

93 FEELING RUNNING HIGH: UMWJ, 16 October 1913.

93 "THE UNION FOREVER": *Foreigners*, p. 109: "The second line was the only one changed. It varied with whomever the miners wanted 'down with.' " The song was composed by Frank J. Hayes. For a complete version see UMWJ, 18 September 1913.

93 SIGNS: UMWJ, 30 October 1913.

95 FLASHY NEW COATS: Mary T. O'Neal, interview.

95 GOVERNOR TOURED THE MINES: *DP*, 23 October 1913.

95 "STRIKE IS NO . . . PICNIC": *DE*, 24 October 1913.

95 ARRESTS AT FORBES: UMWJ, 30 October 1913.

96 MOTHER JONES WAS PREPARING TO LEAVE: UMW Proceedings, 1916, vol. 2, p. 960.

96 DOYLE, WALLACE, TIKAS GO TO DAWSON: UMWJ, 30 October 1913.

96 TIKAS HEADED FOR THE MINE: *DE*, 24, 27 October 1913. Tikas is identified as "Lakas" in the latter account.

96 LOU DOLD AT DAWSON: Louis R. Dold, interviews and conversations.

96 THE RESCUE: *DP*, 23–25 October 1913; *DE*, 23–25 October 1913.

97 BUNDLES OF SOMETHING: Ibid., 24 October 1913.

97 VIC MILLER OF PATHE: *DP*, 26 October 1913.

97 GEORGE MAVROIDIS: *DE*, 23 October 1913. Identified as "George Mavrada." I am assuming Tikas either translated Mavroidis' story for the *Express* reporter, or, as a fellow Greek, spoke with Mavroidis at some other time.

98 FANS COULDN'T HANDLE . . . DUST: *DE*, 27 October 1913.

98 ACCIDENT TOLL: State Mine Inspector of New Mexico, *Second Annual Report for the Year Ended October Thirty-First, 1913* (Gallup, N.M., n.d.), pp. 13–15.

98 JOHN L. LEWIS AT THE HANNA DISASTER: Saul Alinsky, *John L. Lewis: An Unauthorized Biography* (New York, 1949), p. 19; John Hutchinson, "John L. Lewis: To the Presidency of the UMWA," *Labor History* 19 (Spring 1978): 193.

98 DOYLE'S . . . MONEY WAS NO GOOD IN DAWSON: UMWJ, 30 October 1913.

98 SEVENTH STREET SHOOTING: *Coalfield War*, pp. 125–26; CIR, vol. 8, pp. 7334–43; *Depths*, pp. 79–80. For the mine owners' view see CIR, vol. 8, pp. 7152–53.

99 SHOOTING OF OCTOBER 25-26: *Coalfield War*, pp. 126–28; Lawson trial, Farrar, vol. 21, pp. 1613–18, 1641–42.

99 ANNA CAMERON: CCMC, vol. 2, pp. 1485, 1609–10; CIR, vol. 7, pp. 6870–73.

100 GREEKS BURNED . . . SECTION HOUSE: CCMC, vol. 2, p. 1629; CIR, vol. 7, p. 6876.

100 RALSTON PICKS UP BODY: CCMC, vol. 2, pp. 1809–10.

100 STRIKERS HAD TORN UP THE RAILS: CCMC, vol. 1, p. 808; *Coalfield War*, p. 127.

101 DON MACGREGOR: CCMC, vol. 1, pp. 914–19, 922–46, and esp. " 'Colorado Strike,' Statement of Mr. Don MacGregor, Representative of the

United Press," typed ms. marked *confidential*, National Archives, pp. 2–5.

101 SUSAN HOLLEARIN . . . OVERHEARD A CONVERSATION: CCMC, vol. 1, pp. 764–65.

101 PAINT CREEK . . . SHOOTING: Mother Jones had described this shooting her speech at Ludlow on 7 October 1913 and warned that the same Baldwin–Felts "bloodhounds" responsible for it had been shipped to Colorado. Lawson trial, Farrar, vol. 21, p. 1595.

101 DETECTIVE RUNS THE LOCOMOTIVE: *Coalfield War*, pp. 130–32.

102 READY TO DESERT: CCMC, vol. 1, pp. 508–9.

102 BICUVARIS COMES DOWN FROM LA VETA: Las Animas Grand Jury, Farrar, vol. 5, pp. 2533–39.

102 STEVE PAPPAS IN JAIL: *TCN*, 27 September 1913, 21 October 1913.

103 MEN WERE COMING INTO HEADQUARTERS TENT: CCMC, vol. 1, p. 923.

103 TERROR AND . . . DETERMINATION: " 'Colorado Strike' . . . ," p. 5.

103 JESSE SHAW: CCMC, vol. 2, pp. 1743–44.

103 O'NEILL AT TABASCO: Ibid. pp. 1491, 1495–96.

103 SHOOTING AT WOOTEN HOUSE: Ibid., pp. 1579–80, 1583. The bomb did not explode. *New York Times*, 29 October 1913.

104 ROBINSON AND EIGHT HASTINGS GUARDS: CCMC, vol. 2, pp. 1843–44, 1851–52.

104 GOVERNOR HAD CALLED OUT THE NATIONAL GUARD: " 'Colorado Strike' . . . ," pp. 6–8.

104 BICUVARIS CAME DOWN: CCMC, vol. 2, pp. 1749–50; Gus Papadakis, conversation.

CHAPTER 7—THE COMING OF THE MILITIA

107 COMIC BOOK MILITIA: *Depths*, p. 88.

107 GENERAL JOHN CHASE: Ibid., p. 88; *Coalfield War*, pp. 43–45. McGovern and Guttridge trace Chase's overblown militarism to his chagrin at being unable to fight in the Spanish–American war due to an irregularity in his commission. See "Minutes of the Court of Inquiry Established by an Executive Order of His Excellency George A. Carlson, Governor of the State of Colorado, August 26th, 1915," Farrar, vol. 23, p. 570.

107 EDWARD BOUGHTON: *Depths*, p. 92; CIR, vol. 7, p. 6843.

108 PAT HAMROCK: *Coalfield War*, p. 213; Court Martials, Farrar, vol. 20, pp. 80–81.

108 ROOSEVELT ON KETTLE HILL: Edmund Morris, *The Rise of Theodore Roosevelt* (New York, 1979), p. 655.

108 FOREIGN ADVENTURE AND NATIVISM: for a discussion of this psychology see Marilyn Blatt Young, "American Expansion, 1870–1900: The Far East," in *Towards a New Past: Dissenting Essays in American History*, ed. B. J. Bernstein (New York, 1969), pp. 185–86.

108 THE BREAD-WINNERS: first published anonymously in 1883–84 in the *Century Magazine*. Captain Farnham graciously allows his tenants to pay their rent at night, so they won't have to miss a half day's work. In *The Bread-Winners* the strike dissolves when the women march to the barricades to chide their men for behaving so foolishly. The industrial spy system is passed off as a matter of course. Toward the end of the book one of the capitalists is remembered a touch nostalgically for ending an earlier strike by making a little speech to the workers "complimenting Ireland and the American flag, and then they would go away."

108 HENRY ADAMS ON JOHN HAY: Henry Adams, *The Education of Henry Adams* (Boston, 1961), p. 503.

109 PHILIPPINE LEGAL CODE: CIR, vol. 7, p. 6489. Act Number 292 of the Philippine Commission, Section 9 (reprinted in U.S. Congress, Senate, 57th Cong., 1st sess., Doc. 173), set harsh penalties for Filipinos joining or forming secret societies for the promotion of treason, rebellion, sedition, or the promulgation of *any* political opinion or policy. Anyone acquainted with the necessarily secret union locals in the pre-1913 southern Colorado coalfields and the penalties and charges of sedition hurled at those caught joining or trying to organize them, or trying to challenge company-controlled politics in Las Animas and Huerfano counties, should find the comparison of southern Colorado and the Philippines of the Insurrection dismally apt.

109 "A STATE OF WAR EXISTS": UMWJ, 26 March 1914.

109 CHASE AT CRIPPLE CREEK: CIR, vol. 7, pp. 6476, 6482. It is interesting to note, in connection with the role of military enthusiasm in the industrial troubles of this era, that for all his moderation in labor questions President Theodore Roosevelt twice let himself be convinced to send federal troops to a strike zone. Captain Bert M. Lake, quoted in UMWJ, 26 March 1914, was an exception to military excess in the Colorado coal strike of 1913–14: "Government artillery is not intended for use in industrial warfare. I told Chase so, and when he insisted on taking the field guns, I resigned."

109 CHARLES KENNEDY'S SERVICE RECORD: CCMC, vol. 2, pp. 1713–14, 1721.

109–10 EDWIN CARSON'S SERVICE RECORD: *Coalfield War*, p. 205; George P.

West, United States Commission on Industrial Relations, *Report on the Colorado Strike* (Washington, D.C., 1915), p. 125.

110 LINDERFELT IN SOUTHERN COLORADO SINCE OCTOBER: CIR, vol. 7, pp. 6870, 6900–6901.

110 LINDERFELT'S SERIES OF WIRES: Ibid., p. 6873.

112–13 LINDERFELT'S BACKGROUND AND SERVICE RECORD: Ibid., pp. 6866–70.

112 FAMILY OF IMMIGRANTS: Ibid., p. 6832; *Coalfield War*, p. 167, quotes Linderfelt's story that his father was a professor of anatomy at the Sorbonne and died in Paris. See Court of Inquiry, Farrar, vol. 23, p. 1105. George P. West, researcher for the Commission on Industrial Relations, in his typed manuscript, "Report on Ludlow (May 15, 1914)," in the National Archives, claims Linderfelt's father was a Swedish military attaché to the Union Army in the Civil War.

112 THE PHILIPPINES: James Alfred LeRoy, *The Americans in the Philippines* (Boston and New York, 1914), vol. 2, p. 226: "If an officer of one rank might burn a cluster of huts without express warrant of superior authority, or wink at the employment by the Makabebes of methods for obtaining information which could not be mentioned in official reports, why not an officer of another rank. . . ? Under such conditions, unless every American command was officered by prudent, humane and vigilant men, the contagion of guerilla methods would spread from the Filipino to the American camp. And in many, indeed, almost certainly most places it did infect American officers, both high and low, and their soldiers." Van Cise felt he had evidence that, among his other brutalities, Linderfelt had given prisoners in Colorado the water cure. Court of Inquiry, Farrar, vol. 23, p. 318.

112 DAMN, DAMN, DAMN THE FILIPINOS: John A. Lomax and Alan Lomax, *American Ballads and Folk Songs* (New York, 1934), pp. 547–48.

112 LINDERFELT BACK IN THE U.S.: CIR, vol. 7, pp. 6868–69.

112 MISSED COURT-MARTIAL FOR LOOTING: *Coalfield War*, pp. 167–68.

112–13 LINDERFELT ON THE GREEKS: Court Martials, Farrar, vol. 20, p. 280.

113 HAVE . . . SEDITION LAWS TURNED ON THEM: CIR, vol. 7, pp. 6884, 6887.

113 WEST POINT TEXTBOOK: U.S. Congress, Senate, 57th Cong., 1st sess., Doc. 205, pt. 1, p. 19.

113 CANNOT GO AT IT WITH KID GLOVES: CIR, vol. 7, p. 6884.

113 MILITIA COMES TO LUDLOW: *TCN*, 1 November 1913; *Depths*, pp. 93–94.

113 CHASE'S ACCOUNT: Colorado Adjutant General, *The Military Occupation of the Coal Strike Zone of Colorado by the Colorado National Guard, 1913–1914, Report of the Commanding General to the Gover-*

nor for the Use of the Congressional Committee . . . (Denver, n.d.), p. 14.

113 PILED UP . . . WEAPONS: CCMC, vol. 1, p. 281.

115 TIKAS TAKES OVER LUDLOW COLONY: Tikas to the UMW, 10 February 1914.

115 VAN CISE'S SPEECH: *DP*, 28 October 1913.

115 FIRST DANCE: *DE,* 4 November 1913.

115 LINDERFELT GATHERS INFORMATION: Court Martials, Farrar, vol. 20, p. 279.

115 COLLEGE COMPANY: CIR, vol. 7, pp. 6809–10; *DP*, 28 October 1913.

116 COMPANY B: *Ludlow: Being the Report of the Special Board of Officers Appointed by the Governor* . . . (Denver, n.d.), pp. 8–9. pp. 8–9.

116 RAIDED THE LUDLOW COLONY: *DE*, 6 November 1913; CIR, vol. 7, p. 6807.

116 GREEKS AND GUNS: CIR, vol. 7, p. 6985; " ' Colorado Strike,' Statement of Mr. Don MacGregor, Representative of the United Press," typed ms. marked *confidential*, National Archives," pp. 8–9.

118 "LOUIE THE GREEK": *TCN*, 13 November 1913.

118 "EVERY MAN IS A LEADER": Las Animas Grand Jury, Farrar, vol. 5, p. 2244.

118 APOCRYPHAL JOKE: quoted in UMWJ, 13 November 1913.

118 CHASE HAD BEEN ADVISED: *TCN*, 13 November 1913. A post-Ludlow massacre sermon by Newell Dwight Hillis pictures Tikas in the role of anarchist: "A young Greek, knowing little about the Republic and having no stake in the country, and under the influence of the war in the Balkans, organizes his followers, foments hate, and precipitates a war that costs the State $5,000 a day. . . . Alas, for men who follow a leader who points them not to God's pillar of cloud by day and of fire by night, but waves a firebrand before them with which to burn up all ships, all factories, all legislative halls, and the Constitution of the fathers." Quoted in CIR, vol. 9, pp. 8666–67. The sermon was recommended by John D. Rockefeller, Jr., to his publicity agent, Ivy Lee. Ibid., p. 8729. Cf. CCMC, vol. 1, p. 469, on the aliens who have created open insurrection in southern Colorado. The myth of alien lawlessness existed, of course, independent of the fuel of violent industrial struggles. See Henry Pratt Fairchild, *Greek Immigration to the United States* (New Haven and London, 1911), p. 239: ". . . it seems likely that the presence of this [Greek] race in the country will add to, rather than diminish, the growing indifference to law as such, which is one of the most threatening signs of the times. This lack of reverence for

law, and every form of authority, seems to be characteristic of the children of immigrants of every race. But the Greeks appear to have it when they come."

119 GREEK VETERANS FROM THE BALKANS: on the day of the Ludlow massacre, a Greek participant knew of only three such veterans. Mike Lingos, interview.

119 JIM BICUVARIS . . . IN HIS EARLY THIRTIES: State Federation of Labor Investigation, LC, p. 680.

119 MACGREGOR WROTE OF A GREEK VETERAN: DE, 7 November 1913.

120 TIKAS SHOWS UP HIMSELF: Ibid., 11 November 1913.

120 VAN CISE ON TIKAS: CIR, vol. 9, p. 8120.

120 LINDERFELT SAID OF TIKAS: Ibid., vol. 7, p. 6895.

121 HELEN RING ROBINSON ON TIKAS: Independent 78 (11 May 1914): 247.

121 BREWSTER ON TIKAS: CIR, vol. 7, pp. 6664–65.

121 WALSENBURG MOVIE PALACE: TCN, 17, 18 November 1913.

121 CHASE CONFISCATED . . . FILM: Ibid.

121–22 KILLING OF BELCHER: UMWJ, 27 November 1913; Barron Beshoar, conversation.

122 BICUVARIS ARRESTED: TCN, 22 November 1913; State Federation of Labor Investigation, LC, pp. 671–81.

122 ZENI AND ZANCANELLI: Depths, pp. 103–4; CCMC, vol. 1, pp. 60, 229.

122 "UNDER THE WIDE AND STARRY SKIES": reprinted in the TCN, 11 December 1913, from the McDowell County (West Virginia) Recorder.

122 ZANCANELLI CONFESSED: TCN, 25 November 1913.

122 LUDLOW SURROUNDED: CIR, vol. 7, p. 6808.

123 COLONY PEOPLE LINED UP: UMWJ, 4 December 1913; DE, 26 November 1913.

123 LETTER WITH DOYLE'S SIGNATURE: New York Times, 27 November 1913; Coalfield War, p. 151.

123 DOYLE WAS RELEASED: Coalfield War, p. 152.

123 STATE AUDITOR BURNED IN EFFIGY: Ibid., p. 157.

123 LIVODA, PERRETT, AND TIKAS ARRESTED: UMWJ, 4 December 1913.

CHAPTER 8—A GAME OF GOLF

125 A GAME OF GOLF: details of the game come from Elbert Hubbard, The Fra 12, no. 5 (February, 1914): 131–34.

125 ROCKEFELLER'S APPROACH TO GOLF: Allan Nevins, *Study in Power: John D. Rockefeller, Industrialist and Philanthropist* (New York and London, 1953), vol. 2, pp. 292–93.

126 "THE DIVINITY OF BUSINESS": *Cosmopolitan* 44 (March 1908): 333. "Business is human service. Therefore business is essentially a divine calling."

126 A MESSAGE TO GARCIA: East Aurora, N.Y., 1899, 1907.

127 HELD ABOUT FORTY PERCENT OF THE C. F. AND I. STOCK: CCMC, vol. 2, pp. 2841–42.

127 HEEDLESS OF THE LIVES OF INDIVIDUAL MEN: ". . . while the corporation in the new organization of society had grown from a simple financial device to the only apparent doer of things, the law had not yet adjusted itself to the requirements of the new corporate society. You could not jail a *corporation* for a crime, and you did not yet hold directors themselves private persons, responsible for the acts of *other* 'legal persons' " The situation about 1907. Thomas C. Cochran and William Miller, *The Age of Enterprise*, rev. ed. (New York, 1961), pp. 200–201.

127 ROCKEFELLER ON TRADE UNIONS: Allan Nevins, *John D. Rockefeller: The Heroic Age of American Enterprise* (New York, 1940), vol. 2, p. 675.

127 LABOR DAY 1913: *New York Times*, 2 September 1913.

127 ROCKEFELLER ON CHECKERS: Nevins, *John D. Rockefeller*, vol. 1, p. 46.

127 "MAUDLIN SYMPATHY EXPRESSED FOR THE 'DOWNTRODDEN . . . ' ": Elbert Hubbard, *A Message to Garcia* (East Aurora, N.Y., 1899, 1907), pp. 11, 13–14. In print Hubbard had moved from astringent criticism of Standard Oil and John D. Rockefeller, Sr., to slavish praise. Freeman Champney, *Art and Glory: The Story of Elbert Hubbard* (New York, 1968), pp. 121, 167–68, 170–72, 178, 229.

128 HAD NOT BEEN IN COLORADO SINCE 1904: CCMC, vol. 2, pp. 2847, 2850.

130 PASS ON RESPONSIBILITY: CIR, vol. 9, pp. 8691, 8700–8701.

130 BOWERS' FULMINATIONS: Ibid., pp. 8420–21.

130 W. B. WILSON HAD WIRED HIM: Ibid., p. 8422.

131–32 ROCKEFELLER, JR.'S, EARLY LIFE: Raymond B. Fosdick, *John D. Rockefeller, Jr.: A Portrait* (New York, 1956), pp. 19–20, 33, 35–36, 39, 56, 59, 71, 79–80, 90–91, 107–8.

131 GRUMPY, MOROSE, AND GLOOMY: Ibid., pp. 88–89.

131 EARNING HIS WAY: Ibid., p. 87.

131 GLAD TO BLACK HIS FATHER'S SHOES: Ibid., p. 195.

132 LIKED CUTTING LOGS: Ibid., p. 92.

132 "A GREAT POWER TO GIVE": CIR, vol. 9, p. 8299.

132 AMERICAN BEAUTY ROSE SPEECH: excerpted in James Ghent, *Our Benevolent Feudalism*, 3d ed. (New York, 1903), p. 29.

132 RESIGNS CORPORATE DIRECTORSHIPS: Fosdick, *John D. Rockefeller, Jr.*, p. 140.

132 LETTER TO THE PRESS: *New York Times*, 12 December 1913.

133 ROCKEFELLER'S LIBRARY: Israel Shenker, "House That Holds Rockefeller Riches (Papers, Not $$$)," *Smithsonian* 8, no. 6 (September, 1977): 93.

133 "ONE OF THE SOUNDEST . . . PRONOUNCEMENTS": CIR, vol. 9, pp. 8635, 8636–38. The junior Rockefeller took issue with Chairman Walsh of the Commission on Industrial Relations' removal of the line following "Such children should not have been born": "But the assertions are a priori, they can not be proved, and are closely related to the other assertion that poverty is the cause, not merely a cause of crime."

133 GOMPERS WELL UNDERSTOOD: Ibid., p. 8813.

133 WITHOUT TALKING TO A SINGLE PROSTITUTE: CCMC, vol. 2, p. 2865.

134 FAR TOO SENSIBLE: Ibid., p. 2891.

134 WROTE BOWERS: CIR, vol. 9, pp. 8423–24, 8426–27.

134 TRINIDAD JAIL: *DE*, 24 November, 16 December 1913.

134 MARTIAL LAW: CIR, vol. 8, pp. 7332–33.

134 LOUIS KING'S TWO MEALS: Ibid., 24 December 1913.

135 A MATTER OF INDIFFERENCE: CIR, vol. 7, p. 6648.

135 BY HIS COMMISSION: *TCN*, 29 November 1913. General Chase reported that the commission was "a kindly and humane device established for the sole purpose of minimizing the possibility of error in judgment attending to the incarceration of civilians." Of the 172 prisoners held by the commission, 141 were "foreigners." There were fourteen Greeks. Colorado Adjutant General, *The Military Occupation of the Coal Strike Zone of Colorado by the Colorado National Guard, 1913–1914, Report of the Commanding General to the Governor for the Use of the Congressional Committee* . . . (Denver, n.d.), pp. 44–45.

135 THE MEN WERE GRILLED: *DE*, 3 December 1913.

135 THEY CALLED UP TIKAS . . . AND UHLICH: *TCN*, 2 December 1913.

135 "DANGEROUS AND UNDESIRABLE ALIEN": Ibid., 3 December 1913.

135 TRIED TO BARGAIN WITH TIKAS: *DE*, 16 December 1913.

135 MAY HAVE HINTED: see Tikas to the UMW, 10 February 1914, quoted below, pp. 135–36. Cf. Uhlich's letter to the UMWJ, 19 February 1914.

135 LIVODA SANG, UHLICH . . . READ: *DE*, 3 December 1913.

135–36 TIKAS' LETTER: Tikas to the UMW, 10 February 1914.

136 SNOWSTORM OF DECEMBER FOURTH: *DE*, 5 December 1913.

136 BAZANELLE WOKE UP: from interview transcripts in *The Life of the Western Coal Miner* project video tapes.

136 ARRESTED ADOLPH GERMER: *DE*, 5 December 1913.

136 WELBORN WROTE: CIR, vol. 8, 7119.

136 BUNKS COVERED WITH . . . SNOW: *DE*, 16 December 1913.

136 VAN CISE AWAKENED ON THIRTIETH OF NOVEMBER: CIR, vol. 7, pp. 6808–9.

137 AMMONS RESCINDED HIS ORDER: CCMC, vol. 1, p. 414. The order was rescinded 28 November 1913 according to this account.

CHAPTER 9—HIS VOICE

139 WINTER AT LUDLOW: *Foreigners*, pp. 116, 121.

139 MEN WENT LOOKING FOR RABBITS: CCMC, vol. 1, p. 763.

139 "UNION SHOES": Ibid., p. 818. The union bought up shoes by the thousand dollars' worth, supplying the camps in turn. Doyle notes, LC.

139 RUMORS THE UNION WAS BROKE: *Foreigners*, p. 124.

139 HABEAS CORPUS PROCEEDINGS: *TCN*, 15 December 1913.

139 THE MILITIA RELEASED TIKAS: Ibid.

139–40 TIKAS' LETTER IN THE FREE PRESS: *Trinidad Free Press*, 17 December 1913.

140 VULCAN MINE EXPLOSION: UMWJ, 8 January 1914.

140 SEVENTY-FIVE DOLLARS FOR FUNERALS: Ibid., 1 January 1914.

140 DIED OF GAS FROM HIS OWN MINE: *Coalfield War*, pp. 162–63.

140 PHOTOGRAPH OF TIKAS AND MOTHER JONES: *Rocky Mountain News*, 19 December 1913.

140 A LONG RESOLUTION: CIR, vol. 8, p. 7346; UMWJ, 25 December 1913.

143 TIKAS IN UMWJ: 4, 18 December 1913.

143 LETTER . . . TO INTERNATIONAL: Tikas to the UMW, 10 February 1914.

143 CHRISTMAS . . . AT LUDLOW: *TCN*, 24, 26 December 1913; *DE*, 22 December 1913.

143–44 UTAH PHILLIPS' SONG: "Larimer Street," *Songs of the Workers to Fan the Flames of Discontent*, 34th ed. (Chicago, 1973, 1974), p. 40.

144 NEST OF GREEK CARDSHARKS: *DT*, 2 March 1909.

145–46 TIKAS' TESTIMONY: State Federation of Labor Investigation, LC, pp. 335–39.

146 PROFESSOR BREWSTER ON TIKAS' VOICE: CIR, vol. 7, p. 6665.

146 WILSON KILLED KID MORGAN: *TCN*, 31 December 1913.

147 IN THE DEPOT: CCMC, vol. 1, pp. 760–61.

147 LINDERFELT WOULD REMEMBER TIKAS: Court Martials, Farrar, vol. 20, pp. 274–77, 292, 294.

149 LUDLOW SEARCHED: *TCN*, 31 December 1913.

149 SIKORIA'S ACCOUNT: CCMC, vol. 1, p. 685. The man at the machine gun seems to be an ex-guard named Patton. Ibid., p. 242, 381. For Patton's role in the events leading up to the Ludlow massacre, see Chapter Thirteen, pp. 213–15.

149 LINDERFELT ON KENNEDY'S REBUKE: Court of Inquiry, Farrar, vol. 23, pp. 1085–86; CIR, vol. 7, pp. 6880, 6882.

150 BREWSTER AND LINDERFELT: CIR, vol. 7, p. 6645.

150 ORF AND LINDERFELT: CCMC, vol. 1, pp. 975–76.

150 SIKORIA GOT MAD: Ibid., pp. 685–86.

150 THIRTY-FIVE RIFLES HIDDEN: CIR, vol. 7, pp. 6810–11.

150 COMMITTEE . . . WIRED THE GOVERNOR: Ibid., p. 6646, Colorado Bureau of Labor Statistics, *Fourteenth Biennial Report, 1913–1914* (Denver, 1914), pp. 184–85.

150 FELLOW OFFICERS PRIVATELY SUGGESTED: Court of Inquiry, Farrar, vol. 23, pp. 676–77.

151 BEGGED TIKAS TO GET OUT: Tikas to the UMW, 10 February 1914.

151 COMMITTEE CONTINUED ITS INVESTIGATION: a synopsis is printed in the Colorado Bureau of Labor Statistics *Fourteenth Biennial Report*, pp. 177–87. Transcripts of testimony taken by the committee have been referred to earlier and are found in both the Lawson and Farrar collections of the Denver Public Library.

151–52 KOSTAS MARKOS' STORY: CCMC, vol. 2, pp. 2047–48; State Federation of Labor Investigation, LC, pp. 567–70; *DE*, 5 January 1914; Gus Papadakis, interviews and conversations.

152–53 BICUVARIS' STORY: State Federation of Labor Investigation, LC, pp. 671–81.

153 MARKOS DIED IN WALSENBURG: note at the end of his testimony, Ibid., p. 570.

153 AMMONS' COMMENT: *Coalfield War*, p. 169.

153 WELBORN ON SCABS: CCMC, vol. 1, p. 530.

153 50 BULGARIANS: *DE*, 28 January 1914.

154 SCABS . . . RECRUITED IN PITTSBURGH: CCMC, vol. 1, pp. 1249–50, 1255–56, 1395–1400.

154 ADS IN IMMIGRANT PAPERS: cf. an ad said to be put in New York's *Il Progresso Italo-Americano* asking for "1000 men to go to Colorado.

Good pay, splendid working conditions, fare free." No mention is made of the strike. UMWJ, 8 January 1914.

154 YANSENSKI: CCMC, vol. 1, pp. 1450–51.

154 TRIED TO GET OFF THE TRAIN: Ibid., p. 1455.

154 ANOTHER PAPER TO SIGN: Ibid., pp. 72–73, gives the text of the Colorado Deception Act making it illegal to deceive workers about labor conditions during a strike.

154 "TAKE US TO A SLAUGHTER HOUSE": Ibid., p. 1263.

154 TROIO: Ibid., p. 1148.

154 QUANTINO: Ibid., p. 1178.

154 MORELLI: Ibid., p. 1179.

155 NO WORD . . . FOR STRIKE: Ibid., p. 1457. In his appeal for donations after the Ludlow massacre, a correspondent to the Greek-language *Atlantis* called the United Mine Workers a "club." See Chapter 14, Reference Notes, p. 240 MAVROIDIS' TELEGRAM.

155 HAD TO PAY OFF THEIR BOARD: CCMC, vol. 1, p. 653.

155 TOOK AWAY THEIR SHOES: UMWJ, 5 February 1914.

155 SNEAK AWAY: CCMC, vol. 1, pp. 1232, 1264–65.

155 UNION MEN WOULD KILL THEM: Ibid., p. 632.

155 ONE COUPLE . . . NAMED BROCKETT: Ibid., p. 170. Their affidavit of 10 January 1914 is found in the Elias Ammons Correspondence, Division of State Archives, Denver, Colo.

155 CENSUS THE UNION TOOK: UMWJ, 1 January 1914. Lawson shows 20,508 people on relief in Colorado as of January 1914. CCMC, vol. 2, p. 2227.

155 16 BABIES BORN: *DE*, 16 January 1914.

155–57 MAJOR KENNEDY SENT TO . . . FREMONT COUNTY: CIR, vol. 7, p. 6811.

157 LAWSON'S WORDS ON TIKAS' PHOTOGRAPH: CCMC, vol. 1, p. 243. The photograph appears in the UMW pamphlet by Walter H. Fink, *The Ludlow Massacre*, 3d ed. (Denver, 1914), p. 42.

CHAPTER 10—THE WOMEN

159 MARY THOMAS: Mary Thomas O'Neal, interview.

159 HER MEMORIES OF COLORADO: *Foreigners*, pp. 50–54, 59–61 ff.

159 WEDDING PRESENTS: CIR, vol. 7, pp. 6356–57.

160 AS MUCH OF A STRIKER: CCMC, vol. 1, p. 796.

160–61 MOTHER JONES' SPEECH: CIR, vol. 8, pp. 7253–57. For a very interesting view of the psychology of the South Italian peasants and the role of women in their society see F. G. Friedmann, "The World of 'La Miseria,'" *Partisan Review* 20 (March–April 1953). Victor R. Greene, in *The Slavic Community on Strike* (Notre Dame, Ind., 1968), pp. 44–45, 143–44, and Michael Novak, in *The Guns of Lattimore* (New York, 1978), pp. 161–62, 174–77, esp. give accounts of Slavic women in the anthracite fields of Pennsylvania before the turn of the century and their militant participation in the strike of 1897. See also Helen Zeese Papanikolas, "Unionism, Communism, and the Great Depression: The Carbon County Coal Strike of 1933," *Utah Historical Quarterly* 41 (Summer 1973): 269–70, 275, 280, 285 ff.

161 WOMEN AT SOPRIS: UMWJ, 16 October 1913.

161 IN THE FORE OF THE MOB: see Chapter 8 and Reference Notes, p. 136 VAN CISE AWAKENED ON THIRTIETH OF NOVEMBER.

161 "NOT A CHARITY ORGANIZATION": CIR, vol. 8, p. 7256.

161 MARY THOMAS REMEMBERED SINGING: *Foreigners*, p. 12.

161 A CHANCE TO BE TOGETHER: John Reed, "The Colorado War," *Metropolitan* 40, no. 3 (July 1914): 13–14.

163 HELEN RING ROBINSON VISITED THE CAMPS: CIR, vol. 8, p. 7212.

163 OPPORTUNITIES OF THE STRIKE: For many of the strikers, the immigrants especially, the union's most permanent legacy was its function as a school. UMW Vice President Frank Hayes put it this way: "I should say that the United Mine Workers is the only school that a great many miners have. Their trade union hall is their school. . . . I notice the fact that when they [the immigrants] are members of our union for a certain length of time that they speak the language better, they take more interest in our common life, and the life of our country. They are anxious to read and learn; that it awakens new ambitions and new ideals in them, due to contact with the men who are free to think what they please. . . ." Ibid., p. 7197.

163 STRIKE BENEFITS: Ibid., vol. 7, p. 6356.

163 THE WOMEN'S ROLE: Dale Fetherling, in assessing the reasons for Mother Jones' influence, develops the idea that coal camp families, because of the uncertain lives of the men, were essentially matriarchal. Dale Fetherling, *Mother Jones, The Miners' Angel: A Portrait* (Carbondale and Edwardsville, Ill., 1974), pp. 167–68. Cf. Anne Ellis, *The Life of An Ordinary Woman* (Boston and New York, 1929), pp. 261–62, on her experience during the Goldfield, Nevada, strike of 1907: "Day after day, week after week, and the money almost gone. During a strike all suffer, but I think it must be harder on the wife. The husband, tramping and looking for work, sees other men and can talk matters over with them, thereby forgetting himself and gaining a sort of courage, but she, at home, is planning what and how to feed

her children in the cheapest and most nourishing way possible—counting and recounting each penny, so much for fuel, so much for water, so much for a soup bone. They told of a woman who asked a neighbor if she could borrow her yesterday's soup bone. The answer was, 'No. Mrs. So-and-So has it to day.' "

163 MOTHER JONES WAS A CATALYST: details of Mother Jones' early life and career are drawn from *Autobiography*, pp. 11–16.

164 "THE STORY OF COAL": Ibid., p. 231.

164 DISGUISED AS A PEDDLER: Ibid., pp. 95–96.

164 ENOUGH WOMEN TO BEAT THE HELL OUT OF THEM: CCMC, vol. 2, p. 2631. Of Mother Jones' effect as a speaker, Mike Livoda said to the author, "She could do more to arouse a man's nerve in five minutes than the best speaker could in a whole day. She was right now."

164 ORGANIZED . . . WOMEN IN ARNOT: *Autobiography*, pp. 34–36.

164 "AN ARMY OF STRONG MINING WOMEN": Ibid., p. 91.

166 WOMEN ORGANIZED ALONG INDUSTRIAL LINES: Ibid., p. 204.

166 DIDN'T NEED A VOTE: Ibid., p. 203.

166 "IRON RAIN": Ibid., p. 124.

166 "I'VE SAT ON A BUMPER": the anecdote is quoted of Nimrod Workman in the notes to his recording *Mother Jones' Will*, Rounder Records #0076.

166 "THAT IS THE WAY WE . . . PRAY": *Autobiography*, p. 55.

166 WRECKING ANY CHANCE FOR COMPROMISE: *The Military Occupation of the Coal Strike Zone of Colorado by the Colorado National Guard, 1913–1914, Report of the Commanding General to the Governor for the Use of the Congressional Committee* . . . (Denver, n.d.), pp. 45–46.

166 MOTHER JONES DEMANDING STRIKERS KEEP THEIR WEAPONS: UMW Proceedings, 1916, vol. 2, pp. 957–58.

166 PASSING OUT RIFLES: George Paterakis, interview.

166 JUST AN OLD WOMAN: Autobiography, pp. 115–16.

166 ALMOST . . . BETRAYING HER CAUSE: witness her attempt to end the strike in the Northern Field (*Depths*, pp. 32–35) and her ability to be charmed by John D. Rockefeller, Jr., after the Ludlow massacre (*New York Times*, 28 January 1915). See Chapter 14, Reference Notes, p. 244 MOTHER JONES.

166 AWAITED A CALL FROM THE UNION: UMWJ, 18 December 1913.

167 ARRESTED ON THE FOURTH OF JANUARY: *TCN*, 5 January 1914; UMWJ, 8 January 1914; *Coalfield War*, p. 171.

167 ON THE ELEVENTH OF JANUARY SHE WAS BACK: *Autobiography*, pp. 178–82; UMWJ, 15 January 1914; *Coalfield War*, p. 172.

168 GREEKS LIVED A LITTLE REMOVED: O'Neal, interview.

168 BACHELORS: *Ludlow: Being the Report of the Special Board of Officers Appointed by the Governor . . .* (Denver, n.d.), p. 7.

168 HEROIC EXAGGERATION: In the *Coalfield War* they are termed "truculent showoffs," p. 211.

168 GREEKS SLAPPED A CURFEW: CIR, vol. 7, p. 6354.

169 THE GREAT HARILAOS: the Cretan Harilaos Piperakis came to the United States in 1908 and gained his first fame as a professional musician in Cretan communities in the Rockies. "The Little Soap," [*To Sapounaki*] was originally recorded in New York in the late 1940s (Liberty 39). Translation and notes by Nicholas E. Manos in *Songs of Humor and Hilarity, Folk Music in America*, vol. 11, Library of Congress Recording Laboratory.

169 TO HAVE A PHONE: Mary T. O'Neal to the author, 16 February 1974.

169 PRIDED HIMSELF ON HIS . . . FAIRNESS: Tikas to the UMW, 10 February 1914.

169 PREFERRED TO MEET HAMROCK AWAY FROM CAMP: Court Martials, Farrar, vol. 10, p. 386.

169 TAKING HIS MEALS: Las Animas Grand Jury, Farrar, vol. 5, p. 2354.

169 "SHE FORCED HERSELF IN": O'Neal, interview.

170 "COULDN'T GET RID OF HER": O'Neal, interview.

170 PEARL JOLLY: CIR, vol. 7, p. 6348.

170 TESTIFIES FOR UHLICH: *People of the State of Colorado* v. *Robert Uhlich*, Farrar, vol. 22.

170 ARRESTED FOR PICKETING: UMWJ, 5 March 1914.

170 WAY THE COMPANY HAD TREATED HER FAMILY: Ibid., 11 June 1914. For a report that Pearl Jolly's father was a gunman brought up for the 1904 strike see M. McCuster, "Reports on Colorado Situation," typed ms. in Commission on Industrial Relations Colorado Strike Reports, National Archives, pp. 19–20.

170 DRESSED DOWN: O'Neal, interview.

170 TIKAS WAS BEATEN: O'Neal, interview; *Foreigners*, pp. 118–19. These pages also contain Mary T. O'Neal's generous assessment of Tikas. Mary seems unclear on the date of the beating. See Chapter 13, pp. 213–14.

170 COURT-MARTIAL: Farrar, vol. 12, pp. 54–56. It may have been such rumors that prompted L. M. Bowers to term Tikas a "white slaver" (*Coalfield War*, p. 211).

170–71 HELEN RING ROBINSON ON TIKAS: *Independent* 78 (11 May 1914): 247.

171 JOSEPHINE ROCHE ON TIKAS: in Nicholas Von Hoffman's column, *Washington Post*, 24 November 1972. As Gus Papadakis put it, "Louis

was a ladies' man. He had a position, some respect."

171 JOKED WITH HER GUARDS: UMW Proceedings, 1916, vol. 2, pp. 961–62.

171 WOMEN'S MARCH: *Depths*, pp. 132–34.

171 SARAH SLATOR: CCMC, vol. 1, pp. 988–94.

172 MARY THOMAS ARRESTED: Ibid., pp. 794–95, 1445; CIR, vol. 7, pp. 6357–58.

172 LAWSON . . . WIRED THE UNION: UMWJ, 29 January 1914.

172 MILITIA CALLED IT A RIOT: *Coalfield War*, p. 173.

172 WOMEN'S INDIGNATION MEETING: *TCN*, 23 January 1914. UMWJ, 5 March 1914, reported that the "United Women of the Mine Workers," formed around January of 1914, had almost 500 members, and was applying to the State Federation of Labor for a charter.

173 MARY THOMAS . . . AT THE COUNTY JAIL: CCMC, vol. 1, pp. 795–800; *Foreigners*, pp. 158–59. In her book Mary T. O'Neal places her arrest after the Ludlow massacre.

173 GERMER IN WALSENBURG: *Coalfield War*, pp. 175, 338.

174 STRIKERS QUIETLY TOOK UP POSITIONS: *Depths*, pp. 138–39.

CHAPTER 11—THE INVESTIGATION

175 VIOLENT WINDSTORM: CIR, vol. 7, p. 6811.

175 SPOOF: *TCN*, 4 February 1914.

175 TIKAS IN FREE PRESS: *Trinidad Free Press*, 9 February 1914.

176 TIKAS . . . WROTE A LETTER: Tikas to the UMW, 10 February 1910. Another such confrontation over the dispensation of relief supplies took place between Mother Jones and Diamond's assistant Bob Bolton. *Autobiography*, pp. 196–97.

177 DIAMOND HAD WRITTEN TO ED DOYLE: Diamond to Doyle, 10 January 1914, DC.

177 LARGE EXPENSES: Ibid., 5 February 1914.

177 TALK ABOUT HIS BOOKS: Ibid., 10 January 1914. Regular audits of relief accounts had been instituted by Doyle in anticipation of just such criticism. In his letter to Diamond of 31 January 1914, Doyle gives no suggestion that he has any suspicions of Diamond's handling of union funds.

177 HE'D WIRED DOYLE: Ibid., 2 October 1913 (telegram).

177 DOYLE REPLIED: Doyle to Diamond, 31 January 1914, DC.

177 TO DODGE HIS CREDITORS: Ibid., 2 October 1913 (letter).

177 DIAMOND HAD OPENLY BOASTED: Tikas to the UMW, 10 February 1914.

177 GREEKS THOUGHT THEMSELVES MISTRUSTED: Mike Lingos, interview. Cf. Diamond's suspicions of Angelo Zikos that so angered Zikos that he left—or threatened to leave—the union. Las Animas Grand Jury, Farrar, vol. 5, p. 2496.

178 TIKAS HAD OVERSTEPPED HIS BOUNDS: He was experiencing the sort of friction with a member of the Anglo–Saxon union hierarchy that may have played a part in Carlo Demolli's break with the UMW after the 1903 strike and in the long-suffering organizer Frank Bonacci's troubles with John McLennan in the Utah coalfields during the early 1920s. For accounts of Demolli and Bonacci see Philip F. Notarianni, "Smoldering Unionism: The Italian Labor Organizer in Carbon County, Utah," unpublished seminar paper, University of Utah, May 1979.

178 NEW IMMIGRANTS DEFERRED: Melvyn Dubofsky and Warren Van Tine, *John L. Lewis: A Biography* (New York, 1977), p. 22. A sign of the union's real fears of the immigrants' influence, as well as sheer numbers, may be the resolution passed at the UMW convention of 1914 in favor of restricting immigration in light of the unemployment problem. UMW Proceedings, 1914, vol. 2, pp. 656–60. Cf. Ed Doyle's statement that immigrants should not be allowed to intermarry and should sign an oath stating they would not work for less pay than Americans (CIR, vol. 8, p. 7017).

178 DIAMOND'S CRONY BOLTON: in Diamond to Doyle, 6 January 1914, DC, Diamond calls Bolton "a very useful man." For Mother Jones' harsh assessment of Bolton, see Jones, *Autobiography*, pp. 196–97.

178 E. M. SNYDER: CCMC, vol. 2, p. 1745. E. M. Snyder was the brother of the ex-mine guard Charles Snyder, whose account of the Northern Field stockades appears in Chapter 4, pp. 46–47. Charles Snyder and his brother-in-law J. R. Petty, alias Pat Murphy, were working simultaneously for both the union and the Baldwin–Felts agency in the Southern Field and would later testify against John Lawson in the Nimmo case. Lawson trial, Farrar, vol. 21; *Depths*, pp. 274–75.

178 PETE KATSULIS: Las Animas Grand Jury, Farrar, vol. 5, pp. 2208–56.

179 KATSULIS . . . INDICTMENT: UMWJ, 24 September 1914.

179 TALKED ABOUT TIKAS: Gus Papadakis, conversations; O'Neal, interview, stated that the Greeks were going to have Tikas fired because of his relationship with Pearl Jolly. I find this hard to believe.

179 COULD DO THAT JOB MYSELF: Gus Papadakis, conversation. Papadakis implied a certain distance growing between Tikas and the Cretans when he contrasted his popularity to that of Lester Motis (Motakis) who "was more like us."

179 DIAMOND WROTE ED DOYLE: Diamond to Doyle, 5 February 1914, DC.

180 THE OPERA HOUSE: *TCN*, 18 February 1914.

180 JESSE SHAW'S TESTIMONY: CCMC, vol. 2, pp. 1743–56.

180 ACCUSED SHAW OF SPYING: Ibid., p. 1921.

180 SOMEBODY HAD BLOWN UP SHAW'S HOUSE: Ibid., p. 1754.

180 WEITZEL . . . TAKING NOTES: Ibid., pp. 2018–19.

180 ZAMBONI: Ibid., vol. 1, pp. 790–93.

180 COLNAR: Ibid., vol. 2, pp. 2052, 2054–56.

182 QUESTIONS HERRINGTON AND NORTHCUTT COULD HAVE PUT: Adolph
Germer wrote Eugene Debs that the union had not insisted on having
Mother Jones and certain striking miners in the West Virginia strike of
1912–13 testify before a Senate committee because "their movements
are not known minutely and their testimony will not only injure the
case . . . but some of the boys might be involved in serious complica-
tions." Dale Fetherling, *Mother Jones, The Miners' Angel: A Portrait*
(Carbondale and Edwardsville, Ill., 1974), pp. 101–2.

182 JIM FYLER: CCMC, vol. 1, p. 1458, vol. 2, pp. 1506–10.

182 DIAMOND . . . TOOK THE STAND: Ibid., vol. 2, pp. 2499–2509.

182 DIAMOND . . . WAS A TRAITOR: Lawson's and Doyle's views on Diamond
have been passed on privately by a source who knew both men. Their
concern about informers in the union prompted them to feed bits of
information to men they suspected "just to see where they would turn
up." Diamond was certainly aware of the rumors that clung to him.
In the *United Mine Workers Journal* of 15 October 1914, he called
attention to a "well-defined plan" to discredit the International Union
and "the leaders of the strike in particular."

182 ORDERED A SHIPMENT OF GUNS: *Depths*, p. 81.

183 QUESTIONS ON . . . HOW DIAMOND KEPT HIS BOOKS: Diamond to
Doyle, 10 January 1914, DC. See reference note above, p. 177 TALK
ABOUT HIS BOOKS.

183 STORY . . . HE EMBEZZLED: Victor Bazanelle, interview transcripts for
The Life of the Western Coal Miner project video tapes.

183 RENO HATCHED A PLOT AGAINST LIVODA: CIR, vol. 7, p. 6783. That
the immigrant ranks were being worked on in a deliberate effort to
alienate them from the union is also suggested by a report in UMWJ,
30 October 1913, which warns of a letter in Polish being circulated
stating that foreign strikers in Colorado were being given half the strike
aid English-speaking miners were receiving. Cf. also Chapter 11, Reference Notes, p. 177 GREEKS THOUGHT THEMSELVES MISTRUSTED.

183 TAINT . . . CLUNG TO LIVODA: it is privately suggested that these sus-

picions may have been why Livoda was put out of the union automobile at Suffield on the way to Ludlow on 20 April 1914.

183   HOW DID YOU GET RID OF SPIES?: CCMC, vol. 2, p. 2194.

183   DIAMOND WAS PUMPED: UMWJ, 26 March 1914.

183   DIAMOND'S PHOTO: Ibid., 13 August 1914.

183   DIAMOND AS STATISTICIAN: masthead, UMWJ, 6 July 1916.

183   REPLACED BY . . . LEWIS: Dubofsky and Van Tine, *John L. Lewis*, p. 34.

183   DIAMOND'S NAME APPEARED THE FINAL TIME: UMWJ, 13 June 1918.

184   LEWIS IN COLORADO: Dubofsky and Van Tine, *John L. Lewis*, p. 35.

184   LEWIS AND HAYES: Ibid., pp. 39–40.

184   CRETANS WERE TRYING TO PUSH KATSULIS OUT: Las Animas Grand
Jury, Farrar, vol. 5, p. 2222.

184   BILL PAPPAS; PAPADAKIS RIDING . . . TO LUDLOW; "SHOOT-UP . . .
SCABS"; NEELLY: Gus Papadakis, conversations.

184   AMBUSHED OUTSIDE OF LA VETA: *Coalfield War*, p. 140; George P.
West, United States Commission on Industrial Relations *Report on the
Colorado Strike* (Washington, D.C., 1915), pp. 110–11. On the same
day as the La Veta ambush (November 8, 1913) a nonunion miner
was murdered by strikers in Aguilar.

184   WHORES TIP OFF GREEKS: Gus Papadakis, conversations.

185   GALANIS: Gus Papadakis to Helen Zeese Papanikolas, 28 February
1974, conversations.

185   GREEKS FROM BINGHAM CANYON: George Paterakis, interview. Greek
scabs were still being imported from Bingham Canyon in October of
1914. UMWJ, 20 October 1914.

185   PATERAKIS AND SKLIRIS: George Paterakis, interview.

185   AMMONS RECALLS ALL BUT TWO HUNDRED TROOPS: *Coalfield War*,
p. 187.

185   LOU DOLD: Louis R. Dold, interviews and conversations.

186   SCAB HAD BEEN FOUND DEAD: *Trinidad Free Press*, 13 March 1914;
TCN, 9, 10 March 1914; *Coalfield War*, p. 187.

186–87   EMMA ZANATELL'S STORY: Emma Zanatell, interview transcripts for
The Life of the Western Coal Miner project video tapes; *Trinidad Free
Press*, 11 March 1914; UMWJ, 19 March 1914.

187   DOLD WAS WATCHING IT ALL: Louis R. Dold, interviews and conversations; UMWJ, 26 March 1914.

187   OLD MAN JOHNSON: CCMC, vol. 1, p. 960–61.

187   THREE MORE . . . JAILED: *TCN*, 12 March 1914.

187   GRAND BALL: *Coalfield War*, p. 188.

188 LINDERFELT STOPPED THEM: *TCN*, 19 March 1914.

189 LAWSON . . . WAS PREVENTED: Ibid., 24 March 1914. In the light of the subsequent events at Ludlow, the Policy Committee's statement on the Forbes evictions has a chilling ring: ". . . as citizens of the State of Colorado and officials of the Colorado miners' union, we are going to advise every man to arm himself to protect and defend his home, whether it be from attacks of mine owners' hirelings under the guise of Baldwin–Felts gunmen, or the Colorado state militia.

  "A striking miner's tent is his house and is as sacred to him as the mansion of the mine owner." UMWJ, 19 March 1914.

189 DETACHMENT . . . CAMPED ON THE SPOT: *Coalfield War*, p. 190.

189 PHOTOGRAPHS OF ATTEMPTS TO REBUILD THE COLONY: Louis R. Dold, interviews and conversations. Two of these photographs are in the possession of the author.

189 MOTHER JONES WAS RELEASED: *Coalfield War*, pp. 189–90.

189 DOCTOR BESHOAR HAD TRIED: *Depths*, p. 131.

189 PEARL JOLLY HAD TAKEN A ROOM: Court Martials, Farrar, vol. 12, p. 54.

189 MOTHER JONES ARRESTED OUTSIDE WALSENBURG: *Autobiography*, pp. 184–85; *TCN*, 23 March 1914.

190 FREEZING JAIL: *Autobiography*, pp. 185–86.

190 STAYED UNTIL THE SIXTEENTH OF APRIL: UMWJ, 23 April 1914.

190 INCENDIARY LETTER: Ibid., 9 April 1914. The letter is posted from "Military Bastille, Walsenburg," and is addressed to the nation and "to my friend General Francisco Villa."

190 LEGAL STORM: Fetherling, *Mother Jones*, p. 121.

190 KATSULIS ON TIKAS' REMOVAL: Las Animas Grand Jury, Farrar, vol. 5, p. 2223.

190 GENERAL CHASE ISSUED AN ORDER: UMWJ, 19 March 1914.

190 CAVALRYMEN TOOK UP POSITIONS: Ibid., 26 March 1914; *Depths*, p. 159.

190 A SCAB HAD EMPTIED HIS REVOLVER INTO . . . ROBINSON: UMWJ, 2 April 1914.

190 SEARCH THE LUDLOW CAMP: *Depths*, p. 159.

191 SACRED RIGHT OF AN AMERICAN CITIZEN: *Harper's Weekly* 58, (23 May 1914): 3.

191 "A GREAT PRINCIPLE": CCMC, vol. 2, p. 2858.

191 TEN THOUSAND SHARES: Raymond B. Fosdick, *John D. Rockefeller, Jr.: A Portrait*, p. 150.

191 ROCKEFELLER ON YMCA: CIR, vol. 9, p. 8429.

191 TURNED DOWN A REQUEST BY HAYES: *Coalfield War*, p. 204.

191 MILITIA LEAVING THE SOUTHERN FIELD: UMWJ, 23 April 1914.

191 GUNMEN SWORN IN: Ibid., 23 April 1914; *Coalfield War*, p. 205.

191 TROOP A: UMWJ, 21 May 1914. For evidence that Troop A was subsidized by the coal companies and that John D. Rockefeller, Jr., could have been aware of it just before the Ludlow massacre, see CIR, vol. 9, pp. 8429–30.

CHAPTER 12—THE MEMORIAL WHEAT

195 A EUBOEAN: George Rousses, interview.

198 DEATH CERTIFICATE: Department of Public Health, Trinidad, Colo.

198 ONE OF THE BULLETS: Proceedings of the Las Animas, Colo., County Coroner's Inquests, April 1914, National Archives, pp. 12–13; CIR, vol. 8, p. 7364. CIR, vol. 8, pp. 7363–86, contains excerpts from the Coroner's Inquests and affidavits of the Ludlow survivors. In the notes that follow, I will refer to the CIR excerpts or other published sources for this testimony wherever possible.

198 OLD LEDGERS: Records of the Hall–MacMahon Mortuary, Trinidad, Colo.

204 SIXTY-YEAR-OLD DOCUMENT: see p. 226.

CHAPTER 13—LUDLOW

207 THE PHOTOGRAPHS: in the collection of the Denver Public Library, Western History Department.

210 SENATOR ROBINSON'S ARTICLE: *New York American*, 12 April 1914.

210 SHE WENT OUT TO THE TENT COLONIES: CIR, vol. 8, pp. 7212–13.

211 TROOP A: *Ludlow: Being the Report of the Special Board of Officers Appointed by the Governor* . . . (Denver, n.d.), p. 7; *Coalfield War*, p. 205.

211 DR. CURRY'S BOASTING: CCMC, vol. 2, p. 1733.

211 EDWIN CARSON: *Coalfield War*, p. 205.

211 LINDERFELT . . . "RECRUITING": *Ludlow: Being the Report*, p. 9.

211 ROCKEFELLER WAS PRACTICING HIS PUTTING: *New York American*, 19 April 1914.

212 A CROWD SWARMED OUT: Court Martials, Farrar, vol. 12, pp. 41–43.

212 SENATOR ROBINSON IN WALSENBURG: CIR, vol. 8, p. 7213.

212 DETERMINED TO HAVE A BETTER EASTER: Gus Papadakis, conversation.

212–13 GREEK EASTER AT LUDLOW: CIR, vol. 7, p. 6349, vol. 8, pp. 7379–80, 7385, vol. 9, pp. 8185–86; *Foreigners*, pp. 130–31, and Mary T. O'Neal, interview and letters to the author; Court Martials, Farrar, vol. 10, pp. 242–43, vol. 20, p. 143.

213 ZIMMER AND MARTIN . . . FOUND FIGHT: Coroner's Inquests, pp. 43–44. This incident may have happened on the previous Sunday.

213–14 TIKAS BEATEN: see Chapter 10 Reference Notes, p. 170 TIKAS WAS BEATEN.

214 LOUIS TIKAS SAT DOWN TO WRITE A LETTER: see Chapters 4 and 15 and Reference Notes for Chapter 4, pp. 52–53 FIRST NOTES.

214 MORNING OF APRIL TWENTIETH: CIR, vol. 8, pp. 7380–81, 7384, vol. 9, pp. 8186–87; Court Martials, Farrar, vol. 10, pp. 373–75, 386, vol. 14, pp. 393–94; Hamrock to Ammons, 22 April 1914, Elias Ammons' Correspondence, Division of State Archives, Denver, Colo. Coroner's Inquests (Pearl Jolly testimony), n.p. Governor Ammons' records show thirty-six men of the state militia stationed at Ludlow and Cedar Hill on the morning of April 20, 1914. An additional ten men arrived from the militia detachment at Sopris later in the afternoon. CIR, vol. 8, pp. 7415–16.

216 THE MILITIA WOULD REMEMBER, TOO: *Ludlow: Being the Report*, p. 11; Court Martials, Farrar, vol. 10, p. 391; CIR, vol. 7, p. 6895.

216 LINDERFELT . . . WOULD JUSTIFY HIMSELF: Coroner's Inquests (K. E. Linderfelt testimony), n.p.

217 NOW THEY HUNG DRY AS TINDER: Court Martials, Farrar, vol. 12, pp. 49–50.

217 HAD VOWED NEVER TO PERMIT ANOTHER SEARCH: *Ludlow: Being the Report*, p. 13.

217 TAPPED LINE: Hamrock to Ammons, 22 April 1914, Elias Ammons Correspondence; Court Martials, Farrar, vol. 10, p. 405.

217 WANTED TO SEE IF REPORTS: CIR, vol. 8, pp. 7371, 7378–79.

217 MADE GREEKS PROMISE TO DO NOTHING: *Ludlow: Being the Report*, p. 13.

217 TIKAS RECOGNIZED THE WOMAN: Court Martials, Farrar, vol. 10, p. 375.

217 WHAT LOUIS TIKAS HAD OBSERVED FOR HIMSELF: Coroner's Inquests (Pearl Jolly testimony), n.p.

217 MRS. DERR: CIR, vol. 8, p. 7381.

218 HAMROCK AND TIKAS CONTINUED TO TALK: Court Martials, Farrar, vol. 10, p. 375.

218 "WHAT DAMNED FOOLS": *Ludlow: Being the Report*, p. 14.

218 GREEKS GATHERED TOGETHER AND TALKED IN PANIC: Mike Lingos, interview.

219 BEGGED LINDERFELT FOR THE ORDER TO FIRE: Court Martials, Farrar, vol. 11, p. 144.

219 MAGGIE DOMINISKE: CIR, vol. 8, p. 7380.

219 MRS. FYLER WAS THERE: Ibid., p. 7384.

219 THE PEOPLE RAN FOR IT: *Foreigners*, pp. 133–35; *DE*, 30 April 1914.

219 SLAV RIDES OFF: Las Animas Grand Jury, Farrar, vol. 4, p. 1802.

219 CHARLIE COSTA RAN BY: CIR, vol. 8, p. 7380.

219 "I WILL NEVER SEE YOU ANY MORE": Ibid., p. 7384.

220 THE PUMP HOUSE AND ESCAPE: Ibid., vol. 7, pp. 6854–55, vol. 8, pp. 7380, 7384–85.

220 JOHN BARTOLOTTI RAN BACK TO HIS TENT: John Reed, *Metropolitan* 40, no. 3 (July 1914): 11; Coroner's Inquests, affidavits of Virginia Bartolotti and Edith Fyler.

220 SNYDER HAD NO GUN: CIR, vol. 8, p. 7377.

220 CLORINDA PADILLA; JUANITA HERNANDEZ; MRS. TONNER: Ibid., pp. 7383, 7385; Coroner's Inquests, affidavit of Juanita Hernandez.

220 MARIA CZEKOVITCH: John Reed, *Metropolitan* 40, no. 3 (July 1914): 11.

220 TIKAS WANTED PEARL JOLLY TO STAY: CIR, vol. 7, p. 6350.

220 CORPORAL BENEDICT: Court Martials, Farrar, vol. 20, pp. 96, 160.

220 HAMROCK . . . TRYING TO GET A MESSAGE THROUGH: Ibid., vol. 10, p. 377, vol. 20, p. 82.

220 WHERE THE FIRST SHOT HAD COME FROM: Pete Katsulis, who was one of the Ludlow defenders on April 20, claimed a man was hit by fire from the militia before the Greeks reached the Colorado and Southeastern railroad cut. Las Animas Grand Jury, Farrar, vol. 5, p. 2231. Linderfelt maintained that he ordered his men to hold their fire. M. G. Lowe, a noncombatant sympathetic to the strikers, claimed the first shot came from the military position on Water Tank Hill. CIR, vol. 7, p. 6854.

220–21 SOMEONE . . . PEPPERING MILITARY CAMP: Court Martials, Farrar, vol. 10, pp. 376–77.

221 FIRST CASUALTY: Ibid., vol. 13, p. 56.

221 MARTIN'S BODY WAS RECOVERED: Ibid., vol. 20, pp. 135–36.

221 PEARL JOLLY HAD GONE FROM TENT TO TENT: CIR, vol. 7, pp. 6350.

221 A KIND OF SHARPSHOOTING: Ibid., p. 6863.

222 LAWSON GOT TO THE BATTLE: Court Martials, Farrar, vol. 20, pp. 37–48; UMWJ, 4 June 1914.

222 "WE'RE COMING LOUIS": Mike Livoda, interview.

222 TIKAS . . . HAD WASTED A COUPLE OF HOURS: Coroner's Inquests (Pearl Jolly testimony), n.p.

222 LAWSON GOT DOWN THE ARROYO: Court Martials, Farrar, vol. 20, pp. 40–41, 47–48.

222 THE TWO MEN EMBRACED: *Depths*, p. 173.

223 PEARL JOLLY TRIED TO GET TO THE DISPENSARY: CIR, vol. 7, pp. 6350–51.

223 SHOOTING DOGS AND CHICKENS: Ibid., p. 6351.

223 THE MILITIA'S REINFORCEMENTS HAD ARRIVED: Court Martials, Farrar, vol. 10, pp. 316–19.

223 COMMANDEERED AN AUTOMOBILE: CIR, vol. 8, pp. 7368–69; Coroner's Inquests, affidavit of Victor Alarid (reprinted, UMWJ, 30 April 1914).

223 MEN FROM TRINIDAD WORKED THEIR WAY UP THE TRACKS: Court Martials, Farrar, vol. 10, pp. 319–20.

224 LINDERFELT HAD COME IN AN AUTOMOBILE: CIR, vol. 8, pp. 7383–84.

224 MRS. TONNER'S STORY: Ibid., pp. 7383–85.

224 HAD ROUNDED UP WOMEN AND CHILDREN: Ibid., vol. 7, p. 6351.

224 TIKAS GOES TO NUMBER ONE TENT: Ibid., vol. 8, p. 7385; Coroner's Inquests (Pearl Jolly testimony), n.p.

224 TENTS BURNING NEAR THE BLACKSMITH SHOP: Court Martials, Farrar, vol. 10, p. 263.

224 STRIKERS . . . MADE A RUSH: Coroner's Inquests, affidavit of Joe Dominiske (*Trinidad Free Press*, 24 April 1914).

224 CHEWING THE TENTS TO LACE: CIR, vol. 8, p. 7385.

224 BUNCHES OF FIRECRACKERS; MACHINE GUNS LIKE HOSES: Coroner's Inquests, affidavit of Joe Dominiske.

224 MARY PETRUCCI'S STORY: CIR, vol. 8, pp. 7376–77, vol. 9, pp. 8193–98.

225 MILITIAMEN SPREADING THE FIRE: Court Martials, Farrar, vol. 20, pp. 255–57, and the admissions of guards shortly after the massacre found in the anonymous typewritten report "Information About Ludlow," in the Elias Ammons Correspondence, p. 1.

225 TENTS WERE LIFTED OFF FOUNDATIONS: Court Martials, Farrar, vol. 10, p. 399, vol. 20, p. 173.

225 SNYDER'S STORY: CIR, vol. 8, pp. 7370–73, 7377–79.

225–26 CARSON'S STORY: Court Martials, Farrar, vol. 10, pp. 321–25, 332.

226 TIKAS HAD GONE BACK: Coroner's Inquests, affidavit of Joe Dominiske (*Trinidad Free Press*, 24 April 1914); notes in LC; *DE*, 29 April 1914.

226 LIEUTENANT CONNOR: Court Martials, Farrar, vol. 12, p. 71.

226 MCDONALD'S STORY: CIR, vol. 8, p. 7369. Cf. McDonald in Coroner's Inquests for a discrepancy which suggests Linderfelt may have known about Tikas' death at this point.

226–27 IN THE LUDLOW DEPOT: Ibid., pp. 7369–70, 7372; Coroner's Inquests, affidavit of Juanita Hernandez; Las Animas Grand Jury, Farrar, vol. 4, p. 1811; Court of Inquiry, Farrar, vol. 23, p. 1090; Court Martials, Farrar, vol. 10, p. 325.

227 CHARGES AND SPECIFICATIONS: Court Martials, Farrar, vol. 20, pp. 6–29, 32–35.

230 CAPTAIN T. C. LINDERFELT: Ibid., vol. 12, pp. 84–85.

230 SERGEANT DAVIS: Ibid., vol. 10, p. 357.

231 LINDERFELT: Ibid., vol. 14, pp. 358–59, vol. 20, pp. 288–90.

231 SERGEANT CULLEN: Ibid., vol. 14, pp. 382–83. This is probably the Cullen listed as a deputy sheriff in CCMC, vol. 2, p. 2622.

232 DAVIS: Court Martials, Farrar, vol. 14, p. 362.

232 SERGEANT CULLEN: Ibid., vol. 14, p. 383.

232 HAMROCK, RECALLED: Ibid., vol. 20, pp. 297–98.

232 AND THEREFORE: Ibid., vol. 20, pp. 310–11.

233 THE COLONY WAS IN ASHES: DP, 25 April 1914; Trinidad Free Press, 24 April 1914.

233 BAYES' WINDMILL: Coroner's Inquests (Frank Bayes testimony), n.p.; CIR, vol. 8, pp. 7367–68.

233 DEAD WAGONS DRIVEN OFF: Coalfield War, pp. 235–36.

233 WHISKEY BOTTLES: CIR, vol. 7, p. 6853.

233 GEORGE CHURCHILL'S STORY: Ibid., vol. 8, pp. 7381–83.

237 ACCOUNTS . . . ARE GARBLED: Victor Bazanelle, interview transcripts for The Life of the Western Coal Miner project video tapes; New York World, 5 May 1914; Trinidad Free Press, 24 April 1914; New York Times, 22 April 1914.

235 CONFLICTING EVIDENCE: Ludlow: Being the Report, p. 26.

235 A SWORN AFFIDAVIT FROM JOHN DAVIS: Court of Inquiry, Farrar, vol. 23, pp. 1018–20. For medical corroboration that Tikas was shot while falling forward or on the ground, see Coroner's Inquests, p. 10, reprinted in G. P. West, United States Commission on Industrial Relations, Report on the Colorado Strike (Washington, D.C., 1915), p. 129.

237 PHOTOGRAPH SHOWING TIKAS LYING DEAD: reproduced on the cover of Walter H. Fink, The Ludlow Massacre 3d ed. (Denver, 1914). See also CIR, vol. 7, p. 6955.

237 LINDERFELT . . . SAW TIKAS' FEET STICKING OUT: Court Martials, Farrar, vol. 14, pp. 360–61.

CHAPTER 14—SURVIVORS

239 UNION HALL IN TRINIDAD: *DP*, 22 April 1914.

239 PEDRO VALDEZ: *Trinidad Free Press*, 9 May 1914.

239 MRS. FYLER LEARNED FROM MRS. BARTOLOTTI: Proceedings of the Las Animas, Colo., County Coroner's Inquests, April 1914, National Archives (affidavit of Edith Fyler).

239 ALCARITA PEDRAGON: *DE*, 23 April 1914.

239 THE STRIKE LEADERS WERE MEETING: *DP*, 26 April 1914.

239 CALL TO ARMS: *Depths*, pp. 183–84.

239–40 STRIKERS . . . ATTACKED DELAGUA AND AGUILAR: *Coalfield War*, pp. 240–41.

240 THIRTY ARMED GREEKS: *DP*, 26 April 1914; *Depths*, p. 207.

240 SEVENTEEN GREEKS PICKED UP RIFLES: *DE*, 23 April 1914.

240 MANCINI: *Depths*, p. 184.

240 MAVROIDIS' TELEGRAM: *Atlantis*, 25 April 1914. *Atlantis* editors had read of the Ludlow massacre in the American press and on April 23, 1914, printed a telegram from Trinidad replying to their request for news from the southern Colorado Greeks, which confirmed the death of Louis Tikas. A conservative newspaper, usually more interested in Old Country politics than in the problems of Greek workingmen in America, *Atlantis* nevertheless printed a short but passionate editorial on April 25, 1914, stating that the Greeks' responsibilities to their families had forced them to go against the American soldiers and that they fought for the fame and honor of the Greek name and "to show their loyalty to the great workers' union to which they belonged."

240 STREETS OF TRINIDAD: *DP*, 25 April 1914.

240 DRILLING ON THE PARADE GROUND: M. McCuster, "Report on the Colorado Situation," typed ms. in the Commission on Industrial Relations Colorado Strike Reports, National Archives, pp. 16–17.

240 GREEKS HAD FLOWN THEIR . . . FLAG: CIR, vol. 8, p. 7181.

240 STRIKERS . . . DIGGING TRENCHES: *DP*, 26 April 1914.

240 FACE OF FRANK SNYDER: *DP*, 24 April 1914.

240 HEEL PRINTS ON HIS FACE: CIR, vol. 7, p. 6351, vol. 5, p. 2375.

240 RUMOR: Louis R. Dold, interviews.

240 BAZANELLE . . . WENT LOOKING FOR GENERAL CHASE: Victor Bazanelle, interview transcripts for *The Life of the Western Coal Miner* project video tapes.

240 BURIAL OF TIKAS: *DE*, 27 April 1914; *TCN*, 27 April 1914; Frances Wayne, *DP*, 27 April 1914.

242 THE SOUL OF LOUIS TIKAS WOULD WANDER: *Service Book of the Holy Orthodox-Catholic Apostolic Church*, 4th ed., rev., trans. and ed. Isabel Florence Hapgood (Brooklyn, N.Y., 1965), p. 612.

242 THE BURNING STABLE AT FORBES: *Coalfield War*, pp. 263–64; CIR, vol. 8, p. 7362.

242–43 GREEKS RETREATING BALKAN-STYLE: *TCN*, 27 April 1914.

243 LOU DOLD TELLING THE RED-NECKS: Louis R. Dold, interviews.

243 JAPANESE SCABS BURNED TO DEATH: *Coalfield War*, p. 264.

243 BANGING WILDLY ON A PIANO: *The Life of the Western Coal Miner* project video tape "Out of the Depths."

243 ON THE HOGBACK: *Coalfield War*, pp. 265–67.

243 MACGREGOR: Mike Livoda, interview with the author; *Coalfield War*, p. 259.

243 GUS PAPADAKIS . . . STANDING OVER LESTER'S CORPSE: Gus Papadakis, conversation.

243 FEDERAL TROOPS ARRIVED: *Coalfield War*, p. 265.

243 UNION WOMEN ON TOUR: *Foreigners*, pp. 163–72.

243 ACCOUNT . . . IN THE METROPOLITAN: *Metropolitan* 40 (July 1914).

243 CARTOONS IN THE MASSES: see *Masses*, June 1914, esp. John Sloan's cover.

244 ROCKEFELLER HAD WIRED BOWERS: CIR, vol. 9, p. 8430.

244 ROCKEFELLER AND WALSH COMMISION: Ibid., pp. 8592–8715; summarized in *Coalfield War*, pp. 317–19, 326–29.

244 MOTHER JONES: *New York Times*, 28 January 1915.

244 LAWSON ON FOUNDATION'S ACCOMPLISHMENTS: CIR, vol. 8, p. 8006. Lawson's remarks to the Walsh Commission on labor agitation themselves deserve to be remembered: "I expect there would probably be a very great change come over this country and over the world if labor would cease its agitation. I think in a very few years there would not be any so-called unrest amongst the unemployed. They would be beyond that condition of creating unrest" (CIR, vol. 9, p. 8215).

244 UNION HAD GIVEN UP: Ibid., vol. 8, pp. 7073–74. The strike in Colorado had been costly. Doyle's accounts show that between April 1, 1910, and June 1, 1915, the union had spent $3,695,514 on the strikes in the Northern and Southern fields, with well over $2.5 million going to the south (DC). With the union facing the possibility of a major strike in Ohio, the Colorado situation might well appear hopeless.

244 THE POOR GREEKS WANDERED: Gus Papadakis to the author, 30 September 1978.

245 PETE KATSULIS: Las Animas Grand Jury, Farrar, vol. 5, pp. 2208–56; *Coalfield War*, pp. 287–88.

245 BILL PAPPAS: typewritten notes dated 12 August 1914, DC.

245 ROCKEFELLER WAS IN COLORADO: *DT*, 21–24 September 1915.

245 ROCKEFELLER WOULD SELL OUT HIS INTEREST: *Coalfield War*, p. 342.

245 LEWIS CAME TO COLORADO: Melvyn Dubofsky and Warren Van Tine, *John L. Lewis: A Biography* (New York, 1977), p. 35; *Coalfield War*, p. 340. Lewis took great pride in signing an agreement with John Osgood of the Victor–American Fuel Company in 1917. Lewis' father had been blacklisted for his part in a strike against Osgood's Iowa mines in 1882. See John Hutchinson, "John L. Lewis: To the Presidency of the UMWA," *Labor History* 19 (Spring 1978): 199.

245–46 LAWSON AND DOYLE: *Coalfield War*, pp. 338–40; *Depths*, pp. 364–67. According to the UMWJ of 13 June and 1 August 1918, attempts by Colorado coal miners loyal to Doyle and Lawson to obtain a charter from the A. F. of L. and form a dual union "fizzled."

246 DOYLE'S SPEECH: UMW Proceedings, 1916, vol. 2, p. 756. Notes for this speech, and an unfortunately incomplete manuscript, are found in DC.

246 THREE YEARS AFTER: *Coalfield War*, p. 340.

246 "WHO KNOWS WHAT DEEDS": by Frances Gibson Richard, UMWJ, 28 May 1914.

247 HASTINGS MINE EXPLODED: Gus Papadakis, conversation.

247 HUBBARD'S NOTES: CIR, vol. 7, pp. 6675–76.

247 HUBBARD GOT HIS ARTICLES WRITTEN: see "The Colorado Situation," *The Fra*, August 1914, and "In Colorado," January 1915.

247 HE WENT DOWN WITH THE LUSITANIA: A. A. Hoehling and Mary Hoehling, *The Last Voyage of the Lusitania* (New York, 1956), pp. 41–42, 171–72.

247 PAPADAKIS IN FRANCE: Gus Papadakis, conversations.

247 MILITIA OFFICERS IN WAR: *Depths*, pp. 367–68.

247 A GREEK CANDY STORE OWNER: *Rocky Mountain News*, 28 August 1917.

247 LINDERFELT . . . IN MEXICO: UMWJ, 2 July 1914.

247 IN POLICE COURT: Ibid., 13 August 1914.

248 OVERSEAS: *Depths*, p. 368.

248–49 LOU DOLD'S STORY: Louis R. Dold, conversations.

249 DOYLE AND LAWSON: *Depths*, pp. 364–67.

249 HAMROCK ADJUTANT GENERAL: Ibid., pp. 363–64.

249 LINDERFELT IN SAN DIEGO: Ibid., p. 368.

249 PEARL JOLLY: Mike Livoda, conversation.

249 LIVODA HIMSELF: taped interview, interview notes.

249 ROCKEFELLER CONSUMED BY THE FEAR: Herbert Cerwin, "Those Incredible Millionaires," *California Living (San Francisco Sunday Examiner and Chronicle)*, 22 April 1979, p. 7.

249 BOOED . . . BY THE CHILDREN: Barron Beshoar, conversation.

250 FOR A TIME THE COFFEEHOUSE: John Tsanakatsis, interview.

250 SKLIRIS IN PUEBLO: John Rougas, interview.

250 IN ARIZONA: Gus Papadakis, conversation; George Paterakis, interview notes.

250 SPENT MORE THAN A MINER MADE: Helen Zeese Papanikolas, "Greek Workers in the Intermountain West: The Early Twentieth Century," *Byzantine and Modern Greek Studies* 5 (1979): 193.

250-51 SKLIRIS WAS RUNNING THE ICE HOUSE: George Mavrikos, interview notes.

251 THE ARGENTINES, THE PORTUGUESE AND THE GREEKS: by Carey Morgan and Arthur M. Swanstrom (Edward B. Marks Music Company), recorded by Nora Bayes, July 1920. Columbia A-2980.

254-55 THERE HAD BEEN A CUSTOM: John Cuthbert Lawson, *Modern Greek Folklore and Ancient Greek Religion: A Study in Survivals* (Cambridge, 1910), pp. 371-76.

CHAPTER 15—LOUTRA

257 THE LETTER: Emmanuel Marangoudakis to the author, 8 June 1976.

258 LOUTRA: the visit to Loutra and subsequent taped interviews took place 25 June 1978.

258 ILIAS' BEGINNINGS: Emmanuel Marangoudakis to the author, 8 June 1976, and interview.

259 CHRISTIANS AND TURKS: *Times* (London), 22 June 1896. L. S. Stavrianos, *The Balkans Since 1453* (New York, 1966), pp. 105-7.

259 EROTOKRITOS: see Chapter 2, Reference Notes, p. 20 EROTOKRITOS.

259 LOVE-COUPLETS: the example is from *Folk Dances of Greece*, James A. Notopoulos, ed. and recorder, notes by Spyros Peristeres, Folkways Records FE 4467, pp. 5-6, adapted.

259 DIGENIS; DASKALOYIANNIS: see Appendix.

259 ARKADHI: see note on ARKADHI below. The monastery of Arkadhi was blown up in 1866.

259 OUTBREAK OF . . . 1889: *Times* (London), June–August 1889, esp. 8, 12 June; 9, 26 July; 6, 7, 12, 26 August.

259 KAZANTZAKIS: Nikos Kazantzakis, *Report to Greco*, tr. P. A. Bien (New York, 1965), pp. 85-91. *Times* (London), 15 August 1889,

gives details on the massacre. For concise descriptions of the events of Crete in Tikas' youth, see C. M. Woodhouse, *Modern Greece; A Short History* (London, n.d.), pp. 177–86; Stavrianos, *The Balkan since 1453*, pp. 467–71.

260 A REFORM MOVEMENT: Times (London), 14 March, 16 October 1895; 25 March 1896. See 25 August 1896 for the background of the struggle.

260 BURNING EACH OTHER'S VILLAGES: Ibid., 5 June 1896.

260 TROOPS BROUGHT IN FROM ZEITUN: Ibid., 6 June 1896.

260 MOSLEM REFUGEES IN RETHYMNON: Ibid., 26 August, 21 September 1896.

260 A STRANGE QUIET: Ibid., 12 August 1896.

260 IN PYGHI: Ibid., 28 September 1896.

260 STARVING WINTER OF 1897: Ibid., 25 December 1897; 1 February 1898.

260 REFUGEES: Ibid., 8 February, 14 March 1898.

260 SHARP FIGHTING: Ibid., 21 March, 2 April 1898.

260 FOUGHT A DAY OR TWO: Cf. ibid., 2 April 1897.

260 MASSACRE AT IRAKLION: Ibid., 7, 13, 14 September 1898.

260 AN ULTIMATUM: Ibid., 28 September, 6, 17, October 1898.

260 PRINCE GEORGE: Ibid., 28 November 1898.

260 TOUR OF THE DISTRICT: Ibid., 19 May 1899.

261 KAZANTZAKIS ON PRINCE GEORGE: Kazantzakis, *Report to Greco*, pp. 105–7.

261 ILIAS' HOBBY: Emmanuel Marangoudakis to the author, 8 June 1976.

261 RETHYMNON: details drawn from Pandelis Prevelakis, *The Tale of a Town*, tr. Kenneth Johnstone (London and Athens, 1976).

262 ARKADHI: for a contemporary account of the battle of Arkadhi see *Times* (London), 8 December 1866.

262 MELIDHONI: Adam Hopkins, *Crete: Its Past, Present and People* (London, 1977), p. 123.

262 FOUR MARTYRS: Prevelakis, *The Tale of a Town*, pp. 95–96.

262 MET THE RUSSIANS: *Times* (London), 8, 10 May; 1, 7, 31 July; 17 August 1905.

262 "HE FINISHED . . . SCHOOL": Emmanuel Marangoudakis to the author, 8 June 1976.

264 ILIAS' FATHER . . . DIED 1927: Ibid.

SELECTED BIBLIOGRAPHY

The bibliography is arranged by subject under the following categories: *The Greeks in the United States, Mines and Mine Owners, Labor and Labor Organizers, Labor Conflict in Colorado, 1912–14,* and *Crete and Greece.*

THE GREEKS IN THE UNITED STATES

BOOKS

Burgess, Thomas. *Greeks in America.* Boston, 1913.
Fairchild, Henry Pratt. *Greek Immigration to the United States.* New Haven, 1911.
Papanikolas, Helen Zeese. *Toil and Rage in a New Land: The Greek Immigrants of Utah.* Salt Lake City, 1974.
Saloutos, Theodore. *The Greeks in the United States.* Cambridge, Mass., 1964.

PERIODICALS

Papanikolas, Helen Zeese. "Greek Workers in the Intermountain West: The Early Twentieth Century." *Byzantine and Modern Greek Studies* 5 (1979): 187–215.
———. "Life and Labor Among the Immigrants of Bingham Canyon." *Utah Historical Quarterly* 33 (Fall, 1965):289–315.

UNPUBLISHED

Cononelos, Louis James. "Greek Immigrant Labor." M.A. thesis, University of Utah, 1979.

321

MINES AND MINE OWNERS

BOOKS

Fosdick, Raymond B. *John D. Rockefeller, Jr.: A Portrait.* New York, 1956.

Nevins, Allan. *John D. Rockefeller: The Heroic Age of American Enterprise.* New York, 1940.

————. *Study in Power: John D. Rockefeller, Industrialist and Philanthropist.* New York and London, 1953.

Rockefeller, John D. *Random Reminiscences of Men and Events.* New York, 1909.

Scamehorn, H. Lee. *Pioneer Steelmaker in the West.* Boulder, Colo., 1976.

PERIODICALS

Camp and Plant, 1901–4.
Coal Age, 1912–14.

LABOR AND LABOR ORGANIZERS

BOOKS

Fetherling, Dale. *Mother Jones, The Miners' Angel: A Portrait.* Carbondale and Edwardsville, Ill., 1974.

Gutman, Herbert G. *Work, Culture, and Society in Industrializing America.* New York, 1976.

Jones, Mary Harris. *The Autobiography of Mother Jones.* 3d ed. Chicago, 1974.

LABOR CONFLICT IN COLORADO 1912–14

MANUSCRIPTS AND ARCHIVAL MATERIALS

Elias Ammons Papers. Division of State Archives, Denver, Colo.

Edward L. Doyle Collection. Denver Public Library, Western History Department, Denver, Colo. (Especially 1. William Diamond–Edward Doyle correspondence 2. "Proceedings of the Special Convention of District 15, United Mine Workers of America Held in Trinidad, Colorado, September 16, 1913."

Frederick M. Farrar Papers. Denver Public Library, Western History Department, Denver, Colo. (Especially 1. Las Animas County, Hearings of the Grand Jury, June–August 1914, vols. 2–5. 2. "Record of the General Court Martial, Military District of Colorado, in the Matter of Karl E. Linderfelt . . . et al.," vols. 10–20. 3. "Minutes of the Court of Inquiry Established by an Executive order of his Excellency, George A. Carlson, Governor of the State of Colorado, August 26th, 1915." 4. *People of the State of Colorado* vs. *John R. Lawson, et al.*, vol. 21.

John R. Lawson Collection. Denver Public Library, Western History Department, Denver, Colo. (Especially "Transcript of Statements of Witnesses Appearing Before the Investigating Committee Appointed by John McLennan, President State Federation of Labor, Investigating Conduct of State Militia in the Southern Colorado Coal Fields.")

Proceedings of the Las Animas, Colo., Coroner's Inquests, April 1914. National Archives, Washington, D.C.

MacGregor, Don. " 'Colorado Strike,' Statement of Mr. Don MacGregor, Representative of the United Press." Typed ms. National Archives, Washington, D.C.

United Mine Workers of America. District 15 Correspondence, 1913–1914. United Mine Workers of America National Headquarters, Washington, D.C.

UNITED STATES GOVERNMENT DOCUMENTS

U.S. Congress, House. *Conditions in the Coal Mines of Colorado, Hearings before a Subcommittee of the Committee on Mines and Mining.* 63rd Cong., 2d sess., 1914, pursuant to H. Res. 387, in 2 vols.

U.S. Congress, Senate. *Industrial Relations: Final Report and Testimony Submitted to Congress by the Commission on Industrial Relations, Created by the Act of August 23, 1912.* 64th Cong., 1st sess., 1916, Doc. 415, vols. 7–9.

West, George P. United States Commission on Industrial Relations, *Report on the Colorado Strike* (Washington, D.C., 1915).

COLORADO PUBLIC DOCUMENTS

Colorado Adjutant General. *The Military Occupation of the Coal Strike Zone of Colorado by the Colorado National Guard, 1913–1914, Report of the Commanding General to the Governor for the Use of the Congressional Committee* ... (Denver, n.d.).

Colorado Bureau of Labor Statistics. *Fourteenth Biennial Report, 1913–14* (Denver, 1914).

Colorado Special Board of Officers. *Ludlow: Being the Report of the Special Board of Officers Appointed by the Governor of Colorado. . . .* (Denver, 1914).

BOOKS

Beshoar, Barron B. *Out of the Depths: The Story of John R. Lawson, A Labor Leader.* Denver, 1942.

Committee of Coal Mine Managers. *Facts Concerning the Struggle in Colorado for Industrial Freedom*, Series I. Denver, 1914.
————. *The Struggle in Colorado for Industrial Freedom*, Series II. Denver, 1914–15.
McGovern, George S., and Guttridge, Leonard F. *The Great Coalfield War*. Boston, 1972.
O'Neal, Mary Thomas. *Those Damn Foreigners*. Hollywood, 1971.

PERIODICALS AND NEWSPAPERS

Fitch, John A. "Law and Order: The Issue in Colorado." *Survey* 33 (December 5, 1914):241–57.
Reed, John. "The Colorado War." *Metropolitan* 40 (July 1914):11–72.
Robinson, Helen Ring. "The War in Colorado." *Independent* 78 (May 11, 1914):245–47.
United Mine Workers of America. *Proceedings of the . . . Biennial Convention of the United Mine Workers of America*, 1914, 1916.
Atlantis, 1914.
Denver Express, 1913–14.
Denver Post, 1913–14.
The Fra, 1914–15.
New York American, 1914.
New York Times, 1913–14.
Rocky Mountain News, 1913–14.
Trinidad Chronicle–News, 1913–14.
Trinidad Free Press, 1913–14.
United Mine Workers Journal, 1912–18.

VIDEO TAPES

Margolis, Eric, producer. *Toil and Rage in a New Land (Life of the Western Coal Miner Project)*. Institute of Behavioral Science, Boulder, Colo., 1981.
————. *Out of the Depths (Life of the Western Coal Miner Project)*. Institute of Behavioral Science, Boulder, Colo., 1981.

CRETE AND GREECE

BOOKS

Stavrianos, L. S. *The Balkans Since 1453*. New York, 1966.
Woodhouse, C. M. *Modern Greece: A Short History*. London, n.d.

PERIODICALS

Times (London), 1895–99, 1905.

INTERVIEWS

All interviews are by the author unless indicated. Tape recorded interviews on file with the American West Center of the University of Utah are marked with a (UU). The other tape recorded interviews are in the possession of the author.

Victor Bazanelle, interview transcript. *The Life of the Western Coal Miner* project video tapes. Eric Margolis, producer. Institute of Behavioral Science, Boulder, Colo.

Louis R. Dold, tape recorded (UU). Albany, Calif., 27 July, 17 August, 12 October 1974.

Milton Karavites, tape recorded (UU). Denver, Colo., 1 August 1974.

Demetrios Kalergis, tape recorded (UU). Loutra, Crete, 25 June 1978.

Mike Lingos, tape recorded with Helen Zeese Papanikolas (UU). Price, Utah, 23 July 1973.

Mike Livoda, interview notes. Denver, Colo., 27 August 1973 (with the author). Tape recorded interview with Joseph Stipanovich, Denver, Colo., 20 June 1973 (UU).

Peter Loulos, tape recorded (UU). Chicago, Ill., 4 April 1974.

Emmanuel Marangoudakis, tape recorded. Loutra, Crete, 25 June 1978.

George Mavrikos, interview notes. Walsenburg, Colo., 29 July 1974.

Mary Thomas O'Neal, tape recorded. Hollywood, Calif., 4 April 1974.

Gus Papadakis, tape recorded (UU). Oak Creek, Colo., 29 August 1973; 24 July, 1 August 1974; Chania, Crete, 30 May 1975 (with Helen Zeese Papanikolas).

George Paterakis, interview notes. Denver, Colo., 19 June 1979.

John Rougas, tape recorded (UU). Pueblo, Colo., 28 July 1974.

George Rousses, tape recorded (UU). Aguilar, Colo., 28 July 1974.

John Tsanakatsis, tape recorded (UU). Oak Creek, Colo., 29 August 1973.

Emma Zanatell, interview transcript. *The Life of the Western Coal Miner* project video tapes. Eric Margolis, producer. Institute of Behavioral Science, Boulder, Colo.

George Zeese, written. Salt Lake City, Utah, c. 1960.

INDEX

327